R · W · LIGHTBOWN

DONATELLO AND MICHELOZZO

IN TWO VOLUMES

VOLUME I : TEXT

DONATELLO AND MICHELOZZO
is published in two volumes
Volume I contains the Text
Volume II contains Illustrations, Notes, Documents,
Glossary, Tables and Index

R·W·LIGHTBOWN

DONATELLO & MICHELOZZO

An Artistic Partnership and its Patrons
in the Early Renaissance

Volume I : Text

HARVEY MILLER  LONDON

Published by Harvey Miller
20 Marryat Road · London SW19 5BD · England

Distribution: Heyden & Son Ltd., Spectrum House,
Hillview Gardens, London NW4 2JQ, England;
247 South 41st St., Philadelphia PA 19104, USA;
Münsterstrasse 22, 4440 Rheine/Westf., Germany.

ISBN 0 905203 22 4 (SET OF TWO VOLUMES)
ISBN 0 905203 27 5 (VOLUME ONE)
ISBN 0 905203 28 3 (VOLUME TWO)

Printed in Great Britain
Text printed by Latimer Trend & Company Ltd
Crescent Avenue · Plymouth · England
Illustrations originated by Roger Adams · London EC4
Printed by Cheney & Sons Ltd · Banbury

CONTENTS

CONTENTS OF VOLUME TWO

Preface

ONE OF AN AUTHOR'S PLEASANTEST DUTIES, at the end of his task, is to thank all those who have helped him to bring it to completion.

My first thanks must go to those who encouraged and supported my work. I wish to place on record that without the continued interest of Professor Horst W. Janson this book might never have seen the light of day, and I wish to express to him my deep gratitude both for reading and commenting on the typescript and for his generous support. In addition he has allowed me to use his set of unpublished photographs of the Aragazzi tomb.

Like so many others, I also owe a great debt to Professor Ulrich Middeldorf for his unfailing kindness and assistance. Dr Eve Borsook, with typical enthusiasm and generosity, gave me practical encouragement and aid at more than one critical moment in my researches. Dr Michael Kauffmann was kind enough to read the typescript and I thank him for this characteristically helpful act of friendship. To translate a graceful French phrase, may all these friends and scholars find expressed here my recognition of their help.

These are only the first items in my list of obligations. Mrs Diane Finiello Zervas generously allowed me to make full use of the measured drawings of the Cossa and Brancaccio monuments she had prepared for her own researches. The Sindaco of Montepulciano kindly gave me the free range of the Archives of Montepulciano, so granting me an essential facility, as will be seen from the Appendix of Documents at the end of this book. I record here that my first initiation into the courtesy and hospitality of Montepulciano was due to the late Monsignor Emilio Georgi, Bishop of that lovely city. Dr Ilio Calabresi, the local historian of Montepulciano, was most helpful in answering my enquiries and in communicating documents to me: I would like to express to him my gratitude for his invariable interest and kindness. Dr Gino Corti transcribed a number of documents for me from originals and from photocopies: I am only one of many scholars whom he has placed in his debt in this way. Dr Harriet Caplow has kindly allowed me to use her photograph, the only one in existence, of the bronze inscription of the Aragazzi monument. Other friends and colleagues I must also thank are Dr Marco and Signora Françoise Chiarini, Mr Claude Blair, Dr Alvar González-Palacois, Mr Leonard Joyce, Professor Nicolai Rubenstein, and Dr Michael Modell.

Mrs Helen Baz and her firm of Teamwork Typists and Miss Barbara Cole typed the manuscript with admirable care and patience. I am grateful too to

Mr and Mrs Harvey Miller, my publishers, and their staff for their interest in the book and for their encouragement. The index was prepared by Mrs Isabel Hariades.

My final words of gratitude go to my mother and father and to my wife and son. Contrary to orthodox practice, this preface concludes with the dedication of the book, first to Horst Janson and then to the memory of two dear friends, Robert Vernon Hatt (died 4 March 1978) and William George Archer (died 6 March 1979).

The numbers in brackets throughout the text refer to the illustrations, which are all grouped together in Volume II.

Prologue

IN 1425, PROBABLY IN THE SPRING OR SUMMER, two Florentine masters, Donatello and Michelozzo, entered into partnership. Donatello (1386–1466) was already a sculptor of renown, with a series of great statues of prophets and saints on the Duomo and Or San Michele to his credit. Michelozzo (1396–1472) is now chiefly famous as one of the greatest architects of the Early Renaissance, but it was as a sculptor that he became Donatello's partner. The less well-known of the two, his early career is also more mysterious, for what we know of it tells us nothing of how he learnt the two arts of architecture and sculpture. We do not even know when he first began working as an architect, though this was certainly before 1430.

Michelozzo was the son of a tailor called Bartolommeo di Gherardo, nicknamed Borgognone because he came from Burgundy. Bartolommeo obtained Florentine citizenship in 1376. He must have been a man of substance to do so, for one of the conditions of the grant was that he should buy property in Florence and its *contado* to the value of at least 1000 *fiorini piccoli*, a considerable capital sum.[1] Michelozzo was one of several sons. He was probably trained in a goldsmith's shop, for he later worked as a goldsmith, and even in 1427, when he had been in partnership with Donatello for some two years he described himself as an *orafo* in Donatello's tax-return. The craft was held in high esteem, for it was very profitable. When Michelozzo first appears at work, on 28 May 1410, as a die-engraver to the Florentine mint, an office he was to hold more or less continuously until August 1448, it was as a goldsmith, for die- and seal-cutting were branches of the goldsmith's art throughout the Middle Ages and the Renaissance and even later.[2] They demanded precision of hand and a mastery of sculptural design in miniature. As a goldsmith, Michelozzo also knew how to cast and chase and gild copper and bronze, two of the metals in which the medieval and Renaissance goldsmith most commonly worked. Indeed when he is first mentioned in connection with a work of sculpture, it is as Ghiberti's partner in making the great bronze statue of St. Matthew for the Arte del Cambio on Or San Michele and as assisting him in the first bronze doors of the Baptistery. The St. Matthew was commissioned on 26 August 1419 and was finished by 6 March 1423, when the partnership seems to have been dissolved.[3] In early July 1427 the Arte still owed Michelozzo 13 florins as a last payment for it.[4] The general opinion is that Michelozzo's contribution to the St. Matthew was limited possibly to its founding, certainly to its chasing. But its influence can be felt in his later sculpture. And it has been suggested that he was invited by Donatello to enter into partnership when Donatello's statue of St. Louis of Toulouse, cast in bronze for the Tabernacle of the Parte Guelfa on Or San Michele, had to be chased and gilded.

Donatello and Michelozzo put only a small capital into their partnership, according to their tax-returns of 1427,[5] 30 florins in all, over and above the value of their chisels and the other tools of their craft and of a mule, which had cost 10 florins and was needed 'because for our business we have to go about often'. In addition Michelozzo put his yearly salary from the Mint of about 20 florins into the partnership. It can be assumed that Michelozzo was its business manager – his later success as an architect proves him to have had a hard head in matters of organisation. By early July 1427 the partnership was in a big way. It had moved from a first workshop in Corso degli Adimari, rented from Guglielmo di Piero Adimari for 16 florins yearly, into two work-shops in the Via di Santa Reparata rented for 14 florins a year from Tedaldo di Bartolo Tedaldi. In these the two sculptors remained until 1433 when Tedaldo sold the two shops. Another, secondary workshop in Pisa, had been hired from Bartolommeo da Lavaiano for 7 florins and two boats bought from the Florentine Consoli del Mare for carrying marble from Carrara. Michel-ozzo's words in his tax-return of 1427 suggest that as sculptor he remained the junior partner – 'I have practised the art of carving as partner of Donato di Niccolo di Betto Bardi.'

The partnership was not intended to be permanent or even exclusive: temporary partnerships to meet the burdens imposed by important commis-sions were frequent in *trecento* and *quattrocento* Florence, bringing as they did shared risk and labour, and the harnessing of different skills. Indeed, some scholars have argued that Donatello took Michelozzo into partnership because he wanted his skill as an architect as well as his experience in chasing bronze. One of the purposes of this book is to penetrate to a clearer understanding of the partnership between the two, not by way of assumption from too confident a delimitation of their artistic temperaments, but by way of visual and docu-mentary evidence. But this is only one of its purposes. In an effort to recover a fuller knowledge of how some of the greatest and most famous sculptures of the Early Renaissance were devised and executed, it attempts more than purely formal analysis, more than the publication of new documents, though research in the archives and libraries of Italy has yielded, as always, new information and with new information, new insights. Its matter and structure are designed to reflect the nature and intention of the four great works of art which are its principal theme – the tomb of Cardinal Baldassare Cossa, better known as Pope John XXIII, in the Baptistery of Florence; the tomb of Cardinal Rainaldo Brancaccio in the Church of Sant' Angelo a Nido, Naples; the tomb of the Papal Secretary Bartolommeo Aragazzi in what is the modern

Duomo of Montepulciano; and the external pulpit of the Duomo of Prato. It is now realised that the art of the Middle Ages and Renaissance was not a 'pure' art of forms invented by artists independently of their times and patrons. Naturally it would be absurd to search every work of art made in the Europe of hierarchy and Christianity for evidence of a patron's presence. There were always devotees who were content to order or buy pious images painted according to standard patterns; there were always men who were content to be commemorated by effigies cut according to standard patterns in slabs of stone or metal.

But the four great works of sculpture we shall principally be considering were not modest carvings executed to a standard pattern. Each contains to a greater or lesser degree elements which were the deliberate choice of the patrons who commissioned them. In the case of the three tombs even their size and shape were consciously chosen to represent the degree in this world of those they commemorated. However, these are matters we shall explore more fully in the chapters that follow. Although the 1420s and 1430s were the decades when the style of the Renaissance triumphed in Florence over that of the Gothic past, the works of art made during them still contained elements which were new and elements which were traditional. To distinguish among these, to assign them to their true origin, to determine what was modern, what traditional, is one of the tasks of this book. The new has a perennial attraction, but the life and meaning that conventional patterns and images retain after they have lost their first vividness of symbolism are also an absorbing study, especially if we discard the arbitrary notion that in art only invention is important. For they reveal the continuity of a social and spiritual order. And to distinguish them is to help to demarcate the nature and the evolution of artistic styles. We shall explore then not only the formal life of designs and images but their social life, in an attempt to lay bare the motives that prompted so lavish an expenditure on tombs and other works of sculpture.

3

Chapter I · The Life and Death of Baldassare Cossa, Pope John XXIII

THE TOMB OF POPE JOHN XXIII in the Baptistery at Florence, wrote Gregorovius, 'is at once the sepulchre of the Great Schism in the church and the last Papal tomb which is outside Rome itself'.[1] The career of Baldassare Cossa (*c.* 1360–1419), Pope John XXIII, was indeed one of the most dramatic and most controversial of the Great Schism but its dramas are too complex and its controversies too difficult to unravel here at length. Yet something we must know about Cossa's life if we are to understand certain features of his tomb's history and design and how it comes to stand in the Baptistery of Florence.[2] Cossa belonged to a great and noble Neapolitan family, originally from Ischia, which in 1339 acquired the lordships of Vivara and Procida. The Cossa were famous as sea-captains, and Baldassare seems to have fought in one of the civil wars between the Durazzo and Angevin factions for the throne of Naples. But he soon abandoned the knightly life for a career in the Church. He became a student at Bologna, where he took the degree of doctor of civil and canon law and of decretals, and lectured for a year before entering *c.* 1387 the household of Cardinal Pietro Tomacelli, a fellow-Neapolitan and a kinsman who shortly afterwards (2 November 1389) became Pope Boniface IX.

Cossa was greatly valued by Boniface as an able diplomat and for his financial skill and in 1402 he created him Cardinal Deacon of Sant' Eustachio. In the following year he sent him as his Legate to recover Bologna for the Church. This Cossa succeeded in doing, governing the city firmly and well, and becoming a power to be reckoned with in Italian politics. From Bologna he took a leading part in encouraging the cardinals of Gregory IX to rebel against him after he had failed to honour his oath to resign in order to bring about an end to the Great Schism. And he supported them with money, arms and diplomacy during the Council of Pisa (1409), at which both Gregory and his rival, Benedict XIII, the Pope of Avignon, were deposed and Alexander V was elected in their place to reign, it was hoped, over a reunited Christendom. But the deposition did not in fact end the Schism, and when Cossa was elected to succeed Alexander on 17 May 1410 and took the title of Pope John XXIII, he found himself reigning from Bologna over only one of the three obediences into which the West was now divided.

It was encouraging nevertheless that his own obedience was so large that it could be called nearly universal. He was acknowledged by France, by England,

Bohemia, Prussia and parts of Germany, by most of Northern Italy, including Florence and Venice, and by Portugal. But Benedict XIII was still tenaciously entrenched at Morella in Aragon, obeyed by the Kings of Aragon, Castile and Scotland, while Gregory now sat in Gaeta, protected by King Ladislaus of Naples, who had seized a large part of the Papal States, and supported by Carlo Malatesta, whose lordship of Rimini was dangerously near to Bologna. Gregory was also supported, more distantly, by the princes of Bavaria, notably Ludwig, the Elector Palatine, by some parts of Germany and by Poland.

At first John attempted to restore union by negotiating with the Kings of Aragon and Castile, Benedict's chief supporters, and by expelling King Ladislaus of Naples, Gregory's only important supporter, from his kingdom. With the help of Louis of Anjou, the rival claimant to Naples, he returned suddenly to Rome in April 1411 and summoned a Council of the Universal Church to meet in the Holy City in April of the following year. Soon afterwards Louis defeated Ladislaus, and though he failed to follow up his victory, John was able to conclude peace with Ladislaus in June 1412. But the Council of Rome, when it opened on 10 February 1413, was so poorly attended that John himself was obliged to prorogue it. And four months later Ladislaus, alarmed at the movements in North Italy of Sigismund, King of the Romans, whose right to the throne of Hungary he disputed, attacked Rome and expelled John, who was Sigismund's ally. John fled northwards and took refuge in Florence. Sigismund, who was head of the Holy Roman Empire in all except name, now intervened and insisted that John should consult him before convoking the Council again. For Sigismund had come to feel that it was his duty, as advocate and protector of the Church, to bring the Schism to an end. In spite of John's reluctance to place himself in Sigismund's power, he was obliged to accept Constance, which lay in Imperial territory, as the place where it should be held. Accordingly he summoned it to meet there on 1 November 1414.

At Constance John was confronted by determined and clamorous demands from the northern nations for an end to the Schism and for the enforcement of the reforms which had already been called for by the Council of Pisa. Under pressure John declared that he was ready to resign in order to restore unity to the Church, but he stood firm on the point of honour, that he should resign only at a time and in circumstances that did not compromise his right and dignity as legitimate Pope. Led by Sigismund, the northern nations pressed him ever more ruthlessly, until John, angered by insults and fearing for his safety, fled from Constance to Schaffhausen, disguised as an archer, on the night of 20–21 March 1415, under the protection of Frederick of Austria. From Schaffhausen he summoned the Curia to join him.

The violent reaction of the Council was not expected by John, who probably thought his departure would be sufficient to disperse it. Encouraged by Sigismund, the Council proclaimed that it was not dissolved by the Pope's departure and continued its sessions. Sigismund and the Swiss moved against Frederick and John fled from Schaffhausen through the Black Forest to Freiburg, near the Rhine, escorted by Frederick. His intention was to seek the protection of the Duke of Burgundy, whose territories lay beyond the river, but before he could cross it Frederick, cowed by the threats of Sigismund and the expostulations of his kinsman Ludwig of Bavaria, surrendered him into the custody of Sigismund and the Council. Proposals for an accommodation were made, but the Council, now thoroughly angered, was determined to make an end of John and on 1 May formally cited him to appear and answer for himself in the process it now began against him. A tribunal was appointed which collected a great deal of evidence, much of it highly scurrilous, against John, who was brought back from Freiburg to Radolfzell, on the north shore of the Lake of Constance. Here on 27 May he accepted the sentence of deposition pronounced against him by the Council.

He was now handed over by Sigismund into the custody of Ludwig of Bavaria, Elector Palatine, who put him in close confinement first in Heidelberg and later in his castle of Rheinhausen, near Mannheim. In spite of attempts to procure his release, by conspiracy or negotiation, he remained a prisoner until 1419. Meanwhile the Council proceeded with measures to replace him and on 8 November 1417 the Cardinals met in conclave at Constance. One of the earliest acts of the new Pope, Martin V, after his election on 11 November 1417, was to receive Cossa formally and by proxy into his custody and to re-commit him into Ludwig's charge. But when, a few months later, Martin and Sigismund both made attempts to obtain the surrender of his valuable prisoner, Ludwig, who had turned against Sigismund in 1417, declined to give him up. It was the Florentines who succeeded in securing his release. As Legate of Bologna, Cossa had been a personage of importance to the Florentines, whose borders marched with those of the Bolognese. After a first cloud over their relations in 1404, he had been their constant friend and ally. In 1405–1406 he helped them to take Pisa, their ambition of centuries, and in 1409 he joined with them in a league and sent troops to help them resist the advance of King Ladislaus against the Council of Pisa. Indeed it was Cossa who was chiefly responsible for inducing the Florentines in 1408 to allow the Council to be held in Pisa. In July 1415, shortly after his deposition, the Florentine *Signoria* debated whether they ought not to intercede with the King of France for his liberation, since he had always been a true friend and benefactor of the Republic, but decided that the step was too dangerous at this time. Nevertheless some of the most powerful merchants of the citizen oligarchy felt themselves bound to Cossa by strong ties of friendship and interest, for both as Legate and Pope he had used Florentines as his bankers. Chief among them was Giovanni de Bicci de' Medici, whose fortune had been made in transactions with the Papal Curia.

In November 1415, rumours were circulating in Constance that the ex-Pope had more than a million florins deposited in Florence.

By the late summer of 1418 Cossa had made up his mind to surrender himself into Martin's hands. Accordingly, on 29 September, the Florentine *Signoria* instructed the envoys they were despatching to Martin to congratulate him on his election, to negotiate with the Pope for Cossa's release and restoration to high estate. Martin was only too relieved to have Cossa renounce of his own free will all claim to the Papacy in favour of Martin's right, for there were still many, especially in Italy, who thought that John had been badly used at Constance, and that his deposition had been violent and illegal. Accordingly, a treaty was set on foot for Cossa to be surrendered into Martin's hands and brought to his feet in Italy. As the price of his consent Ludwig demanded 38,500 Rhenish gulden, disguising this huge ransom under the customary fiction of charges and expenses incurred for the maintenance of his prisoner. Cossa wrote at once to Giovanni de' Medici to pay the money on his behalf, and Giovanni immediately despatched northwards to act as his agent in the business a young Florentine named Bartolommeo de' Bardi (1397–1428) of whom we shall hear more in later chapters. In April 1419 Cossa was brought to Basle, escorted by Bartolommeo, and consigned into the hands of the Bishop of Lubeck, who had been deputed by Martin to receive him into his custody. Three days later he was on the road to Italy, to make submission to Martin, who was now residing in Florence as the guest of the Republic.

All went smoothly until the party reached Parma, when Bartolommeo received a letter from Giovanni de' Medici warning him not to allow Cossa to go on to Mantua, for there he was to be arrested and consigned to prison for the rest of his life. This seems to have been a false rumour, but Cossa was not unnaturally alarmed. With typical resourcefulness he contrived to make his custodians drunk, and then escaped by night over the mountains to Sarzana, on the Ligurian coast, where his old friend and ally Tommaso Campofregoso, Doge of Genoa, was lord. The news of his escape created consternation in the Curia, which knew only too well that he could call up a strong body of supporters at a nod. But Cossa now gave a last and greatest proof of his sincerity in the cause of unity. Having sought and obtained assurances for his own personal safety, he came on to Florence and on 14 June solemnly made submission to Martin in general consistory, acknowledging him as true Pope. In return Martin, in spite of opposition from some of his cardinals, treated him generously, creating him Cardinal Bishop of Tusculum. According to contemporaries, it was the Florentines who were chiefly responsible for persuading the Pope to act magnanimously. So grateful was Cossa for their aid that he ordered himself to be called, not the Cardinal of Tusculum as custom prescribed, but the Cardinal of Florence.[3]

He now led the ordinary life of a Cardinal. But the hardships and shocks he had endured – he was now aged about sixty – were too much even for his strong constitution and in the early morning of 22 December he died, in the house where he had taken lodging in Florence, that of Antonio di Santi Chiarucci beside the Church of Santa Maria Maggiore.[4]

On the day of his death Cossa, firm and energetic to the last, 'sound in mind and understanding by the grace of Christ Jesus, though languishing in the body' drew up with his own hand the final form of his last will and testament. First he devoutly and humbly commended his soul to the Most High Creator, God Omnipotent, to His Mother, the glorious Virgin Mary, and to all the Court of Heaven. Next, he left the choice of his burying-place, whenever he passed from this life, to his executors, or to any two of them, who were also to determine how much should be expended from his estate on his funeral exequies, his tomb and the founding and endowment of a chapel. There followed two small pious bequests to the Duomo, then still building, a gold florin to the *Opera*, a florin towards the construction of the new Sacristy, and another bequest of a florin towards building the new walls of Florence. These three legacies were bequests to favourite civic causes of a kind customary with pious and loyal Florentines born during these years. Next came those bequests to convents and works of charity 'for the love of God and the remedy of his soul', which he intended should promote his soul's welfare after death. Each of the orders of friars in Florence, the Franciscans of Santa Croce, the Dominicans of Santa Maria Novella, the Carmelites of the Carmine, the Augustinians of Santo Spirito, the Servites of the Annunziata, the Camaldolese Hermits of Santa Maria degli Angioli – this last a convent he had much favoured as Pope – were to receive whatever legacy his executors thought fitting. So too were his faithful attendants, the Olivetan monks Fra Matteo da Viterbo and Fra Giovanni.

His charitable bequests followed the classic pattern of pious legacies in the later Middle Ages: he dowered poor girls, and left money for the four great works of mercy, clothing the naked, feeding the hungry, visiting the sick and succouring prisoners. Here too he chose to benefit Florentines. 'For the love of God and for the remedy of his soul' his executors were to nominate fifty poor girls, who were to receive dowries of 10 florins each after their marriage. 'For the love of God and the remedy of his soul' they were to lay out 100 florins on freeing poor prisoners, to be chosen by them from the *Stinche*, or prisons of the Comune. 'For the love of God and the remedy of his soul', they were to choose fifty poor persons of Christ and clothe them in garments to the value of 10 lire (part of a florin) per person. And lastly, 'For the love of God and the remedy of his soul' he left 100 florins to the Hospital of Santa Maria Nuova 'in aid of the poor of the said Hospital'.

These bequests made up a very considerable sum, but they were small compared with the sums he left to his nephew Michele, son of his elder brother Pietro, Lord of Ischia (d. 1416), formerly the Captain-General of his fleet, and from 20 December 1420 Captain-General of the Neapolitan fleet, and to his young nephew Giovanni (1400–1476), son of his brother Gaspare, who had died in Rome on 23 September 1411. To Michele he bequeathed 5000 florins, to Giovanni 10,000, in compensation 'for many labours and many expenses borne for the Church of God' by Michele and Gaspare. A letter of 25 January 1420 from Michele to Giovanni de' Medici proves that these phrases were far from being a mere empty disguise for blatant enrichment of his nephews. During his uncle's wars as Legate and Pope against Ladislaus, wrote Michele, the family estates in the Kingdom of Naples had been greatly reduced and impoverished. Michele had lost revenues to the value of 10,000 florins during a seven years exile from Naples, and he and his uncles Gaspare and Marino had been obliged to sell estates to the value of 10,000 more. On the family's return to Naples they had found all their property laid waste and themselves deep in debt. Far from his uncle's having enriched them, Michele and his father had never received anything but ill from him – even on his death-bed he had left Michele 5000 florins less than Giovanni, though Michele was burdened with five children, two of them daughters to be dowered.[5]

In observance of a customary courtesy from dying cardinals to the Pope, he left a legacy to Martin, consisting of a white horse and a ring. Whether the Pope was gratified by these is not recorded: he is reported to have said on being told of Cossa's death: 'Now we are sure of our estate and of the mitre on our head.' And if the contemporary Lucchese chronicler Giovanni Sercambi is to be believed, Cossa himself was under no illusions about the pleasure and relief his death would bring to the Pope. 'A sickness came upon him,' he writes, 'and seeing himself in evil state and in case of death, he sent one of the Panciatichi, who was one of his household, with a message to Pope Martin, saying, 'Go and tell him, Baldassare Cossa is dying.' The said familiar answered him: 'How can you wish I should go and tell such things to the Pope?' He said, 'Go, for thou wilt take him the best news he can have.'[6]

To the Baptistery of San Giovanni Battista in Florence Cossa left what in medieval eyes was his most splendid legacy of all, no less a relic than the right index finger of St. John the Baptist, the patron saint and protector of Florence, being that finger with which the Baptist pointed to Christ and said, 'Behold the lamb of God.' This most glorious relic was said to have been presented to Pope Urban V by Philotheos, Patriarch of Constantinople, in 1363. From him it had descended to his successors Gregory XI and Urban VI by whom it was also held in great veneration. From Urban it had been stolen during the siege of Nocera and had later been redeemed by Cossa with much trouble for 800 florins, a great sum. If this story is true, it is typical of the medieval passion for relics that he did not restore the finger to its rightful owner, but kept it to wear about his person. In 1413, before going to Bologna, he deposited it secretly in the monastery of Santa Maria degli Angioli, only his confessor Matteo da Viterbo and Cosimo de' Medici being privy to its hiding-place.[7] Since doubts have been voiced as to whether Cosimo was at all well acquainted with John, it is worth recalling here that in 1413 John granted two abbeys at Cosimo's instance to Cosimo's favourite convent of Santa Maria degli Angioli and that on 27 September 1414 he granted Cosimo a safe-conduct to Constance.[8] He ordered that the relic was to be placed in San Giovanni 'in that part of the Church which shall best please the Priors and Gonfaloniere of Florence'. But first it was to be enshrined in a reliquary after the fashion on which Fra Matteo da Viterbo and Cosimo de' Medici had already decided and for this purpose he made a bequest of 200 florins. All the residue of his estate he bequeathed to the 'poor of Christ and pious places.'

The last clause of the will named as his executors Bartolommeo Valori, Niccolò da Uzzano, Giovanni de' Medici and Vieri Guadagni, with powers to any two of them to act on behalf of all four and full rights of administration over his estate. In choosing four Florentine citizens for this great honour he gave a signal testimony of gratitude to the city as well as to the four men themselves. An even greater honour was his desire to be buried in Florence, rather than in his native Naples, where he would lie in the daily sight of relations, friends and descendants, who would offer up prayers for his soul whenever they saw his tomb in the family chapel.

His four executors were the men who had been principally instrumental in securing his release. Giovanni de' Medici was Cossa's old and confidential friend and banker. When he was on his flight from Constance, it was to Giovanni that he sent for safe-keeping by the hands of Niccolò Piscicelli, Archbishop of Salerno, a rich Papal mitre set with gems and precious stones. He also deposited in Giovanni's care a number of Papal registers and writings. Giovanni was also the trusted friend and banker of all the Cossa family. Making his will in Pisa on 21 October 1417, Marino Cossa, who had also found refuge under Florentine protection, made Giovanni and Michele Cossa his heirs, and appointed Giovanni de' Medici executor of his will and guardian of Giovanni Cossa until he should come of age.[9]

With Niccolò da Uzzano, one of the most powerful of Florentine citizens, Baldassare had long been on the best of terms. Their friendship was probably promoted by mutual interest and we know from the Florentine chronicler Buonaccorso Pitti that it was already strong in the time of Cossa's Legateship of Bologna. In 1409 Buonaccorso had set his eye on the wealthy Hospital of Altopascio, near Pisa, whose master appeared to him to be dissipating its property, conduct of which Buonaccorso's own nephew would be incapable.

He broached the affair to Cossa, who encouraged him to petition Pope Alexander for the Hospital and promised him his influence. But Niccolò da Uzzano, Pitti's bitter enemy, got wind of the affair and pressed Cossa not to support the petition. Cossa then told Pitti frankly that for nothing in the world would he, Cossa, do anything contrary to Niccolò's wish but said he did not want to do anything against Buonaccorso either, and urged him to get someone else to support his petition. Even after he became Pope, '*per la grazia o disgrazia di Dio*' wrote the angry Buonaccorso, he still refused to grant the petition, though Pitti went in person to Bologna to solicit his favour. None the less, he did his best to reconcile Niccolò and Pitti, but Niccolò first deceived Pitti with fair words and promises, or so Pitti claims, and then secretly procured the benefice for a friend. In compensation John offered Pitti any benefice he liked, 'even a good bishopric', but Pitti sulkily refused and left Bologna in a rage at having wasted both his time and his money.[10]

Bartolommeo Valori (1355–1427) had been a convinced supporter of the Council of Pisa and of the league between Florence and Cossa against Ladislaus. Valori had served John so loyally that he left him a large bequest of money; indeed he was another man of whom John declared that he could refuse him nothing. It was his influence with John which was said to have obtained a cardinal's hat for his cousin, Alamanno Adimari. When John was returning from Lodi to Bologna, Bartolommeo and Giovanni de' Medici met him at Ferrara, having been deputed as envoys to him by the *Signoria*. Bartolommeo, foreseeing the perils that awaited John in Constance, warned him about them, only to be told by the Pope that he too knew well how foolish it was to trust himself to unknown hands, and that the Council would not be on his side. 'But what can I do, if destiny draws me there?'[11]

Vieri di Vieri Guadagni (1369–1426), a wealthy banker, had been a friend and associate of Cossa from as early as 1403 when the Florentines sent him twice to Ferrara to concert measures for the recapture of Bologna. In January 1409 he was one of the ambassadors despatched by the *Signoria* to the marquis of Ferrara and a number of Lombard lords to persuade them to support the Council of Pisa. Later that year he was sent by the *Signoria* to Cossa to promise him the help of Florence against Ladislaus and was at the same time commissioned to order all the Florentine subjects living near Bolognese territory to obey the Legate's commands. In the expedition of Louis of Anjou and Cossa against Rome in the autumn of 1409 he was one of the two Florentine commissaries. During the summer of 1411 he went on an embassy to Carlo Malatesta to ask him not to ravage the Bolognese territory. After John's expulsion from Rome in 1413, it was he who was sent by the Florentines to Ladislaus to reproach him for having broken his faith and to ask him to restore Rome and the Papal States to John. He was to offer him a league with Florence and Siena if he did so, and when Ladislaus made it a condition that Venice too should enter the league, Vieri went to Venice in February 1414 to negotiate for this and to tell the Venetians that Florence had appealed to John to mediate between them and Sigismund. On 19 May 1414 he was sent to warn John of Ladislaus' advance against him and of the peril in which the Florentines stood and to urge him to grant the King the Vicariate of Marittima and Campagna – unsuccessfully, as it proved. He died on 9 August 1426, while acting as Florentine commissary in Arezzo during the war against Filippo Maria Visconti, in consequence of a blow from a bombard ball.[12]

In return for the honours done them by Cossa his executors and the Florentines did him magnificent honours after his death 'which has touched and grieved every citizen,' wrote Giovanni de' Medici on 31 December 1419 to Michele Cossa.[13] On the evening of the day of his death[14] his body, uncovered, with a white mitre on the head and a cardinal's hat on a pillow at the feet, was laid on a bier draped in a white pall and carried in solemn procession into the Baptistery by the canons of the Duomo preceded by three crosses, that of the Baptistery, that of the Duomo and that of Santa Maria Maggiore. They laid it on the flat top of the font – a place of great honour, for here the relics of the Baptistery were set out on feast days – and recited the office. Then they took it up and set it beneath the pulpit, where it lay in state, surrounded by many burning torches (*doppieri*).[15]

On 27 December the *Priori* and *Consiglio* of Florence voted by 157 votes to 34 a provision in honour of Cossa's memory.

> The Lords Priors and Gonfaloniere of Justice of the people of Florence, desiring to show more especially in the sepulture of his body how dear and acceptable to all the people of Florence were the love and long-standing goodwill displayed in continual benefits by the most reverend father in Christ and lord, the lord Baldassare Coscia, Cardinal of Holy Roman Church, of his own affection named in the vulgar tongue Cardinal of Florence, towards the magnificent and potent Comune of Florence, as well in the time of his felicity while he held the papacy as before and afterwards, loving all Florentines and their good estate as himself and his own, most evidently demonstrating his love the more clearly and fervently by proofs at his departure from this life. Having therefore solemnly deliberated among themselves and together with the officers of the Gonfaloniere of the People and of the Dodici Buonuomini and finally being congregated in sufficient number in the palace of the Florentine people, and having first held and conducted a solemn and secret scrutiny and passed the resolution by means of black and white beans according to the ordinances of the said Comune, of their own motion and for the utility of the said Comune, and by every way and custom by which best they could, they provided and ordained and determined on the twenty-seventh day of December 1429 . . . That his body and exequies should be honoured at the expense of the Comune of Florence to the honour of God and the fame of his happy memory and that for the expenses of the said exequies and the things thereunto pertaining or annexed, the Lords Priors of the Arts and Gonfaloniere

of Justice together with the officers of the Gonfaloniere of the People and the Dodici Buonuomini of the said *Comune* ... may assign and cause to be paid ... so much money as shall best please and seem proper to them ... saving only and excepting that in virtue of the present provision no more than 300 florins may be expended or assigned or paid, but up to that sum according as it shall have pleased and seemed proper to the *Signori* and *Collegi*.

Next day this provision was ratified by 138 votes to 12.[16]

The obsequies began on 30 December. The day before the *invitatore* had gone round to all who were to attend and announced: 'My lord Cardinal of Tricarico[17] and the executors of the will notify you to be present tomorrow at 16 hours in Santa Maria del Fiore, where the obsequies of Messer Baldassare Cossa Cardinal of Florence will be held.' In Santa Maria del Fiore stood a catafalque set with burning tapers and hung round with a black cloth decorated with Cossa's arms. Around the catafalque ran a wooden bench on which sat all the mourners, each with a burning taper in his hand. Under the catafalque lay a bier covered with a black pall on which were placed two pillows, one bearing Cossa's Cardinal's hat. The body had not been brought into the Duomo but had been left beneath the pulpit in San Giovanni, which was filled with burning tapers, some fixed to wooden supports set up round the tribune and above the three doorways. The choir of the Duomo was filled with *doppieri* and the nave with tapers. Mass was said by Cardinal Antonio Correr, the nephew of Gregory XII and Cossa's former enemy, and twenty cardinals were present, besides many archbishops and bishops.

The *Signori* and *Collegi* of Florence attended, and gave Cossa a hundred torches and a pall of cloth of gold, whose lappets were adorned with the arms of Cossa, of Pope Martin and of Florence. This was laid on the bier and the *Signori* then took their places in the choir. Then came the *Capitani* of *Parte Guelfa*, together with many of the greater citizens, judges and knights, and gave him eighty torches and a pall of black cloth with lappets adorned with his arms and those of the *Parte*. Then came the *Sei della Mercatanzia* together with all the *Capitani* of the *Arti*. The *Sei della Mercatanzia* gave Cossa forty torches together with a pall of black cloth with lappets adorned with Cossa's arms and those of the *Mercatanzia*. These two black palls were also laid on the bier. Each of the greater *Arti* gave him four *doppieri* and each of the lesser two, making fifty-six torches in all. During the ceremony the cardinals, the *Signori*, the *Capitani* of *Parte Guelfa* and the *Sei della Mercatanzia* all held a burning torch in their hand, while the rest held tapers. After mass and the funeral sermon, preached by the Dominican friar Maestro Domenico da Figline, the cardinals, wearing white mitres, assembled round the bier holding their lighted torches and said the office for the dead, and then the canons of the Duomo carried it into San Giovanni.

Next day the same ceremonies were repeated at the cost of the *Signori*, and in the presence of the same dignitaries, except that this time Tommaso Brancaccio was the only cardinal present. But the Vice-Chamberlain of the Church and many archbishops and bishops and high prelates of the Curia attended, all bearing torches or tapers, and mass was said by the Bishop of Florence. After the ceremonies the bier was once more carried by the cathedral canons into San Giovanni. Next day the Bishop of Fiesole said mass at a *rinovale* or anniversary held for the dead man in San Giovanni. The bier lay on the font, surrounded by many torches, and Cossa's relations and household sat round it dressed in black, each holding a taper. Then came forty-four poor men whom the executors had clothed in white, according to the instructions of Cossa's will, 'for love of God and for his soul'. They stood upright round the font, holding lighted candles. After mass had been said and the office for the dead, those present escorted the dead man's relations back to their house and then returned home. This ceremony was repeated on the six following days, until the nine days' exequies prescribed by the *Ordo Romanus* for cardinals were completed. 'I say', wrote Giovanni de' Medici to Michele Cossa, 'that such great honour has been done him by the *Signoria* here that no greater could be done to any Lord.'[18] According to custom the body was then given temporary burial in the church, until a more honourable sepulture was made ready.

The condition of Cossa's estate was not so satisfactory as these splendid and costly funeral ceremonies, described significantly by the sixteenth-century historian Scipione Ammirato as honourable '*à guisa di Papa*', might suggest.[19] Giovanni de' Medici told Michele Cossa in his same letter of 31 December that 'when the expenses of the funeral are deducted it will be a struggle to give effect to the legacies.' This was in fact a by no means uncommon occurrence with the wills of great ecclesiastics. They were apt to make bequests with a stately disregard for the real amount of their wealth, though this was of course less easily calculated in that age than now. Indeed if Ammirato is to be believed, Cossa himself was aware that his estate might well be insufficient to pay all his legacies. In another minute of his will which Ammirato had seen he ordered that if there was not enough to meet them all, those to his nephews and to Valori should at all costs be paid in full. Besides, wrote Giovanni to Michele, many persons had now come forward to demand payment of debts which they claimed John had contracted with them while he was still Legate of Bologna and Pope, and the Spini, Florentine bankers and Giovanni's rivals were threatening to take steps to have the Auditor of the Papal Camera order the executors not to pay the legacies. As they were Martin's bankers, the threat was serious. Moreover the creditors were declaring loudly that if they could get no justice from the Curia they would sue Cossa's heirs. Giovanni and the executors were anxious to do all they could to give Cossa's will effect, and he advised Michele that it would be a

14

good thing if it could be shown that Cossa had drawn on his own or on the family patrimony for money before and after he became Cardinal and also that Michele and Giovanni had suffered losses on his account. If a lawsuit arose it would also be useful to have the advice of some men of weight and legal learning in Naples.

Michele and Giovanni were at once alarmed and angered at the possibility of losing their legacies. In instant reply Michele, addressing Giovanni as 'Egregie Pater' and signing himself 'vester filius', set out all that the Cossa had lost in the service of the Church and of their uncle.

> Wherefore I pray you and the other executors, that with my faith and hope and similarly of Giovanni, that it may please you to display to us the good will you felt towards our late uncle, of happy memory, and also for your honour as the executor which you are, that it may please you to cause us to be given the moneys which our uncle has left us by his will, and also to send us a copy of the will. And when we have had the money, should any person ask us for some of it opportunity will be given to him. I for myself and similarly for Giovanni we pray you that it may be your will and that of your companions to be our defenders in these matters, for we do not wish neither ought we to plead at law with anyone, for it would be a great sin after we have lost our possessions and have been ruined by our uncle, since this that he leaves us is for losses received through him.

Another letter from Giovanni Cossa written on 15 June 1420 reveals that both he and Michele had still received little or nothing from their legacies and that he had had to borrow money from Michele, who could ill afford it, to pay his widowed mother her dowry.[20] For many months, perhaps for more than a year or a year and a half the estate could not be satisfactorily wound up: indeed, according to Ammirato, the *Signoria* ordered all moneys from it to be paid into Vieri Guadagni's bank, no doubt to protect it from the claims of importunate creditors.[21]

And the history of the reliquary of St. John the Baptist's finger implies that it was some time before the estate was cleared of all claims. The relic itself was formally presented to the *Arte di Calimala*, which had charge of the Baptistery, on 13 January 1421, after the Prior of Santa Maria degli Angioli had handed it over to the executors.[22] The *Signori* carried it with their own hands to the Baptistery, accompanied in solemn procession by all their colleagues and by the clergy of the city with much expense of wax candles and pennons, and there handed it over to the six *Consoli* of the *Arte*.[23] Within a year it had been enshrined in a reliquary 'all adorned with gold, silver and pearls',[24] for it was in 1421 (s.f.) that the goldsmith Giovanni del Chiaro was paid 40 florins by the *Opera* of the Baptistery as a half-share of the cost of gilding the reliquary, the other half-share being provided by the executors. This must have been by agreement between the two parties since a document of 1423 records that the reliquary had cost 80 florins more than Cossa's bequest of 200 florins. And it was only in 1423 that Giovanni del Chiaro was paid those 280 florins.[25]

These facts are essential for the history of Cossa's tomb, all the more so because the truth of its history depends on fixing its chronology accurately. Unfortunately, most of the records of the *Arte di Calimala* for the 1420s have been lost, and it is known that they contained much concerning the tomb. But some important facts can be culled from one little book of the *Deliberazioni* of the *Consoli* which has escaped the general destruction, and others can be deduced from notes made by seventeenth-century antiquaries who went through the *Arte*'s other records while they still survived. The first known date in its history is 9 January 1422.[26] On that day, Niccolò da Uzzano, Bartolommeo Valori and Vieri Guadagni appeared before the *Consoli* of the *Arte di Calimala*. At the end of his life, they declared, Messer Baldassare Cossa had told his executors secretly that he longed for the favour of being buried in the Baptistery of San Giovanni Battista on account of the great devotion he felt for the church, of which devotion they were well apprised from the relic of the Baptist's finger which he had bequeathed to it. But from modesty he had not spoken of this wish concerning his tomb in his will. He had also expressed a desire to have a chapel built as well as a tomb, and the executors now petitioned the Consuls for license to erect both.

From all this it is clear that Cossa well understood how greatly the Baptistery was revered by the Florentines as their '*bel San Giovanni*' the cradle of Christianity in the city, and their ancient cathedral, built, so they firmly believed, by the Romans. There were no tombs in it save for the sarcophagus of Bishop Ranieri (d. 1113) and two Roman sarcophagi re-used as tombs in the thirteenth century, and the interior was then as now spacious and un-cluttered with graveslabs set in the pavement or grander monuments on the walls. Palla Strozzi replied for the *Consoli*. He said that by no manner of means would they allow a chapel to be added to the church, because it would spoil it. He gave other reasons as well, which have not been reported. But we can still see for ourselves that a protruding chapel would have broken the unity of that harmonious octagon. On the other hand, he said, the Consuls were prepared to allow a tomb to be erected, but it must be '*breve e honestissima, sichè non occupi dell' adito della Chiesa*', that is, it must not take up room on the open floor of the church and was to be very beautiful, so as to be an ornament to it. For it was no small honour to Messer Baldassare, Strozzi ended, to be buried in the Baptistery. The honour was indeed so signal that it was an unspoken testimony to the affection the Florentines felt for Cossa's memory and a vindication of his claim that he had once been rightful Pope that they allowed it at all. And we shall discover that the two conditions imposed by the *Consoli* were of paramount importance in the design of the tomb.

It should not be thought that Strozzi and his fellow *Consoli* spoke such words because they had recently been illuminated by the new aesthetic light of the Renaissance. Already in the thirteenth century, St. Thomas Aquinas had praised tombs as ornaments to churches, declaring that since it was a good work to ornament a church the erection of a tomb must also be regarded as a good work. The principal purposes of a visible tomb, he continued, were to honour the dead man, to affirm faith in the doctrine of the Resurrection and remind the living of a dead man and so inspire them to offer prayers for the suffrage of his soul, which might be lingering in Purgatory. Burial in a holy place was profitable to the dead man himself, if he had ordered his own tomb, and even more to the living who had a tomb made for him, for his soul was thereby committed to the patronage of some saint 'by whose prayers on this account it is to be believed he is assisted,' and also to the prayers of those serving the holy place, since they would pray more often and more especially for those interred in their house.[27]

The saint was only voicing the general belief. The inscription on the tomb of Cardinal Guillaume de Braye (d. after 27 April 1282) in Viterbo is partly couched as a prayer to God, Christ and the patron saint of his Cardinal's church: 'May Guillaume de Braye, adorned with the Cardinal's title of Mark, who is buried here, be acceptable to Christ; may he be placed through thee, O Mark, in the citadel of Heaven: I pray thee, God omnipotent, spare him.'[28] On 24 August 1297, Cardinal Hugues de Billon ordered that he should be buried before the high altar of the monastery of Santa Sabina in Rome 'and let there be laid above us a copper tomb level with the pavement so that when the brethren see it, they may remember us in their prayers'. Cardinal Guillaume Teste willed on 1 September 1326 that he should be buried in the church of the hospital of Saint Jacques which he had refounded near Condom 'in a suitable and fitting place, and in a tomb neither very precious nor humble, by the sight of which together with its epitaph men may be encouraged to pray for his soul more willingly and devoutly.'[29] Cardinal Guillaume de Chanac desired what all those men desired who raised splendid tombs to themselves, honour to his memory, but he too wanted prayers for his soul. 'I will and ordain that for my body should be made an honourable tomb of alabaster such as benefits my estate: on it shall be placed my statue, my arms and other necessary ornaments, so that my relations and friends and those whom I have known as they pass by it, may remember me and take care to implore Almighty God for my soul.'[30]

Only by the end of the High Renaissance was imitation of the antique both in the design of tombs and in their spirit to erase from them all direct summons to prayer, the honourable commemoration of the dead to become their sole ostensible intention. It is this religious purpose which partly explains why executors so often strove long and anxiously to honour the obligation of erecting an expensive tomb when the will of a testator had imposed it on them. Not only were they applying his estate to the fulfilment of his desire and the honouring of his memory; by interring his body and erecting his tomb they themselves were performing good works which would earn them some remission of their sins. Indeed burial of the dead was regarded as one of the Seven Works of Mercy. In Cossa's case they were not able to gratify his desire for a special chapel to house his tomb and an altar where priests might say prayers and mass for him daily. But they were careful not to leave his soul without those spiritual suffrages on which late medieval men, racked by fear of pain and punishment in Purgatory, relied with conscience-stricken calculation for swifter redemption. For on 2 May 1426 the *Arte di Calimala* appointed two chaplains at a salary of 2 florins a month with the obligation of saying masses every day in the Baptistery for Cossa's soul.[31]

The *Consoli* probably gave permission for the tomb to be erected in the Baptistery because of the general reverence felt for Cossa by the Florentines, and because of his legacy of so great and precious a relic as the index finger of their patron saint. On receiving their permission the executors must have commissioned a design for the tomb. In the circumstances it is virtually certain that having procured one they submitted it to the *Consoli* for their approval: we shall consider later whether they also consulted Cossa's relatives in Naples. Whoever designed the architectural part of the tomb – a question that must be left unopened for the moment – there is every reason to think that they obtained their design from or through Donatello, to whom all early writers unanimously attribute the tomb. According to Vasari, it was not Giovanni but Cosimo de' Medici who chose Donatello for a work which he must have known would make the sculptor famous throughout Italy if he wrought it successfully.[32] Since Giovanni was now sixty and had already retired from active life in 1420, handing over his bank to his two sons, Cosimo and Lorenzo, it is more than possible that Vasari was recording a true tradition. Moreover, as we saw, it was Cosimo who together with Fra Matteo da Viterbo was entrusted by Cossa with devising or supervising the form which the reliquary of the Baptist's finger was to be given. But the most convincing argument of all for his intervention is a document of 14 February 1426, in which Cosimo de' Medici, who is described as one of Cossa's executors, appears with Bartolommeo Valori before the Consuls of the *Arte* to act concerning the tomb.[33] However, that same document suggests that Bartolommeo Valori may also have had some hand in awarding the commission. The price for the tomb as stipulated in the contract with Donatello was 800 florins, to include all expenses.[34]

Some time must have been spent making the design, which because of the conditions imposed by the Consuls offered special problems. More must have gone in obtaining marble after the design had been accepted and ap-

18

proved both by the executors and by the *Arte di Calimala*. Documents and the evidence of the tomb itself suggest that the marble was obtained piecemeal, not procured in one great order from Carrara. Probably this was because of the financial difficulties with which the executors had to contend. Nevertheless, work must have progressed fairly rapidly and during 1424 part of the tomb was set up in the Baptistery. We can assess how far it had risen by the last two months of 1424 from a remarkable episode whose significance for the dating of the tomb has not been understood. It so happens that the seventeenth-century antiquary Ferdinando del Migliore printed the substance of a note of it made by the Florentine notary Ser Pietro di Lodovico Doffi, while serving a bi-monthly term as the official notary who recorded the *Deliberazioni* of the *Signoria*.[35] Unfortunately Del Migliore omitted to print the date of Doffi's record. To make things worse his own copy or note of it is untraced, and the original *Deliberazioni* of the *Signoria*, from which he took it, have long been lost. Fortunately, we possess a full list of those who held the office of notary to the *Signoria* during the 1420s,[36] and from this we learn that Doffi held it only twice, once in 1420, much too early for what he records concerning the tomb, and once again in 1424, which must therefore be the date of his record. The two months of his term of service in 1424 are given by a contemporary chronicler as November and December and the original *Deliberazioni* for May to August 1424, which do survive, confirm that he was not notary during those terms.[37]

According to Doffi, then, as reported by Del Migliore, Pope Martin was much displeased when he heard of the epitaph that had been carved on the tomb. This read and still reads:

IOAN*n*ES QVO*n*DAM PAPA

XXIII*us*. OBIIT FLORENTIE A

N*n*O D*omi*NI MCCCCXVIIII XI

KALENDAS IANVARII

To Martin it seemed that there was an ambiguity in the QVONDAM, in that it appeared to suggest that Cossa had died, not a Cardinal, but a Pope. He concluded that the Florentines, whose behaviour to him during his residence in their city had greatly offended him, intended to imply a doubt as whether he himself was truly Pope. In his defence it must be admitted that the honours paid to Cossa after his death were universally held to be exceptional: Scipione Ammirato remarked ironically that had Cossa truly been Pope at his death, the *Signoria* would have paid him less honour.[38] Martin may well have felt during these ceremonies that their magnificence was a flout to his dignity; in any case it is not surprising if he was anxious and sensitive in all matters concerning Pope John. Accordingly a Papal emissary appeared before the *Signoria* to require that the epitaph should be removed, and that one beginning with the words *Baldassar Coscia Neapolitanus Cardinalis* should be substituted: for this had been Cossa's title at the end of his life, when he no longer enjoyed that title of Pope of which he had been lawfully deprived by a Universal Council of the Church. The Priors were taken aback by this request, but refused to be bullied into depriving of its full splendour the memory of a great man of whose burial in their city they would always be proud. Martin, they decided, was making too much of too little, and they replied that what was written was written. In fact they were not behaving so insolently as it might seem, for after his deposition it had been the universal practice to describe Cossa in letters and other documents as Messer Baldassare Cossa 'formerly Pope John' (*olim Papa Johannes*) a phrase which stated exactly both what he had been and what he then was.

The offending epitaph is still inscribed on the sarcophagus of the tomb, and the conclusion to be drawn from the episode is that by the date of Martin's protest the sarcophagus had been hoisted into its present position in the Baptistery and had been visible for some time to the generality. It is lucky that the date of Doffi's record can be fixed with precision, because another document which has been used to date the tomb happens not to bear out the interpretation that has been placed on it. By great good fortune another seventeenth-century antiquary, the Senatore Carlo Strozzi, went systematically through the books of the *Arte di Calimala* before they were lost and made notes of their contents. In his *Spoglio Secondo*[39] of these records he wrote '*Sepultura di Mr Baldassar Coscia si fabbrica in S. Gio 1424*' and noted as his source '*Deliberazioni dal 1424 al 1426, (f.) 2*'. Now this is the one little book of *Deliberazioni* of the *Arte* from the 1420s still surviving. Not only is it labelled *Deliberatione dall' anno 1424 al 1426*, but on f. 2 there is indeed a document about the tomb. Unfortunately Strozzi was misled by an early hand which has added the date 1424 after the second entry in the book, that for 2 January. The addition is unmistakable because it is written in a different ink from the rest of the book. And if we read the entry above, we find that the true first date in the book is 1 January 1425 Florentine style, that is 1 January 1426 modern style. The subsequent entries in the book all confirm that it contains the deliberations of the first six months of 1425/6: possibly the mistake was made as early as the fifteenth century when some careless notary, making up the book for deposit in the archives of the *Arte*, misread the *vigesimoquinto* of the first entry as *vigesimoquarto*, and added the wrong year to the rubric of the second entry, the first where there was space.

The document itself has already been mentioned in passing.[40] On 14 February 1426 Bartolommeo Valori and Cosimo de' Medici appeared before the *Consoli* of the *Arte di Calimala* as 'commissaries and executors of the Lord Baldassar Cossa'. Cossa, it will be recalled, had empowered any two of his four executors to execute his will and Bartolommeo and Cosimo had evidently been deputed by the other two to supervise the execution of the tomb. They declared that they were in need of money 'for the expedition of the tomb which they are having made for the body of the said Lord Baldassare, and they cannot obtain it elsewhere save from the *Arte* or *Opera* of San Giovanni, that is, from the money which the said *Opera* received in deposit from them'. Accordingly they petitioned the *Consoli* to allow them to take at least 400 florins from that deposit. The Consuls consented 'wishing to please the said executors and or commissaries and also most of all because to do otherwise would be contrary to right and without any profit to the said *Arte*'. They therefore decided, having taken a vote by means of black and white beans 'as is the custom', to withdraw 400 florins from Filippo di Bernabò degli Agli and partners and Antonio di Messere Niccolò da Rabatta and partners, the bankers into whose hands the *Arte* had paid the deposit made by the executors. Guccino da Sommaria, the treasurer of the *Opera*, was then to pay this sum over to the executors. The whole transaction suggests that the *Arte* had at first been doubtful as to whether Cossa had left enough to pay for the tomb, and so had insisted on the full price of 800 florins as agreed by contract being deposited in their hands by the executors before work began. It is hardly surprising if they were afraid they might be obliged to produce a large sum of money for the completion of the tomb, if only to prevent its being an unsightly object in their '*bel San Giovanni*'. After all they had been obliged to find half the cost of gilding the reliquary of St. John's finger.

It is impossible to say whether this vast sum of 400 florins, half the price of the tomb, was needed to pay for work already done or for work to be done, since the words 'for the expedition of the tomb' could mean either. But the probability is that it was in payment for work already done, since for most of 1426 Donatello was in Pisa, working or supervising work on the tomb of Cardinal Rainaldo Brancaccio. The document of 2 May 1426 which records the election of two chaplains by the *Arte* to say mass daily for Cossa's soul, speaks of him as 'sepultured in the church of San Giovanni' (*seppulti in ecclesiam Sancti Johannis*), and could be interpreted as implying that work on the tomb was expected to be complete before too long.

When we next hear of the tomb, it is 28 January 1427, and the *Operai* of the Duomo are agreeing to allow their *capomaestro* to sell four panels of white marble from their store 'at the usual price' to Bartolommeo Valori 'for the tomb of Pope John XXIII.' In early July Michelozzo enters the story, listing the tomb in his *catasto* return first among all the works which he and Donatello have had in hand during the two years or thereabouts they have been partners. So far they have received 600 florins for it, every one of which they have spent on the work and still the tomb is not finished. Hence they can make no estimate of their profit. But they are bound to stay within the limit of

800 florins. This is a significant clause if we remember the posthumous difficulties concerning Cossa's estate and the transaction between the executors and the *Arte* in February 1426.[41] Further on he notes that the workshop owes the brick-maker Benedetto di Marco da Terrarossa 5 florins for lime and bricks supplied for the tomb of Pope John.

On 2 September 1427 Bartolommeo Valori died, after making a retreat that summer with the friars of Santa Croce, so as to detach himself wholly from the affairs of this world.[42] The supervision of the tomb must now have fallen entirely in Cosimo's hands since Niccolò da Uzzano seems to have taken no interest in it and Vieri Guadagni had been dead for a year. The date when it was completed can only be conjectured. H. W. Janson proposes 1428, partly on the ground that the marble-carver Pagno di Lapo Portigiani, who is known to have spent eighteen months working for Donatello and Michelozzo in 1426 and 1427, began working in Siena early in June 1428 under Jacopo della Quercia on the great font in the Duomo. And as we shall see in the next chapter, the tomb of Raffaele Fulgosio (d. September 1427) in the Santo at Padua, which is a close copy of the Cossa tomb, is known to have been designed before 5 March 1429, when it was formally commissioned from the Florentine sculptor Piero Lamberti.

The probability that the tomb was completed between July 1427 and June 1428 is also strengthened by a fragment of indirect documentary evidence. Carlo Strozzi has left a list of the references he found in the *Libri Grandi*, or main records of the *Arte*, to wills in which it was concerned. All six of those which concern the execution of the will of Messer Baldassar Coscia he assigns 'to the *Libro Grande* marked G'. According to him, this book was begun in 1425 and closed at the end of 1428, in other words, since he keeps to the original Florentine style, it ran from early in 1426 to early in 1429. Between these dates any matter raised with the *Arte* about Cossa's will can only have concerned either his chaplains or his tomb. Strozzi refers to folios 265, 279, 285, 294, 320 and 350, numbers which suggest that the documents he found came late in the book, and therefore under the years 1427 and 1428/9.[43] But since the completion of great and costly works of sculpture was often protracted by reason of their very expensiveness and the difficulty of finding money to pay for them, it is worth mentioning that the tomb was surely finished by 1432. For in that year the *Arte* decided that a jewel consisting of a ruby set between two diamonds, which formed part of Cossa's estate and was now deposited with the *Spedalingo* of Santa Maria Nuova, should be sold,[44] after composition made with Cosimo de' Medici and others who claimed to own part of it. The proceeds were to be applied to buy shares in the *Monte* or public debt of Florence, the interest to be used for the *Opera* of San Giovanni. The jewel was bought by Cosimo, who declared that seven twenty-fourths of it belonged to him, at a price of 300 florins 'although much more had been offered for it at other times', complained the *Arte*, and with these shares to the value of 1000 florins in the *Monte* were bought to provide *paramenti* for the Baptistery altar. The proceeds of the sale would surely have been applied to finishing the tomb had it still been incomplete. It would be interesting to know how the *Arte* came to acquire a title to the jewel. Certainly it was not from Cossa's will. Had it after all advanced money to make it possible for the tomb to be completed? And what was Cosimo's own title to part of the jewel? Del Migliore says that the tomb cost 1000 florins in all, 200 more than the 800 specified in the contemporary documents, of course too round a figure to be accepted unhesitatingly, especially as it seems a little high for the quantity of figure-work on the tomb. Altogether the loss of the *Arte*'s books is a great misfortune.

Chapter II · The Cossa Tomb

THE TOMB OF POPE JOHN XXIII (no. 2) is set against that wall of the Baptistery which runs from Ghiberti's North Door to the tribune on the east, between the two central pillars and just before the sarcophagus tomb of Bishop Ranieri. During the thirteenth and fourteenth centuries three types of tomb in the interior of churches were used in Italy for different estates of society. The tomb slab was for the unaspiring merchant, professor, jurist, notary, or knight, for abbots, priors and priests of lower degree and for those who from humility desired no more splendid form of commemoration. Such slabs were set in the floor, or much less commonly in the wall. They might be either plain or elaborately carved in low relief with an effigy of the deceased, usually shown standing or lying beneath a canopied framework. The canopy was a motif borrowed from the most splendid type of Gothic standing tomb, and slabs of this kind were sometimes executed in costly bronze or marble. Yet the choice of a slab set level with or only slightly raised above the pavement was nonetheless a true token either of the estate of the deceased in the hierarchy of society or else of his humility. For the distinguishing sign of degree and of posthumous honour was the height to which the tomb rose from the ground. This connection between height and honour was already established by the middle of the thirteenth century. Aldobrandino Ottobuoni, an *anziano* of Florence who had refused to betray the city's interests to the Pisans for a bribe, was given splendid obsequies by the city after his death *c.* 1260 and buried in the Duomo, 'at the expense of the Comune in a tomb of marble loftier than any other',[1] says the chronicler Giovanni Villani. Naturally the association of honour with height entailed some distinction among degrees of height according to degrees of estate or merit: in his will Gian Galeazzo Visconti of Milan (d. 1402) ordered himself to be buried in his foundation of the Certosa of Pavia in a tomb behind the high altar 'to be raised for excellence seven steps from the ground and on it to be set up to him an image in his likeness, seated in ducal habit in a chair'.[2]

Accordingly, we find the intermediate order of wall-tombs either rise to a moderate level above the ground or are set against the wall on brackets. Such tombs were erected for members of knightly families, for bishops and great abbots, for personages whose distinction or whose aspirations obtained for them such an honour. Their design and iconography might be more or less elaborate according to the means and wishes of their patrons. But often they were reduced or curtailed versions of the largest and most magnificent of all wall-tombs, those reserved for the highest secular and ecclesiastical estates of feudal society; Popes, cardinals, archbishops and greater bishops, princes, great lords and personages whom it was especially desired to honour. In Italy the standard scheme of such tombs appears in the middle of the thirteenth century. It was derived from French Gothic tombs. The tomb rises from the ground to a great height, varying of course according to the means or importance of the patron, factors which also decided whether the tomb was of greater or lesser size, of greater or lesser elaboration. It projects well forward, so that there may be room for its complex structure of sculptures and for a deep space above the effigy. The sarcophagus, usually carved with a scene or figures of devotional significance to the deceased and with heraldry, rests on figures of Virtues – usually cardinal Virtues for laymen, and theological Virtues for ecclesiastics. On the sarcophagus lies the effigy of the deceased, either on a bier or more usually on a pall spread over the sarcophagus, which then symbolises the death-bed or bier on which the corpse was laid out after death. Two angels draw back the curtains from the bed of the deceased or perform some other office in praise of his merits – but their meaning and purpose must be reserved for later, fuller discussion. Above rises a canopy, supported on columns. On or under this canopy are set figures of the Virgin and Child, of the patron saint or saints of the deceased and of Christ in Glory.

The only rival to such grandiose wall-tombs was the free-standing tomb raised to a greater or lesser degree above the floor. Jacopo della Quercia's tomb of Ilaria del Carretto, wife of Paolo Guinigi, lord of Lucca, where the effigy rests on a free-standing sarcophagus, is an unrecognised early fifteenth-century example of this type, which again was introduced into Italy from France. In such tombs the prominence due to great rank was proclaimed both by their height – which was sometimes very great, as in the tomb of Bernabò Visconti in San Giovanni in Conca at Milan – and by their isolated setting. Inside churches such tombs seem to have been the prerogative of secular rulers and of Popes – the tomb of Pope Martin V (c. 1431) in St. John Lateran (no. 96) was originally just such a tomb. Of course there are variations in all these types of tomb and it would be a great mistake to force all surviving monuments into conformity with them or suggest that each estate kept rigidly to that form which was its right. As in matters of clothes and jewellery, where sumptuary laws had constantly to be made forbidding certain articles of dress or adornment to the lower orders or reserving them for the higher, vanity and the love of display broke through all the gradations imposed by hierarchy. Moreover, since it was a good work to erect a tomb, affection and family pride often prompted expense and magnificence. Nevertheless, in a general sense, and allowing for differences in individual choice and local usage, the distinctions we have just made are valid and were surprisingly well observed.

With these considerations in mind, we can now examine the Cossa tomb itself. It rises 24 ft. high (7·32 metres, in Florentine measurements of the day twelve *braccia* or thereabouts) from the ground, and at the time of its erection was the loftiest tomb in Florence.[3] Except for the plinth and base, four sections of the canopy and some plain panels, which are of white or whitish-brown marble, it is cut from a brown marble which has white patches here and there.[4] This marble is found in other Florentine *quattrocento* sculptures, though not generally of so deep a brown as in the Cossa tomb: an example is Antonio Rossellino's bust of Giovanni Chellini (1456) in the Victoria and Albert Museum. Fitted between the columns is the low plinth on which the tomb rests, with moulded front and sides. It measures 6 ft. 6$\frac{7}{8}$ in. (2 metres) at the base, expanding to 7 ft. 5$\frac{5}{8}$ in. (2·28 metres) at the top, and is 1 ft. 2$\frac{5}{8}$ in. (38 cm.) high. On it rests a base (no. 4) whose projecting cornice and foot have concave mouldings which in the case of the foot are set slightly back from the base in relation to the plinth. The front of the base is carved with three winged cherub heads decorated with ribbons ruffling out to either side and beneath. Between the cherub heads hang swags of fruit and foliage, suspended on stalks faceted spirally which pass behind the heads at the level of the ear. The same motif of cherub heads and swags is used again on the frieze of the *Tabernacolo di Parte Guelfa* (now of the *Mercatanzia*) on Or San Michele (no. 100) which once housed Donatello's statue of Saint Louis of Toulouse. This is known to have been completed by 1425, when the Saint Louis was set up in it. On the *Tabernacolo*, because of the height of the frieze, the swags are composed of leaves and the ribbons are ruffled into higher ruckles. Among the swags on the tomb there are differences in the fruit, leaves and flowers which compose them. The ends of the ribbons curl illusionistically in depth, a device already used on the sarcophagus of Nofri Strozzi (no. 101) carved by Niccolò di Piero Lamberti in 1418–19.[5] Putti bearing a long swag, it may be noted in passing, decorate both sides of the vault above Nofri's sarcophagus. The length of the base is 7 ft. 7 in. (2·31 metres) receding to 7 ft. 5$\frac{1}{2}$ in. (2·27 metres) and its height is 1 ft. 9$\frac{5}{8}$ in. (55 cm.). Its top is made up of several slabs of marble: a long narrow slab at the front, two short narrow slabs at the sides, and several pieces of marble fitted between these, one on the left with rather awkward effect.

Set back on the base is a great vertical slab of marble (no. 3) carved with four fluted Corinthian pilasters supporting a moulded cornice. Between the pilasters, enclosed in receding moulded frames, are sunk three shell-topped niches with curved backs. They contain figures in very high relief of the three theological Virtues, Faith on the left, Charity in the middle, Hope on the right. Each of these three figures moves freely in the space of the niches, and each puts out her right foot on the platform formed by the top of the base, so linking these two sections of the tomb. The slab, which for convenience we may call a pylon, is 4 ft. 6¾ in. (1·39 metres) high and 6 ft. 5⅜ in. (2·02 metres) wide. The capitals of the pilasters are 6½ in. (16 cm.) high, the pilasters 3 ft. 5¼ in. (1·05 metres) high and the base 2½ in. (6 cm.) high. From the cornice of the pylon four consoles of very classical type rise 1¼ ft. (38 cm.) to support the sarcophagus (no. 19). They are decorated on the underside with fluted acanthus leaves, whose ends and edges curl downwards with illusionistic effect. The volutes end in rolls shaped as bunches of leaves with a rope tied round them, a motif found in the consoles supporting the *Tabernacolo di Parte Guelfa* and also used in different forms on the Brancaccio tomb, where the three Virtues support the sarcophagus on rather similar *fascinae*. The sides of the consoles are carved with Gothic foliated stems.

The caissons above the consoles are carved in the base of the sarcophagus: they are decorated with Gothic ornamental motifs of flowers set in foliage. Each flower is different, though the foliage is arranged to form more or less the same pattern. Between the consoles, which are 1 ft. 3⅜ in. (39 cm.) high, are set three oblong panels of whitish marble, each with sunk grounds in moulded frames. On them are carved three shields shaped as painted ovals. It is important to read these shields in the heraldically correct order, from dexter to sinister, that is from left to right. The shield on the left (dexter) bears Cossa's family arms, *party per fess, in chief azure a leg or, in base, bendy vert and argent, all within a border dancetty or*,[6] surmounted by a Papal tiara. The centre shield bears the arms of the church, the keys of Peter, again surmounted by a Papal tiara. The right (sinister) shield has Cossa's arms as a Cardinal, that is, his family arms surmounted by a cardinal's hat with four tassels. The shields project on to the frame below and the tiaras and hat on to the frame above. They stand out in deep and sharp relief with the usual deliberately illusionistic effect, casting a shadow on the sunk ground: indeed their surfaces are made slightly convex so as to stand out all the more. The scarves embroidered with crosses of the first two and the tassels of the third emerge from behind, their lower relief graded to the depth of space the sculptor has created for them. The illusion of space is augmented by hollowing out the tiaras and cardinal's hat so that they seem three-dimensional.

The sarcophagus, which measures almost 7 ft. (2·13 metres) wide by 2 ft. 3½ in. (70 cm.) high is set slightly back on the consoles. Its base is of unusual form, for instead of rising with an inward slope, as is customary, it rises outwards in a series of projecting mouldings. It is in fact shaped as an architrave, and a member of the same form is used correctly as an architrave on the *Tabernacolo di Parte Guelfa*. The purpose of its unorthodoxy is to create a ledge, a natural space on which the two child angels carved on the front of the sarcophagus can sit. The surface of the ledge slopes a little upwards, suggesting receding space, and to increase the illusion of depth behind the angels and the parchment they hold, a narrow oblong panel with moulded border is sunk behind their chubby bodies, which are seen to be carved in surprisingly high relief if looked at from the sides, and their wings. The effect is of a lively yet formalised illusionism. The two angels have unrolled their parchment, in contemporary parlance a brief (*breve*)[7] or short Papal letter, which is inscribed with the epitaph, and hold it stretched out between them. The conceit is that they have brought a missive which they have unfolded for the visitor to read. Its upper edges have curled inwards, springing back with such force on the left that the edge of the parchment is torn. Both angels, though similar in pose and smiling expression, are different in face and body, one fat and dimpling, the other slenderer and slighter. This attention to diversity in symmetry is constant throughout the tomb.

The sides of the sarcophagus are decorated with plain sunk panels. On its top the bronze effigy of Cossa rests on a bier which stands almost 2 ft. high (58 cm.) on two lion legs (no. 12). The bier is in fact slightly tilted to make the effigy more visible from below, but this device can be detected only from the back. To bring the head even more into view the feet of the bier are of unequal height, the foot on the left being made $22\frac{7}{8}$ in. (58 cm.) high, 2 centimetres higher than the right foot. Here too the designer's fancy has exercised itself. On a real bier, as on any piece of furniture, the legs were made exactly alike, but on this bier one lion looks straight forward and the other turns his head to the right. Such a detail suggests, it may be thought, a design from an artist with a sculptor's interest in animated form rather than one from a more architecturally-minded hand – all the more so because the lions are unmistakably the work of an assistant.

The bronze effigy of Cossa, measuring 6 ft. $3\frac{1}{4}$ in. (1·91 metres) long, lies on a great fringed pall spread over the bier. The head is supported by a pillow enclosed in a cover embroidered with a border of linked circles enclosing rosettes, with fringed tassels hanging from the corners (no. 18). In order that his features shall be visible at so great a height the head is turned outwards, not laid flat on the back of the head with the face in vertical profile, as was customary in effigies. Behind rises a second pylon, 4 ft. $4\frac{3}{4}$ in. (1·34 metres) high, decorated with three panels enclosed by sunk moulded borders in a plain framework surmounted by a cornice. Above it rises a third pylon, of the same height or nearly so, for it measures 4 ft. $5\frac{1}{4}$ in. (1·35 metres) high by 7 ft. $8\frac{7}{8}$ in. (2·36 metres). It is topped by a heavy cornice and carved with a sunk half-oval shell-topped niche in which is a half-length figure of the Virgin holding the Child. The niche repeats the form of the niches below, even to the cornice which separates the shell-top from the space (here supposed) below, with slightly awkward effect.

From a ribbed bronze ring attached to the ceiling above hangs a great canopy, richly painted on the inside with a pattern of stemmed flowers and with heavy fringes (no. 1). It is important to appreciate that it is not a canopy of state or *baldacchino*, which had a standard form, like that depicted by Pinturicchio (no. 99) hanging above the throne of Pope Eugenius IV in his fresco of *Eugenius despatching Aeneas Sylvius to the Emperor Frederick III* in the Libreria Piccolomini in the Duomo of Siena. The Cossa canopy is a bed-tester of rich stuff, as we might expect, for this part of the tomb figures the death-chamber of the deceased. This type of bed-tester was described in the fifteenth century as of *baldacchino* shape: so the inventory of Palazzo Medici taken in 1492 after the death of Lorenzo de' Medici lists, '*Vno sparviere a Vso di padiglione di panno Lino con pendenti frangiati sopra la cornice di detta spalliera.*' We can form an idea of the sumptuousness and cost in the early fifteenth century of the cloth of which the Cossa tester is shown as made from what is recorded of the *baldacchino* under which Pope Gregory XII made his entry into Siena on 4 September 1407. It was of 'cloth of gold of taffeta' and cost the Sienese slightly more than 124 florins, a huge sum. For painting it Maestro Taddeo di Francesco was paid 14 florins and later it was given to Gregory as a present.[8]

The Cossa canopy has two tent-like summits, one behind the other, though only the front summit hangs from the ring. Both are fastened by a broad fringed band. The two fringed breadths of the canopy extend to either side of the tomb, where they are looped up against the pillars, and then hang down almost to the level of the bottom of the bier. At the apex of the back of the canopy its inner edges are made to curve inwards and upwards with naturalistic irregularity and the stuff is creased along the inner edge of the breadth. Below the apex the fringed sections are carved in narrow blocks of white, not brown marble, unlike almost all the rest of the tomb, and so are the sections of the hanging drapes immediately beneath them. The painted decoration does not disguise the difference in colour between the two marbles: indeed, it has not been very logically applied in the drapes, which are left white with rather odd effect.

Seen from the sides the base has a plain framework. The pylon is framed by two fluted Corinthian pilasters like those on the front, containing a sunk panel. Above is a plain oblong corresponding to the consoles, and above this again is a plain framework enclosing a sunk panel with rounded corners at the top and surrounded by a raised border. The sides of the last pylon lack even this austere ornamentation and are left quite plain and flat. Merely to the naked eye it is obvious that the three pylons are the same size, and that the monument was designed by superimposing them on each other, the consoles being interposed in order to emphasize the sarcophagus. The plinth and canopy therefore break what would otherwise be a rather dull repetition of a single architectural form. The proportions of the monument, including those of the figures, are governed by a system which relates all the parts to each other – to cite a single instance, the measurement of the head of Charity

29

from brow to chin is the same as that of the capital of the pilasters framing the Virtues.

It is sometimes suggested that the tomb has been scrubbed of much of its original gilding and colour. There appears to be no early description which records anything of these enrichments, so important for the final aspect of the tomb. A late fifteenth-century drawing of the tomb (no. 97) in the manuscript *Libro* of Buonaccorso Ghiberti (f. 70v) which is sometimes cited as evidence for them is of no value whatsoever as evidence for early colouring. It is one of a series of designs for tombs contained in Ghiberti's book, some purely inventions, some adapted, like the drawing of the Cossa tomb, from existing monuments. It depicts the tomb as set in a chapel, framed by Corinthian pilasters with a rich moulded base beneath and a monumental cornice above. Two shields are added in the spandrels between the cornice and the canopy. Like the other drawings in the group it is coloured in red, blue and yellow, the red representing the rich red marble so frequently used for architectural inlays in the *quattrocento*, the blue that favourite adornment of a gay and costly azure pigment, the yellow gilding. On the Cossa drawing the shields, the ring from which the canopy hangs, the Madonna, the effigy, the putti, the epitaph, the consoles and the shields between them, the three Virtues and the pilasters are coloured yellow. The capitals of the pilasters are yellow too: the pilasters themselves are lightly shaded with it, as is the canopy. The space between the tomb and the frame and the frieze of the base are coloured pink: the sunk caissons of the ceiling and the frieze of the cornice are coloured blue. These patterns of pigmentation are repeated in other drawings, notably in those on ff. 67v and 69v, and apart from suggesting rich effects of colouring, their purpose is to give relief to the design, not to reproduce reality.

It is better to scrutinize the tomb itself for evidence of original colour and gilding, using what we know of the colouring of other tombs as a guide. It is most unlikely that the base and the three figures of the Virtues were ever coloured, either wholly or in part. Nor is there any trace of gilding on the attributes held by the figures, such as appears for example on the Aragazzi tomb. The marble of the base is white Carrara marble but the brown marble in which most of the tomb is carved already has a rich variety of surface without the addition of colour, and it has been given a high, smooth, shining polish which is a finish in itself. On the other hand it is not impossible that the capitals of the pilasters and the shell tops of the niches were partly or wholly gilt in order to set off the figures, but again no trace of any such gilding remains.[10] It might be supposed that the shields were given their proper heraldic colours like those on the sarcophagus of the Brancaccio monument. If so, they would have been coloured gold, azure, green and silver, the colours of the Cossa arms. But again there are no traces of colour or gilding, either on the shields themselves or on the tiaras and hat which surmount them, and it must be remembered that many shields on *trecento* tombs had no colouring. It does not even seem that any of the mouldings of the frames were gilt. The front of the sarcophagus is unlikely to have been coloured or gilded and again there is no sign that any of its mouldings were ever gilded.

It seems in fact that as on the Brancaccio tomb the costly enrichments of gilding and colouring were deliberately reserved for the upper half of the monument, where they not only illuminated the effigy and the canopy but marked them out more distinctly to the eye, which looks up to them from some distance below. The bier itself is painted red, a dark terracotta red, but the brownish marble of the lion supports is left uncoloured. The pall on which the effigy lies is a deep rich blue except for its fringes, which are gilt, and the pillow supporting the head is also blue where it shows through the embroidered cover. The underside of the cover is gilt to represent cloth of gold, and gilt too are its fringed tassels, but on top it is left white in order to set off the richness of the bronze effigy, which is entirely gilt. The great canopy has gilt fringes – fringes were a costly piece of magnificence in the Middle Ages, especially fringes of gold thread. We are meant to imagine it as made of lined stuff. The outer stuff is white, and has a border above the fringes consisting of a broad band of flowers outlined in blue between two thick red lines decorated with Gothic crocketing. The lining is decorated with stemmed flowers, painted in blue with red centres, and arranged in rows of three, the stems of one row rising from the heads of another, just such a design as is found in woven stuffs. The patterning, colour and gilding very effectively suggest a real medieval canopy of sumptuous splendour such as hung above the state beds of the greatest personages of Christendom.

The ring from which the canopy hangs and the bands that loop it are also gilt. The Virgin and Child were never gilt: it is possible that the moulded frame around them was once wholly or partly gilt and that the shell behind was outlined in gilt. But it is also possible that they were left plain because of the rich gilt fringes hanging immediately above. The taste of the *quattrocento* was always elegantly discriminating in the colouring and gilding of marble, preferring to set off its white lucency against details in gold and colour so as to reveal the beauty of the stone. Indeed, the designer has skilfully contrasted the white stuff of the canopy against the rich gilding of the capitals of the two framing pillars. All in all then it is probable that not so much of the original colouring and gilding has been lost as might be imagined. Begrimed and dust-laden now, when the tomb was in its pristine state it must have been lit with a very International Gothic splendour of gold and blue and floral magnificence.

The *Consoli* of the *Arte di Calimala*, we remember, expressly forbade a tomb that projected deeply into the church, as a grandiose canopied tomb of the usual sort would have done. But the designer of the tomb, though he could not raise up a real pillared canopy, ingeniously contrived to suggest one for the tomb while abiding by the condition imposed. The projecting upper storey of the Baptistery is supported on each wall by a pair of majestic columns in the centre and a pier at either end. By fitting the tomb between the pair of columns on the wall allotted as a site for the tomb he made them substitutes for the columns which support the canopy in canopied Gothic tombs. To weld them even more tightly into his design he shaped the mouldings of the platform which supports the superstructure of the tomb to match those of the bases of the pillars. And the ends of the platform are cut so as to fit flush with the bases of the columns. As a result of his contrivance, bases and platform seem a single element. For the upper part of the monument it was not possible to create such a unified feature, but the pillars are once again integrated into the design by making the ends of the great canopy rest against them.

The problems of setting out the elements of the tomb in a rational and appropriate space within the limits set by the *Arte* are solved with masterly elegance. The front of the two pillars fixes the front plane of the design. In the space between and behind them the tomb is made to recede, recede again, then at the level of the consoles project, so bringing forward with eloquent emphasis sarcophagus, bier and effigy. The projection simultaneously creates here the effect of greater depth demanded by tradition for a part of the tomb symbolising the death chamber. The depth is increased and room is made for the great drapes of the heavy canopy by setting back the plain panelled pylon behind the sarcophagus to the extent of the width of the foremost fluted Corinthian pilaster carved on the side of the pylon of the Virtues. The space between the sarcophagus and drape and the panelled pylon is filled with plain stone. The heavenly being of the Virgin is suggested with equal ingenuity: the pylon on which she is carved is set back from the projecting cornice below, so creating an effect of visionary distance. The same dexterity of solution converted the Virtues from free-standing supports into high relief figures which seem to move with three-dimensional life, and for the architectural canopy that was precluded by the *Arte*'s restrictions a substitute was found in a magnificent bed-canopy, a motif of similar outline and of weighty symbolism.

There has been much dispute as to whether it was Michelozzo or Donatello who achieved this masterpiece of design, in which all the salient features of the canopied tomb are retained without intrusion beyond the two pillars on to the floor of the Baptistery. But the arguments of the dispute were all drawn from the old documentation of the tomb, which is delusive, as we have seen. On a strict interpretation of all the documents as we have them now, the designer of the tomb must have been Donatello, since the tomb was commissioned in 1422 and was well under way by the end of 1424, which is surely to be taken as the earliest plausible date when Donatello and Michelozzo can have entered into partnership, and then only on the assumption that the '*due anni o incircha*' of which Michelozzo speaks early in July 1427 should be interpreted as meaning that the two masters had been partners for more, not for less than two years. All the fifteenth-century writers who mention the tomb attribute it to Donatello; even Vasari, who knew that Michelozzo had worked on it, assigns to him only the figure of Faith.

It has been argued that the tomb cannot have been begun before Michelozzo and Donatello entered into partnership, since Michelozzo listed it in his *catasto* return. But this is to misinterpret the arrangement between the two men. Michelozzo did not list the works on which they are engaged as commissions received after the date when they had entered into partnership, but as commissions in hand from that date, a rather different matter. It is far more likely that when the two invested capital in a joint workshop and tools, Donatello agreed to share with Michelozzo the responsibility and the profits of one or two large-scale commissions he had already received but which were not yet finished or begun. We know that Donatello abandoned, no doubt gladly, the commercial side of the partnership to the capable and business-like Michelozzo. Not only did Michelozzo draw up Donatello's *catasto* return for him in 1427, but on 9 May of the same year he signed jointly with Donatello a letter demanding a payment of 50 florins from the *Opera* of the Duomo of Siena for Donatello's work on the font, work in which Michelozzo had no part, and for which Donatello received all the payments. As was natural in a tax-return Michelozzo listed in his *portata* all those joint works from which he expected a share of the profit, but without other proof it cannot be assumed that because they appear in his list they had not been begun before *c.* 1425. If anything is clear from fifteenth-century documents about works of sculpture, it is that the costs of procuring material and labour ate away most of the large sums that were spent on them, and that the artist only saw his profit with the last payment. The history of the Brancaccio tomb, as set out in the next section of this book, suggests that it was the commission for this great tomb which induced Donatello to take a partner, not the commission for the Cossa tomb.

Yet there still remains the possibility that Donatello turned to Michelozzo or to some other architect for the general architectural design of the tomb. Because of this possibility, no conclusion about the attribution of the design can be advanced as entirely certain. But it must be remembered that as a sculptor Donatello was trained to undertake tombs and other sculptural work involving architectural design and construction. He must certainly have been known to possess the knowledge and skills required to design and erect such works, otherwise he would hardly have been commissioned to execute a great monument like the Cossa tomb. Most tombs in fact demanded no special architectural expertise beyond the competence of a mason. Yet although it is now customary to emphasise that Donatello was primarily a sculptor, it is a great mistake to suppose that he could have worked successfully as a master sculptor in the *quattrocento* without some knowledge of architectural design and technique, so tightly linked were the carver's and the builder's art. And if Brunelleschi's late fifteenth-century biographer is to be believed, Donatello, far from being modest about his architectural knowledge, was presumptuous enough to carp at the great Brunelleschi 'though he had no great understanding of architecture, as can be seen from his pulpit in Santa Maria del Fiore and his other pulpits and from other similar works, in which he worked in architecture.'[11] The same writer does indeed report that when Donatello and Brunelleschi went to Rome together, Donatello studied only the antique sculpture which had been their original goal without sparing a glance for the secrets of antique architecture, whereas Brunelleschi sought to penetrate into the mysteries of its proportions and construction. But he also says that Donatello worked with Brunelleschi in making rough drawings and taking the measurements of almost all the ancient buildings of Rome and many buildings in the Campagna, so that his words cannot be interpreted as meaning that Donatello took no interest at all in architecture.[12] On the contrary he complains that Donatello insisted on making his own designs for the framework of his sculptures, as in the stone surrounds of the bronze doors of the Old Sacristy in San Lorenzo, for all that he had so little aptitude for architecture and only a superficial knowledge of its true antique forms, except in his own opinion.[12]

We must ask then whether the tomb itself is so ambitious architecturally that it must have been designed for Donatello by Michelozzo or some other architect. In working out the answer to this question the ingenious brilliance of the solution to the problem posed by the *Arte*'s restriction should be set out of consideration, for with one exception, to be considered, it did not create any problems of structure. We must ponder only the structure itself. This consists of a number of panels and members of marble applied to an understructure of brick, and of the canopy. If the canopy is excluded the construction is simplicity itself and it is difficult to believe that it demanded any expertise beyond that normally at the command of medieval and early Renaissance sculptors, who were always setting up heavy wall tombs on brackets. The canopy, on the other hand, may have required consultation with an architect, since it had to be fixed so securely that its great weight would not bring it crashing down. Here then Donatello, if it was he who made the design, may well have consulted with Michelozzo or Brunelleschi in order to be certain that a single bronze ring and mortaring to the great pillars on either side would be enough to sustain the canopy in place.

In reality its form has the advantage of distributing the weight very evenly.

If there is nothing except the canopy in the structure of the tomb which suggests a technical expertise beyond that which we may assume Donatello to have possessed, there is nothing at all in the formal elements of the design which implies reliance on an architect. The tomb consists of a series of superimposed horizontal oblongs, three of them, the pylons, identical in size. The members are all simply and elegantly designed, but the purely architectural elements, pilasters, cornices and the like, are kept subordinate to the sculptural elements for which they merely provide a framework and a background. So the pilasters framing the Virtues are kept low, with an effect of flatness surely very different from the stronger relief with which an architect would have articulated the structure of such a design. Except for these pilasters, with their plain flutings and flatly carved capitals, there is hardly any architectural ornament on the tomb: no attempt has been made, as on the Brancaccio monument, to enrich it profusely with antique ornament. Moreover, as we have seen, there is an unorthodoxy in the design of the base of the sarcophagus, where an outward sloping pedestal is used instead of the usual inward one so as to create a logical space for the two reliefs of angels, and another in the lion supports of the bier, made asymmetrical so as to please the sculptor's fancy. The simplicity and comparative want of variety of the members also seem to point to Donatello as designer – to be in fact just what might be expected from a sculptor whose primary interest was sculpture, but who had learnt or was learning from ancient works of art and from a master like Brunelleschi the architectural vocabulary of the antique manner in order to use it decoratively and appropriately, not as an architect, but with an architect's emphasis.

These characteristics also suggest a rather earlier date for the tomb than the *Tabernacolo di Parte Guelfa*, which in spite of such fantasies as the folded mat between its consoles and its base and the strange over-dominant heads ornamenting the corners of the base, is more strongly articulated and more richly decorated with antique ornaments. These seem significant differences, in spite of the allowances which must always be made for differences in the purpose and function of works of art in order to avoid confusing variations of treatment with stylistic development. Whatever assistance or advice he received from Brunelleschi and Michelozzo, the *Tabernacolo* was surely designed by Donatello. No architect would have tolerated such usurpations of a sculptural fancy on the clarity of his structure: even those who maintain the contrary are obliged to agree that some of the sculptures are from Donatello's hand. But although the *Tabernacolo* has the same sculptor's decorativeness as the architectural parts of the Cossa tomb, it is a profuse, not an austere decorativeness.

35

The decoration of the plinth was adopted from an antique sarcophagus, probably of that favourite type with genii holding a long swag which was copied by Jacopo della Quercia on the sarcophagus of Ilaria del Carretto and used again and again in Florence during the first half of the *quattrocento*, by Piero Lamberti on the vault above the tomb of Nofri Strozzi, by Michelozzo on the Aragazzi monument, by Bernardo Rossellino on the tomb of Leonardo Bruni. Here the motif is more emphatically Christianised, in that cherub heads have been substituted for naked putti – not that the other sculptors who copied the motif with exact naïveté from the antique intended to deserve the accusations of neo-paganism that nineteenth-century Romantics, moved by the transcendency of Gothic art, would bring against their beautiful antique forms. The carving is competent, and more justice would be done to the modelling if it were cleaned of the dirt that has filled its hollows. But it is clearly by the hand of a well-trained assistant: he and other assistants no doubt carved the other architectural members and their ornaments to Donatello's design.

Of all the sculptures on the monument it is the Virtues which have proved the great crux of attribution. Together with the Virgin and Child above they were already distinguished by Francesco Albertini in 1510 as the work of Donatello's assistants: 'the sepulchre in bronze of Pope John (is) by the hand of Donatello, the ornaments of marble (are) by his disciples.'[13] Probably Albertini was here repeating a current tradition about the authorship of the tomb. From the moment of its creation it was one of the most celebrated of Florentine monuments, and the history of its making was certainly familiar to the city's artists and literati during the *quattrocento*. Albertini was born no later than 1470 and so may well have learnt what he reports from men who had known Donatello himself. But it is in the nature of traditions, particularly verbal traditions, to become confused as time passes. A few years later Andrea Billi (1481–1530) records for the first time a tradition that Michelozzo carved the figure of Faith, and in 1550, as we have seen, this attribution was repeated by Vasari, who gave the Hope and the Charity to Donatello[14] and the Faith to Michelozzo. About the same time Gian Battista Gelli recorded that many in his day did not believe the tomb to be by Donatello at all.[15] In the second edition of his *Vite*, published in 1568, Vasari again declared that the Faith was by Michelozzo, calling it 'very beautiful, and in company with a Hope and a Charity by Donatello of the same size: it does not lose in comparison with them.'

The great significance of the Doffi document is that it fixes a firm date for the completion of the sarcophagus. Now if the sarcophagus was in position by November or December 1424, it is obvious that the plinth, the base, and the pylon carved with the Virtues were also in position by that date, since all three of them give structural support to each other and to the sarcophagus.

But since Michelozzo was not in partnership with Donatello until the follow-ing year at the earliest, these dates in themselves seem to dispose of the notion that he participated in the carving of the Virtues. Evidently it was already realised in the early sixteenth century that the Faith was less well executed and by a different hand from the other two figures, and since it was remem-bered that Michelozzo had had a share in the tomb, it seemed an obvious deduction that this least perfect of the three was from his hand.

But before forming any conclusion it is important to look first at the figures themselves. They do not look out at the spectator with an independent pose of their own, in the manner of older Virtues, but are gracefully linked, Faith and Hope turning in their niches towards the central figure of Charity, who is slightly taller than her companions. For Faith is 3 ft. 5⅜ in. (1·05 metres) high and Hope is 3 ft. 5¾ in. (1·06 metres) high, while Charity is 3 ft. 6⅛ in. (1·07 metres) high. They move easily in their niches and in the space before them, as we noted when looking at the general aspect of the tomb. Charity (no. 5) carries a flaming vase or brazier, symbolising the love of God, in her right hand and a cornucopia filled with grapes, roses, pears and vine-leaves, symbolising love of one's neighbour, in her left. In earlier iconography Charity's cornucopia had been one from which flames issue: this type of cornucopia, first found on Niccolò Pisano's Siena pulpit, had later been developed in the Pisano workshop into a motif of two flaming cornucopiae, one pointing heavenwards, one earthwards. Andrea Pisano seems to have been the first artist to substitute a classical cornucopia of fruit and flowers for a flaming cornucopia: the Charity on his bronze doors for the Baptistery holds one in her left hand and a flaming heart in her right. A flaming heart is also held by Charity on Orcagna's tabernacle in Or San Michele. Donatello, while deriving his iconography from these local Florentine exemplars, has, significantly, classicised it: the flaming heart, so medieval an emblem, has been replaced by an antique two-handled brazier.

Clearly Donatello has assimilated his Charity as much as possible to an antique representation of Abundantia or Ceres or Juno, all of whom carry cornucopiae in the left hand in just such a fashion. She stands in the centre, for from the time of St. Paul onwards Charity had been exalted as the mother of the Virtues.[16] Faith (no. 6) is placed in the post of honour on her right hand, Hope (no. 7) the daughter of Faith and Charity, on her left. Charity wears a robe with tight-fitting bodice and a heavy mantle, which is wound across the body, brought over her right shoulder and arm and again across her body. It hangs down her left side in deep folds, but is stretched out in tension on her right by the movement of her right arm as it holds out the brazier. Hope is winged. Her hands clasped in prayer, she looks outwards with inclined head and pensively trustful expression. She wears a sleeved robe, buttoned at the wrist, and over it a heavy mantle with chaperon. She too is shod in antique sandals. Her long tresses are braided with a ribbon. Faith wears a heavy robe and over it a mantle clasped at the neck by a brooch (*fermaglio*) set with precious stones, probably pearls. With her right hand she proffers a chalice, more or less a true Italian Gothic chalice of the time, with a sloping bowl held in a calyx of pointed lobes, a polygonal stem, a knob set with lozenge-shaped bosses, which on a real chalice would have been enam- elled, and a round lobed foot (see no. 8). The right side of her cloak is pulled round to the front and held beneath the right wrist, while she holds up a bunched up piece of the left side, using two fingers to help keep up the right side beyond. All three figures rest their weight on the left leg, the right foot being raised and pointed outwards to the left in graceful rhythm, though only in Hope is the flexion of the leg which should follow this action clearly expressed.

It is all-important to distinguish between the design and the execution of these figures. Unmistakably they were designed by the same hand, which also made models for them. That hand was Donatello's and the style they reflect, smoothed and weakened in the Hope and Charity, in the Faith translated with lumpish insensitiveness, is Donatello's style. There is even external evidence to support this contention, for as Lord Balcarres pointed out long ago, the Charity and Hope closely resemble the small bronze figures of Faith and Hope on the Siena Font for which Donatello was paid between 1428 and 1 April 1429 (nos. 132–133). Hence H. W. Janson's conjecture that Donatello adapted the Siena Virtues from models made for the Cossa Virtues is more than likely to be correct, particularly as the necessities of iconography imposed limits on the possible variations of pose and form in such allegorical figures. Besides, there is good reason to believe that Donatello was hard pressed for time between the summer of 1427 and the spring of 1428, as we shall see when we come to the history of the Brancaccio tomb. Although the Siena Virtues are beautiful small figures, instinct with a life that only Dona- tello could give to the forms of bodies and draperies, there is no reason to suppose that Donatello scorned such useful economies of invention any more than other great artists struggling to finish a great commission. And after all, they were intended for Siena, not for Florence, and so would not stir the bitter tongues of his fellow-citizens to carping sneers.

In design then the three Virtues are beautiful, but their execution is inferior to their design. However, there are differences among them in quality. The sculptor who carved the Charity and the Hope was a competent artist, who worked carefully, even with a certain preciosity. But he did not have Donatello's infallible sense of how to merge the figure with the ground; indeed the right side of Hope's drapery is so rendered as to have a double edge, the rear edge forming a plane from which the figure rises awkwardly. And for all his competence and the glistening polish of his figures, there is a certain dry neatness, a certain insensitive laboriousness, which betrays the careful copyist, the reliable *aiuto*, with talent but no genius for plastic form. The Faith is a much cruder figure (no. 6). As Billi noted in the early sixteenth century, the right arm is shorter than the left. The face instead of being the elegant oval of the two companion figures (nos. 5, 7) is lumpish and inexpressive, and the folds of the drapery are cut with the dry mechanical manner of an assistant who is copying a model without understanding the vitality of its rhythms. The entire figure is poorly related to the niche in which it stands and is certainly the work of a second assistant, trained in a workshop where the traditions of the *Trecento* still lingered. The working of the left hand (no. 8) suggests that he may have been helped in this conspicuous form by the more capable sculptor who carved the two companion Virtues.

Beyond what has been pointed out there is nothing exceptional in the iconography of the Virtues. But we may pause for a moment to consider their meaning in the context of the tomb. According to orthodox Catholic doctrine the three theological virtues are infused into man by God, unlike the cardinal or moral virtues whose beginnings are in us naturally, though their perfection must proceed from God. Allegorical figures of the three supporting a man's sarcophagus may seem therefore to declare that his virtues have earned him a place in Heaven. But in fact such a statement cannot be made without careful qualification. In the first place, the three theological virtues are only present in man while he is in this life or in purgatory. When he is blessed with the Beatific Vision, the prime object of faith and hope, these virtues are ended, for he no longer has need of them. Their presence in a man is therefore a ground of pious belief in his salvation, not a proof of it. Hope, for instance, according to St. Thomas Aquinas, 'does not principally rest on grace already received, but on the divine omnipotence and mercy, by which even he who has not grace, may obtain it so that by it he may attain eternal life: and whoever has faith has certain knowledge of God's omnipotence and mercy.' But the action of hope, says the saint, can be impeded by man's free will, which interposes the obstacle of sin.

Since Cossa's last will, made on the day of his death, contained provisions testifying to his faith, his hope and his charity, in setting figures of these virtues on his tomb his executors were justified by contemporary belief, which laid great store on a 'good death', that is one in which God allows a man time to repent of his sins, to make amends for them by works of faith, hope and charity, and to receive the last sacraments of the Church in a good disposition. It is typical of the thirteenth, fourteenth and fifteenth centuries, when posthumous honour in the form of a magnificent tomb was just as eagerly sought as in the Renaissance and later, that praise should be couched in the form of abstract allegorical figures. The difference between such medieval

39

tombs and their successors is one of outward forms, not one of underlying purpose.

Although the tomb was ordered by Cossa's four Florentine executors, the motif of the three Virtues raises an interesting problem as to whether its design was worked out entirely in Florence by the executors and by Donatello or whether Cossa's two surviving nephews, Giovanni and Michele, were also consulted. For while tombs supported by Virtues were commonplace for the great nobles and ecclesiastics of Naples, having become traditional in the city during the *trecento*, the only Florentine precedent for such a design was the tomb of Francesco and Simone de' Pazzi in Santa Croce, the work of an unknown sculptor of *c.* 1340–5. We have seen that Giovanni and Michele Cossa had not merely been brought accidentally into correspondence with Giovanni de' Medici, but were intimately acquainted with him, as confidential family friend and banker in the case of Michele, as guardian in the case of Giovanni. Since the two were Cossa's principal heirs, it is highly likely that they were consulted about the design of their uncle's tomb. If so, in all probability they would have suggested the form of tomb traditional in their native city, perhaps keeping in mind the tomb of their grandfather Giovanni erected in 1397 in the Cathedral of Ischia.[17] For this rested on figures of three Virtues. The unusual form of a relief given to the Virtues, perhaps for structural reasons of support, must on the other hand be Donatello's own invention.

The Virtues are easily recognised as traditional features on tombs, but it is perhaps more difficult to see immediately that the two angels on the sarcophagus also belong to an old iconographical tradition, for their forms, placing, poses and action are influenced by the new humanistic imitation of antique sculpture. As we have seen, the type of ancient sarcophagus on which two winged geniuses hold a laurel wreath was already known by 1418, when it was copied by Piero di Niccolò Lamberti on the tomb of Nofri Strozzi (no. 101), where two winged child angels hold a shield with the Strozzi arms. Although it may now seem a strange, even presumptuous form of tribute to the dead, thirteenth- and fourteenth-century piety did not shrink from representing angels as mourning over the deceased or performing the last rites over his body. Such angelic witnesses to the hope of the dead man or to the hope of his relatives that his soul, by the Divine mercy, might be received into heaven, there to enjoy the Beatific Vision, had their origin in those simpler representations which showed the soul of the deceased being carried up to heaven by angels, an iconography which was also developed into one figuring a hope or assurance of Christ's mercy. But since these themes are much more prominent on the Brancaccio and Aragazzi tomb, full discussion of them is better reserved: here we need only consider the use of angels in the subsidiary role in which they are represented on the sarcophagus.

There were Gothic precedents for this motif. Usually they take the form of small angels bearing a shield blazoned with the arms of the deceased, as on the tomb of Cardinal Carbone (d. 1405) in Naples (no. 102). From the original tomb of St. Catherine of Siena in Santa Maria sopra Minerva in Rome there still survives a fragment of an angel holding an unrolled scroll with the epitaph of the saint, which must date from *c.* 1383, the year when her disciple the Blessed Raimondo da Capua obtained permission to lay her body in the tomb.[18] In the early fifteenth century, as we learn from documents, such small angels were known as *spiritelli*.[19] There can be no doubt that these are classical forms adapted to Christian iconography, for the motif of two winged angels holding a laurel wreath is repeated on the bronze shrine of San Proto, San Giacinto and San Nemesio, commissioned by Cosimo and Lorenzo de' Medici for the monastery of Santa Maria degli Angioli. The only difference is that Ghiberti has given the angels albs in order to indicate their degree in the hierarchy of heaven. In this classicised form the motif of child or youthful angels holding a shield of arms, an inscription, or some other emblem continued to be a commonplace of *quattrocento* sepulchral art.

Donatello's angels praise Cossa by holding up his epitaph (nos. 13, 14, 15). Their smiling faces express the same joy at the entrance of a soul into Heaven as the trumpet-sounding angels on the Brancaccio tomb. This interpretation is not arbitrary or far-fetched, but is, on the contrary, fitting, as shall be seen, to the devotional purpose for which fourteenth- and fifteenth-century tombs were erected. It is echoed on the twin marble tombs of the Beato Giovanni da Salerno (d. after 1231) and of the Beata Villana delle Botti (d. 1361), set up for veneration in Santa Maria Novella in 1451–2. On both of these two angels (*angnoli*) hold out scrolls with the epitaphs or rather praises of the two Beati while above divine hands hold their heavenly crowns (no. 109). Later the motif became a commonplace of *quattrocento* funerary art.

There has been some dispute as to the authorship of the two angels on the Cossa tomb. In the artful complexity of their pose, so skilfully adapted both to their placing and to display the sculptor's virtuosity in foreshortening, they are conspicuously the invention of Donatello. Angels, according to orthodox doctrine, were individuals, so that the difference in type between the two can be explained either in terms of a learned iconography or simply by Donatello's preference for diversity in symmetry. The left-hand angel (no. 14) was certainly executed almost wholly or indeed entirely by Donatello: only he was capable of the soft, smudgy forms of the hair which are shaped in the marble with his incomparable sensibility to the translation of texture. The body too is compact with life in its soft forms of a child's body. But as the arms are less well-shaped than the rest of the figure and the left arm is a little flat, these parts may have been executed by an assistant. The other angel (no. 15) offers the same combination of merits and defects, but is perhaps a little more mechanical than its companion, and the hair is much less sensitively described.

D

Perhaps the true explanation of these figures is that they are by Donatello working with an assistant and executing or finishing parts with his own hand. The crown of the head of the right-hand angel, which is in higher relief than the crown of the head of the companion figure, is left in the rough because it is invisible from the front – an economy of workmanship frequent in *quattrocento* sculpture.

The arrangement of the three shields between the consoles is heraldically significant. Cossa's arms as Pope are on the dexter side, the nobler side in heraldry, a position whose significance was immediately conspicuous to a fifteenth-century eye. His arms as Cardinal are relegated to the humbler sinister side. The emphasis of such a placing is even more apparent if it is remembered that a husband's arms were always placed on the dexter side, the wife's on the sinister. And the presence in the centre of the arms of the Church surmounted by a Papal tiara reduces the sinister shield to even greater unimportance. Yet such an arrangement could easily be justified by Cossa's supporters. No-one in his old obedience doubted that John had been true Pope. Martin himself only contended that the inscription on the tomb should not seem to imply that he was still Pope when he died. It was the emphasis which the Florentines had placed on John's Papacy that angered him, since it seemed to voice the thoughts of those who still believed he had been wrongfully and violently deposed.

By contrast, the bier and its lion supports need not detain us long, since they are certainly the work of assistants, though Donatello's hand is evident again in the design of the lion supports, which recall the famous Marzocco or lion of Florence he carved *c.* 1418–19 for the staircase built to connect the apartments of Pope Martin V in Santa Maria Novella with the Chiostro Grande of the convent (no. 94). It might be tempting to think that there is some allusion in this motif to the links of affection between Cossa and Florence, but lions were traditionally used as supports; the tomb of Lapo de' Bardi (d. 1342), for example, now in the Bargello, rests on lion-headed brackets. The decorative motifs on the pillow and pall are chiselled with that sharp decisive relief typical of early *quattrocento* sculptured ornament of this kind, where the intention is to define the pattern strongly and firmly, even more strongly and firmly than on *quattrocento* textiles themselves.

The splendid gilt bronze effigy has always commanded admiration, and unlike the rest of the tomb has always been regarded as a work by Donatello and as one of his masterpieces. A number of effigies in the round, of gilt copper or latten, sometimes with details in enamel, were made in Northern Europe during the later Middle Ages, but they were the privilege of the greatest personages, unlike the flat brasses which have survived in such numbers. The vicissitudes of European history have left most of the surviving examples in England: the effigy of William de Valence (*c.* 1290–1300) in Westminster

Abbey, that of the Black Prince (*c.* 1377–80), in Canterbury Cathedral, those of Edward III (*c.* 1377–80) and Richard II (1384–6) in Westminster Abbey. By contrast effigies in the round in metal seem to have been almost unknown in medieval Italy.

The choice for Cossa's effigy of so expensive a material as bronze may of course have been influenced by the interest in antique art of contemporary Florentine humanists, who were certainly familiar with some at least of the many references in ancient authors to the nobility and durability of bronze. But it must also be borne in mind that the tradition of large-scale works in bronze had persisted in Italy throughout the Middle Ages, probably under Byzantine influence, and that bronze and brass, the metal preferred in the Gothic North, are not so different in their composition, indeed are so alike that it is dangerous to be too precise in applying the terms to medieval works of art. It was as well known in the early fifteenth century as it is now that the ancients were entombed in sarcophagi of marble, not in canopied tombs with effigies in bronze. Hence it would be rash to assume that Cossa was commemorated in bronze because of the *antiquisant* spirit of Florentine humanism rather than because of the prestige traditionally attached to effigies in costly metal from the twelfth century onwards. The bankers and merchants of Florence, travellers themselves and masters of factors who travelled far and wide in their service, knew as well as the goldsmiths and founders of France, England and Low Countries what magnificences were prized as honourable expenditure in the tombs of kings, princes and cardinals of that lordly Europe north of the Alps. A man who had been Pope, the executors may well have felt, deserved an exceptional effigy in regal metal rather than in marble. For it must be remembered that John was the first Pope to be buried in Florence, that it was a signal honour to the city for him to be buried there, and that the executors felt an especial desire to honour his memory because of his affection for themselves and their city. In favour of this interpretation is the fact that the bronze was not given a brown patina, *all'antica*, but was gilt in the best medieval tradition. The 80 florins required to pay for the gilding of the comparatively small reliquary of the Baptist's finger give us some notion of the expense of gilding so large an effigy as Cossa's. And the vast sum entailed by gilding of itself suggests that what the executors wanted was not so much an effigy in antique bronze as an effigy in gilded metal, the gilding adding a last coat of splendour to what was already the most costly of the non-precious metals.

Cossa's effigy (nos. 16, 95) as we saw, measures 6 ft. 3¼ in. (1·91 metres) from the top of the mitre to the feet, so that Donatello has shown Cossa as about 5½ ft. (1·68 metres) tall, in other words as the small man we know him to have been. He must have seen Cossa while he was alive, and seen him as the strong stout man who is described by contemporaries as 'a man robust and dark,' and as 'a stout man'.[20] Certainly robust strength is the impression stamped by the face (no. i) with its bushy eyebrows, knitted forehead, firm mouth and strong chin. Donatello has unquestionably executed a portrait of the real man, made from a death-mask taken by commission of the executors immediately after his death, as was customary when it was known that an effigy was to be made. This has been denied, but Cossa's executors, as we have seen, knew from his own mouth the importance he attached to sepulture in an honourable tomb. Hence one of their first cares would have been to have had his features recorded in a death-mask. Donatello has vitalised every feature of the dead man, yet the expression still betrays that he used a death-mask.

The dead were customarily buried in the ceremonial costume of their rank – in Cossa's case, that of a Cardinal Bishop – and accordingly their effigies were shown attired in the same costume. In the case of great men like Cossa, the body generally lay in state dressed in its ceremonial costume before interment. 'If the cardinal is a Cardinal Bishop,' says the *Ordo Romanus*, 'he must be wholly clothed in sacred vestments wholly of black or violet colour, like the Pope, with a white mitre, gloves and sandals with a Pontifical ring and a veil of silk covering his face.'[21] Johann Burckhardt, the Papal master of ceremonies some sixty years later, has left a vivid description in his diary of this custom of clothing the corpse in ceremonial dress. Immediately after his death on 12 August 1484 Pope Sixtus IV was laid on the bed in his chamber, dressed in a long robe over a shirt, with a cross on his breast and his hands 'composed', that is, crossed over each other on his stomach. Then, after the cardinals had come to do it honour, the body was laid naked on a long table in the middle of the room. Its orifices were stopped up and it was washed and then clothed in a long robe of white or red damask. 'In this,' noted Burckhardt, 'I erred, for he ought to have been interred in the habit of St. Francis, in whose order he professed, with his sacred pontifical vestments above. And since he had no rochet, we clothed him in sacred vestments as above, sandals, amice, alb, a rope girdle, a stole in the manner of a cross across his breast, since I could have no pectoral cross for him, a tunicle, dalmatic, gloves, a white and precious *castile*, a pallium, a simple mitre and a ring with a sapphire ... And thus adorned we laid him on a bier which we set in the middle of the chamber on the aforesaid table, with cushions at his head and a pall of brocade, where he remained until the hour of his interment.' Burckhardt was clearly following time-honoured custom, for in a second note about his error in not dressing Sixtus in the Franciscan habit he remarks that Alexander V (d. 1410) had been clothed in it after his death. The whole passage explains illuminatingly the design of the central portion of the tomb, with the effigy laid in ceremonial dress on a bier with a pall and cushions.[22]

Del Migliore relates that Cossa's sarcophagus was opened during the first decade of the sixteenth century to satisfy the curiosity of Cardinal Francesco

Soderini (1453–1524), brother of the Florentine *Gonfaloniere* Pier Soderini. His body was found whole and entire, with one eye open and shining as if he were still alive, a mitre on his head and the whole of his pontifical vestments still intact. Only the ring he had used for sealing when Pope had fallen from his finger.[23] Del Migliore took all his information from Bellaccio Scarfagni, Cardinal Soderini's auditor, who was present at the opening, and so there is little doubt that Cossa was buried in the full pontifical robes of a cardinal, the same robes in fact in which, according to Del Corazza, he had lain in state. But there has been some confusion because both Carlo Strozzi and Del Migliore, writing in the middle of the seventeenth century, use the technical term *pontificali*, that is full pontificals, meaning simply full mass vestments, to describe the costume of Cossa's effigy, and it has even been suggested that the executors had him represented in Papal dress. That would indeed have been a deliberate insult to Pope Martin, however highly set the effigy, but the executors were not so audacious. It is worth examining the costume more closely to demonstrate this point and to illuminate certain details of the design.

On the head (see no. i) is a mitre of the type known in the Middle Ages as a *mitra pretiosa*, worn only by great ecclesiastics. Its border is embroidered with lozenges, each containing a cross, alternating with roundels. The spandrels contain two medallions which on a real *mitra pretiosa* would probably have been enamelled or set with precious stones. Around the neck (see no. 16) is an amice, tucked in at the front under the broad down-turned collar of the chasuble. Underneath the chasuble is a long dalmatic (see no. 95) fastened by a girdle (*subcingulum*) richly embroidered with rosettes in medallions, whose fringed ends emerge from either side of the chasuble, on the left lying flat as such an end might be expected to do in life, on the right parallel to the side (best seen in no. 95). The orphrey of the collar is embroidered with lozenges and half-lozenges containing crosses. The same motif, this time contained in a frame of interlaced quatrefoil cartouches, reappears on the orphrey of the left sleeve. The orphrey of the right sleeve is not visible since this sleeve has been turned back to reveal the magnificent episcopal glove which Cossa wears on his right hand (no. 16). The glove has a border of imitation Cufic lettering and is set with a medallion simulating a silver-gilt medallion set with precious stones such as decorated episcopal gloves in the Middle Ages – the design of a large stone surrounded by eight smaller ones is typical of the period. Beneath we can see the matching glove on the left hand: in both gloves the modelling admirably suggests that they are of the thinnest material, such as silk. The great Tau-shaped orphrey down the front (nos. 16, 95) again of a sort worn only by high ecclesiastics, is decorated with a pattern of circles linked by rosettes and interlaced with lines which form a lozenge pattern. Clearly Donatello was at pains to imitate or reproduce a

Gothic embroidery of his day, just as in the chalice held by Faith a true Gothic chalice is copied. For as yet artists made no attempt to impose antique design and motifs on these subsidiary features. Cossa's feet are shod in the high buskins worn by bishops and cardinals, with a band of lozenges running down them.

The differences between this costume, which is certainly that of a cardinal bishop, and the costume of a Pope can be seen at a glance if we compare Cossa's effigy with the effigy of Martin V on his tomb in the Lateran, in which Donatello is traditionally supposed to have had a hand (no. 96). The tiara and fanons and the pallium worn by Martin are conspicuously absent from the Cossa effigy. On the other hand, there can be no doubt that, as Del Migliore remarks,[24] the canopy hangs above the tomb 'to express a certain magnificence due to the person buried in it.' Whenever a Pope rode in procession or made a ceremonial entrance into a town a *baldacchino* was carried over his head. When he presided on great occasions, a canopy hung over his chair: at the Council of Rome in 1412 it was taken as an evil omen when an owl settled on John's canopy. Because of the restrictions imposed on the design of the tomb, it may be wrong to see the canopy as more than an ingenious translation of the formal Gothic architectural canopy into the naturalistic motif of a stately bed-canopy. But everything we now know of the tomb and its history suggests that it too deliberately emphasises that Cossa, if he died a Cardinal, had been a Pope.

The Virgin standing half-length in the niche on the topmost pylon (nos. 17, 20) is present as the Divine Mediatrix, that is, as intercessor for the soul of the deceased with her Son that it may be admitted into Heaven. In his will of 25 October 1360 Cardinal Talleyrand de Périgord expresses very clearly the sentiment of this motif. '*Imprimis*, commending our soul with humble devotion to Almighty God and Our Lord Jesus Christ, we pray Him supplicatingly that He, who desired to be born and suffer for the salvation of mankind, may receive us propitiously and mercifully when we pass from this vale of tears after the dissolution of our body of clay into the true life, and that He will not reward us according to the sins we have done, but according to His mercy may cause our soul to be saved and deign to place it in the bosom of his Patriarch Abraham. And because at times another's intercession is able to obtain that which we cannot obtain by ourselves, we pray with humble orisons that by the prayers and intercession of the holy and glorious Virgin Mary, Mother of Our Lord Jesus Christ, and of all the saints we may obtain these things which we beseech and ask with devout mind and contrite heart.'[25] The iconography of the tomb, like that of all such tombs intertwines, as we shall see more fully later, a hope that the soul of the deceased has been found worthy to enter Heaven with a reminder to the faithful that they must pray for its salvation, in case it still languishes in purgatory. It expresses the medieval Catholic's pious trust that Christ would be merciful to the dead if they had made their end in faith, charity and contrition and at the same time his pious fear of divine judgment, whose sentence can never be known to man, except in the case of the saints, until the Last Resurrection. For paradoxically it was orthodox both to trust in and to fear for a man's salvation.

The Virgin and Child therefore look down on the effigy so as to express the spiritual drama of intercession. Set at so great a height, they are less carefully finished than the other figures on the tomb, and moreover, there is no doubt that they are by Michelozzo. The type and proportions of the Virgin's face (nos. 17, 20) and its austere, contemplative nobility are those of the Virgin and the two angels on the tomb Michelozzo carved some years later for Bartolommeo Aragazzi (no. 50). The Child too is very like the children on the Aragazzi tomb, particularly the child on the right of the Virgin's throne in the relief of the Virgin blessing Aragazzi (no. 50). And the combination of great beauty in the two figures with some awkwardness in relating them correctly to each other in their different planes is typical of Michelozzo's strength and weakness as a sculptor.

The problem of the internal chronology of the tomb is at least partly solved by all that we now know about its history. The plinth, pylon, consoles and sarcophagus were completed by the end of 1424 and set up in position. Donatello designed these parts of the tomb, and made models for the three Virtues, but left the execution entirely to his assistants, except for the angels on the sarcophagus. He himself concentrated his energies on the most important part of the tomb, the gilt bronze effigy of Cossa. By July 1427 Michelozzo and Donatello had received 600 florins for the tomb and in February 1426 Cosimo de' Medici and Bartolommeo Valori urgently demanded 400 florins of this sum. The hugeness of their demand suggests that the money was in whole or part payment for the effigy, and although the appointment of two chaplains to say mass for Cossa's soul in May 1426 cannot be pressed to mean too much, it can be read as implying that the body was by that date in its sarcophagus and the effigy set on the bier above.

It has been suggested that Michelozzo cast and chased the effigy for Donatello. But if the chronology I propose is correct, then H. W. Janson's suggestion that it may equally well have been cast by Giovanni di Jacopo, who cast Donatello's bronze reliquary bust of San Rossore, begun after 1422 and completed by 1427, becomes even more plausible.[26] Moreover Michelozzo, even though he had the technical knowledge, did not have the material resources of a large workshop and assistants for founding a large work of this kind.[27] The reliefs for the Siena Font, in whose casting and chasing he very likely had a share, and the bronze capital of the Prato pulpit, which he cast in 1433, do not provide a fair parallel, since they are so much smaller and demand so much less of a founder's skill. But it is more than likely that he took an important part in the chasing. The contrast in style between the effigy and the figure of St. Louis of Toulouse which dates from the years *c.* 1423 to 1425, does not conflict with this dating, since Donatello necessarily applied different canons in creating the idealised figure of a youthful saint, resplendent with heavenly beauty, and the portrait effigy of a man whose forceful energy had moved some of the greatest events of the age.

The Virgin and Child – 2 ft. 1¼ in. high by 1 ft. 9⅞ in. wide (64 cm. by 58 cm.) – in the upper part of the monument are by Michelozzo, so that the stylistic evidence combines with the documentary to prove that this was the last part of the monument to be executed, probably in 1427 or early in 1428, though certainly not before. The canopy and the pylon behind are to be attributed to assistants, working under the supervision of Michelozzo, who was as we have seen almost certainly in charge of the Florence workshop now that Donatello was busy on the Brancaccio tomb in Pisa. Since the effigy was incomparably the most expensive part of the tomb, its cost explains in itself why all the rest of the tomb was executed by Donatello's assistants rather than by Donatello himself. If Donatello had carved them himself, his handiwork would have been valued too highly in the final *stima* which fixed a just valuation of the tomb for the price to be kept within the limit imposed by Cosimo on the sculptors of 800 florins.

We know of at least two assistants who were working for the two masters during 1427 and 1428 and so may have helped Donatello and Michelozzo with the Cossa tomb. One, Nanni di Miniato, was born *c.* 1398. He was a client of the Strozzi and their bank in both the Roman and modern sense, and had caught sufficient of the enthusiasm for antiquity of Donatello and his *brigata* to write to Matteo di Simone Strozzi on 28 September 1428 advising him that two small sarcophagi, one carved with the history of Bacchus, were lying for the taking between Pisa and Lucca.[28] They had been seen by Donatello who had praised their workmanship. Nanni was writing to Matteo from Naples, where he had gone to work on the tomb of King Ladislaus, as appears from a second letter he sent to Matteo on 10 December 1430 enclosing a copy of the King's epitaph. In the same letter he complains that Michelozzo was in arrears of payment to him, and his *catasto* return of early 1431, filed from Naples, discloses that the debt was one of about 8 florins due for some days' work put in for Michelozzo three years before, which takes us back to 1427.[29] In this and in all his other tax-returns Nanni describes himself, not as an *intagliatore* or sculptor, but as a *scarpellatore* or stone-mason, and indeed the only work he is known to have executed during these years is purely decorative. On 23 December 1433, for example, he was paid 40 *lire piccole* for a stretch of 10 *braccia* of cornice which he had carved for Luca della Robbia's Cantoria (*pergamo*) in the Duomo.

The other assistant was Pagno di Lapo Portigiani, whom Vasari mentions as having in his youth helped Donatello to carve certain figures, including some in San Miniato al Tedesco.[30] As a result his ghost haunted art-historians for many long years, and they made a habit of assigning to him those parts of works executed by Donatello and Michelozzo which were obviously by a different or inferior hand. In 1942 Janson pointed out that although Pagno was certainly regularly employed by the two masters, they employed him as an architectural mason, not as a figure-carver, and documents subsequently discovered about the Prato pulpit have only proved his contention. Pagno was much younger than Nanni, for he was born in 1408, and so can only have been about eighteen years old when first hired by the two masters. Nanni di Miniato seems to have worked for Michelozzo in Florence, but Pagno may have been taken on for both the Cossa tomb and the Brancaccio tomb, the next large commission received by Donatello and Michelozzo, which was executed in Pisa. Pagno's father declares in his *catasto* return of 8 August 1428 that 28 florins were still due to his son as part of the salary he had earned during eighteen months work with the two in Florence and Pisa. He also implies that the work for which Pagno had been hired was finished: 'The said masters have not reckoned his salary, and have not come to an agreement with him about it, and they have had words over it: they believe and maintain that there is little between what he owes them and they must pay him. No judgment can be made until the account is made out, for the said Pagno is away and the said masters are in Pisa.' In fact, Pagno was at this moment in Siena, where he had begun work as a carver on the font early that June.[31] Other assistants too must have been taken on by Donatello and Michelozzo, most, like Nanni di Miniato, as casual journeymen rather than as full-time workshop hands.

From the first the Cossa tomb was admired and imitated. If Courajod and Fiocco are to be believed, it was already being copied in Venice in 1423–4, when the Florentine sculptors Piero Lamberti and Giovanni di Martino da Fiesole carved the tomb of Doge Tommaso Mocenigo (d. 4 April 1423) in Santi Giovanni e Paolo (no. 110). The Mocenigo tomb was signed and dated 1423 by the two sculptors, and since the Venetian year ran from 1 March to 1 March it must have been executed between April 1423 and 1 March 1424. The front of its sarcophagus is carved with five round-arched, shell-topped niches containing Virtues which are very like those of the Cossa tomb, and the effigy is surmounted by a great canopy, again as on the Cossa tomb. The discovery that the plinth and sarcophagus of the Cossa tomb were executed before the last two months of 1424 does away with the anomaly of so early an imitation, which has puzzled art-historians. Some indeed have denied any relationship between the two tombs; others have suggested that Piero Lamberti made drawings after Donatello's preliminary designs or models for the tomb, while Janson has pointed to the precedents that undoubtedly exist in North Italian sculpture for the shell-top niches, precedents not found in Tuscany, and suggested that Donatello may have made a journey to Venice during which he saw and took a fancy to this motif.

There is nothing improbable in the notion of such a journey, but the shell-topped niches of the much-restored tomb of Doge Antonio Venier (executed between 1403–10), also in Santi Giovanni e Paolo, which Janson cites as the immediate inspiration of the Mocenigo niches, are Gothic in design, with pointed arches, whereas in the Mocenigo niches not only the design but the proportions and the placing of the figures seem to be imitated from the Cossa tomb. The figure of Faith in one of them conspicuously reflects the Faith of the Cossa tomb, though in coarsened form, while the statue of St. George to the left of the sarcophagus is a blatant plagiarism from Donatello's St. George (c. 1416) and the corresponding figure on the right of another warrior saint has a pose borrowed from Donatello's David (c. 1416). And according to Paoletti, the first and best historian of Venetian sculpture, the canopy, later to become a familiar motif on Venetian tombs, appears here for the first time. Yet the canopy, unlike the niches, is not closely similar in design to the Cossa canopy, and moreover the niches, as Janson has pointed out, are separated, not by Corinthian pilasters, but by ornamental strips. This makes rather plausible the suggestion that Lamberti saw the design for the Cossa tomb at an early stage, before much of it was executed.[32]

Certainly the majestic tomb of John XXIII's celebrated jurist Raffaelle Fulgosio (d. September 1427) in the Santo at Padua, designed by Lamberti before 5 March 1429, when Fulgosio's widow formally commissioned it from him, is much more closely copied from the Cossa tomb, so closely that, as we have seen, it is a strong pointer to the date when its prototype was completed. Curiously enough the technical problems were rather the same in the case of both tombs, for the Fulgosio tomb was to stand between two pillars of the choir behind the high altar of the Santo. However, in conformity with Paduan tradition it is raised on four columns, one at each corner with two half-columns between at the sides, and because of its position has two faces, not one. But from the columns upwards it is more or less a copy of the Cossa tomb. On each side is a plinth with three niches, separated by Corinthian pilasters and containing figures of Virtues, an oblong frieze with two standing angel putti (*spiritelli*) holding an illusionistic scroll (*breve*) inscribed with the epitaph. Above is a bier resting on lion heads and surmounted by a canopy draped very much in the manner of the Cossa tomb, but with a horizontal top. In the Fulgosio tomb, which was finished by 11 October 1430, Lamberti had the help of the Florentine sculptor Giovanni di Bartolommeo. We must suppose then either that Lamberti had recently seen the Cossa tomb, which is perhaps most probable, or else drawings of it brought from Florence by his partner.[33] Jacopo della Quercia too was so strongly impressed by the tomb that the tabernacle he designed for the Siena Font in or after September 1428 clearly shows its influence. All the more striking then are the differences between the Cossa tomb and the tomb of Cardinal Brancaccio, to which we must now remove.[34]

Chapter III · Cardinal Rainaldo Brancaccio

CARDINAL RAINALDO BRANCACCIO was born into one of the noblest and most ancient of Neapolitan families, ancient and noble even in the fourteenth century.[1] The Brancacci belonged to that exclusive citizen aristocracy which had governed Naples until the advent of the Angevin dynasty in the second half of the thirteenth century. Both St. Candida the elder and St. Candida the younger, traditionally the first Christian martyrs of the city, were believed to have been members of the family. Their bones lay in the ancient monastery church of Sant' Andrea a Nido, close to the family palace, and the abbacy of Sant' Andrea was often held by a Brancaccio. During the late thirteenth century the family had produced a Cardinal in Landolfo Brancaccio (d. 1312), confidential counsellor of Boniface VIII and his Legate in the Kingdom of Sicily. Landolfo, or so it has lately been suggested, was the Brancaccio cardinal who commissioned the frescoes which decorate the family chapel of Sant' Andrea in the convent church of San Domenico Maggiore,[2] near the Brancacci palace. San Domenico, which is intimately linked with the Brancacci family, and especially with Cardinal Rainaldo, was consecrated in 1255 and was extended in the late thirteenth or early fourteenth century by the addition of another church dedicated to the Magdalen which had been founded in 1289 by King Charles II of Naples.

Under the Angevins by a process of amalgamation Naples came to be divided into five *seggi* or districts. An institution peculiar to the city, the *seggi* (also known as *sedile*, *platea*, *piazza* and *tocco*) were more or less informal gatherings of local notabilities who met in a special room, or *seggio*, to administer the affairs of their district. Originally they seem to have been associations of persons living in a particular street or round a certain square, perhaps formed for pious rather than administrative purposes. A Ferrarese envoy sent to Naples in 1444 has left the first and best description of them after they had developed into large wards: 'The city is divided into five parts and five *seggi*; the Seggio of Capuana, which is first, the Seggio of Montagna, the Seggio of Portanova, the Seggio of Porto, the Seggio of Nido. These *seggi* are loggias, finely worked and adorned, to which the gentlemen of those streets and that part of the city resort, and whereas in other cities the gentlemen gather in the squares and palaces, the Neapolitan gentlemen spend all day in these *seggi*, from morning after mass until the hour for eating, and after dining until supper-time, and they do not foregather in any other squares or loggias. But no-one other than the said gentlemen would ever go to the *seggi* for they would be thrust and driven without.'³ Originally the *seggi* had numbered many more than five, but gradually the wealthier and more powerful associations had absorbed the less powerful. Even among the five great *seggi* there were distinctions; the *seggi* of Capuana and of Nido in the heart of Naples were the noblest and haughtiest of all and often joined together during the fourteenth century in faction fights against the others. The Brancacci belonged to the Seggio di Nido, whose original members were a consortium of *militi* or nobles with palaces lining the long straight street of Nido, the admiration of fourteenth- and fifteenth-century visitors to Naples for its width and stateliness. In fact their great family palace lies between the Via Donnaromita and the Via Fontanula (the modern Via Mezzocanone), off the little Piazza di Nido into which the street expands half-way along its length, behind that hospital of Sant' Andrea which in 1426 became Cardinal Rainaldo's hospital and chapel of Sant' Angelo a Nido. Possibly then they had originally belonged to the piazza or *seggio* of Fontanula which by 1366 had become amalgamated with the Piazza di Nido. The ties between members of the same *seggio*, in spite of local disputes, were very close, and were strengthened by intermarriage. Outside Naples, away from internal rivalries, they were drawn even tighter, strengthening the intense loyalty felt by all Italians to the city of their birth and, outside its walls, to their fellow-citizens.

Although so splendid in nobility, the Brancacci, unlike most great Neapolitan families, were not lords of vast fiefs in the Kingdom of Sicily of which Naples was the capital. From early times they were divided into four main branches. Rainaldo's branch was known as the Brancacci Dogliuoli or Glivoli, and after his death sometimes also as 'del Cardinale', so great was his prestige. Rainaldo was born *c.* 1360. We know something of his physical appearance. He was remarkably tall, taller by a head's length than other men – writing about him in 1424, two Florentine ambassadors gave him the code-name of *Lunghissimo* – and had a big mouth, an aquiline nose, and blue-grey eyes.⁴ His grandfather Filippo (d. *c.* 1326–7) had been a courtier and palace grandee of King Robert of Anjou, serving him as a *maresciallo* and as *maggiordomo*. Rainaldo's father was Paolo, of whom little is known, except that in 1346 he was *Capitano* or governor of Durazzo in Albania, then held by the branch of the Angevins which was later to rule Naples from 1380 until 1435.

Rainaldo was created a Cardinal by Pope Urban VI, the stocky, dark-complexioned, fiery-tempered Pope whose imperious behaviour to his cardinals after his election caused the Great Schism. Urban was a Neapolitan, born Bartolommeo Prignano. He was certainly a kinsman of Rainaldo, for his mother was a Brancaccio named Margherita. Brancaccio's creation took place at a promotion held on 14 December 1384, at Nocera, near Naples, where Urban was then residing in a state of semi-siege, in open discord with Charles of Durazzo, whom he himself had made King of Sicily, and the

Queen-Regent Margherita.[5] At the time of his promotion Rainaldo Brancaccio was only a Papal acolyte and an abbot – the latter a title frequently found among the Neapolitan secular clergy in the fourteenth and fifteenth centuries. The presumption is that he was still a very young man, possibly younger than twenty-three, the earliest age at which acolytes, according to canon law, might be ordained deacons, unless they had received a special dispensation. As a Papal acolyte[6] Rainaldo was a personal attendant of the Pope and so on the road for future promotion, but there must have been other reasons for creating so young a man a Cardinal, especially if he had only entered the Curia after the Pope's arrival in Naples, as seems quite possible. Possibly Urban hoped to attach the powerful Brancacci family more closely to his own cause. Alternatively, or in addition, he may have wished to place a near kinsman of his own in the College, for as we have seen Urban's mother was a Brancaccio. Unfortunately there is no means of tracing how closely Rainaldo and Urban were related, but in a brief of 18 June 1386, Urban describes Carlo Brancaccio, Count of Campania, one of the most important and trusted officials in his service, as his *consanguineus*,[7] that is, as a cousin, or kinsman of near degree. Dietrich von Nieheim speaks contemptuously of the five new Neapolitan cardinals of this promotion[8] and says they did not dare assume the red hat for fear of King Charles, but lurked in their family palaces to avoid the mockery of the vulgar. In such matters Dietrich is not to be trusted, but probably because of their youth, four of them had to wait for some time before Urban published their promotion in open consistory, the final stage in the creation of a cardinal. Among these four was Rainaldo Brancaccio.

Trouble broke out when at the end of a consistory on 11 January Urban had six of his cardinals arrested on a charge of conspiring to depose him. Queen Margherita moved promptly to assist them. On 13 January she imprisoned Urban's sister and niece. There followed plots and counterplots, and in March Charles of Durazzo laid siege to Nocera. The Pope escaped on 7 July, crossed over to the Apulian coast where on 19 August he boarded six Genoese galleys waiting for him between Barletta and Trani, and sailed for Sicily and then onwards to Genoa. On his way northwards Urban stopped at Capri, and sent an envoy to demand the release of his nephew, sister and niece, the return of the Papal registers he had left at Nocera, and licence for the five Neapolitan Cardinals he had recently created to leave Naples and join him in Genoa. Charles, anxious for peace, conceded these demands. Henceforward Brancaccio's fortunes were to be indissolubly linked with those of Urban and his successors.

Urban entered the port of Genoa on 23 September, and took up residence in the Hospital of St. John. Here, on 16 October, he at last announced in public consistory his promotion of the four cardinals whose names he had not yet published. That same day the four boarded a Genoese galley at Naples and sailed to join the Pope. On 20 December Urban gave them their titles,[9] and the red hat which was the symbol of their dignity. Brancaccio was made Cardinal Deacon of San Vito in Macello. Although Urban surely chose to make him a Cardinal Deacon in the first instance because of his youth, a Cardinal Deacon he remained for the rest of his life. The distinctions between the three orders of the Cardinal Bishops, Cardinal Presbyters and Cardinal Deacons were by now much blurred, since the most resplendent duties of the College, the election of the Pope, the right to counsel him on the affairs of the church in consistory, were performed in common. Yet they still regulated precedence on solemn occasions. To the Cardinal Deacons belonged certain special liturgical and ceremonial tasks. It was their duty to attend the Pope whenever he celebrated pontifical mass, preached or performed any especially solemn liturgical function, and throughout such ceremonies they assisted and supported him. Whenever the Pope celebrated pontifically one of them read the Gospel and performed all the other tasks proper to a deacon. It was the privilege of the senior Cardinal Deacon to place the Papal mantle on the shoulders of a newly created Pope, to publish his election to the people, and to crown him. Whenever the Pope went out in procession, he marshalled the cortege on foot or on horseback, holding a wand in his hand. At public consistories the two junior Cardinal Deacons, as belonging to the lowest of the three orders of the Sacred College, summoned those who had been cited to appear before the Pope. At secret consistories the most junior of all read out letters, shut or opened the doors and windows of the chamber, and brought a bell when one was needed.[10] By 1406 Brancaccio had risen to be senior Cardinal Deacon, and on 19 November that year he ascended a platform erected in front of St. Peter's with the newly elected Gregory XII 'and as senior Cardinal Deacon took from his head his old mitre and placed on it the papal mitre with three crowns.'[11] After the union of the colleges of cardinals of the rival Popes in 1408 before the Council of Pisa he yielded his seniority to Cardinal Amadeo da Saluzzo, but resumed it again after Amadeo's death on 28 June 1419.

The standing and privileges of the Sacred College had steadily augmented from the middle of the twelfth century.[12] While the Holy See was vacant the cardinals were the ultimate tribunal of the Church. The canonists had given legal form and clothed in all the splendour of metaphor their analogical arguments for the greatness of the cardinalate. Though cardinals are not the head of the Church, said Huguccio, they nevertheless act as its head. The Glossa Palatina argued that they shared the government of the Church with the Pope and collectively were superior to him. The great canonist Henry of Susa (Hostiensis) comparing the government of the Roman Church to that of other churches, declared that its government was shared between

55

Pope and cardinals as between a bishop and his cathedral chapter. Cardinal Lemoine declared that the full authority of the Church, the *plenitudo potestatis*, belonged to Pope and cardinals as a corporate body.

The prestige and influence of the Sacred College perhaps reached their height in 1408-9, when the united cardinals of Popes Benedict XIII and Gregory XII deposed those two rival Popes, temporarily constituted themselves the supreme authority of the Church and convoked the Council of Pisa. Even in the second quarter of the fifteenth century, when the Popes were busy reimposing their absolute supremacy, their estate was still among the greatest of earthly dignities. 'The Lords are the hinges (*cardines*) of the earth and he has set them over the world.' With this verse from 1 Kings 2, St. Antonino[13] opens the section of his *Summa Major* that treats of cardinals. The Pope, the saint declared, is the hinge of the earth (*cardo terrae*); so too are the cardinals,

> . . . for as the whole door turns on its hinges, so all the business of the church and of the world which requires counsel turns on the cardinals, for they assist the Pope as his familiars and counsellors, in as much as the cardinals show divers ways of treating the business preferred before him on which he wishes to receive counsel. Afterwards it pertains to the Pope to choose and determine what he deems most expedient for the church. They are said to be lords for three reasons. Firstly because they are peculiarly God's lords from perfect goodness, secondly because they are the brothers and familiars of the Lord Pope from their exalted dignity, thirdly because they are lords who govern the world because of their counsellorship . . . As regards the first point, cardinals are and ought to be lords who are singular friends of God in the perfection of their lives . . . As regards the second, Augustine of Ancona in his book *De Potestate Ecclesie* says that the cardinals assist the Pope as the Apostles did Christ. For the Apostles are called the brothers of Christ, according to that word of the Psalmist: *I shall speak thy name to my brothers*, and also princes of the world, according to that word of the Psalmist: *Thou shalt make them princes over the whole earth*. As indeed the Pope when he makes cardinals promotes them to this double dignity, saying to them: *Be my brothers and princes of the world*. For the Pope himself acts the part of Christ. And although bishops too succeed to the place of the Apostles . . . yet they do so in another manner from cardinals. For the apostles stood in two relations to Christ. Firstly as attending on him penitentially, as at his Passion and Ascension, secondly as sent by his command through the world, which happened after the advent of the Holy Spirit, when scattered through the world they separated from one another, each receiving a province or a kingdom as his lot for preaching. The Cardinals represent the part of the Apostles as regards attending on Christ, for they attend on the Pope as Vicar of Christ penitentially. The bishops represent the part of the apostles in the second manner, being called to their share of toil in the governance of different cities, or else of provinces as archbishops. And this is well fitting, for as in the hierarchy of heaven some

angels attend on the Lord, others are frequently sent to us, so in our hierarchy of the Church it is proper that some should attend, like cardinals, some be sent as bishops . . . And since even the Apostles were not always with Christ as bishops, but as ministers in other acts, for in the Last Supper and after the Resurrection when he said *Receive the Holy Spirit* he made them bishops: therefore it is not unfitting that all cardinals should be bishops and some priests and some deacons. They receive the red hat from the Pope as a sign of the burning charity which they ought to have, such that they may be ready to shed their blood and to die for the good and defence of the Church . . .

As regards the dignity of the office. As the Roman Church is prior to and worthier than all others and is the lady and mistress of all . . . so it is fitting that its clerics and ministers should shine before others with a certain singular dignity, and hence that the cardinals of the Roman Church should be preferred before all other prelates in the dignity of honour. First on account of the privilege and excellence of the dignity it is enacted that whosoever attacks a cardinal, or captures him or causes him to be captured, or strikes him, over and above the excommunication he incurs . . . also falls into other very heavy penalties according to the crime of injured majesty. He is rendered an outlaw, infamous, detestable, incapable of receiving an inheritance and banished from all hereditary succession: his houses are pulled down, his goods are confiscated and he is deprived of all his fiefs and benefices. His sons and grandsons in the direct line are deprived of all worldly or ecclesiastical dignities, and excluded from all legal acts, and many other things . . .

In 1352 there had been a movement among the cardinals to exalt themselves to an even loftier estate and force the Pope himself to defer to them in certain matters of government, including their own appointment and discipline. Their motives were not entirely selfish: they were alarmed by the arbitrariness of Papal absolutions, by the increase of nepotism, by their anxiety to keep the Papal States and the Church's revenues under ecclesiastical control. One of the constant demands both of the Sacred College and of reformers was that the number of cardinals should be limited to a fixed number, the cardinals in their desire to prevent the Pope from swamping opposition by making new cardinals who would be creatures of his own, the reformers anxious to reduce the number of a class of dignitaries of whose usefulness they were dubious.

The ordinary duties of the cardinals arose from the nature of the Roman Curia itself. First and foremost it was a tribunal of last resort. All appeals were referred to it and certain sorts of case were specially reserved for its judgement. The Pope frequently committed the trial or examination of cases to the cardinals, so that they were obliged to reserve a chamber in their palaces for a court (*audientia*), and to employ one, two or three auditors, often doctors of decretals, one or more clerks (*secretarii*) and notaries together with humbler officials such as ushers. The auditors, besides citing witnesses and hearing their evidence, could give reproofs and light punishments to the members of a cardinal's household. The clerks and notaries recorded the acts of the process and the evidence given: the usher carried the citation to the witnesses. According to the instructions they had received the cardinals either passed judgement themselves, or else made their report to the Pope.[14] The cases they tried were very varied. Some were inquisitorial, and concerned heresy, magic and alchemy or appeals from sentences passed by the inquisition on persons accused of these crimes. So seriously were offences of this sort regarded that generally the Pope himself passed sentence after a report from a commission of one or more cardinals. Heretics pronounced their formal abjuration before a tribunal of cardinals and its president then lifted the sentence of excommunication they had incurred. Brancaccio was one of the cardinals deputed by John XXIII to inquire into the Hussite heresy in 1410 and 1411–12, and to examine Huss himself at Constance in 1414.

The cardinals might also try criminal and civil cases involving ecclesiastics. Much of their time was taken up in determining quarrels concerning rights of jurisdiction between bishops and their cathedral chapters, for example, over benefices, or else in adjudicating in cases of disputed election to a bishopric or to the dignity of abbot. From time to time causes of great political import were committed to them, as when Kings and Queens or great vassals of the Church had disobeyed or rebelled against the Pope. In such causes it was customary to open the process by a trial, so that the Church might not be accused of unjust or precipitate action. After the offender had been cited to appear in person, usually several times and in vain, evidence was taken, and then the Pope pronounced sentence, generally of excommunication. Brancaccio was one of the three cardinals deputed by Boniface IX in 1399 to try Onorato Caetani, Count of Fondi, for conspiracy and rebellion.[15]

The cardinals also took part in the day-to-day administration of the Church. They were frequently called on by the Pope to accept resignations from benefices, to inquire into exchanges of benefices, and to verify that there had been no taint of simony in such transactions. In 1426 or thereabouts Brancaccio was commissioned by Martin V to hear the final appeal made by a certain Thomas Donegan, a clerk of the diocese of Meath in Ireland, against the institution of Nicolas Jurdan into the rectory of Rathwere.[16] It was also the task of cardinals to inquire into the suitability of candidates elected or proposed for a bishopric or abbacy before they were confirmed by the Holy See, and into cases where persons made uncontested suit to the Pope for the grant of rights and privileges. On such matters they prepared reports for the Pope, often in great detail. In the case of aspirants to promotion, sworn evidence had to be collected as to their birth, career and conduct and recorded in authentic form before the report was compiled. The cardinal then read it, bare-headed, before the Pope in consistory. They might also discharge certain formalities necessary for institution. In April, 1427, for example, it was to

Brancaccio that Thomas, Bishop Elect of Ossory in Ireland, swore his oath of fealty to the Papacy.[17]

Naturally such duties gave the cardinals great influence in the conferring of benefices and monasteries and in the appointment of bishops. In the winter of 1407, for instance, while Pope Gregory XII was residing in Siena, the bishoprics of Siena and Grosseto fell vacant. The Sienese tried to obtain them for clerics of Sienese birth, principally through the intermediary of Brancaccio.[18] In fact they were unsuccessful, and Gregory conferred the two sees on his nephew, Gabriele Condulmer, later Pope Eugenius IV, though he had not yet reached the canonical age of twenty-five. The responsibility of examining the written evidence submitted in processes of canonisation was also committed to cardinals. Usually the Pope appointed a special commission of three, one from each order of the Sacred College, for each cause: at its conclusion they submitted a report to him in consistory together with written evidence concerning the life, virtues, merits and miracles of the individual whose canonisation was sought. Brancaccio was one of the three cardinals who were ordered by Boniface IX in February 1391 to inquire into the life and virtues of John of Tweng, prior to Bridlington in Yorkshire, for whose canonisation many Englishmen, King Richard II and Queen Anne at their head, had made repeated petition.[19] And finally the Pope took counsel with his cardinals in consistory on all the great affairs of the Church, such as the proclamation of a crusade, or the definition of a heresy. Ideally it was necessary for a cardinal to have a profound knowledge of theology and law, a judicial mind and a practical sense of affairs. In practice the Popes tended to appoint cardinals from the two classes of specialists produced by medieval universities, theologians and jurists, the jurists being civilians, canonists or decretalists, or else doctors of both civil and canon law. Whether Brancaccio was a theologian or a lawyer I have not been able to establish; but in no document which I have traced is he given any legal title.

A cardinal was attended by a great household and by other persons who augmented his state, discharged certain duties in the household and ministered to his soul. The head of the household was the *camerarius*, who was often an ecclesiastic of rank. It was his duty to supervise the rest of the household and to see to the cardinal's financial affairs, including the administration of his accounts. The cardinal's clerics and chaplains received their office in virtue of documents sealed with the cardinal's own seal. They were much envied, for entry into the household of a cardinal was the first and greatest step towards high office in the Curia or to rich benefices. They recited the hours daily with their lord and served him when he celebrated the office. It was their duty to ride in his train, to keep him company until he retired to bed, to be present at grace before or after meals, and to attend him when he received a state visit from ambassadors or other dignitaries. The chaplains said mass with or before their lord in his chapel, which might be served by choir-boys, singers, and a choir-master (*magister capellae*). The chamberlains (*cubicularii*) had in their charge the cardinal's plate, his clothes, beds, sweet-meats, and the contents of his chamber. They also looked after the wax torches and candles required for lighting – wax was costly in the Middle Ages. Theirs too was the honour of carrying the cardinal's train. One or more secretaries wrote the cardinal's letters and records of the causes tried before him: naturally their posts were of great trust. An almoner daily distributed the left-overs from the cardinal's tables to the poor, and attended to his other charities. Most of the offices in a cardinal's household were regarded as being more suitable for ecclesiastics than for laymen, particularly those of *emptor*, *dispensator*, *panetarius*, *buticularius* and almoner, and might sometimes be doubled with other offices, like that of singer in the chapel. The cardinal's toilet was the task of his barber, who cut his hair and shaved him: one or two doctors and an apothecary cared for his health. Young noblemen, often his nephews or relations, might also enter his household as pages, bringing to it an increase of honour and state.

The services of all these persons, high and low, were rewarded by a yearly salary, provided they were active members of the household and had been taken into it by the cardinal on a salaried footing. For it sometimes happened that familiars and others were allowed to enter a cardinal's household without salary so as to prove their devotion in time for the next vacancy. The cardinal also clothed, fed and lodged his familiars and domestics. As was usual in the Middle Ages and for centuries later, the salaries of the household were gener-ally in arrears, partly because receipts of money came in very irregularly, especially as so many payments were made in kind, not in coined money. It was usual for cardinals to provide anxiously in their wills for the full discharge of these arrears: Brancaccio did so when making his in 1427. In theory, cardinals lodged in the palace attached to their titular church in Rome. But during the residence of the Popes in Avignon most of these, including the Lateran and the Vatican palaces themselves, had suffered damage by fire or fallen into disrepair, for the cardinals, like the Pope, built new palaces for themselves in Avignon. In some cases the Roman palaces must have been refurbished after the return of the Popes in 1378, but sig-nificantly Brancaccio seems never to have occupied his titular palace of San Vito in Macello, but to have lived instead in that attached to Santa Maria in Trastevere, a benefice he held *in commendam*. The two principal rooms in a cardinal's palace were on the first floor (the *piano nobile*). One was the state or tapestry chamber (*camera paramenti*) hung with tapestries, whence its name, and often very large. The other was the dining-room, (*tinellus*). The furniture of these rooms would now seem astonishingly simple and sparse. On the same floor or on the next were the bedroom, study (*studium*), the chapel, the wardrobe and other rooms. On the ground floor were the kitchen, storerooms, cellars, and other offices of the kind.[20]

If cardinals lived in the state and with the ceremony befitting their exalted rank, they differed in the degree of splendour according to their pride or austerity of spirit. Partly of course their large households consisted of clergy and officials who were necessary to them for the discharge of their duties and who would not now be lodged, fed and clothed by their patrons. So Cardinal Branda da Castiglione, cited by Vespasiano da Bisticci as an example of plain-living even for the old days, when a cardinal's servants wore no livery and carried no torches to light the comings and goings and the meals of their master, had a bishop, auditors and other men of condition in his house. Only a bishop who was also Branda's nephew and his own guests sat at his table: the auditors and chaplains sat at another table placed opposite, while the Cardinal's two lay nephews ate standing, each with a towel over his shoulders ready to wait on their uncle. Vespasiano calls this seigneurial *vita in comune*, one befitting a prelate of such high rank. In the 1430s the household of Cardinal Cesarini, who is represented by Vespasiano as a pattern of Christian humility and charity, consisted of about thirty persons, some fifteen of whom were servants, the rest being chaplains and *uomini da bene* maintained by the Cardinal.[21] But most cardinals displayed all the pomp and appurtenances of high rank, gold and silver plate, rich tapestries, fine horses, stately mules, often to the resentment and scandal of the laity.[22]

Brancaccio's career in the Curia is too entangled with the history of the Great Schism to be narrated at length here. He was naturally much favoured by Urban's successor, Boniface IX, who was both a fellow Neapolitan and a kinsman. He played an important part in the rebellion of the cardinals against Pope Gregory at Lucca in 1408, in the convocation of the Council of Pisa, and in the election of a new Pope, Alexander V, in 1409. In January 1410 he accompanied Alexander to Bologna. After Alexander's death in May he was one of the sixteen cardinals who elected John XXIII and, in the absence of Amadeo da Saluzzo, the Avignon cardinal who had replaced him as senior Cardinal Deacon, it was he who crowned the new Pope. John and Rainaldo were connected by ties of kinship. John's sister had married a Brancaccio, and in 1412 John made her son Tommaso a cardinal. Rainaldo and Tommaso have recently been confused in an important article on Masaccio and it should perhaps be made quite clear that Rainaldo was always known to his contemporaries as the Cardinal de' Brancacci (*de Brancatiis, de Brancacciis*). Tommaso on the other hand was invariably called the Cardinal of Tricarico (*Tricaricensis*) from the little town in Basilicata of which he became Bishop in 1405.

On 28 May 1410 John confirmed Rainaldo in his *commenda* of Santa Maria in Trastevere, no doubt at his own petition. He stood high in John's favour, and was greatly trusted, for it was he who in 1412 negotiated the all-important peace with King Ladislaus of Naples by which John hoped to buy off his most dangerous enemy. John recognised Brancaccio's services by making him Arciprete of Santa Maria Maggiore, the greatest, most revered, most ancient of Roman basilicas dedicated to the Virgin. He was granted this dignity in 1412 after the death on 17 July of the previous Arciprete, his fellow-Neapolitan Cardinal Enrico Minutolo.[24] Two years later he accompanied John to Constance, where he was one of the cardinals who remained loyal to the Pope until the last moment. Then like the other cardinals he bowed to the Council and after the election of Martin V on 11 November 1417 it was he who ten days later crowned the new Pope in the cathedral of Constance. On Friday 22 April 1418, Martin commending and the whole Council consenting, he dismissed the fathers with the resonant words: *Domini ite in pace*, to which all those present replied *Amen*.[25]

From the first Brancaccio was one of the two or three cardinals who were among Martin's most confidential advisers. He was also one of the five cardinals who accompanied the Pope on his slow journey southwards in 1418 and 1419.[26] During the year and a half Martin spent in Florence Brancaccio lodged in the Fondaccio, a district which a Lucchese envoy describes as a '*buon luogo*', with honourable houses. His host was one of the Florentine Brancacci, a fact which has been overlooked in the discussion as to whether there was any relationship between the Neapolitan Brancacci and Felice Brancacci, the Florentine merchant who commissioned from Masaccio and Masolino the famous frescoes in his chapel in the Carmine. Since the Cardinal lodged in the house of a Florentine Brancacci clearly some sort of kinship was acknowledged by both sides.[27]

Art historians have been tempted to speculate as to whether the Cardinal was in any way associated with the frescoes. There are many proofs, as we shall see in a moment, that he was the especial protector and advocate of Florentine interests with Martin, though unfortunately Peter Meller has been misled by a slip of the nineteenth-century scholar Cesare Guasti into crediting each and all of them to Cardinal Tommaso Brancaccio, John XXIII's nephew. Meller has suggested that Rainaldo's charitable magnificence in founding the Hospital of Sant' Angelo a Nido is reflected in the five scenes of the fresco in which Peter heals the sick, raises the dead and distributes alms. He has also claimed that the Cardinal may well have devised the programme for the frescoes, especially as Felice Brancacci is known to have been a faithful son of the Popes and on excellent terms with both Martin and Eugenius. Felice was also a friend of Giovanni di Bicci de' Medici, who was Rainaldo Brancaccio's banker and one of his executors. Meller believes that Rainaldo may be represented in the *Distribution of goods to the poor* in the figure dressed in scarlet and wearing a skull-cap who kneels behind St. Peter's sleeves and

62

represents the rich man whose goods were being distributed by St. Peter. But it should be emphasised that Felice Brancacci's devotion to the Popes is of itself enough to explain why he chose scenes from the life of St. Peter to decorate his chapel – their assertion of the supremacy of Peter's successors in opposition to the doctrine of conciliar supremacy would have been obvious in the 1420s.[28]

The Florentine vintner Bartolommeo del Corazza mentions Brancaccio several times in his descriptions of the splendid papal ceremonies and services held in Florence during Martin's residence there. On the Easter morning of 1418, for example, during the celebration of Pontifical High Mass in Santa Maria Novella, he kissed the Pope's foot and then recited the Gospel.[29] As Cardinal Protector of the Camaldolese Order, a lucrative office to which he had been elected in 1389, he frequented their much revered convent of Santa Maria degli Angioli, then a centre of fervent devotion and Christian humanism under the impulse of Frate Ambrogio Traversari, whom we shall meet again in later chapters. On 13 July 1419, he endowed the convent with a 100 florins *de camera*, in return for which 'we are obliged to say every day in perpetuity a Mass for his soul and for the souls of all those who had made gifts to the benefices he possesses, and the said moneys are to be put into the purchase of some possession which may be a reminder in perpetuity of the said mass, and we promised so to do, and burden the conscience of our successors with the duty to do this devoutly, considering the devotion which the said Cardinal has for our monastery and for the whole Order'.[30]

This anxiety for the welfare of his soul was to express itself again in the following year, after Brancaccio had returned to Rome, this time in the fostering of works of mercy. In 1420 he revived the Neapolitan confraternity of the *Disciplinati della Croce*, originally founded between 1290 and 1321 in the oratory of SS Elena and Constantino, near the convent of Sant' Agostino alla Zecca. The confraternity had dwindled away when Brancaccio took it up, revised its statutes, set it on an ampler footing and erected the little church of Santa Croce for it on the site of the old oratory. The obligation which the *Disciplinati* principally imposed on themselves was the succouring of prisoners, one of the four great works of mercy; they undertook, for example, to provide prisoners who died in the prison of the Vicaria or on the royal galleys with funeral rites and burial.[31]

When Martin made his solemn entry into Rome on 28 September 1420 a new era began for the city as well as for the Papal States. The Babylonish Captivity at Avignon and the strife of the Great Schism, during which Rome had been repeatedly occupied by troops or torn by revolts and faction fights had reduced the city to a wretched state of neglect and disrepair. 'He found Rome', writes Platina, 'so ruined and waste that it had nothing of the face of a city. You could see its houses collapsing, its churches collapsed, the streets deserted, the city deep in mud and obliterated, suffering under the dearness and want of everything.' Martin took vigorous measures to repair the streets and churches. By a bull of 28 November 1423, he deputed Cardinal Orsini, Cardinal Fillastre and Brancaccio, together with the Bishops of Adria and Trani and other reverend personages to make a visitation of the Roman churches. In a second bull, following their report, he commanded the cardinals to repair their titular churches, with the result that all of them, or so it is said, not only repaired, but decorated and enriched them.[32]

Brancaccio's confidential standing with the Pope emerges conspicuously from the reports of Florentine ambassadors. For Brancaccio was a warm advocate of Florentine interests with Martin; 'he publicly declares himself a citizen of Florence', reported Rinaldo degli Albizzi on 8 August 1424. He was one of the two cardinals deputed by the Pope in 1424 to mediate between Florence and Milan. 'Yesterday morning', wrote Albizzi on 5 October, 'and again after dinner we went to court, and having had much discourse with the Holy Father, at last he told us that he had deputed Cardinal Brancaccio and the Cardinal Sant' Eustachio, the one as a confidant of the Duke, the other for us, because he knows that Cardinal Brancaccio is your friend'. It is in a private letter from Albizzi to Guadagni dated 9 October that the Cardinal is given the code-name of *Lunghissimo* – 'very tall' – because of his striking height.[33]

Something of Brancaccio's manner of life during the 1420s can be pictured from contemporary documents, above all from his will.[34] He lived in the palace attached to Santa Maria in Trastevere, and had for his own use part of the garden belonging to the canons of the basilica.[35] The principal room was his *camera paramenti* or chamber of state. For its decoration he had several sets of hangings. One set 'worked with men', and two others, one green, one white, he bequeathed to his nephew Messer Paolo Brancaccio. A second nephew, Messer Giovanni, also known as Giovanello, was to receive his new red set, while to a third, Messer Fusco, he left the 'old hangings which he uses now'. He also had books which had belonged to his former chaplain, the Papal Scriptor Messer Niccolò de Senatibus:[36] these he left to Andrea di Bennozzo Brancaccio, a cousin of his nephew Giovanni. At one time or another his household included three nephews whom he had brought to live with him, in the accepted manner, so as to advance them at the Curia. Two predeceased him, Ponello, of whom nothing else is known, and Filippo, in reality his great-nephew, who died in 1423 at the Cardinal's palace at Rome, leaving Rainaldo by his will, dated 4 January 1423, a house in the Contrada della Sellaria in Naples. He also asked to be buried in his uncle's chapel in San Domenico, a wish that was still unfulfilled in 1427, when Rainaldo ordered that after his own death the bodies of Filippo and Ponello were to be conveyed together with his own to Naples 'if this can conveniently be

64

done'. The third nephew, Messer Giovanello, for whom the Cardinal procured the office of subdeacon to Pope Martin, survived him and was one of his two heirs-general.[37]

Naturally Brancaccio's household also contained a number of ecclesiastics. Possibly we should recognise some of these in certain of the witnesses to his will: Giovanni, abbot of the Benedictine monastery of Santa Maria at Positano and nephew of his former master, Pope John XXIII;[38] Bartolommeo, abbot of another Benedictine monastery, that of Santa Maria Rotonda outside Ravenna; and Antonio or Antonello di San Bartolommeo, archdeacon of Vulture. All three were Neapolitans, for cardinals, like Popes, preferred to surround themselves with their compatriots. Also Neapolitans were two other witnesses, Paolo della Valle and Aloisio Mutiliano, doctors of theology, who were surely maintained by the Cardinal to assist him in cases submitted to his judgement. Besides these men and his chaplains, his household contained a number of those aspirants to preferment or to offices in the household who entered the service of a cardinal on speculation and without a salary. Two Neapolitan physicians, Maestro Antonio de'Summonte and Maestro Aloisio cared for Rainaldo's health, and a German, Pietro Schoeme, Imperial and Apostolic notary, was his secretary. Of his other lay servitors, numerous as these probably were, there is no special mention in his will, though a Paolo Scaura of Naples who witnessed it and received a legacy of 50 florins jointly with his brother Onofrio may just possibly have occupied some important post in his household. In his stables the Cardinal kept his household mules: the two best he bequeathed to Pope Martin. In addition to the wine in his cellars he owned in March 1427 certain casks, imported or stored for him by Bartolommeo de' Bardi, of *vina greca*, the sweet white wine considered the noblest of all wines in his day, and that best fitted for a great man to drink, which he bequeathed to his nephew Paolo.[39] Two of the other witnesses to his will, Poncasio, Count of Monte Odorisio and Gentile d'Aiello, Bishop of Sessa and a *consiliarius camerae* or member of the council which supervised the Church's finances, were probably friends or kinsmen rather than members of his household.[40]

Since the history of Brancaccio's hospital and tomb is bound up with his revenues and possessions, we must look at the sources of his income as a cardinal. Besides a portion in the half-share of the regular revenues of the church which Pope Nicholas IV had granted the college in 1289, the extraordinary sources of a cardinal's income were of several kinds.[41] Immediately on his promotion the Pope would confer on him a large number of benefices of all kinds and in all countries, at the same time conceding him dispensation from residence, from personal visitation and from the canonical laws forbidding plurality of benefices. The Pope might even give a cardinal one or more bishoprics or the administration of a diocese. At one time Brancaccio held two dioceses, that of Aversa, and that of Taranto, which John XXIII gave him in 1412, though at that date the honour must have been purely nominal, for Taranto was ruled by Ladislaus. Brancaccio can have drawn as little profit from the archdeaconry of Palermo, which John also gave him.[42] The Pope might also bestow on a cardinal another Roman church *in commendam* in addition to his own titular church, as Innocent VII gave Brancaccio Santa Maria in Trastevere. Obviously the possibilities of abuse in this system were flagrant, and in the fourteenth century complaints of the cardinals' extortion and neglect were loud, frequent and often too well justified. Some cardinals were over eager in that favourite pursuit of members of the Curia, the greedy hunt after benefices. The worst of them accumulated a huge number, far more than they needed, as Audouin Albert admitted on his death-bed. One or two of the stricter Popes tried to eradicate such abuses by refusing their cardinals leave to make a will unless they left funds for any repairs to their churches that their own neglect or the neglect of their proctors had made necessary. Other cardinals were more restrained: some, like Brancaccio, salved their consciences by including in their pious foundations an obligation to say masses for the souls of those who had founded their benefices.

For Brancaccio was evidently one of that sort of cardinal who pursued benefices with more than usual avidity at the Curia, though he sometimes found it much easier to obtain a Papal grace than actual possession in the face of stout local resistance. Sometimes another person advanced a better or prior claim to a benefice, or even went to law with him at the Curia and he did not always win. His kinsman Boniface bestowed many benefices on him, enriching him greatly. In the Empire and in eastern Europe he came to hold numbers of churches and monasteries and even single altars in churches, especially as John XXIII unsealed a fresh fount of liberalities after what must have seemed the rather poor years which had followed the death of Boniface. On 25 August 1410 he granted Brancaccio and two other cardinals 1000 florins from the revenues of two Hungarian bishoprics. Two years later, on 15 February 1412 Brancaccio received the parish church of Woggenheim in the diocese of Utrecht together with a dispensation to hold it with his other benefices. And when he died, he also held the archdeaconry of Condroz and a canonry in the Cathedral of Liège: the canonry at any rate he had certainly held from 1395. He also held a few benefices in France, for *c.* 1413, when cardinals holding benefices in the kingdom of France and in Dauphiné were compelled to make a subvention of 500 florins to the King of France, he paid 10 florins, one of the smallest sums.[43]

In England he had quite a number of benefices. Urban VI gave him a canonry and prebend of Lincoln valued at 270 gold florins. To this Boniface added the canonry and prebend in the same church, that of Coringham, which he himself had held at the time of his accession. In 1391 Brancaccio was seeking to exchange both canonries because he had not yet been able to obtain possession. In 1393 we hear that he had been engaged in a law suit at the Curia with William Langbrok over a canonry and the treasurership of Wells. Some years before Langbrok had been provided to the canonry and prebend of Wormestorre in Wells and to the treasurership by the ordinary, whereas Urban had provided Rainaldo with them as benefices reserved to the Apostolic See. The papal auditor to whom Urban committed the case found for Rainaldo, but William had contumaciously refused to give up either treasurership or canonry, so incurring sentence of excommunication, suspension and interdict and later of deprivation and disablement. From these awful penalties Boniface released him, granting him provisional dispensation from the spiritual consequences, and on Rainaldo's resigning them into his hands, made provision of them to William. In 1394 Rainaldo sought to exchange yet another of his English benefices, the canonry and prebend of Beckingham in St. Mary's, Southwell. On 1 February 1395 Boniface gave him the reservation of the canonry and prebend of Bychull cum Knaresborough in York, made void by the consecration of a new bishop of Exeter, and on 1 May 1400, granted him yet another canonry in Lincoln, void because John Topp had failed to pay in time for the Papal letters of provision, granting him at the same time a dispensation to hold it together with a second canonry and prebend and the archdeaconry in the same church, to which the Pope was also providing him, as well as his other benefices.

The Cardinal plunged once more into litigation when Innocent VII gave him the canonry and prebend of Stransall in York and the archdeaconry of York. He was opposed by Roger Coringham. The cause was introduced in the Curia under Gregory and was still pending in April 1412, when Roger having died, John XXIII ordered that Brancaccio should be provided with the benefices at once, and at the same time gave him the usual dispensation to hold them in plurality. However, the cause had put Roger and Roger's two proctors to great expense, and in September 1414, after they had petitioned the Pope, Brancaccio disgorged Stransall to one of them, having also in the meantime surrendered the archdeaconry to William Pilton, canon of Exeter, who had been lawfully provided with it after Roger's death by the ordinary.[44]

Another, occasional source of income for cardinals was the gift customarily made by a new Pope to the cardinals who had elected him.[45] Many of the Avignon Popes distributed enormous sums on these occasions; sums varying from the 6000 florins given to each cardinal by Clement VI to the 2000 given by Urban V. Boniface IX was too poor to be so munificent after his election, but on 10 November 1389 he ordered the moneys still owing to him from his *servitia communia* as a cardinal and those belonging to dead or deprived cardinals for a year from that date to be distributed among his electors, among them Brancaccio.[46] The slowness with which rents and dues and revenues were collected in the Middle Ages generally meant that on the death of a cardinal money was still due to him from his benefices, both from the *servitia communia* and from other sources. The Pope could allow such sums to be paid into the dead man's estate rather than take them for himself. Moreover, since cardinals often left legacies which were too numerous or too heavy for their estate, the practice grew up of allowing the revenues of their benefices to be used for some years after their death to meet them. We shall find that Brancaccio's will assumes the concession of one or both of these privileges.

Our first record of a pious foundation by Brancaccio illustrates the tenacity with which his feelings clung to his native city throughout a long life at the Curia. In Aversa, near Naples, whose diocese he governed as Papal administrator from *c.* 1404, he caused a deed to be drawn up on 5 June 1406 by which he solemnly gave an endowment to his family chapel of Sant' Andrea in the church of San Domenico Maggiore in Naples. For this purpose a judge, notary and witnesses were summoned to the episcopal palace, where the Cardinal awaited them in his state chamber (*in quadam camera ornamenti*). There he declared to these persons assembled, that from devotion to the church of San Domenico and the chapel, he was making over to two proctors, Feulo Brancaccio and Fra Saverio da Napoli, representing the Dominican friars of the convent, certain properties in Naples and its district, to wit a bath and large houses adjoining it in Via di Fontanula, a *bottega* in Piazza di Pontone, a piece of land planted with vines and olives in the *villa* of Melito, and the sum of 37 *oncie* which the two proctors had already used to buy two *poderi* near Naples. In return for these gifts the Dominicans were to say mass daily in the chapel of Sant' Andrea, to keep a lamp perpetually burning in it, and to celebrate in it the feast days of St. Vitus, the patron saint of Brancaccio's titular church, and of St. Andrew. After his death they were also to celebrate his anniversary. Every year they were to present a wax candle of a pound's weight to the Cardinal, and after his death to the eldest of his descendants in the paternal line in acknowledgement of the *giuspatronato* of the Brancacci over the chapel. If they failed to fulfil these obligations, then the Cardinal's endowment was to pass to the church of Sant' Andrea in Piazza di Nido. His endowment then was made with the usual medieval intention of honouring his patron saints and ensuring perpetual masses for the salvation of his soul.[47]

In the Cardinal's will he testifies that he and his family had always felt a particular devotion to the Dominicans. He himself was the Cardinal Protector of the order from at least as early as 1403 until his death. San Domenico, the convent of the order in Naples, besides being so near to the Cardinal's family palace, was an illustrious foundation. St. Thomas Aquinas had entered the order in Naples as a novice in 1243: after his great career in Paris he returned there in 1272 as superior of the newly founded *Studium Generale*. The presence of the *Studium* made San Domenico a great centre of learning in medieval Naples: in addition the convent was also the headquarters of the Inquisition in the Kingdom.[48]

We saw that already in 1419 and 1420 the Cardinal's thoughts were busy with works of piety for the welfare of his soul after death. And with each year that passed he felt death drawing nearer. On 15 October 1422 he obtained the reversion of his bishopric of Aversa for Pietro Caracciolo Cassano, a canon of the Duomo of Naples, a member of a noble Neapolitan family and probably a kinsman. In 1425, feeling that his mortal life was drawing to its close, his thoughts turned even more to the life after death, fixing themselves on works that might help his soul to salvation and speed its journey into heaven. He began by providing for more masses in his chapel in San Domenico at Naples. On 26 July his secretary Pietro Schoeme drew up in the palace of Santa Maria in Trastevere an instrument by which Brancaccio confirmed and renewed his donation to San Domenico of the house in the Contrada della Selleria left him by his nephew Filippo.[49] In return the friars were to celebrate three masses daily in his chapel of Sant' Andrea, and to discharge other obligations.

The first known documents concerning the Cardinal's intention to refound and rebuild the Hospital of Sant' Andrea which stood at the bottom of Piazza di Nido, just in front of his family palace, date from 1426. Sant' Andrea had originally been founded in the thirteenth century for sick students of the Emperor Frederick II's University: the site on which it and the neighbouring buildings stood was originally so rocky that it was known as '*lo scogliuso*'.[50] Perhaps it was only devotion and local sentiment that inspired the Cardinal to refound Sant' Andrea. But there does exist a document which suggests that he may have also had another reason for his charity. A commission which had been deputed *c.* 1416 at Constance to consider the reforms that were needed in the Church had advocated among other things that the cardinals should forthwith resign 'all hospitals, leper-houses, *xenodochia* and other pious foundations which are to be used as hospices.' But in a marginal note to its memorial it had added: 'Let the petition of the Lord Cardinal de' Brancacci about the hospital also be referred to the nations'.[51] If this hospital was that of Sant' Andrea in Naples, then possibly its ruinous condition had so pricked the Cardinal's conscience that already he had resolved to save up the great sum of money required to rebuild and re-endow it. In fact the commission's recommendations were never given effect.

There was, it should be emphasised, nothing unique in Brancaccio's magnificence of charity. It was customary for cardinals to found, towards the end of their lives or by their wills, churches, convents or hospitals, so cleansing their consciences of any timorousness that the revenues of their benefices

69

had not been spent in the service of God, and at the same time assisting their salvation by making a foundation where prayers would be offered for their souls in perpetuity. In 1318 Cardinal Arnaud d'Aux (d. 1320) endowed with a large part of his patrimonial estate and with precious relics a collegiate chapter, consisting of a dean and eighteen secular canons, in his native village of La Romieu in Gascony. In 1333 Cardinal Arnaud de Via gave his whole fortune to the collegiate church of Villeneuve-les-Avignon, endowing twelve canons, twelve priests, two deacons, two sub-deacons, two acolytes and four servitors. The Franciscan Cardinal Vidal du Four endowed a convent at Toulouse for the prostitutes he had converted.[52] Cardinal Elie Talleyrand de Périgord (d. 1360) founded a chapel served by twelve chaplains in the Cathedral of Saint-Front at Périgord. The tradition continued unbroken into the early fifteenth century: Cardinal Branda da Castiglione (d. 1443) Brancaccio's colleague and contemporary, founded in 1422 two churches in his native place of Castiglione Olona, that of Corpo di Cristo known as della Villa, and the collegiate church, completed in 1428. Lesser prelates of the Curia were sometimes as munificent: the Apostolic protonotary Hermann Dwerg, hoping to purge himself of his sins – and usury must have weighed on his conscience – bequeathed his great fortune to works of charity and mercy, including the foundation of a hospice for the poor in his native town of Herford in Westphalia.[53]

The Cardinal was careful to petition the Pope that after he had refounded and endowed his hospital it should be forever exempt from the jurisdiction of the Archbishop of Naples and also from that of the Abbot of Sant' Andrea a Nido, who like the Archbishop was immediately subject to the Pope. The request for exemption from the Abbot's jurisdiction is tantamount to an admission that he then possessed rights over it, though during the bitter and prolonged lawsuits fought over the *giuspatronato* of the hospital in the middle of the eighteenth century these were claimed to have lapsed. And indeed, a document of 1294 which mentions Bartolommeo Brancaccio as beneficed with the church of Sant' Andrea also describes him as rector of the hospital.[54] Martin answered Brancaccio's petition in a bull of 24 April 1426.[55] 'When we carefully attend' it read 'to the searching diligence of your circumspection, and weigh with paternal consideration that by the greatness of your merits you honour the Roman Church of which you are an honourable member, we deem it meet and due that we should condescend as favourably as we may in God to your prayers, especially those that are seen to regard the salvation of your soul, the increase of God's worship and the advantage of poor and miserable persons. Your petition produced to us contained that it is your intention to reconstruct and rebuild with the goods conferred on you by God the poor persons' hospital of Sant' Andrea in the Piazza di Nido at Naples, now under the *giuspatronato* of laymen, which is wholly collapsed and ruined, or laid

70

waste, in all its buildings and other necessary offices on account of the plagues, wars and other calamities which have so long afflicted the city of Naples, together with an oratory and altar in honour and under the invocation of St Michael the Archangel and of the same Sant' Andrea, together with other necessary offices of this kind so that divers works of piety may there be performed and to endow it sufficiently to maintain the needful ministers and servitors of the said Hospital. Wherefore you have made humble supplication unto us to grant our licence unto you to execute the aforesaid things, and also for the sake of their tranquillity to remove and free the said hospital with its offices, garden, and all its other adjacent property and its rights and appurtenances, and also the persons at any time dwelling therein and its rectors from all jurisdiction, dominion, power and visitation of the Archbishop of Naples and also of the secular abbot of the church of the same Sant' Andrea di Nido of Naples, to the holders of which office the government of the said hospital while in flourishing state was known to appertain, and to subject it immediately to the Holy See, also to deign to commit perpetually the government of the said hospital to that person or persons whom you by your last will shall deem fit to depute for this purpose.'

The bull then grants to Brancaccio all the privileges and exemptions he had begged for his hospital. That same year the Cardinal began buying lands and houses in and around Naples for its endowment, acting through two proctors, his nephew Paolo Brancaccio and Artusio Pappacoda.[56] Artusio was one of the greatest nobles of late fourteenth- and early fifteenth-century Naples. The Pappacoda had originally been ship-builders and merchants, and by the middle of the fourteenth century had risen to the rank of *milites* or nobles. But the first member of the family to achieve some distinction was Linotto or Lionetto, of Seggio di Porto: Artusio was either his son or, more probably, his brother.[57] Both he and Linotto were firm supporters of Charles of Durazzo. From 1390 onwards Artusio bought a number of fiefs from King Ladislaus, so procuring for his family the higher estate appertaining to the feudal possession of land and at the same time contributing much-needed money to the young King's treasury for his campaign against the Angevins. About this time Ladislaus made him a familiar, councillor, Chamberlain of his table-cloth (*nappe sue prepositus*) and seneschal of his household. He was in equally high favour with Queen Giovanna II, the King's sister and successor, all the more because he was an old and intimate friend of her favourite the Gran Siniscalco Sergianni Caracciolo. Artusio built a great family palace in the *Vico Mezzocannone*, so that he was a near neighbour as well as a friend of the Brancacci family. After his death on 3 May 1433, he was buried in the family church of San Giovanni dei Pappacoda in Piazza San Giovanni which he had founded and for which he commissioned the grandiose late Gothic portal, dated 1415, which still decorates it (no. 104).

Work on the rebuilding of the hospital probably began shortly after the issuing of the Papal bull, for on 11 March 1427 the Cardinal's secretary drew up a formal instrument in which the Cardinal laid down the rules to be observed in the government of his hospital and chapel.[58] Addressed to the nobles of the Seggio di Nido, on whom the Cardinal intended to bestow the *giuspatronato* of the foundation, it sets forth both its spirit and its purpose.[59]

> Rainaldo, by divine mercy Cardinal Deacon of Santo Vito in Macello of the Most Holy Roman Church, named in the vulgar tongue of the Brancacci, desires eternal salvation in the Lord to the Magnificent and Noble Members of the University of Nobles of the Piazza di Nido of Naples. When the sight of our consideration is extended, and we weigh with sleepless and devout intention of mind that God the giver of all good things hath raised us up with a title of dignity, and also the number of the good things He hath conferred on our littleness, we deem it discordant and impious not to repay Him, who needeth none of the good things, by some token of gratitude from the good things He hath given us. When therefore we sought in the secret of our heart for the means of doing so, our intention settled itself by preference on attempting a work by which we might at one and the same time satisfy two of the Lord's commandments, on which depend all the law and the prophets, and our mind acquiescing in this deliberation, lest the effect of our desire should suffer a long delay, for the execution of the aforesaid work we have had constructed and built near the church of San Andrea a Nido in the place called *lo largo di Nido* a hospital with its houses and necessary and useful offices, and within it a chapel under the invocation of St. Michael the Archangel and St. Andrew and have provided for the suitable maintenance of its ministers by the purchase of revenues. However, in order that this work now begun may not perish in the course of time and may last through all the revolutions of days, it is expedient to take measures for the sincere faith and faithful goodness of its regents and governors. And after our mind has long revolved in this cogitation, at last our affection turns and fixes itself to your magnificence and nobility which is wont to employ a skilful zeal in the construction, maintenance and defence of pious foundations, thinking and beseeching that you will deign to understand, pursue and accept the form of this pious work in order that you may the more richly deserve the rewards of divine justice.
>
> The form of the aforesaid government and rule shall be according to the manner and terms written below, which we have ordained by the Apostolic authority granted to us in this matter, and we have made the statutes written below, which we desire to be inviolably observed, to wit: Because it seems impossible that the entire University of Nobles should exercise this government, we ordain that each year the aforesaid University shall elect two nobles, worthy and approved men, of whom one shall always be of the house of the Brancacci, who shall have power to demand, seek and receive all the fruits, revenues and profits, offerings and legacies pertaining or which shall pertain to the said Hospital and Chapel, and to give quittances for their receipts, and to expend and dispense the receipts as shall seem proper to them for the advantage and utility of the said

Hospital and Chapel and ministers and infirm dwelling therein. And if it were necessary to act in any law-trial, to despatch and reply and forward all business just as our own person might as principal in its own behalf. *Item*, the said University or the two persons to be chosen by the said University as is permitted, shall choose an honest cleric, who shall have power and jurisdiction over the priests and clergy listed below, and shall have the right of correcting, punishing, excommunicating and exercising all ecclesiastical jurisdiction should it befall that they or any one of them commit a crime or any other offence. *Item*, the said Rectors shall choose a worthy man or a God-fearing woman, of good fame and mature age according to their will and inclination who shall serve in the said Hospital in the reception of the weak and infirm poor of either sex, and in the care and service of the same, and shall ever attend to their preservation and cleanliness. *Item*, that the said Rectors shall choose some priests of good fame and life and of decent family after the fashion that shall most approve itself to the said Governors, and these shall so accord together concerning the celebration of masses, that each day in the said chapel of St. Michael the Archangel and St. Andrew they shall celebrate three masses, of which one shall be that of the feast or day then falling, one of the Blessed Virgin, and one for the dead. But on the sixth day let there be said a mass of the Cross, that which ought to be said on that feast or day, and let a mass of the Cross be said unless it be a double feast or one having its own mass, or a day of Quadragesima, or of the four times or a vigil having a fast, and if for this reason the mass of the Cross is omitted, let it be said plainly after the mass of the day without the sacrifice commonly called holy. *Item*, that on the underwritten feast-days of our Lord Jesus Christ, to wit, those of His Nativity, Circumcision, Epiphany, Resurrection, Ascension, of Pentecost, the feast of the Trinity and Corpus Christi. *Item*, on the single feast-days of the Blessed Virgin, that is of her Conception, Nativity, Annunciation, and of her Visitation, which is on the second day of the month of July, of her Purification, Assumption and of the Madonna of the Snows (*delle Nevi*). *Item*, on the feast-days of the Apparition of St. Michael and of his Dedication, of St. John Baptist, St. John the Evangelist, and on the feast-days of the Holy Apostles Peter and Paul, of the Conversion of St. Paul, of St. Andrew, of St. Stephen Protomartyr, of St. Laurence, of St. Vitus the Martyr, which is on the fifteenth day of the month of June, of St. James, which is on the twenty-fifth day of the month of July, and that also on the feast of the dedication of the said chapel of St. Michael and St. Andrew shall be celebrated a solemn mass with prime Vespers, with singing, and all the priests who are appointed to the said Hospital shall meet together to sing the said Mass with the said Vespers. *Item*, that the said priests who are to be chosen and also the man or woman hospitaller shall not be instituted nor shall any title be given them, but they shall be appointed and dismissed with or without the salary for which they have agreed at the inclination and will of the said Rectors. *Item*, that the said Lord Rectors shall provide for the weak and in-firm a competent doctor or doctors according to the choice of the said Rectors: they shall also provide for spiritual medicines and for all other things necessary for all poor folk in the said hospital according as the said doctor or doctors shall

F

prescribe. *Item*, that the said Piazza or the Governors by them to be deputed cannot and must not sell, alienate or remove anything from the possessions and from the precious furnishings of the said chapel and hospital nor pledge any of them, neither shall it be lawful for them to lend to anyone or to take outside the hospital any of the moveable goods belonging to the said hospital and appointed for its use, but shall be content with the fruits, revenues, pensions, dues and emoluments arising from the said possessions or contingent on them, and shall use them solely for the government, augmentation and repair of the Hospital and for the celebration of the divine offices. *Item*, that since our most holy Lord Pope Martin V has exempted this Hospital and its officers and members from all subjection to any Ordinaries whatsoever and has subjected it immediately to the Roman Church, let the Rectors take good care that neither the Archbishop of Naples nor the Abbot of San Andrea use any jurisdiction over it and that of the legacies made to the said Hospital or to be made in after time, no fourth or canonical part be paid to them, nor shall they receive any visitation from them nor render account to them of their administration, but let the Apostolic Bull and concession of our said Lord Pope be observed in all things. *Item*, that the office of the Rectors or Governors of the said Hospital, who are to be chosen by the said Piazza di Nido into the government of the same shall last no longer than a year, and when the year is finished, by that same fact it shall expire, and they shall be bound to render reason and account of their receipts and disbursements, acts and administration to their successors and to no other, and to assign them what remains. And if (may it never come to pass) they have done or administered aught evilly, or if any discord has arisen between them, they shall be brought to order by the University of the Nobles of the said Piazza, or by those five nobles who hold its protection at the time and shall be compelled to make satisfaction as they are bound. *Item*, that by day and by night there shall burn in the said chapel a lamp before the image of the Glorious Virgin Mary. *Item*. The same Lord Cardinal desired that the priests of the same chapel shall hold and say once a year on the day of his death for the good of his soul solemn vigils with vespers and commendations of the dead, and in the morning masses also for the dead with commendations, candles, wax lights and little torches as shall most approve itself to the said Rectors, and this from year to year on the said day of the death of the said Lord Cardinal. *Item*, he willed and ordained that the said chaplains and priests of the said Hospital shall be able and authorised to hear the confessions of the infirm persons dwelling therein and to administer the Holy Eucharist and the Holy Oil and to do all the other things necessary and fitting in such matters. *Item*, he willed and ordained that the Noble Rectors of the said Hospital should give and offer from year to year in perpetuity on the feast-day of St. Michael in the month of May a small wax torch of a pound's weight to his nearest relative of the male sex of the house of the Brancacci.

The instrument ends with a formal declaration that the Cardinal has ordered it to be subscribed and published and certified by the addition of his seal.

Fifteen days later, on 27 March, the Cardinal made his will.[66] It opens with one of the customary solemn formulae.

> Considering in regard to the last things that nothing is more certain than death and less certain than the hour of death, and that the last day should ever be before our eyes, and desiring while still of sound mind to dispose seriously and in time of those things which have been given to him by God, so that he may deserve to hear that word of Scripture: Well done, thou good and faithful servant &c, and considering that word of Holy Scripture which warns us of the last things, lest any forsooth, being taken captive by the deceitful pleasures of this world forget that eternal life for which the Most High created us, and that it is difficult for those living in the flesh so to dispose of themselves and their possessions before death that there is no need of the body of testaments, by which we leave some things to be executed after our death which either human weakness had left undone in this most rapid course of life or . . . . [sic] reclaimed of its goods, having first called on the Redeemer's aid, he made a will. And first he commended his soul to the Most High Creator, to the most glorious Virgin Mary, to St. Michael the Archangel, to St. John Baptist, St. John the Evangelist, to the Holy Apostles Peter and Paul and Andrew, to St. Laurence and St. Vitus Martyrs, and to the whole court of the holy inhabitants of heaven above.

Like many of its kind the will now jumps backwards and forwards in rather desultory fashion and it will simplify matters to sort out its various provisions into groups.

Five members of the Brancacci family were the principal recipients of property and sums of money. The Cardinal's two nephews, Paolo and Giovanello, whom we have already encountered, received the largest share, as his heirs-general. They were the sons of his brother Filippo: since Giovanello was only a subdeacon in 1428, he cannot have been very old, and was possibly the child of a second or third marriage. Paolo was not only his elder, but had had a more eventful career. He is described by King Ladislaus in a document of 1406 concerning some feudal estates of which he had been wrongfully deprived as *miles familiaris et fidelis noster dilectus*. Ladislaus made him Count of Nocera, but after the King's death he was obliged to surrender this particular fief to its previous possessors, the Zurlo. He was still living in 1452, when King Alfonso granted him some property in Naples. To these two the Cardinal bequeathed all that he had inherited from his mother and father. To Paolo he left in addition 1000 florins as a dowry for his daughter, a sum of the order expected with a girl of great family. Fusco, a third nephew, brother of Paolo and Giovanello, received a legacy of 200 florins. Andrea Brancaccio, not a direct descendant of the Cardinal, as we have seen but some sort of cousin, was much more generously remembered, for he received 600 florins as well as the books already mentioned. Almost

75

certainly this Andrea was a priest for he was also left a breviary that had belonged to a bishop of Todi. The Cardinal's great-niece Maria, daughter of Filippo Brancaccio's son Giacomo, was to receive enough black cloth to make herself a mourning dress in the Neapolitan fashion. To three of the clerics who witnessed his will, Giovanni, abbot of Santa Maria at Positano, who as we have seen was no other than Giovanni Cossa, brother of Michele and nephew of John XXIII, Bartolommeo, abbot of Santa Maria Rotonda and Antonello di San Bartolommeo, he left copes or money to buy a cope. According to custom he ordered that all arrears of salary were to be paid to the salaried officers of his household, recommending especially his two doctors Maestro Aloisio and Maestro Antonio to the goodwill of his executors. Again according to custom he desired that a subvention might be paid to all those who had entered his household without salary in hopes of an office. Any debts were to be satisfied within two years. With a prudent eye to the ways of heirs, he ordained that should any one of them take anything away forcibly from his palace, contrary to the will of the other executors – Paolo and Giovanello and Fusco were executors as well as heirs – he was to forfeit all his legacies and share in the inheritance.

The Cardinal also left money for certain posthumous expenses proper to his exalted dignity, for the costly black mourning his household was to wear at his obsequies, for white dresses to clothe thirteen poor persons (at least one of whom was to be a woman) who were also to attend them, and for his tomb. Legacies for such expenditure were sanctioned by tradition and were made by all great ecclesiastics – though as always, some exceeded in pomp, others wanted only the humblest of interments. Brancaccio also left certain pious bequests for the repose of his soul. On the day immediately after his death two or three priests were to begin singing masses of St. Gregory: to pay for these he left 3 gold florins. For the celebration of other masses and for the distribution of alms he bequeathed 100 gold florins. He left another 100 florins for dowries to be given to two or three girls – a favourite type of pious legacy at this time as we have already seen, though Brancaccio seems to have left larger dowries for fewer girls than was usual. To various churches and monasteries in Rome and Naples he left sums of money with which to make repairs or buy chalices and missals for the service of the altar. Santa Maria Maggiore was to receive 35 florins for a chalice, Santa Maria in Trastevere 25, the Spedale di Santo Spirito in Sassia 20. With 16 florins owed him by Matteo di Benedetto of the Curia a missal was to be bought for the monastery of St. Saba. To St. John Lateran he left 25 florins, to the monastery of San Sisto 15. His titular church of San Vito in Macello received 25 florins for repairs or for any other evident need. To Santa Sabina, the chief convent of the Dominicans, of whose order he was Protector, he left 25 florins and ordered all its treasures (*jocalia*) including a cross and a mitre, and each and every one of its documents and privileges to be returned to it. His only benefaction to a church outside Rome was a legacy of 5 *oncie* to the church of San Falcone in Piazza di Nido in Naples.

Each and every one of his other bequests of money and goods, exceeding these private legacies in value by far, was made either to his hospital and its chapel or to his chapel in San Domenico, which he had re-dedicated to St. Vitus, probably because St. Andrew was to share the dedication of his hospital chapel. From the terms of the will it is plain that work on the hospital was not yet complete, perhaps was not as yet far advanced. In speaking of it as finished the statutes were evidently using the language of anticipation.

'*Item*, he willed and ordained that the Hospital of Sant' Andrea which is in Piazza di Nido shall be rebuilt with all necessary and useful places and offices and a garden and that in it shall be made an altar or chapel under the invocation of St. Michael the Archangel and St. Andrew, in which chapel divine service shall be done precisely as described above in his chapel in the church of the Preaching Friars (i.e. San Domenico), and that priests are to be chosen for it, to be appointed and dismissed at the will of the Rectors and of the same Hospital, and that in the said Hospital be made beds, separated by partitions and supported on legs, to the number of thirteen, twelve for the poor and one for the hospitaller, and for the completion of the said Hospital and chapel and of all other needful things he left five thousand gold florins *de camera* in coined money.' This was a huge sum, and to it the Cardinal added 'for the use and sustentation of the said Hospital and of the poor persons thereto resorting' as much as would buy enough lands and property to produce a yearly rent equal to that produced by the property he had already bought for the hospital, to wit 48 *oncie* and some lands.

In the last part of the will he rather modified these dispositions. He now declared that Cosimo de' Medici, who was present in person, held a *cedula* for a deposit of 6000 florins, from which were to be drawn the funds for building and finishing the Hospital and Chapel. This does not mean that the Cardinal left 11,000 florins to complete the Hospital and chapel, but that the sum was not now limited to the 5000 florins provided in the first part of the will, but more loosely fixed within the limit of 6000 florins. Any moneys remaining from this sum were to be restored to his heirs – a clause possibly not without significance for the history and state of his tomb. Property yielding an annual revenue of 2 *oncie* of *carlini* was to be bought to supplement the endowment of the Hospital, notwithstanding that some lands might prove superfluous. Also to be bought was a vineyard to produce wine for the poor persons and servitors in the Hospital. The number of beds was increased from thirteen to sixteen, each to rest on strong supports and to be supplied with a coverlet and a pair of sheets. And other things needful were to be purchased – stools, benches, chests, bandages, floor-coverings, all 'for the conservation of the property and goods belonging to the aforesaid Hospital'.

The Cardinal then added – was it in increasing terror of death? – yet another bequest of 3000 ducats to the Hospital over and above all his other legacies. Of these 1482 ducats were deposited with Bartolommeo de' Bardi – now head of the Medici bank in Rome – for which the Cardinal held a *cedula* from Bartolommeo. The remaining 1518 ducats were to be found from the dues appertaining to the Cardinal's benefices and to his Cardinal's hat which still remained unpaid at his death, but were to be taken only from his nephew Messer Giovanello's share of the inheritance. The 3000 ducats were to be handed over to the nobles of the Seggio di Nido, to be employed by them in conjunction with Paolo Brancaccio in the purchase of more property for the Hospital. And as a final proviso Rainaldo added that all moneys or emoluments rightfully pertaining to his Cardinal's hat and still owing to him at his death were to be paid over to Cosimo and his brother Lorenzo de' Medici, in other words, the Medici bank; for this he had obtained a papal letter of permission.

For the adornment and furnishing of the hospital chapel the Cardinal left both moneys and instructions. It was to be 'as beautifully painted as the chapel of Messer Artusio and that of Maestro Antonio della Penna'. Messer Artusio can be identified without difficulty as Artusio Pappacoda and his chapel as San Giovanni dei Pappacoda, the church which Artusio had built in 1415.[61] The frescoes Brancaccio so much admired were destroyed during the general restoration of San Giovanni in 1772, but we know that they were in a *trecento* style, for in 1524 Pietro Summonte wrote to Marc' Antonio Michiel that *La cappella che si dice di messer Artuso, iuxta San Ioan Maior, è tutta depinta per mano delli descendenti dalli discepoli di Iocto ad tempo del nostro re Lancelao.* According to those Neapolitan historians and topographers who have left some record of them, they represented scenes from the life of St. John the Evangelist and from the Apocalypse[62] and were already much faded by the end of the seventeenth century.

Maestro Antonio della Penna was another great official of the Neapolitan court. He had been secretary to King Ladislaus, and in 1406 built Palazzo Penna, one of the finest surviving late Gothic secular buildings of Naples.[63] By Penna's chapel Brancaccio meant his tomb-chapel in Santa Chiara, commissioned c. 1413 by Antonio's nephew Onofrio from the sculptor Antonio Baboccio. Its tall canopied framework still survives on the left of the main doorway of the church (nos. 106–107). The tomb is decorated with a fresco showing the Virgin and Child adored by Antonio and Onofrio della Penna. The discovery in 1627 of an older fresco of the Trinity below this scene caused the dismemberment of the tomb, Counter-Reformation sentiment being scandalized that a sarcophagus should have been placed against a representation of so sacred a subject (no. 106).) The sarcophagus (no. 108) was accordingly removed into the first chapel on the right of the church, and in its place an altar was erected. The fresco of the Virgin and Child adored by Antonio and Onofrio is in a style influenced by Lombard art, and has lent its name to a small group of paintings attributed by Ferdinando Bologna to 'Il Maestro di Antonio ed Onofrio Penna'. It is noble and severe, but with a certain lively expressiveness. The Cardinal must have seen and admired both the Pappacoda and the Penna chapels after his return to Rome in 1420.

In addition to frescoes his hospital chapel was to have windows glazed with iron and glass – an expensive matter in the early fifteenth century. With the exception of a cloth of gold 'after the fashion of the Lords Cardinals' he also transferred to it most of the furnishings in the chapel of his Roman palace, all his altar-coverings, his silver cross, his 'beautiful' silver censer and an incense-boat, a pair of silver altar cruets, four great silver candlesticks, a small copper hand-bell, in fact everything necessary for the service of the altar except a chalice and paten and a pyx. He also provided it with books, the breviary in which he himself recited the office, a small missal, a service-book, a gospel book bound in green leather. Besides these costly gifts, he ordered that his vestments 'of whatsoever form and colour', both those in the rooms of his palace and those in its chapel, should be divided into two equal lots, one to be given to his chapel of St. Vitus in San Domenico and one to the hospital chapel. He also left to the hospital chapel other vestments which he had commanded to be made for it, namely 'three chasubles . . . which are still with the tailor'. To these gifts he added a painting 'with many relics', possibly one of those fourteenth-century devotional tablets or diptychs painted with small rows of saints, with a relic set under each figure. He also gave a large twenty-four-hour clock and ordered bells to be bought for the more perfect observance of the hours of service.

His commands concerning his exequies were positive and careful. 'He willed that his exequies should be held according to that rite of the Roman Curia which is customary for Cardinals, the expenses to be discharged from the money and goods to be collected by the under-mentioned executors and trustees as in duty bound, whom he begs and exhorts in the Lord Jesus Christ to abstain from all pomp and superfluity. And he desired the said exequies to be held if he died in Rome in the church of Santa Maria sopra Minerva, or else in Santa Maria Maggiore, of which church he is Arciprete, according as shall seem fitting to his executors. And in whatever place the exequies are held, there let his body be laid for deposition only. If he dies elsewhere, then let them be held in the principal church of the Preaching Friars (i.e. the Dominicans) in whatever place death has befallen him, and let his body be laid there until removed to Naples. But if there should be no convent of the said Order in the place of his decease, then let his body and exequies be removed to some decent place close by belonging to the said Order, or let all be performed in the principal church of his place of death, if it shall seem expedient to his executors, but the testator desired that the removal of his body to Naples remain always firm.'

To transport the body of a Cardinal to its final resting-place was in fact no light task. It was escorted by members of his household and by priests, whose expenses had to be defrayed from the estate by the executors and might well amount to a considerable sum, quite apart from the cost of the exequies themselves, of a stone to cover the temporary resting-place (*depositum*) of the body, and of the procession and services that accompanied the final interment. For even if the testator, like Brancaccio, expressly desired no superfluous magnificence – thirteen poor persons was a very modest funeral escort, some cardinals left money for clothes and candles for as many as a hundred – even if he made no special bequests to the celebrants, yet the expenditure necessary for a state funeral was still great. Cardinal Pierre de Cros left 1000 florins to pay for his, a sum equivalent in value to the entire fortune of a small Florentine merchant. And if Brancaccio did not wish for any extravagant expense, neither did he wish to forgo the honour proper to his high estate.

Besides his three nephews Paolo, Giovanello and Fusco, Brancaccio appointed several other executors. Two were Cardinals, Angelo de Anna de Sommaripa, Cardinal de Laude, a Camaldolese friar who had been made a Cardinal long ago by Urban VI in the same promotion as Brancaccio, and Ardicino de Porta (d. 9 April 1434), a consistorial advocate who was promoted Cardinal Deacon of St. Cosmas and Damian on 24 May 1426. Ardicino, also known as the Cardinal of Novara (*Novariensis*) was to be consulted in everything concerning the execution of the will, a task for which his legal experience made him especially suitable.[64] The other four executors were Messer Paolo di Giovinazzo, who had been deputed by John XXIII in 1414 to receive with Brancaccio the ambassadors of Queen Giovanna II of Naples, Giovanni Cossa, Abbot of Santa Maria in Positano, Frate Tommaso, Prior of Santa Sabina and Giovanni di Bicci de' Medici of Florence. Giovanni, father of Cosimo and Lorenzo, had retired, as we have seen, from any active part in the Medici bank in 1420, yet although Cosimo and Bartolommeo de' Bardi evidently managed all the financial side of winding up the Cardinal's estate, Giovanni no doubt received the honour of being named an executor in the will because he was the Cardinal's old banker and the head of the family.[65]

According to the inscription placed on the Cardinal's tomb more than a century and a half later Rainaldo died on the same day that he drew up his will. This was a false assumption, all the more surprising because the will is self-evidently not a death-bed will, but one made by a man who feels that the hour of his death is drawing closer and desires to put his affairs in order lest death take him suddenly. There exists or existed until the last war in the Archivio di Stato of Naples a document, dated 14 May 1427, in which the Cardinal, having petitioned the Pope to confirm that Aversa was a diocese immediately subject to the Holy See, contrary to a claim put forward by the Archbishop of Naples that it was a suffragan diocese of his archbishopric, received a favourable sentence.[66] But by early May he was already mortally sick, for on the 16th of that month Frate Ambrogio Traversari, the shining light of the Camaldolese order in these years, wrote urgently from Santa Maria degli Angioli in Florence to Rinuccio da Castiglione, a Florentine familiar of Cardinal Condulmer (later Pope Eugenius IV): 'We need your help very greatly. For just causes we desire that the protectorship of our order should be conferred on our common father, the Lord Bishop of Siena, now that the Lord Cardinal de' Brancacci is dying. And because the protectorship carries emoluments of money, we are fearful that one less fitting may obtain it on that account from his Holiness our Lord . . . and so we ask him by letters to confer our protectorship on the Bishop of Siena.' And in another letter written simultaneously to the Bishop himself, Antonio Casini, he tells him that the order, hearing that Brancaccio lies gravely sick, implores him to undertake its protectorship, so that it might no longer decline and return instead to its old regular observance.[67] Brancaccio died in Rome on 5 June, and by July the ledgers of the Medici bank in Rome show his account as in the hands of his executors.[68]

As with the tomb of Pope John XXIII, some of the elements of the design of the Brancacci tomb symbolise the ritual that was followed after death for the exequies of a cardinal. There still survive descriptions of such ceremonies and the *Ordo Romanus* compiled in the late fourteenth century by Pierre Ameilh (Pietro Amelio) records the rite that was followed in Brancaccio's day – we can be certain that this is so because the chapter on the exequies of cardinals contains an addition describing the forms used at the exequies of Ardicino da Porta, Brancaccio's executor, in 1434.[69] The body of the dead man lay in state in his palace or in a convent church – we saw how anxious Brancaccio was that in his case it should be a Dominican convent – for nine days. If it lay on a bier, then the pall was of cloth of gold, and the bier was surrounded by burning candles. After the *novena* it was taken to the church, escorted by the members of the household dressed in mourning and by the poor persons hired and clothed for the purpose, all bearing torches. The service was held in the evening in the nave of the church. The body lay under a catafalque, placed on a bier covered with a cloth of gold, and with hanging lappets of black decorated with the arms of the deceased. The richness of such funeral palls can be judged from that laid over the bier of John XXIII and from that laid under the body of Martin V on his tomb (no. 96) in St.

John Lateran (1431). At least one hundred torches illuminated the ceremony, held by the dead man's household, as it sat weeping and lamenting around the catafalque, which was set with candles. If the Cardinal had been a Cardinal Bishop, his body was clothed entirely in vestments of black or violet colour, like a Pope, with a white mitre, gloves, sandals, a pontifical ring, and a silk veil over his face. A Cardinal Priest was also dressed in these vestments, but a Cardinal Deacon like Brancaccio was vested 'in the habit of a deacon, without a chasuble, and without gloves or pontifical rings, but with other tunics, small gloves and a small ring.' A big black pillow was set beneath his head. At his feet was placed another on which two red cardinal's hats were laid. The funeral mass was said by a cardinal. Either he or a master in theology then delivered a sermon, usually a panegyric on the virtues of the deceased, after which the cardinal who had said mass and four of the older cardinal priests vested themselves in white amice, stole and cope, with rings but without gloves and sandals. The cardinal who had said mass then went to the catafalque, followed by the three or four others, while the choir sang a psalm. When the chant was ended they took their places to either side of it, and the cardinal who had said mass prayed and then asperged the body or bier with holy water and censed it, repeating the Pater Noster and giving the first absolution followed by the others, each in due order. All the other cardinals and clergy present meanwhile remained seated in the choir, the cardinals and patriarchs holding great wax torches, of at least four pounds in weight, while those of lesser rank held ones of a pound or two pounds in weight, according to the means or magnificence of the testator and his executors.

Chapter IV · The Brancaccio Tomb (1)

AMONG CARDINALS, as indeed among other great ecclesiastics and laymen, there were three intentions of feeling about the kind of tomb in which they wished to be buried. Some wanted only a humble memorial, so that they might not imperil their own souls or those of others by seeming to covet the vainglory of wordly honour even after death. In 1364 Cardinal Pierre de Colombiers declared in his will that 'since funeral pomp, long trains of mourners at exequies, sumptuous diligence of sepulture and opulent construction of monuments are some sort of consolations to the living, but of no assistance to the dead, they are to be performed with much moderation, and it is of more moment to attend rather to the prayers and salutary sacrifice of Holy Mother Church and to the alms which are bestowed for their souls, by which things there is no doubt that the dead are assisted.' Accordingly he chose to found a monastery and ordered that he should be buried in its church or chapel under a plain stone level with the ground, bearing neither image nor inscription. Cardinal Audoin Albert of Limoges, who lamented in his will of 3–5 May 1363 that he had accepted too many benefices from his patron Pope Innocent VI, commanded that his body should be laid under a plain stone, with only a verse epitaph carved round the edge. The stone under which Cardinal Philippe Cabassole was to be laid by his will of 27 August 1372 was to be set before the altar, under the feet of the celebrant, with no arms, but only his image and name and his cardinal's hat beneath his feet in memory of his dignity. In the will of the ascetic St. Pierre de Luxembourg (29 June 1387) humility became self-humiliation. He ordered 'that my rotting body . . . after my soul has been delivered from it and from the bonds of the flesh, shall be buried in the cemetery of St. Michel at Avignon, in the public ground, without the chapels, together with the other public corpses.'[1]

Other cardinals chose the middle way between humility and pride. Cardinal Pierre Desprez, for example, desired in 1361 that he should be buried in the church of St. Martin at Montpezat 'not too sumptuously but moderately, according to what is fitting to our estate.' But many were anxious that their tombs should perpetuate their exalted degree in this world with becoming splendour. Cardinal Guillaume de Chanac (d. 30 December 1383) commanded in his will: 'I will and ordain that for my remains there may be made an honourable tomb of alabaster, fitting my degree, that on it may be placed my statue, my arms and other necessary ornaments, so that my relations and friends and those whom I have known, as they pass by it, may remember me and take care to implore the All-Highest for my soul.'[2] By the 1420s the tradition of grandiose tombs for cardinals was already an old one. Among the earliest was the tomb of Cardinal Guglielmo Fieschi (d. 1256) in San Lorenzo fuori le Mura, in Rome (no. 120) but the tomb of the French cardinal Guillaume de Braye (d. 30 April 1282) in San Domenico, Orvieto, by Arnolfo di Cambio, is the earliest to survive in something of its original majesty.[3] The dismembered tomb of Cardinal Riccardo Annibaldi (d. *c.* 1275) in St. John Lateran is possibly some years earlier, and already pretends to magnificence, with a carving of the last rites at the solemn exequies of the Cardinal represented in figures in high relief on a mosaic ground which extends behind the entire length of the effigy.

These two majestic tombs have recently been shown to be inspired in iconography and design by French thirteenth-century Gothic tombs,[4] and it is no accident that Italian tombs reached their most gigantic proportions in Naples, under the rule of the French Angevin dynasty. A number of cardinals ordered or were given splendid tombs during the fourteenth century: Cardinal Riccardo Petroni (d. 1314) in the Duomo of Siena, Cardinal Luca Fieschi (d. 1336) in the Duomo of Genoa, Cardinal Matteo Orsini (d. 1340) in Santa Maria sopra Minerva, Rome, Cardinal Adam Hartford (d. 1397) in Santa Cecilia in Trastevere and Cardinal Philippe d'Alençon (d. 1400) in Santa Maria in Trastevere. In design their tombs did not differ from the tombs of Popes and other great personages, although they too naturally vary within a general pattern according to the means, devotion and taste of the patron and the style of the sculptors.[6] The sarcophagus is set under a canopied framework. Angels draw back curtains to either side of the effigy: above is a figure of the Virgin and Child, often with a kneeling figure of the deceased being presented to them, and a figure of Christ in glory giving His blessing.

In Naples itself the Brancaccio tomb was immediately preceded by two imposing tombs erected to themselves by cardinals who were contemporaries, colleagues and probably kinsmen of Brancaccio. Cardinal Francesco Carbone (d. 8 June 1405) had built for himself in the Duomo of Naples a funerary chapel dedicated to San Tiburzio and Santa Susanna together with a splendid tomb in which he was buried with a laudatory epitaph (no. 102).[7] In the Minutolo chapel, also in the Duomo, Cardinal Enrico Minutolo erected an even more grandiose tomb (no. 103) for himself between 28 February 1402 and his death on 17 July 1412.[8] There is no doubt that Brancaccio commissioned his tomb in emulation of these.

Surprising as his indifference may seem, he left it to his executors to decide whether he was to lie in San Domenico or in his Hospital. Ordaining that his body and those of his nephews were to be carried to Naples 'the said testator willed that in the said chapel (of San Domenico) or in his other chapel of the Hospital of Sant' Angelo and Sant' Andrea shall be placed his tomb, which the said testator has had made through the hands of Cosimo de' Medici and Bartolommeo de' Bardi.' Both Cosimo and Bartolommeo have already figured in this book, in connection with John XXIII, and we have seen that both of them are mentioned elsewhere in Brancaccio's will. But now it is clearly crucial to discover the exact nature of their connection with the Cardinal. It was financial. The fortunes of the Medici had been founded on Giovanni's services as banker to the Papal Curia, which his bank accompanied on its various migrations. When John XXIII went to Constance, Ilarione de' Bardi, head of the bank's Roman counter, followed him, and Cosimo de' Medici was also sent there by his father. He may well have encountered Brancaccio in Constance, or they may already have met in Rome or Florence. But the probability is that the two became acquainted through Giovanni's bank, which Brancaccio used both for the collection of revenues from his far-flung benefices and for the deposit of money. His relations with Giovanni must have been of long standing, if only because he made him an executor of his will.

When Giovanni withdrew from active business after the death of his partner Benedetto di Lippaccio Bardi in 1420, his sons Cosimo and Lorenzo entered into a new partnership with Ilarione, Benedetto's brother. Bartolommeo de' Bardi, Giovanni's confidential agent in the ransom of John XXIII, now became head of the bank's branch in Rome. His instructions, drawn up by Cosimo, Lorenzo and Ilarione on 15 September 1420, just before his departure from Florence, reveal the close ties of friendship and mutual interest that bound Brancaccio and the Medici.[9] The partners were not at all eager to involve themselves in financing the Pope or in dealings with members of the Curia, as business with the citizens of Rome was much more profitable. They authorised Bartolommeo to lend any cardinal sums up to 300 florins provided he was in receipt of the annual provision to which he was entitled from the revenues of the Church. The Pope's long-term credit was limited to 2000 florins, but before any more loans were made to him, he was to repay the sums he had already borrowed, which the partners considered quite large enough already. By contrast Brancaccio, whom they named first of some six dignitaries of the Curia to whom Bartolommeo might turn for help in case of need, was to be allowed 'all that he wants for his expenses or for anything else, and should you pay him up to 3000 florins, advise us of it, but if he wants more then pay it him.' His credit was thus far greater than that of the two other cardinals whom the partners also regarded as protectors, Alamanno Adimari and Branda da Castiglione. Alamanno, whose revenues were all paid into the bank, could only draw up to 1000 florins without reference to the partners, while Branda was to have money, but also to be reminded of his great debt to the bank.

In reality, for all its cautions to Bartolommeo, the bank's principal business was with the members of the Curia, for its position as official *depositario* to the Camera Apostolica (Papal Treasury) attracted into its coffers deposits from wealthy prelates who were anxious to place their funds in safe hands – the bank promised secrecy to depositors and so offered a defence against sudden seizure by a new Pope anxious to recover misappropriated moneys and from the hazards of sudden death, when the property of clerics escheated to the Pope unless he had already given licence to make a will or was pleased to grant their relatives a dispensation. In exchange for deposits made for a fixed period, clients received a *scritta* which entitled them to share in any profits made by the banker. Since this practice was a disguised form of usury, it was much denounced by theologians, but was resorted to nonetheless by many high ranking members of the Curia, among them Brancaccio's executor, the Cardinal of Novara. By no means all deposits were *a scritta*: many were deposits pure and simple, and we cannot be certain whether the 6000 florins for which Brancaccio held a *cedula* from Cosimo were earning him interest or had simply been lodged in the Medici bank for safe keeping. If they were earning interest, then he may possibly have had an additional expiatory motive in making his pious foundation, just as the influential Westphalian protonotary Hermann Dwerg evidently hoped by his pious foundations in his native Herford to soften or escape the penalties that awaited him in the after-life for his usurious transactions.[10]

It would be pleasant to think that the Cardinal commissioned his tomb from Donatello and Michelozzo because of his admiration for the novel Renaissance style, but in reality the transaction was probably rather more prosaic. Antonio Baboccio, the leading sculptor of Naples in the first two decades of the fifteenth century, had been much patronised by the great courtiers and high ecclesiastics of the city, and Brancaccio certainly knew his relatively crude but vigorously expressive work, if only because it was he who carved the Penna Chapel tomb whose frescoes Brancaccio admired. But Baboccio was already seventy in 1421, when he carved the tomb of the Grand Admiral Luigi (Lodovico) Aldemorisco, and even if he was still alive *c.* 1425, was too old to undertake such a grandiose tomb as that the Cardinal meditated. No new South Italian sculptor of importance had emerged to take Baboccio's place, and for the enormous tomb of King Ladislaus in San Giovanni a Carbonara (no. 105) his sister Queen Giovanna summoned in 1428 a Florentine sculptor, Andrea di Onofrio. The truth is that the sculptors of Florence, even the stone masons, carvers and builders trained in the quarries of Fiesole and Settignano, were in universal reputation throughout Italy; in 1434 Jacopo della Quercia stipulated with the Sienese for the same rate of payment 'as is customarily given to those famous masters that at present work and have worked in the city of Florence'.[12]

This reputation for fine workmanship attracted patrons who probably knew or cared little about the new cult of the antique in Florentine art. What they wanted was craftsmanship of a higher standard than was offered by local artists, and they were prepared to pay accordingly. Even though Brancaccio must have seen and perhaps admired some of the new sculpture of Florence during his residence there in 1419–20, Ghiberti's north doors, for instance, or some of the statues of prophets and evangelists carved by Donatello and others for the Duomo – by that date none of the great tombs of the Renaissance had been even so much as begun. On the other hand, he must certainly have taken some interest in the tomb of his old lord Pope John XXIII. Accordingly he may well have asked to have his own tomb carved by Donatello: in which case what little we know of his artistic taste – his admiration for the frescoes of the Pappacoda and Penna chapels in Naples – suggests that if anything it was Donatello's general reputation, not his style, which attracted him. But it is also possible that he simply sent a request through Bartolommeo de' Bardi to Cosimo asking him to find a sculptor for his tomb and when one was found contented himself with making stipulations as to its size, form and iconography. What the words of his will prove beyond doubt is that Bartolommeo and Cosimo were his agents throughout the business of its making.

They also settle beyond doubt the old debate as to whether the tomb was begun before or after his death, even if the past tense of *fecit fieri* is to some extent anticipatory, as was only natural in a will drawn up before the testator was on his deathbed, or even, so far as we know, seriously ill. In early July 1427 Michelozzo listed the tomb in his *catasto* return as one of the four works he and Donatello had had in hand during the two years of their partnership: 'One tomb for Naples of Messer Rinaldo Cardinal de' Brancacci of Naples. We are to receive eight hundred and fifty florins *di camera* and we have to complete and take it to Naples wholly at our expense. We are making it in Pisa and we estimate that a quarter of it is done and we have received as part of our expenses for making the work three hundred florins, that is three hundred florins of gold, or thereabouts. I cannot make an estimate of the profit it may bring, it being so much behind as it is.' From these last words it is safe to assume that the commission for the tomb had been given quite some time before, since work was now for some reason lagging. And other documents exist to confirm that this was the case. The two set up a workshop in Pisa, obviously to avoid the double expense and risk of carrying marble to Florence and conveying the finished pieces of the tomb back to Pisa. We know that it was under the supervision of Donatello. He was certainly working in Pisa by 16 April 1426, when he drew 10 florins from a deposit of 30 which had been paid ten days before by Cosimo and Lorenzo de' Medici into the Pisan branch of the bank of their cousin Averardo di Francesco de' Medici, which held Donatello's account. From these 30 florins more payments were made both to Donatello and on his behalf on 16 April, 30 April and 20 June; three of them were for marble. Donatello was also in Pisa on 24 July, when Masaccio paid over to him 10 florins which, he Masaccio, had just received on account from his Pisan patron, Giuliano di San Giusto for the altarpiece he was painting for Giuliano's chapel in the Carmine. A document of 14 October, recording Donatello's presence as a witness at a payment made by Giuliano to Pippo di Giovanni di Gante, the mason-architect of his chapel, expressly describes him as living in Pisa. He was still there on 18 December, when he witnessed yet another payment by Giuliano to Masaccio.[13]

We can identify the approximate location of the workshop in Pisa from the Pisan *catasto* returns of 1429–30. These record that Bartolommeo, natural son of Gaspare di Ser Benvenuto da Lavaiano, had inherited two houses in the Quartiere di Kinzica from the late Giovanni da Lavaiano, one in the Cappella di San Sepolcro and one in the Cappella di San Cristofano. The latter had been used by Giovanni for his trade as a maker of white lead (*biacca*). Bartolommeo, aged thirty, lived with his father in another house in the Cappella di San Sepolcro which was evidently close to the one in the same Cappella which he had inherited from Giovanni. Giovanni's widow lived in another house nearby. We can deduce then that the workshop was one of the two empty houses belonging to Bartolommeo and that it was hard by the churches of San Sepolcro, which still exists, and San Cristofano, now destroyed, which in fact stood near together just off the south bank of the Arno, in the centre of Pisa. Its nearness to the river made it convenient for the landing of marbles and no doubt Donatello and Michelozzo took it for this reason. The renting of the house was not arranged by the sculptors themselves but by the bank of Andrea de' Bardi, Donatello's kinsman and a partner of Averardo de' Medici in the Pisan branch of the Medici bank. For Andrea de' Bardi & Co. are listed in the tax-return of Gaspare da Lavaiano, Bartolommeo's father, and a man of very considerable wealth, first among the names of his debtors.

In their *catasto* return of 12 July 1427 Cosimo and Lorenzo de' Medici list Michelozzo and Donatello as their debtors for 188 florins, 1 *soldo* and 11 *denari* advanced *per una sepultura del Cardinale Branchacci*.[14] As we saw, according to Michelozzo himself, by early July the partners had received a total sum of about 300 florins for their expenses in making the tomb. We know that for the Aragazzi tomb, a work of comparable grandiosity, the two received an advance of 100 florins towards the purchase and transport of marbles, and from a comparison of figures it seems a fair deduction that by the end of the summer of 1426 they had brought to Pisa quite a quantity of the marble they needed for the tomb, in the two boats they had hired to transport it from Carrara to Pisa. If we subtract 100 florins for marbles, we are left with 200 florins paid for work, a sum which corresponds very well with Michelozzo's declaration that in July 1427 the tomb was about a quarter finished. In all probability then the tomb was commissioned in 1425, when Cardinal Brancaccio was busy renewing and augmenting the endowment of his chapel in San Domenico and was beginning to turn his thoughts to the foundation of his hospital.

The tomb of Cardinal Rainaldo Brancaccio[15] now stands in a chapel to the right of the high altar of the church of Sant' Angelo a Nido, formerly the chapel of his hospital. The church has been much altered since the mid 1420s, for in 1700 it was enlarged and richly redecorated inside and out in the Neapolitan Baroque style by the architect Guglielmelli. Among other alterations Guglielmelli raised the roof and added a cupola. And his was not the first hand that had been laid on Sant' Angelo. During the second half of the fifteenth century a stately Gothic portal was erected on the façade, with a lunette containing a fresco of the Cardinal kneeling before the Virgin between St. Andrew and San Bacolo,[16] a holy seventh century Bishop of Sorrento who was believed to have been a member of the Brancacci family. Probably contemporary with this portal was the pavement of maiolica tiles,[17] ornamented with the Brancaccio arms surmounted by a cardinal's hat, and with motifs of foliage, birds and hares, which was torn up in the nineteenth century and of which some fragments are preserved in the Museo Industriale of Naples. A doorway in the Renaissance style, surmounted by a statue of St. Michael, was opened in the side of the church facing the Piazzetta di Nido some decades later, probably during the early sixteenth century.[18]

The first point to note about the tomb then is that it has been moved from its original position. Dr. di Stefano has recently argued that the apse of the present church, that is, the presbytery with the high altar and the two side chapels, was not part of the Cardinal's foundation at all. He claims that these parts of the church were originally a secular building, no less a monument than the original *seggio*, whose site has long been a mystery, in which the nobles of Nido conducted the business of their ward, and suggests that they were only incorporated into Sant' Angelo after the completion of a new *seggio* in 1507.[19] According to the reconstruction he proposes, the Cardinal's chapel at the time of its foundation consisted only of the three arched recesses which are still marked off on both walls of the nave by four large pilasters. The Renaissance doorway surmounted by St. Michael opens into the central recess of the three on the Piazzetta di Nido side, and faces a corresponding doorway opening on to a courtyard at the bottom of which is Palazzo Brancaccio. The side of this courtyard facing Via Mezzacannone, between the palace and Sant' Angelo, was formerly the Cardinal's hospital. Dr. di Stefano is inclined to think that these three recesses and their framing pilasters were originally a portico, and that the Cardinal's builder converted them into a chapel by the simple expedient of walling them in to form an oblong space.

G

There are difficulties in accepting this hypothesis about the origins and early history of the church, at least in its entirety. All the documentary evidence goes to show that the Cardinal did not build a new foundation on a new site, but refounded and rebuilt the decayed hospital of Sant' Andrea. We do not know whether the original hospital possessed a chapel or not, but medieval hospitals usually did have chapels, if only because their inmates were too old or too sick to attend mass outside its walls. The document of 6 July 1428 which records that Brancaccio's heirs handed over possession of the hospital and its chapel to the Seggio di Nido seems to imply, as we shall see, that the chapel had been new built rather than converted from an existing structure, since it was handed over with windows unglazed and walls un-frescoed, contrary to the Cardinal's instructions. A *seggio* normally consisted of a portico, some 33 feet in length (10 metres) and nearly square in shape, where general meetings were held, and a small room adjoining which was reserved for more secret deliberations. It is difficult to believe that there was enough space in the area of the present apse of Sant' Angelo for a portico and a room of such dimensions. Nor can Dr. di Stefano's suggestions about the original form of the nave be accepted without reserve. The lower bays of the nave were evidently built as a single unit, since they are identical in their design, structure and material, which is peperino marble. But di Stefano must be correct in thinking that in its present form the upper storey, a composition of pilasters in stuccoed stone and windows, is the work of Guglielmelli. Is he also correct in suggesting that the original roof must have been much lower, and may even have rested on the heavy cornice which runs above the pilasters separating the bays of the nave below? The Cardinal's monument rises higher than the cornice, and whatever its original situation, must always have had a little free space above it. Since the monument was carved in Pisa, not in Naples, the specification given to Donatello and Michelozzo must have included instructions about height, so that the chapel must already have risen or been designed to rise above the cornice. Besides, we know that the windows for whose glazing the Cardinal provided in his will, were certainly pierced in the walls of the chapel, for the notary who recorded the donation of hospital and chapel in 1428 was careful to observe that they were not glazed. Now windows in Italian churches of this date were pierced high in the wall, the space below being reserved for altars with their accompaniments of altar-pieces or sculptured figures, and the bays on either side of the lateral doorways in Sant' Angelo, perhaps originally the bays containing the doorways themselves, were surely destined for altars rather than windows. And since the Cardinal also intended that the chapel should be frescoed, this again argues that it was the upper wall which was pierced by windows. All these considerations suggest that the present Baroque upper storey is merely an enlargement of the original upper storey.

Di Stefano suggests that the tomb was removed from its original position because of the enlargement of the church. The new Seggio di Nido was completed in 1507, but he is inclined to date his hypothetical enlargement to 1535, when, so he says, there is documentary evidence of work in the church. But the break-front plinth on which the tomb now rests evidently dates from the second half of the sixteenth or from the early seventeenth century. The tomb was certainly standing where it now stands well before 1692, when Canonico Carlo Celano (1617–93) describes it in his guide to Naples as standing in the chapel to the right of the high altar, with no mention of any recent alteration in its position.[20] Originally no doubt it stood against the wall immediately behind the high altar of the church, as di Stefano suggests, for this was the customary position in Naples for the tombs of founders of churches and convents, and even of chapels. In so conspicuous a place those they had benefited were daily reminded to pray for the souls of their founders and benefactors. So the tomb of King Robert the Wise stands behind the high altar of his church of Santa Chiara and that of King Ladislaus (no. 105) behind the high altar of San Giovanni a Carbonara, and Brancaccio's executors surely chose to set up his tomb in Sant' Angelo rather than in his chapel in San Domenico because the hospital was by far the more important and imposing of his two foundations.

Its removal from behind the high altar is most likely to have been the work of Counter-Reformation devotion, so much stricter in its notion of the proprieties of church decoration than medieval piety. For the probability is that it was moved in 1565 when Marco del Pino, also known as Marco da Siena, painted his altar-piece of St. Michael trampling on Satan for the high altar of the church. Presumably the tomb was originally fronted, like so many tombs in chapels of the kind, by a simple table-altar left without an altar-piece so as not to conceal the tomb of the founder, an arrangement most distasteful to Counter-Reformation notions. Hence the transfer of the Cardinal's tomb to a place of lesser honour is best accounted for by two characteristic impulses of the Catholic reform in Italy: the desire to make of a resplendent high altar containing a religious image the load-stone of devotion in churches and that severity of scruple which sought to disjoin the altars of chapels from the too close association into which they had often been brought with the tombs of founders in the funerary chapels of the later Middle Ages. None of the Angevin royal tombs was so moved, but then it was a rather less serious matter to move the tomb of a cardinal, even of a cardinal-founder. Nor would the Brancacci family necessarily have objected to the change: under the Counter-Reformation some devout Brancaccio might even have proposed it in a movement of piety.

It is perhaps time for us to form an impression of the general design and appearance of the tomb (no. 22). It now measures 29 ft. 9½ in. (9·07 metres) high by approximately $12\frac{3}{4}$ ft. (3·87 metres). Because of its removal the joints of the different sections of which it is constructed have been loosened and here and there a little parted. As several scholars have pointed out, in design and iconography it follows the tradition introduced into Naples during the early fourteenth century by the Pisan sculptor Tino di Camaino. That tradition also appears in other places where Pisan influence was felt during the fourteenth century, and H. W. Janson is inclined to think that Michelozzo and Donatello took as models certain tombs in Florence, such as Tino's Orsi tomb (no. 117) in the Duomo (1321), the Aliotti tomb in Santa Maria Novella (*c.* 1336) and the Pazzi tomb in Santa Croce (*c.* 1340). This view assumes that the two artists received only very general specifications from Brancaccio. As we shall see, there is some reason to think that the instructions they received were on the contrary rather precise, at any rate as regards form and general aspect, even if the Cardinal left the style of execution to the two sculptors. Certainly he must have approved the design proposed for a work of such expense, which was to honour his memory to all posterity.

The lower part of the tomb consists essentially of a deep recess resting at the front on Roman composite columns with rich acanthus capitals and scrolling volutes. The back wall is a composition of four fluted pilasters forming three sunk blind panels whose recessed areas are set with blocks of stone with roughened surface. Columns and pilasters are 13 ft. $5\frac{1}{4}$ in. (4·09 metres) high. The general design seems to have been inspired by an antique portico and the space at the sides between the columns and pilasters is open. Above runs a majestic entablature, complete with architrave, frieze and cornice. From this springs an arch, hung at the front with a rich fringed curtain, looped up along the upper edge and falling at the sides in two long drapes down to the level of the base of the column capitals below. At the rear is an arched lunette. In the space so defined is set the sarcophagus (no. 32) supported by three female figures holding *fascine* which are really the scroll ends of the volutes of the John XXIII tomb and the *Tabernacolo di Parte Guelfa* detached by an unorthodox fancy from their decorative function and shaped into pseudo-antique motifs. The effigy of the Cardinal lies directly on the sarcophagus, with no intervening pall, but with the head supported on a tasselled pillow, and with another pillow at its feet.

The front of the sarcophagus is composed of three sunk panels framed by four pilasters, so echoing the composition of the rear wall of the recess. The panels at either end are square and carved with the Brancaccio arms surmounted by a cardinal's hat: the central panel is an oblong and is carved with Donatello's celebrated *stiacciato* relief of the *Assumption of the Virgin*. A youthful angel stands at the head and another at the feet of the Cardinal; each holds an end of the curtain. Above, in the lunette (no. 24), carefully demarcated from the space below by the heavy entablature, is a group of heavenly personages, St. John the Baptist on the left, in the centre of the Virgin and Child, St. Michael on the right. To either side of them the arch is carved with a motif borrowed from ancient sarcophagi – a two-leaved door, with one leaf, that nearest to the front of the tomb, ajar. Each of the leaves is carved with six panels, and the motif is crowned by a scalloped arch like those above the Virtues of the Cossa tomb. All are half-length figures carved in relief. Above the arch runs a strong horizontal cornice, supported at either side by twin pilasters which frame the arch below. The spandrels so formed are decorated with medallions containing rosettes (no. 27). At either end of the cornice stands an angel – this time not in the form of a youth, but in that of a *spiritello*, a winged *putto* – triumphantly sounding a trumpet (nos. 25–6). Between rises a great International Gothic canopy, richly crocketed, framing a laurel-wreath medallion encircling a half-length figure of Christ in Glory, His right hand raised in blessing, His left holding the book (no. 23). In the bottom corners of the canopy, to the right and left of the medallion, are scallop shells enclosed in semi-medallion frames on a sunk ground.

The foliage of the capitals, the frames of the sarcophagus, the halo and faldstool of the Virgin and the wings of the angels in the relief, one of the mouldings of the arch, the inner moulding of the two small panels set at the base of the pairs of twin pilasters, the vase-shaped motif set at the top of the inner pilaster of each pair, the carved moulding of the cornice, the inner frames of the rosettes and the inner moulding of the spandrels containing them, the decorated mouldings of the canopy, the decorated moulding and the laurel wreath of the medallion encircling Christ, and Christ's hair, beard, and the edge of His sleeve and mantle, the wings of the angel *putti* and the crockets are all richly gilt. In addition the two scallops are outlined in gilt. Hence the upper, heavenly section of the tomb glows with gold, all the more celestially because the tomb is not gilt overall, but rather as if touched on its edges and outlines with golden light. The effect of heavenliness is enhanced by the background of the lunette, which is painted blue. On it once shone golden rays emanating from the Virgin and Child, but these have been obliterated by time. Around Christ two golden rays once also shone. Although some of this gilding and blue have been restored during the centuries – they must certainly have been so when the tomb was moved – they undoubtedly date from the fifteenth century, when gold and blue were the costliest and most admired of enrichments.

Since the tomb still is so bright with gilding and colour and since much of the architectural framework and its ornament are richly wrought and highly finished, the state of many parts of it has escaped attention in the general magnificence of its aspect. In the first place the present plinth, as already mentioned, is not the original, which was evidently broken up during the transfer of the tomb. The present break-front plinth is in a different stone and is late sixteenth or early seventeenth century in design. The original plinth must have been quite different in form, but although some of its marble has been used to re-pave the floor of the monument, nothing can be deduced about its appearance from these fragments. This is to be regretted, for the height of the monument would have been strikingly different from its present height if like the Cossa tomb it was raised on a carved base as well as on a plinth. But the probability is that it rested simply on a low plinth, perhaps slightly taller than the present plinth, if only because it seems unlikely that the supports of the columns were significantly larger than their capitals. The three figures which support the sarcophagus are carved in one with low pedestals. All that can be seen of these is the broken outline of the upper surface, and indeed it is more than likely that they were always sunk flush with the floor of the tomb, since they are set on a level with the bottom of the square bases of the columns.

The pilaster wall at the rear of the tomb presents two disconcerting features of a different kind. The ground of the recessed panels between the pilasters is set with roughened blocks of stone. This cannot have been intended by Michelozzo and Donatello: the contrast between rough and smooth textures was not an effect sought in tomb architecture by fifteenth century sculptors. The roughened stone, roughened to take mortar, was clearly meant to be covered with a thin panel of some more precious material: from the oblongs of red marble inset in the ends of the entablature we may conjecture this was to have been red marble, as so often in fifteenth-century monuments. It might be argued that all three of these panels were broken when the tomb was moved were it not for another surprising feature which proves that the decoration of the architectural part of the tomb was never finished. This is the epitaph, which was added between 1560, when Pietro di Stefano[21] recorded that the tomb was still *senza alcun Epitaphio* and 1624, when another antiquary, Cesare d'Engenio Caracciolo,[22] remarked that originally there had been no epitaph, but that one had been put up by the Brancacci family 'in our days'. In all probability it was added to the tomb in 1605 by Ottavio Brancaccio, for it was he who in that year set up a long inscription in Sant' Angelo a Nido with a list of the members of his family buried in the church, headed by Cardinal Rainaldo. The epitaph reads:

RAYNALDUS BRANCATIUS

S.R.E. CARDINALIS HVIVS

ECCLESIE ET SACRI

HOSPITALIS FVNDATOR

OBIIT XXVII MARTII

A(n)O . D . M . CCCCXXVII

To make room for the block of stone on which this epitaph is inscribed the upper part of the central recess was cut away and the block itself shaped – none too competently – at the top to fit the edge of the capitals on either side. It has been argued that the tomb cannot have been left without an epitaph for so long, and that the present epitaph must be original. But quite apart from the explicit testimony of di Stefano and Caracciolo, the crude shaping of the block, its stone, which is different from that used in the rest of the tomb, its vertical oblong form and its epigraphy all make it impossible for it to be earlier in date than the late sixteenth or early seventeenth century. Furthermore, as we have seen, 27 March 1427 is the date of the Cardinal's will, not that of his death, and it has already been pointed out that a confusion between the two dates would not have been made at the time when the tomb was being carved.[23] The insertion of the block of stone with the epitaph has in fact impaired the fine architectonic design of the rear wall and with it some of the spatial effect originally intended by the sculptors – the eye is too attracted by the inscription.

According to the traditional iconography of tombs like the Brancaccio tomb the three female caryatid figures are to be identified as three Virtues. No good reason appears for doubting that Virtues they are, in spite of the strange absence of any attribute by which each might be identified, and although not one of the three gives any clue to her identity by pose or expression.[24] Since all three of the Virtues on the tomb of John XXIII name themselves clearly by emblem or pose or expression, the omission is even more puzzling; the fixity of their eyes becomes troubling in its mystery. It must none the less be assumed that they represent the three theological Virtues of Faith, Hope and Charity, since these were conventional for the tomb of a great ecclesiastic. As Virtues they were certainly regarded in the mid fifteenth century, if only because they were copied wholly or in part by an unknown Neapolitan sculptor for the caryatid virtues he carved for the monument of Cristoforo Caetani (d. 4 May 1441), now in San Francesco, Fondi.[25]

There can be no doubt of the artistic reasons which persuaded their designer to the audacity of suppressing any identifying motif, for the overriding consideration in the pose of these figures is to represent them as absorbed, even straining in the action of bearing the sarcophagus. All the effort of the two figures at the ends is exhausted in sustaining the heavy load: only the central, axial figure supports it with effortless majesty. As Burger saw in 1904,[26] there do exist precedents in the *trecento* for this treatment, notably on the tomb of Francesco de' Pazzi (d. 1341) in Santa Croce But on most earlier tombs caryatid Virtues are pier-figures that stand stiffly or serenely upright, sustaining without sign of stress the burden of the sarcophagus, holding their emblems in tranquil dignity. In the Pazzi tomb the action is so violent in its expressiveness and the figures enacting it are so solidly cubic in conception that the effect seems forced and grotesque. In the Brancaccio tomb, though there is still a certain forcedness, the greater naturalism of the style harmonises the action of the figures.

The central figure is very slightly shorter than her companions, measuring 5 ft. $7\frac{1}{8}$ in. (1·7 metres) to their 5 ft. $7\frac{1}{2}$ in. (1·72 metres). Each of the three wears a robe and mantle and they are composed with careful attention to symmetry, though the strictness of the symmetry is varied, as it was varied in the tomb of John XXIII, in the interest of a lively naturalism. The figures on the left and right both stretch up an arm to bear a volute roll and support their action by bringing the other arm across the waist. But the figure on the left has wrapped her upstretched arm and hand in her mantle for strength and protection and supports them beneath the elbow with the other hand. Her companion on the left sustains her load with bare hand and arm and for better support presses her other hand against her hip. The bodies of both are flexed under the burden of the sarcophagus, but the figure on the left thrusts her left shoulder upwards and her right foot outwards, so that the right side of her body is thrown into a concave curve. The figure on the right thrusts her left foot backwards and the middle of her body outwards, and is turned at a sharper angle to the front plane of the tomb than her companion.

Certain other differences and certain conclusions will emerge as we examine each of the figures of the tomb in turn. To begin with the caryatid Virtue on the left (nos. 41, 43). Her weight rests on her left foot. Her right shoulder is bared by the slipping on to her breast of the short-sleeved robe she wears, a motif which helps to express the strain of her action and is at the same time a borrowing from the antique – it occurs in innumerable classical figures of both gods and goddesses. It is also found in Donatello's statue of the Prophet Jeremiah, which he carved for the Duomo at some date between 1423 and 1425. The sandals in which she is shod are also of classical type. The breasts are firmly marked, as they are in the Virtues of the Cossa tomb, – a point whose relevance will appear when we come to consider the identity of two of the statues from the Aragazzi tomb – so firmly that the robe is prevented from slipping any further by the protrusion of the right breast. The forms of the heavy stuff are bold, simple and naturalistic. The robe is gathered in ruckled folds at the top because the material is crushed together by its slip-ping movement; the heavy mantle is drawn up by the action of the arms, so that the lines of its folds move into a classic V-shaped form which stresses the forward thrust of the right knee in flexion. Although there is so much contrast of action in this figure, inward-bent head, outward-thrust shoulder, knee and elbow bent inwards, right leg turned outwards, it curves only on the right side, the left being kept more strictly vertical so as to emphasise the architectural function of the figure.

96

Although the movement of curves in the body expresses the stress of the figure's action, her face (no. 43) is nobly serene and contemplative, with no suggestion of physical strain or tension. The eyes are a little uplifted. The hair is braided and two crinkled bands of ribbon lie on the neck. And here is found most conspicuously a striking feature of the entire figure, its absence of finish. The hair is extremely roughly modelled, indeed is wholly unfinished, except for one curl at the front to the left of the parting. Otherwise it is only marked out in preparation for the strokes which would have given its strands of hair precision of form and for the polishing which would have given them smoothness and lustre. The eyes too, though they are shaped, and have deep drill holes in the inner corners, have no iris and pupil, an omission that might perhaps not be significant if these features were not so clearly incised and drilled in the eyes of the central Virtue (see no. 44). If we look again at the rest of the figure, we find that nowhere has it received the shining polish which was the last perfection of fifteenth-century sculpture, that the texture of the surface is uniformly a little too rough for us to believe that it is in its intended final state. This conclusion is strengthened by the back, which in this figure has been brought nearer completion than in its two companions. The left hand and arm supporting the volute roll were to have been seen from behind as naked, but are only sketched out. Although a break at the bottom left side of the mantle was probably caused by an accident during the removal of the tomb, when the part of the left foot which is now missing may also have been lost, the rough state of the figure cannot be attributed to abrasion suffered at the same time. It has none of the characteristics of abrasion, it is too universal, and as we shall see, it is common to other parts of the tomb. However, it does not explain the obvious defects of the figure. The execution of the drapery is not equal to its conception: the folds of the robe are exaggeratedly crumpled, those of the mantle are heavily insensitive. The right arm is too flattened, and the wrist and hand are poorly formed and disproportionate. The protrusion of the volute roll and the lateral extension given to the chest by the upraised left arm add an awkward breadth to the upper part of the torso.

The central Virtue (nos. 39–40) is the most classical of the three in general aspect, if only because of the solemn dignity of her frontal pose and the rhythmic verticals of the heavy folds of her mantle. Her weight, like that of the left-hand Virtue, rests on her left foot. Her long-sleeved robe is pulled up on her right arm in heavy wrinkled folds. The upper edge of her mantle slants downwards over her chest in a band of slender ridged folds, but beneath it falls in the simple verticals just mentioned, except on the right side, where it is arranged in a pattern of V-shaped forms. The mantle ends in a desinence of serpentine curves which gently and skilfully effect the transition to a horizontal plane. It was pointed out by Kauffmann in 1935 that the general

97

arrangement of mantle and drapery is related to that of the celebrated statue of Habakkuk (*Lo Zuccone*) carved by Donatello for the Duomo (no. 134); the relationship is close only in the sense that the mantle in both figures is adapted from an antique toga. Yet the comparison is instructive because it shows how much more schematic, how much less instinct with vitality of form is the drapery of the Virtue, even when allowances are made for the greater monumentality demanded by her architectural function.

The hair of this Virtue is finished or nearly finished in front – showing how much work still remained to be done by the sculptor on the hair of the left-hand figure – but is unfinished behind. The drapery is quite obviously unfinished, particularly on the lower left side. And the volute roll that she holds has not received even the beginnings of form except in the roughly carved rosette at the front. In those areas which need only a final polish for completion, a final polish is wanting. Aesthetically, the figure is more satisfactory than its companion on the left. The drapery is more gracefully disposed with more rhythmic patterning, though for this the pose of rest largely accounts. Since the iris and pupil have been drilled and incised, the expression of the face is not only noble and serene but compelling.

But it is the right-hand Virtue (no. 42), her hair bound by the broad fillet of virginity, her long tresses falling on her shoulders, who holds the spectator by the strangeness of her aspect and because the gaze of her blank eyes is directed on him so fixedly. She wears a costume which differs slightly in its details from that of her two companions. The tight-fitting sleeves of her robe are buttoned and her mantle is heavily fringed – evidently it is of some rich and valuable stuff. Her feet are unshod. Her weight rests on her right foot, the left being gracefully drawn back, an exact reversal of the distribution of weight in the Virtue at the other corner of the sarcophagus. The drapery is once more disposed so that the few bold, simple folds into which a thick material naturally falls follow the curve of the body as it flexes under the weight of the sarcophagus. In this last figure the contrast between finished and unfinished parts is even more acute than in the other two, which have only one principal view, the frontal view, whereas here, because the figure stands at so much of an angle, the view of the left side is indeed equally important. The hair is fully finished only where it is most visible, at the front and on the right (see no. 45). It is significant that so much care was taken to shape these conspicuous tresses into some fullness of form, even if the rest had to be left unperfected. The broad fillet is decorated only on the front and on the left – the ornament is of ruching with a band of material running over it. On the right side of the figure, which is turned away from the spectator, the drapery is merely roughed out. Everything then that can be seen by someone standing directly in front of the tomb was finished off, not to a lustrous smoothness of polish, but to the same pitch of relative smoothness as the comparable areas of the companion figures, and the rest was left rough. Again there is an indication that the execution of the figure was not pushed as far as was intended. The volute roll she holds is bound by a twisted cord, not by a band, like the two others, and the designer would hardly have bothered with such a variation had he not intended to surprise and delight the closely inspecting eye.

The defects of this figure are more or less those of its companion at the other corner: heavy disproportionate arms, the awkward breadth added by the right arm to the upper part of the torso. To modern eyes moreover the strain the figure endures is rather strangely exaggerated by so heavy a forward thrust of the belly. Such a thrust was not, of course, so disturbing, was even a beauty in fifteenth-century eyes, though it was usually set off by a tight-waisted dress rather than by a loose mantle. As in the companion figure, the inclination of the head moves the muscles of the neck into creases, though they are patterned incisions rather than true modelling of form, as a comparison with the creases in the neck of Donatello's earlier St. George makes plain.

These three figures are an interesting document of fifteenth-century working methods – they were obviously blocked out and carved to more or less that stage where they were ready for the strokes of the chisel that would model and sharpen in detail where necessary, and for the final polishing. Except in the case of the left-hand figure, the backs are only roughly blocked out, but since the left-hand figure was brought up rather further and since the sides of the monument are open, making it possible for the backs to be inspected, it is a fair assumption that even behind all three figures were meant to be finished to a fairly high degree, if not quite to the perfection of the front. A curious feature is a small oblong hole cut in the back of each figure two thirds of the way down and containing the remains of a metal fitting, presumably all that survives of bars added at some time for additional support, like the bar which still runs across the tomb at the height of the first cornice. If so, such bars must have been right-angled supports, for there are no corresponding holes in the wall behind.

The front of the sarcophagus, measuring 7 ft. 8⅞ in. (2·36 metres) wide by 3 ft. 4 in. (1·02 metres) high, is made in three sections – that carved with Donatello's relief includes the pilasters on either side. There is little to say of the shields except to admire their handsome armorial blazonry, red in the hats and their tassels, blue in the field, gold on the lion paws. Donatello's relief (no. 33) is another matter. Its position is first to be noted, in the centre of the sarcophagus, between the two shields bearing the Cardinal's arms. Such a placing was not decorative or casual: the subjects of reliefs carved on sarcophagi were always intimately connected with the devotional hopes of the deceased whose body lay within. But the Cardinal's reasons for choosing to have the *Assumption of the Virgin* carved on his sarcophagus must wait for a discussion of the iconography of the tomb: at the moment it is more pressing to point out that if the caryatid Virtues are incompletely finished, Donatello's relief is a minutely and perfectly worked masterpiece in the exacting technique of *stiacciato*, a type of relief so low that it needs the most delicately precise sense of the relativity of forms in space to set off those which are to be in slightly higher relief accurately against those which are to be lower. In Donatello's hands it is a technique pictorial, almost sketchy in effect, suggesting recession by contrasts of relief, pursued to a point where certain forms are incised, so that they appear to be just emerging from what lies behind.

The swelling U-shaped mandorla in which the Virgin is enframed consists not of a radiant stylised almond-shaped form, as was customary in *trecento* and early *quattrocento* art, but of true clouds, and is set against a background of clouds. In this way Donatello at once suggests the infinite airy depth of the sky and transposes the setting of the miracle from the transcendent world of Gothic art, golden and glittering but stylised and formal, to the plane of reality. He has chosen the moment when Mary is being borne from the earthly world here below to the heavenly world above, not that when she is lifted upwards from the ground, nor that when she is crowned in Heaven, both scenes much favoured in representations of the *Assumption*. The bodies of the seven archangels who carry the mandorla and the heads and hands of lesser angels appear and disappear among the clouds with marvellous effects of fore-shortening and a limitless probability of movement. The Virgin is turned sideways in an attitude of profound humility: the emotional force of the composition is concentrated on her praying hands, which are set precisely on the central axis and carved in higher relief than the rest of the scene. They are forced even more on the eye by the deeply hollowed inverted triangle formed beneath them by the arms and sleeves.

The Virgin herself is represented as an old woman, though it was the convention to represent her, even in her Assumption, as a young woman, a mirror of celestial beauty. Presumably the reason for this departure from traditional iconography was first and foremost verisimilitude, for at the time of her Assumption, the Virgin was no longer the young mother of the Infant Christ. Yet here Donatello was not an innovator, for Orcagna had already represented the Virgin as a woman of mature age in the *Assumption* on his Tabernacle in Or San Michele (no. 111). Orcagna has chosen the moment when the Virgin is lifted from the ground on her heavenward journey, but he has seven archangels support her mandorla: and since his influence can be seen in the looped curtain of the tomb, which is copied from the looped curtain of the Tabernacle (no. 111) we can be certain that Donatello had studied his relief with care. It seems indeed that Orcagna set a trend, for in the *Assumption* which Ghiberti designed and which Niccolò di Piero executed in stained glass in 1405 for the oculus of the façade of the Florentine Duomo the Virgin is also represented as an austere and aged figure.[27]

Stylistically, of course, there is a great difference between the bold, confident forms with smooth rounded planes and the sharply defined and richly patterned background of Orcagna's relief and the shrinking humanity and atmospheric unity of Donatello's. Even in Ghiberti's *Assumption*, in which the figures are more freely and naturalistically disposed, the design retains a Gothic formality and still obeys that medieval convention, abandoned by Donatello, which dictated that the Virgin should be much larger than her ancillary angels. But Donatello has considered not only terrestial but also celestial verisimilitude; the Virgin's glory as the Mother of God is symbolised by her gilt halo and by her faldstool, which must have shone out against the surrounding clouds when it still retained the full splendour of its original gilding. And the golden wings of the angels are another intimation of the transcendent world of heavenly beauty to which they are bearing the Virgin.

Like the caryatid Virtues the effigy of the Cardinal (no. 30), measuring 6ft. 8¾ in. (2·05 metres) long, is unfinished. This, together with its partial invisibility from ground level, has prevented general recognition of its remarkable quality, except by some scholars. The Cardinal is shown without ceremonial gloves, wearing the white dalmatic of a deacon, a fringed cingulum and liturgical sandals, exactly the costume, except for the omission of ordinary gloves and a small ring, prescribed by the *Ordo Romanus*[28] for the corpse of a Cardinal Deacon as it lay on the hearse during the celebration of the exequies. A pillow is set at the Cardinal's feet, as demanded by the *Ordo*: on it once lay Brancaccio's cardinal's hat, which in old photographs of the tomb can be seen suspended from the transverse metal tie-rod which crosses the tomb at the level of the entablature (no. 21). Probably the custom of hanging up this most characteristic emblem of the deceased's dignity was commoner than might now appear: certainly a cardinal's hat of metal still hangs from the canopy of the tomb of Cardinal Longhi (d. 1319) in the cathedral of Bergamo.[29]

Brancaccio's austere head (no. ii) would have been as great a masterpiece of forceful realisation as the head of John XXIII had it been finished – but it has been left with ear and hair only roughed out and without the last detailings and sharpenings of the chisel and the plane-uniting smoothness and depth given by polishing. The eyes are partly open, like those of Pope John, and allowing for differences of feature and finish, the two faces are constructed and treated in the same manner. Had the roughly defined lines of Brancaccio's eyebrows, for example, been sharpened and smoothed, they would have had exactly the same wavy outline as those of John. The Cardinal's hands (no. 30) have a shapely fleshiness over a correctly understood inner structure which is quite different from the schematic, approximative forms of the hands of the Virtues. The drapery is unfinished in the flat folds that lie along the side of the body, where they have formed – a little too neatly for nature, but not for art – a graceful pile in consequence of the fall of the heavy stuff from the legs. The drapery's simple disposition has a cunning natural-ness which is subtler than the heavy folds of the Virtues' drapery. Even the mitre is shown bent upwards at the front by the pressure of the hard pillow beneath. Although the pillow may have suffered a little damage during the removal of the tomb, this cannot be held to account for the unfinished state of the tassel on the left corner or the unfinished state of the right corner. Significantly, the edge of the sarcophagus has been crudely hollowed out to accommodate the tassel at the left corner. An interesting point for naturalism of representation is that we know the Cardinal to have been exceptionally tall, whence his code-name of *Lunghissimo*. And the effigy is clearly that of a tall man about six feet high.

The two angels who stand one behind the head, one behind the feet of the effigy, holding the drapes of the curtain are youths, divine in their beauty, but in everything else humanised. Both look down on the Cardinal's head, in poses that partly are symmetrical, in that each stands with flexed outer leg, holding a drape of the curtain they have just looped up to the arch, and partly varied, for the angel at the Cardinal's feet (nos. 34, 35) is turned to the left in three-quarter profile, holding a fold of his tunic with two fingers of his left hand, while the other (nos. 32, 36) stands frontally, his right hand pressed on his breast in a gesture which is probably one of sorrow. By means of this play of similarities and differences, they are made to seem like two living beings, and yet to add their verticals to the verticals of the architecture. This successful balance between sculptural vitality and architectonic line is one of the greatest achievements of the tomb, and is realised more perfectly in the two angels than in the three Virtues below. Their grave emotion binds them in dramatic unity with the effigy they contemplate, making a scene that is deeply moving in its restrained nobility of expression.[30]

Neither angel has wings, evidently because their placing did not admit of room for them – apart from anything else, wings would have broken the solemn rhythm of the pilasters. Over shirts, whose tight sleeves are worn buttoned at the ends by the angel on the right, they wear long tunics, gathered round the waist by a plain cincture. In details, however, their costume is carefully differentiated. The left angel's tunic has a pleated hem round the neck and is split for a little way down the front of his chest, the two sides of the split being fastened together by a round brooch decorated with a double rose, probably intended to be partly gilt in its final state, when it would have represented a gold brooch bearing a white enamelled rose of a type worn by the great or wealthy in the early *quattrocento*. The tunic of the other angel has a plain hem and is not split at the neck, and his cincture is not plain, but ruched. Their hair is differently dressed, and the bandeau of the angel on the left is bound over his forehead, while that of his companion passes behind the roll of hair on his forehead and falls in long ribbons on his neck.

Like the figures beneath, the two are unfinished. The eyes of both are blank, and some attempt has been made to compensate for this by painting irises in the eyes of the right-hand angel. Their hair too wants the sharper definition of a last shaping. The angel on the right is only roughed out behind – admittedly its back was never intended to be seen, but this does not explain the want of all final polish on the figure. And conspicuously unfinished is this angel's left arm: the tunic ends in an abrupt line at the junction of arm with shoulder and in the arm-pit underneath its edge is unshaped. The angel on the left is partly finished on its left side, but again not under the arm.

The arch above the two angels is decorated with four panels of coloured stone, so matching the painted background of the lunette it encloses. The construction of the lunette (see no. 24) offers one curious feature: the Virgin and Child are carved from a separate block surrounded by small oblong blocks at the sides and along the base – a saving of a large single block which implies haste or shortage of money or both. The Virgin, 3 ft. 3½ in. (1 metre) high wears a robe with an embroidered neck under a gold-fringed mantle which is pulled up over her head. With her left hand she clasps the naked Child and an end of her mantle, with her right she points to the effigy below in a gesture of intercession with her Son for the salvation of the Cardinal's soul, in accordance with medieval belief, as we have seen, and we might add with the prayer of the Mass: 'for as much as we are not able to please thee by our own acts, may we yet be saved through the intercession of the Mother of Thy Son, Our Lord.' The Child raises His right hand in blessing, a gesture symbolising that He has granted her petition for mercy on the soul of the dead man. The relief is set on clouds, so that the two seem to float as a vision in the blue of heaven, though the effect is slightly less ethereal than it sounds because the clouds are rather coarsely shaped and rest directly on the cornice below. It is however a question whether these clouds in their present form are not a later restoration: they seem to be in a different stone from the rest of the tomb.

On either side of the Virgin are two saints of the same height (2 ft. 8⅜ in. (82 cm.)), each carved from its own block. To the left is St. John the Baptist, pointing inwards to the Virgin and Child. He is often wrongly identified as St. Andrew the Apostle, but the hair-shirt that he wears under his long cloak is the unmistakable attribute of the Baptist. No doubt the scroll he holds in his left hand was, as usual, to have been inscribed with the words: ECCE AGNUS DEI to explain his gesture of pointing: either they have been rubbed off or were never added. On the right is St. Michael, the Sant' Angelo of the hospital's dedication. The conductor of souls, Brancaccio here invokes his aid as his own soul begins its journey after death. Over Roman armour the arch-angel wears a breast-plate of a type current by the second decade of the fifteenth century. In design these accoutrements resemble the armour of Donatello's St. George, where the same breast-plate is fitted over the same Romanised pauldrons, though in the St. George the laminae are a double row of equal length, not as here, a row of long laminae lying over two other rows whose emerging ends alone are visible. St. Michael's cloak is not knotted over his chest, like that of St. George, but slung from his left shoulder, wrapped round his right shoulder and arm, and brought across his belly. He holds upright a one and a half-handed sword, a great ceremonial weapon which was carried in procession before great rulers. Here Michael is figured as the signifer or standard-bearer of the Court of Heaven, a title he is given in the Mass for dead souls, armed as becomes the warrior-prince of the arch-angels. The group of figures is unified into a single composition by the device of showing the two saints in profile – St. John Baptist in three-quarter profile, St. Michael in full profile – turned towards the Virgin and Child. All four are in high and bold relief.

Above, on either side of the canopy, stand two winged angels sounding trumpets (see nos. 25–6). This time they are *spiritelli*, that is child angels, not youths. There was a recent Neapolitan precedent for the placing, though not for the iconography of these two figures, in the two figures of the Annunciation which are set on the pinnacles flanking the canopy of Cardinal Minutolo's tomb in the Duomo of Naples. The angels are the same height, 4 ft. $1\frac{3}{4}$ in. (1·26 metres) including wings. Like the older angels below they are carefully differen-tiated: their hair is differently dressed and the one on the right wears his fillet over his brow, while his companion has bound it over his curls. In their poses the same care has been taken to avoid replication, and even the trumpets they blow are differenced, for the angel on the left has a trumpet from which hangs a blue pennon, whereas his fellow has only a plain trumpet. Their bodies are fleshily treated, that is, in so far as they are finished, for in the left-hand angel the stone has not even been cut away between the lower legs or from the underpart of the left arm. They sound their trumpets with the same dynamic naturalism that animates the other sculptures of the tomb – but the meaning of this triumphal greeting will be considered in the next chapter.

In the medallion in the centre of the canopy, whose diameter measures 2 ft. 10 in. (86 cm.), is set a half-length figure, bearded, with right hand raised in blessing and left hand holding a book, which is invariably and wrongly identified as a representation of God the Father. He wears a robe and a heavy mantle fastened across his breast by an almond-shaped morse. Behind his head is a cruciform nimbus. On the open pages of his book are inscribed in Lombardic letters the words: *Ego sum lux mundi, via ver* ('I am the light of the world, the way of truth' *or* 'the way, the truth'). They are painted, not carved, and so were added in Naples, not in Pisa and not by Donatello and Michelozzo,[30] who in any case would surely have used antique lettering. The inscription disposes once and for all of the mistaken identification of this figure as God the Father. It must represent the Son, as prescribed by the traditional iconography of such tombs as this. Possibly the confusion arose and has been perpetuated because it was customary to make the Father and the Son in Glory resemble each other physically so as to emphasise their relationship and their consubstantiality, and also because as two persons of the Trinity they share some of the same attributes, a cruciform nimbus, a mantle fastened by a morse.

The hand raised in blessing, the book inscribed *Ego sum lux mundi* (John, 8, 12) are the normal attributes of Christ in such representations. He appears with them for instance on the façade of Santa Maria Maggiore, the great Roman basilica of which Brancaccio was Arciprete, in Filippo Rusuti's mosaics executed to the commission of Pope Nicholas IV and Cardinals Giacomo and Pietro Colonna during the last years of the thirteenth century.[31] The figure is set a little back from the front of the laurel frame, so creating an illusion of a divine being immanent in space. The aureole of golden rays once painted behind images the words written on Christ's book, that he is the Light of the World, and the symbolism of light and glory is continued in the gilded laurel wreath encircling the medallion, a Renaissance version of the medieval mandorla.

Chapter V · The Brancaccio Tomb (2)

VIRTUES, SAINTS, ANGELS, THE VIRGIN AND CHILD appear so often on fourteenth- and fifteenth-century monuments that it is tempting to regard them as merely conventional elements, without considering that even in their universality, indeed because of it, conventional elements must have a significance, however muted from the intensity which was theirs at the moment of their invention. On the Cossa monument, as we saw, the full company of allegorical and heavenly beings was reduced to those symbolising the pleas of medieval man for justification at the judgement of Christ and a speedy admission to the Beatific Vision. The figures of the Virtues beneath the sarcophagus represented the deceased's works of faith, hope and mercy which made it justifiable to hope for his ultimate salvation, while the relief of the Virgin and Child expressed trust in the intercession of the Virgin with her Son. The same hopes are expressed in the Brancaccio tomb, but far more elaborately.

To the statues of the Virtues and the relief of the Virgin and Child are added St. John Baptist and St. Michael, the first two saints of the nine to whom the Cardinal bequeathed his soul by name in his will and so the foremost of those for whom he felt an especial devotion. The Baptist was invoked in one of the prayers of the service of commendation of the dead in the Roman Breviary as a special intercessor: 'May St. John the Baptist, elect Apostle of God, to whom were revealed the secrets of heaven, intercede for him.' The Cardinal's devotion to the Archangel was probably exalted as he neared his end by Michael's role of *psychopompus*, or chief conductor of souls after death, a role which caused him to receive many dedications of funerary chapels. 'Praise God, all his angels,' runs a responsorium in the Mass of the Angels in the Roman Breviary, 'may all his Virtues praise him. We pray thee, St. Michael, Archangel of God, to snatch us from the snare of death. Pray for us, all angels, archangels and Virtues of Heaven.'[1] A prayer in the Mass for the souls of the dead beseeches God: 'May thy standard-bearer St. Michael bring the souls of the dead into the light of holiness.' The belief that Michael fought for the souls of the dead with the Devil and brought them into heavenly bliss was founded on a verse in the Epistle of St. Jude (9): 'But Michael the archangel, when contending with the devil he disputed about the body of Moses, durst not bring against him a railing judgement, but said, The Lord rebuke thee.' His image and that of the Baptist invited the living to pray to the saints to continue that work of merciful intercession for the soul of the dead man which they had begun when he himself had first commended it to their care.

Pairs of angels appear both with and without attributes on thirteenth-, fourteenth- and fifteenth-century monuments. In Italy, the tradition of representing angels on tombs went back at least to the late twelfth century, for *c.* 1200 Magister Buoncompagno wrote in his *Candelabrum Eloquentiae* that angels or saints are depicted on tombs 'presenting the souls of the deceased to the Divine Majesty.'[2] Angels were believed to carry the souls of the dead to heaven because of the verse in Luke (16:22) describing the deaths of Dives and Lazarus: 'And it came to pass that the beggar died, and was carried by the angels into Abraham's bosom: the rich man also died and was buried in hell.' For this reason the service in commendation of the dead of the Roman Breviary invokes them again and again. 'Remember not, O Lord', begins one prayer 'the sins of his youth and ignorance, but be mindful of him in the glory of thy light according to thy great mercy. May Heaven be opened unto him, may the angels rejoice with him. Take up thy servant, O Lord, into thy kingdom. May holy Michael, the Archangel of God, who has merited the princedom of the army of heaven, take him up. May the holy angels of God come to meet him and lead him into the city of the heavenly Jerusalem.' And in a response 'Come forth to his help, saints of God, come forth to meet him, angels of God, taking up his soul and offering it in the sight of the Most High. May the choir that has called take thee up and may the angels conduct thee into Abraham's bosom.' And again, 'it is a work of mercy, O Holy Lord, Almighty Father, Eternal God, to pray for others, even in us, who are not sufficient to make supplication for our own sins. We pray thee, take up the soul of thy servant which now returns to thee. May Michael, the angel of thy testament assist it, and by the hands of thy holy angels mayest thou deign to place it in the bosoms of Abraham, Isaac and Jacob, thy holy patriarchs. Deliver it, O Lord, from the princes of darkness and the place of punishment: let not thy servant be confounded by any of the errors of his early life and ignorance. May he be acknowledged by those that are thine and by the mercy of thy goodness brought to the place of rest and quiet in Abraham's bosom.'[3]

Because confusion has recently sprung up between the particular judgement which according to Catholic doctrine awaits every soul immediately after death and the Last Judgement, when the bodies of the dead shall be resurrected and the final doom pronounced, it cannot be emphasised too much that a medieval Catholic believed that after death his soul would be conducted by the angels before Christ for judgement. There it would be admitted to the Beatific Vision, or condemned to purge itself in Purgatory for a term of years, or else thrust down into the torments of hell. Although the doctrine of a particular judgement[4] was never explicitly formulated during the Middle Ages, the beliefs on which it rests were universally held throughout Catholic

Christendom. The profession of faith offered in 1274 by the Second Council of Lyons to the Emperor Manuel II Palaeologus declared that the souls of those who died exempt from sin are shortly received into Heaven and the souls of those who die in mortal sin are shortly received into Hell. *Mox*, the Latin word used by the Council to express the notion of time here rendered as shortly, is usually taken to mean immediately, but the Church allowed a certain imprecision in its interpretation and contented itself with insisting that reward and punishment come swiftly after death and do not wait for the last and general Day of Judgement.

Modern Catholic theologians argue that even if the doctrine of a particular judgement is not as yet explicitly affirmed, it is nevertheless implied in the Council's profession of Faith. However, only fifty years after the Second Council of Lyons the whole doctrine was impugned by no less a personage than Pope John XXII. His interest in the problem of the state of the soul after death seems to have been aroused about 1325, when a noblewoman of Provence claimed that the soul of her dead husband had appeared to her again and again for several months. After she had offered up many prayers in suffrage, it came again for one last time to her and revealed that it was about to ascend into Heaven to partake of eternal bliss with the angels and saints. On All Saints' Day 1331 John preached a sermon in which he declared that the souls of the saints rest after death in the protection and consolation of Christ's humanity and that Christ will raise them up to the enjoyment of the Beatific Vision after the Day of Judgement. On the Third Sunday in Advent he repeated and elaborated the same doctrine, resting it on the authority of the Gospels and the fathers. The Beatific Vision, he argued, is the whole recompense of man, and so cannot be given to the soul alone or to the body alone, but only to the whole man, after he has been reconstituted on the Day of Judgement. And in a third sermon on 5 January 1332 he added that until Christ comes in judgement the bad shall not sink into Hell nor shall the good ascend into Heaven. The scandal and outcry caused by these teachings were enormous, and the Pope retracted them, though rather captiously, on his death-bed some two years later. On 2 February 1335, shortly after his election, they were denied by John's successor, Benedict XII, who reaffirmed that the soul goes to Heaven, to Purgatory or to Hell after death, and on 29 January 1336 published the constitution *Benedictus Deus* defining the doctrine as an article of faith.

As the shortest and most authoritative summary of the eschatological beliefs imaged in tombs like those of Rainaldo Brancaccio *Benedictus Deus* deserves to be read in full. 'In this constitution, to be for ever valid, we by apostolic authority define; That according to God's common ordinance the souls of all the saints who departed this life before the Passion of Our Lord Jesus Christ, and also of the Holy Apostles, martyrs, confessors, virgins and the other faithful who departed after receiving Christ's holy baptism and in whom there was nothing to be purged when they died, nor shall be when they die in time to come, or indeed if there was or shall be anything to be purged, when they have been purged after death, and also the souls of children who have been born again by the same baptism of Christ and of those to be baptised, and if they have been baptised then dying before the use of free-will, shortly after their death and the aforesaid purgation of those who required such purgation, even before resuming their bodies and the general judgement were in Heaven after the ascension of Our Lord Jesus Christ, are and shall be in Heaven, in the Kingdom of Heaven and the celestial Paradise with Christ, aggregated to the company of the angels and saints. And that after the passion and death of Our Lord Jesus Christ they saw and see the divine essence by intuitive vision and also face to face, no creature interposing itself as the object seen, but the divine essence showing itself to them plainly, clearly and openly, and that in thus beholding they enjoy the same divine vision, and also that from such vision and enjoyment the souls of those who are already dead are truly blessed and have life and eternal rest, and also the souls of those who shall die in future shall see that same divine essence and shall enjoy it before the general judgement. And that the vision of the divine essence and the enjoyment of it end in themselves the acts of faith and hope, according as faith and hope are properly theological virtues. And that after their intuitive vision face to face of these same things has or shall have begun, that same vision and enjoyment is continuous without any intermission or termination of the aforesaid vision and enjoyment and shall continue until the last judgement and from thence unto eternity.

We also define that according to the common ordinance of God the souls of those dying in actual mortal sin shortly after their death descend into Hell, where they are tormented by infernal punishment, and that nevertheless on the day of judgement all men shall appear with their bodies before the tribunal of Christ, in order to give an account of their own deeds, so that each may receive those things proper to his body according as he did good or evil.'[4]

This doctrine explains why pairs of angels appear so often on tombs north and south of the Alps during the thirteenth, fourteenth and fifteenth centuries.[5] They appear in two main roles. Sometimes they are messengers from heaven come to fetch the soul of the deceased. They symbolise their mission by drawing back the curtains from his death-bed. As such they are generally actors in the first scene of a drama whose next scenes will be enacted above, when the dead man or woman appears before the Virgin and then before Christ. But the medieval tomb was also designed to honour the deceased, and it honoured him, not merely by commemorating his greatness in the world, as in the costume of his effigy, or even as on the tomb of Guido

Tarlati, Bishop of Arezzo (d. 1356) by depicting his secular triumphs and conquests, but by expressing the pious belief that through faith and good works he had obtained salvation. Accordingly angels appear in a second role, as mourners for the deceased, bearing candles or torches, like human mourners round the catafalque at the exequies of the deceased, or performing the same ritual acts of censing and asperging his body which the earthly officiant performed at the termination of the exequies.

This iconography was originally French, like so much else in Italian Gothic art. A pair of angels holding censers and another holding candles already appear to either side of the effigy on the great bronze slab of Bishop Evrard de Foulloy (d. December 1222) in the cathedral of Amiens. The motif spread to Italy, when we cannot now tell. On the tomb of Teodice Aliotti, Bishop of Fiesole, (d. 1336) in Santa Maria Novella, for example, and on that of Cardinal Enrico Minutolo in the Duomo of Naples (see no. 103) one angel bears a censer and the other a stoup of holy water. According to the doctrine of angels first elaborated by the Pseudo-Dionysius and generally accepted in the medieval West, they discharged these priestly offices with perfect right, for the hierarchy of angels in heaven was held to correspond with the hierarchy of the priesthood on earth, and it is for this reason that they are so often represented in medieval art as dressed in vestments. The censing angel on the Aleotti tomb is even shown as tonsured. The pious belief that angels came to mourn for those dead in the Lord was authorised by an epistle on the Assumption of the Virgin falsely attributed to St. Jerome and professing to be addressed to Paula and her daughter Eustochium. This was familiar to all medieval ecclesiastics because it was read during the octave of the Feast of the Assumption. 'We read' it says 'how often angels have come to the funerals and interment of certain saints and have added exequies to their exequies, and also have borne up the souls of the elect into heaven with hymns and praises.'[6]

On the Brancaccio tomb the angels have come as carriers of the Cardinal's soul, and hold the drapes of the curtain after looping it up. Such curtains, usually drawn back rather than drawn up, have sometimes been interpreted as symbolising the veil which hangs between this life and the next, but it is surely more probable that they represent the bed-hangings which were drawn round the death-bed after decease, according to a very ancient and long-lived custom. The allegorical interpretation, which reflects a Romantic rather than a medieval view of the after-life, has arisen because in such tombs the sarcophagus and the area above it rather confusingly came to represent the death-chamber with motifs which are partly symbolic, partly literal.

The action of the tomb moves upwards from the sphere of earth to that of Heaven. The Virgin shows the dead Cardinal to the Child with a powerful gesture of intercession, while the Baptist and St. Michael stand on either side adding their prayers. The Child grants her prayer by raising His right hand in blessing. The open door motif was carved on ancient sarcophagi as an exit for the soul: carved here in the side of the canopy it must represent the doors of Heaven. One leaf is represented ajar to signify the admission of the Cardinal's soul into Heaven. For when the action ascends, it ascends to the figure of Christ in Glory, His hand raised in blessing, receiving the Cardinal into Heaven. It is for Christ to do so – whence a further absurdity in identifying His figure as that of God the Father – because it is He whom the Father has appointed to judge mankind, as He himself revealed to his disciples in the verses of John (5:21–7). 'For as the Father raiseth up the dead and quickeneth them, even so the Son quickeneth whom He will. For the Father judgeth no man, but hath committed all judgement unto the Son: That all men should honour the Son, even as they honour the Father. He that honoureth not the Son honoureth not the Father which hath sent Him. Verily, verily I say unto you, he that heareth my word, and believeth on Him that sent me, hath everlasting life, and shall not come into condemnation; but is passed from death unto life. Verily, verily, I say unto you, The hour is coming, and now is, when the dead shall hear the voice of the Son of God; and they that hear shall live. For as the Father has life in himself; so hath he given to the Son to have life in himself; And hath given him authority to execute judgement also because he is the Son of man.' The verse, also from John (8:12; 12:46) inscribed on Christ's book is pertinent to the theme of judgement, for it promises that those who truly believe in him shall see him face to face, that is, enjoy the Beatific Vision: 'I am the Light of the World: he that followeth me shall not walk in darkness, but shall have the light of life.' And the angels standing on either side of Him are trumpeting in joy at the entrance of the Cardinal's soul into Heaven.

Conventional as its elements were, the Cardinal's attitude of mind in ordering a tomb with such a meaning is difficult to recapture, so much more hopeful and fearful was medieval devotion than ours. On the one hand it was just as much a heresy during the Middle Ages as before or since for a man to believe himself in a state of grace. Yet the belief in the efficacy of works of faith, hope and charity, in the church's right to grant indulgences and in the sacraments of penitence and extreme unction prompted men to put their trust in a 'good death' which would enable the soul to go to Heaven, even if after a time of purification in Purgatory. One of God's punishments of the wicked was to deprive them of a good death by taking them suddenly in the lust of their hearts, one of his mercies to the penitent that of allowing them time and warning to prepare themselves for death by repentance and works of expiation. It was possible to have a pious belief that a man had gone to heaven, and yet to pray for his soul after death, the paradox being justified by the inscrutability of the human heart and of the judgements of God. As we saw, tombs were intended not only to honour the deceased – and to the honouring of his memory Cardinal Brancaccio certainly attached all due importance – but to remind men to pray for his soul and so hasten its journey into Paradise. It can be seen from his will that Brancaccio's hopes for his soul were only those of the devout medieval believer. He had fear enough of hell to turn in his last years to works of mercy for his salvation, and probably more fear of a long sojourn in Purgatory, whence his great gifts of money and property to found abundant masses for his soul's health. It is his hopes and fears for his soul after death, not a boastful confidence in his own state of grace, that are expressed by the tomb, a trust in the merits of Christ and of the saints and in the prayers of the faithful, a trust that death was God's merciful call to sinful men to enter into the peace of Heaven.

The image of the Virgin often appears on tombs to invoke her intercession with her Son. The *Assumption of the Virgin* is a scene which is exceptional on a medieval Italian tomb, with no recorded precedent to suggest that it was a conventional emblem like the *Pietà* or *Passion*, which were frequently carved on the central panel of sarcophagi, where they confessed the deceased's faith and hope in Christ the Redeemer. Hence there has been much puzzlement as to why the Cardinal should have chosen to have the *Assumption* set on his tomb. In fact scenes expressing devotion to Mary and trust in her intercession were probably not so rare as has been imagined. At least two important tombs were decorated during the fourteenth century with reliefs of the *Death of the Virgin*, that of Doge Francesco Dandolo (d. 1339) now in the Frari, Venice, and that of Cardinal Philippe d'Alençon (d. 1397) in Santa Maria in Trastevere in Rome (no. 123).[7] These cannot have been the only two examples of the motif, and it is clear that the ordinary believer felt an analogy between the death or dormition of the Virgin and her assumption into heaven and his own hope that he too would be received into Paradise after his death. Brancaccio must have been familiar with Cardinal d'Alençon's tomb since he held the benefice of Santa Maria in Trastevere and lived in its palace from 1419 onwards.

Yet there also existed what was for him a most powerful motive of devotion to prompt his choice of the *Assumption* for his sarcophagus. The most illustrious of all his benefices was the dignity of Arciprete of Santa Maria Maggiore,[8] one of the five basilican churches of Rome (the others were St. Peter's, the Lateran, San Paolo fuori le Mura and San Lorenzo), which he had held from 1412. According to legend, this greatest and most venerable of Roman basilicas dedicated to the Virgin was founded by an ancient patrician named Johannes and his wife, who were rich and childless and desired to dedicate their wealth to some work in honour of the Mother of God. They had long prayed to the Virgin to reveal what manner of work this should be. On the night of 5 August 352 A.D. snow fell on the summit of the Esquiline, and the

Virgin appeared to Johannes and his wife and told them to dedicate a basilica to her on the spot where they would find next morning a fall of snow. Johannes found the snow, and hastened to tell Pope Liberius of the miracle, only to discover that the Pope had been vouchsafed the same vision during the night. Liberius, followed by Johannes and a great company of priests and laymen, went to the Esquiline, and with his own hand traced the outline of the new basilica on the still unmelted snow. This scene from the legend of Santa Maria ad Nives was represented by Masolino and Masaccio on the altarpiece they painted for a Colonna chapel in Santa Maria Maggiore during the *arcipresbiterato* of Cardinal Brancaccio.[9]

It is now thought that in sober historical fact Pope Liberius did build a church on the Esquiline, but that the present basilica of Santa Maria Maggiore, though often called the Basilica Liberiana, is not his church, but one erected by Pope Sixtus III (432–40), close to Liberius' foundation, in celebration, so it would seem, of the decision of the Council of Ephesus in 431 that the Virgin was truly the Theotokos or Mother of God. Sixtus decorated the church with a celebrated cycle of mosaics representing the life of Mary and Jesus. The Sixtine basilica soon came to be known as 'Santa Maria ad praesepe', seemingly because it contained a much venerated subterranean oratory shaped like the Cave of Bethlehem. Later, in the seventh century, the basilica acquired the Cradle of the Holy Child, whereupon it became the custom for the Pope to celebrate the three Christmas masses in the subterranean oratory. The possession of so holy a relic also brought rich offerings to the Church, and from its size and splendour it came to be known as Santa Maria Maggiore.

The primacy of the basilica in the Roman cult of the Virgin was enhanced again during the late seventh century by Pope Sergius I (687–701) who ordained that on each of her four great feasts, the Annunciation, Nativity, Assumption and Purification the people of Rome should go in solemn procession from San Adriano to Santa Maria Maggiore. And from the pontificate of Leo IV (847–55) it was the Assumption that of all these feasts was celebrated at most length and with greatest splendour. This was because in 851, while the Saracens were besieging Rome, a great fire broke out on the feast of the Assumption in the Borgo Vaticano. The *acheiropitos* painting of the Virgin Hodegitria belonging to Santa Maria Maggiore was brought in procession to the Borgo and miraculously put out the flames – an event also commemorated in Raphael's *Incendio del Borgo* in the Stanze of the Vatican. In gratitude Leo ordered that henceforth the feat of the Assumption should be celebrated every year in Santa Maria for eight days. Already on the eve of the Assumption it was customary to bring the painting of Christ *acheiropitos* preserved in the Sancta Sanctorum of the Lateran in solemn procession to Santa Maria to visit the *acheiropitos* image of the Virgin, according to a ceremony said to have been first performed in 754 by Pope Stephen II during the panic of a Lombard invasion. And from at least as early as the twelfth century the Pope himself, attended by all the Curia, celebrated vespers and vigils of nine lessons in Santa Maria Maggiore on 14 August, one of the feast-days of the Assumption.

The especial association of the basilica with the feast of the Assumption continued throughout the later Middle Ages. The programme of the great mosaics commissioned from Jacopo da Torrita by Pope Nicholas IV (1288–92) and Cardinals Giacomo and Pietro Colonna to decorate the apse is a glorification of the Assumption. In the centre of the hexedra is a grandiose representation of the first scene of the Assumption cycle, the *Dormitio Virginis*. On either side are smaller scenes in which the Virgin figures as the Mother of Christ – the *Annunciation*, the *Nativity*, the *Adoration of the Magi*, the *Presentation in the Temple*. To either side of these, on the face of the triumphal arch, are two other scenes, one showing St. Jerome expounding to Paula and Eustochium the epistle concerning the Assumption of the Virgin from which some of the homilies for the feast of the Assumption in the Roman Breviary were taken in the Middle Ages,[10] the other St. Matthew preaching to the Jews. In the centre of the apse, between adoring choirs of angels, blazes the great circular scene of Christ crowning the Virgin. In His left hand He holds a book inscribed with words taken from a mass for the feast of the Assumption in the Roman Breviary: VENI ELECTA MEA ET PONAM TE IN THRONVM MEVM. Also taken from masses for the Assumption in the Breviary are the two inscriptions below the medallion: MARIA VIRGO ASSUMPTA EST AD ETHEREVM THALAMUM IN QVO REX REGVM STELLATO SEDET SOLIO, and EXALTATA EST SANCTA DEI GENETRIX SVPER CHOROS ANGELORVM AD CELESTIA REGNA. The second inscription in particular is a recurring *leitmotiv* from the introit of the first mass.

Nicholas restored as well as decorated the basilica, and devotion to it as a centre of the cult of Mary if anything increased during the fourteenth century. On the feast of the Assumption in 1347 Cola di Rienzo went in great pomp to Santa Maria Maggiore and received a crown of olive from the dean of the chapter. A little earlier his admirer Petrarch had lauded the basilica in his epistle to Pope Clement VI pleading with him to return from Avignon to Rome and to shorten the interval between the Jubilees. In his will Petrarch even expressed a pious wish to be buried in the church.

Some thirty years after Petrarch's epistle a Jubilee brought new glory to Santa Maria Maggiore. In his bull of 1300 instituting the Jubilee Boniface VIII had imposed on pilgrims two obligations, to receive the sacrament of penance with true devotion and to visit St. Peter's and San Paolo fuori le Mura for a certain number of days. To the basilicas of the Apostles Clement VI added in 1343 the Lateran and Gregory XI, in 1373 Santa Maria Maggiore. When Gregory returned from Avignon to Rome in 1377, he celebrated mass at Pentecost on the high altar of the basilica, gave it money to begin building a great campanile, and granted it the magnificent privilege of a *Porta Santa*, hitherto possessed only by St. Peter's and San Paolo. Throughout the fourteenth century the Assumption remained the great feast of the basilica. A guide-book for English pilgrims to Rome written during that century says that the pious pilgrim may hope for an indulgence of fourteen thousand years if he visits Santa Maria during the eight feast-days of the Assumption:[11]

> 'On our Lady's Assumption
> Then is there great pardon
> Unto the day that she was born
> Never a day shall be forlorn.
> In that time, there is fourteen thousand year
> To all that come to that Minster'

It is not surprising then if Cardinal Brancaccio, who as the chief dignitary of Santa Maria Maggiore must have taken a leading part in its greatest festival from the time of his return to Rome with Pope Martin V until his death, elected to have the *Assumption* carved on his tomb. There it symbolised not only his association with the greatest of Marian basilicas, but also his deep devotion to the Virgin – in both his chapels in Naples, it will be remembered, he ordained that a lamp should burn perpetually before her image. There is, as it happens, another proof that the *Assumption* relief commemorates in part his office as Arciprete of Santa Maria Maggiore. His predecessor as Arciprete, Cardinal Enrico Minutolo, had also been a Neapolitan, and as we have seen had caused a tomb (no. 103) to be erected for himself in the Duomo of Naples between 1402 and a date before his death in 1412. On it, as the central relief of his sarcophagus, he had chosen to have sculptured the *Nativity* (the Presepio) obviously in commemoration of Santa Maria's subterranean oratory and the relic of the Holy Cradle. Any lingering doubt we might feel about this is dispelled when we find that the saint who presents the Cardinal as he kneels in adoration immediately to the left of the relief is St. Jerome. In all probability it was the *Nativity* of the Minutolo tomb which prompted Brancaccio to choose the *Assumption* as the subject of the central relief of his own sarcophagus.[12]

The probable history of the commissioning, carving and transportation of the tomb to Naples can now be reconstructed. The general size and design of the tomb, conventional in Naples and the Regno from the second decade of the fourteenth century, were prescribed by the Cardinal, who must also have caused the sculptors to be provided with the approximate measurements for its height and width. He seems to have taken hints from the monuments of Cardinal Carbone and Cardinal Minutolo when giving his commands, and there are important resemblances between his tomb and those of his two colleagues. The Carbone tomb (no. 102) is supported by three Virtues, set in much the same relationship to the sarcophagus as in the Brancaccio tomb, (only two Virtues, set at either end of the sarcophagus, support the Minutolo tomb). On these two tombs, moreover, the angels are shown drawing back the curtains from before the effigy of the deceased, though rather as inviting prayers for the deceased than as participants in the great drama of judgement after death. It is likely that Brancaccio had it in mind for them to be represented in this manner, inviting worshippers to prayer, rather than in the intimate, closed relationship of his own tomb. The relief of the *Assumption* was also prescribed by the Cardinal, who must have given at least a general command concerning the other figures on the monument, the saints, the Virgin and Child, and the Christ in Glory.

We know that the tomb was carved in Pisa and was begun by or in April 1426, under the supervision of Donatello. But, according to Michelozzo's declaration in his *catasto* return, at the end of June 1427 only a quarter of it had been finished. There is, of course, an ambiguity in Michelozzo's words. They do not necessarily mean that only a quarter of the tomb had been begun and completed by June 1427 but that only a quarter of the tomb could be described as finished. Other parts may perfectly well have been roughed out by that date, in all probability were so. Since Donatello spent quite a considerable part of 1426 in Pisa, the question arises, what did he occupy himself with personally. The answer comes from the tomb itself. As we have seen, parts of it are fully finished, others are not. The architectural framework, which must have been executed by skilled masons hired for the job, is fully finished only in the lower part and even here the three unfilled panels between the pilasters have not been faced. The upper part is only partly finished in the section above the arch, where the curtain is merely blocked out in the three sections at the top and on the left, and only roughly finished in the cornice, mouldings and ornaments of the canopy – this even allowing for possible damage in the dismantling and re-erection of the tomb. The five sculptures in the round, the effigy, in near-round relief, and the figures in relief of the two saints, the Virgin and Child and Christ in Glory are all in various stages of incompleteness, ranging from roughing-out to hasty finish. Of all the carvings only the relief of the *Assumption* has been fully and minutely perfected. In all likelihood then Donatello divided his time in Pisa between supervision of the work in general, work on some of the other sculptures on the tomb – to what degree will be discussed in a moment – and a patient labour over the part of the work that interested him most, the exacting subtleties of his *stiacciato* relief. During 1426 and the first half of 1427 neither he nor Michelozzo can have felt any pressing urgency to finish the tomb, for the Cardinal was not yet dead. No more did the Cardinal himself, to judge from the size of the payments, 300 florins or thereabouts, that the sculptors had received by early July 1427. Indeed a letter of 9 May 1427 written by Michelozzo and Donatello to the *Operaio* of the Duomo of Siena presses him for payment of 50 florins and asks him what figures are still needed for the Siena font 'since we shall now have leisure to give them despatch.'[13]

What happened after the Cardinal's death? Here any interpretation of events must explain why so much of the monument was set up in Naples unfinished. This can only be done by determining whether Donatello and Michelozzo fully intended to go to Naples to complete the tomb there, but for some reason never went, or whether instead they gave a hasty finish in Pisa to those surfaces most likely to strike the eye before packing off their work to Naples, never to see it again. As we have seen, certain areas of the caryatid Virtues, like the hair and fillet of the figure on the extreme right, suggest that the second is the true explanation, since they are moderately finished from the front view, but not at all elsewhere. Had Donatello and Michelozzo intended to go to Naples, they would surely not have taken the trouble to bring up these parts more fully than the rest. For even if the backs of fifteenth-century carvings in the round, when not meant to be seen from behind, were left without the smoothness and shining glow of a final surface polish, it was usual to bring them up to a fairly – even deceptively – high finish, as can be seen from Michelozzo's two statues in the round for the Aragazzi tomb.

There are two other features of the tomb which also imply that it left the sculptor's workshop incomplete. The three sunk panels between the pilasters were certainly intended to be filled with coloured marble. But since such an enrichment was expensive and not called for until the last stages of the work, Donatello and Michelozzo evidently waited before procuring it, only to find that there was not time, or as we shall see, more probably not money enough for it to be added. The omission of an epitaph is even more significant, for the epitaph was an essential part of a tomb, not only commemorating the name and honours of the deceased, but reminding visitors and worshippers to pray for him. Its omission cannot have been intentional, and is the strongest possible argument for believing that the tomb never received the last strokes from the hands of the sculptors and was set up hastily in Naples. By a coincidence, Cardinal Minutolo's tomb, put up a few years earlier, also lacks an epitaph, and in 1560 Pietro di Stefano explained that this was because he died in Bologna[14] 'where rendering up his soul to God, there his body remained.' Michelozzo may have gone to Naples to supervise the erection of the tomb, but it is also possible that he and Donatello never saw it again after they had packed it up in cases and barrels at Pisa.

Such documentary evidence as there is points to shortage of money as the explanation for the unfinished state of the tomb. We have seen that when complete it was to cost 850 florins, including all the expenses of marble, workmanship and transportation. By early July Michelozzo and Donatello had received only 300 florins, or little more than a third of this sum. Now it so happens that the balance of the Medici bank in Rome on 12 July 1427 is known, and it shows that if Cardinal Brancaccio's executors were in credit in the *mastro-libro* to the amount of 1068 florins, 6s 10d, they were in debt to the *quaderno di cassa* to the tune of 1328 florins, 9s.[15] Even if this balance was subsequently righted, it was not righted sufficiently to allow the Cardinal's disposition about the glazing and decoration of his chapel to be fulfilled, for we have already seen that on 6 July 1428, when his nephews and heirs Paolo and Giovanni, solemnly assigned the hospital and its chapel to the Seggio di Nido for ever, the notary who drew up a record of the transfer specifically noted that the windows of the chapel had not been glazed and that its walls were unpainted.[16]

The mere fact of the transfer would of itself suggest that by the same date the Cardinal's tomb had already been set up inside the chapel even if other parts of the transaction did not tend to corroborate that this was so. For by it Paolo and Giovanni Brancaccio declared that as their uncle's executors they were now handing over the hospital and chapel he had built from his own goods to the *Seggio*. In token whereof they had given the keys of both chapel and hospital to Malizia Carafa, the representative of the *Seggio*. Malizia in turn had given them to Marino Brancaccio and Errichello de Lamberto, who had been appointed first governors of the foundation. As such, Marino and Errichello now took possession of all the property that had been bequeathed to the hospital. In all probability then the executors discovered late in 1427 or early in 1428 that the building of hospital and chapel had cost too much for the chapel to be decorated as the Cardinal had intended or for more work to be done on his tomb, and brought the sculptors to a halt by sending to Pisa for the tomb. In Pisa it was hastily made as presentable as possible – the sculptors had after all their reputation to consider – and despatched in the spring of 1428 to Naples, where the Cardinal's executors had it erected, painted and gilded, and then hastened to get rid of responsibilities that had become embarrassing.

It was quite usual for a cardinal's estate not to be able to meet the charges imposed on it by the testator's will, especially if those charges were heavy and made more with an eye to a posthumous parade of magnificence and piety than to financial realities. It seems very likely that this was what happened in Brancaccio's case, especially if he made his will in the expectation of clearing off some burdens, like the building of his hospital and chapel and the making of his tomb, to a rather greater extent during his life-time than was possible in the event. The past tense of the words *'fecit fieri'* which he used concerning his tomb and his large bequests of money and valuables to his hospital and chapel, which tied up most of his disposable property, seem to imply such a hope. Or it may be that his nephews found themselves torn between the necessity of purchasing property to complete the endowment of hospital and chapel and a demand for more money for their uncle's tomb, and thought it preferable to complete the endowment, since not to do so would profit his soul far less and dishonour his memory far more. Certainly purchases of property for the endowment are recorded in 1428.[17]

In the sixteenth century Brancaccio was thought to have provided splendidly for his hospital: 'This was that Cardinal,' wrote the Neapolitan historian Angelo di Costanzo (c. 1507-91) 'who built the Church and hospital of Sant' Angelo a Nido, endowing it with so many possessions, that they suffice not only for the maintenance of many priests to celebrate divine office, but also for the care of many sick persons who are cared for there with great charity.'[18] By an Apostolic Brief issued in November 1428 Martin V[19] granted indulgences to all those who being truly contrite after confession, visited devoutly the hospital and chapel of St. Michael and St. Andrew on the feast-days of those saints, and this 'by reason of the great concourse of the faithful to visit the said oratory.' Such a grace seems to have been conceded by established custom to those whom the Popes wished to honour: in March 1405, for instance, Innocent VII granted an indulgence to all who made their devotions at Christmas and on St. Peter's Day in Cardinal Arrigo Minutolo's chapel of St. Peter and St. Anastasia in the Duomo of Naples.[20]

The traditional attribution of the tomb was always to Donatello. Vasari mentions it in 1550 in the first edition of his *Vite* as a work by him 'In Naples too he made a tomb of marble for an archbishop, which was sent there by water and placed in the church of Sant' Angelo of the Seggio di Nido: in which tomb are three figures in the round, which support the sarcophagus of the dead man with their heads, and on the body of the sarcophagus is a history in bas-relief, so marvellous, that infinite praises are fitting for it.' In Naples itself there lingered a vague tradition that Cosimo de' Medici was somehow connected with the making of the tomb. In 1692, for instance, in his famous guide-book to the city, Canonico Carlo Celano followed a long, rambling and inaccurate account of the foundation of Sant' Angelo with: 'The said Cardinal Rainaldo passed to a better life in the city of Florence in the year 1418, and left the great Cosimo de' Medici as executor of his will, who caused Donato or Donatello, the Florentine sculptor, to make for him a tomb of white marble which is that which is seen in the church on the Epistle side, consisting of a tomb-chest well-worked with bas-reliefs supported by three Virtues and accompanied by other ornaments, and when the body of the said cardinal had been transported to the Church he sent the same Donato to set up the tomb.'

From 1742, the history of the Cardinal's foundation, like that of so many other buildings and works of art in Naples, was confused by the romancings of that unscrupulous historian of Neapolitan art, Bernardo De' Dominici.

These could be passed over without notice if they were still not often cited as serious evidence for the date of the foundation of the hospital, though so early as 1746 the great Neapolitan advocate Carlo Franchi published or summarised documents which refute each and every one of De' Dominici's inventions. De' Dominici claimed to have found in his notorious 'manuscript compiled by the notary and painter Giovanni Agnolo Criscuolo' that Sant' Angelo a Nido was built for the Cardinal *c.* 1387 by De' Dominici's fictitious architect Masuccio the Younger, and that the fresco in the lunette of the portal representing the Cardinal kneeling before the Virgin and Child between St. Andrew and San Baculo was painted by Colantonio del Fiore. There is no need now to expose the elaborate forgeries by which De' Dominici sought to bolster up his conjectures about the date and attribution of hospital and fresco: his sole contribution of value was to save the fresco when it was threatened with destruction in 1729.

With the early nineteenth century began that systematic search for documents in Italian archives which has led to the revision of so much of the traditional history of art. In 1839 the Danish scholar Johann Gaye first published the extracts from Michelozzo's *catasto* returns which proved that he had been in partnership with Donatello, not only for the tomb of Pope John XXIII but also for the Brancaccio and Aragazzi tombs. But it was not until the second half of the nineteenth century that any division was attempted between Michelozzo and Donatello of the several parts of the monument. Schmarsow seems to have adventured one first: in 1886 he assigned the left and right caryatids to assistants and the head of the central caryatid to Donatello himself. Donatello had also carved the *Assumption* relief – an attribution with which no one has since disagreed – and the head of the effigy. The lunette reliefs were by Pagno di Lapo or by Pisan assistants. Bode thought the tomb was largely by assistants working under the supervision of Michelozzo: shortly afterwards Lord Balcarres claimed for the first time that the three Virtues were by Michelozzo. The angels and effigy he assigned to Donatello. His attribution of the Virtues found favour with Schubring in 1907 and has enjoyed a certain vogue ever since, though Venturi in 1923 returned to Schmarsow's suggestion that the middle Virtue might be more or less by Donatello. Colasanti also believed that Michelozzo was responsible for all the tomb excepting the effigy, the *Assumption* and perhaps the two standing angels, while in 1935 Kauffmann reverted to Bode's suggestion that the entire tomb was the work of assistants supervised by Michelozzo. Harriet Caplow attributes all the sculpture of the tomb to Michelozzo and his assistants, with the exception of the relief of the *Assumption*. Other scholars have advocated opinions more or less similar to these. Meanwhile so far back as 1904 Burger had emphasised the dramatic, tableau-like effect of the composition, and stressed that for him the tomb was largely conceived by Donatello and executed under his supervision. Michelozzo carved the body of the effigy, the figure of 'God the Father' and the middle caryatid, and designed the sculptures of the lunette, which Pagno di Lapo executed. The left-hand angel was by Donatello.[24]

It will be seen from all this that the attribution of the tomb is no simple matter. The first problem to settle is how much of the design and execution of the tomb should be given to Donatello, how much to Michelozzo. The architecture of the tomb must have been designed by Michelozzo, since he used the same design only a very few years later for the façade of the church of Sant' Agostino in Montepulciano (no. 141) as we shall see in a later chapter. Its richness and its orthodoxy also argue in proof of his authorship: it has neither the sameness nor the simplicity of structural members that are so marked in the Cossa tomb, nor the strange decorative fantasy of the *Tabernacolo di Parte Guelfa*, with its neatly folded matting interposed as a cushion between consoles and base. Only in the design of the sarcophagus is it possible to see the hand of Donatello: not only because it is set with his *Assumption*, but because its pilasters are of exactly the same design as those of the Cossa plinth. We have already noted that the execution of the architecture was without doubt left to skilled mason assistants, according to custom.

The attribution of the sculptures is a far more complex question. They did not receive any really close and probing stylistic dissection until Martinelli made one as late as 1958. Martinelli was the first scholar to realise that the tomb was unfinished, though from the sole part of his study which has appeared in print it is not quite certain if he understood just how unfinished it is. But he drew the right conclusion, that the monument was completed in great haste, and that any assessment of its sculptures must take this into consideration. His other important contribution was the enlargement of Donatello's share in the tomb. He saw and demonstrated that not only the relief of the *Assumption* but also the head and hands of the effigy were by Donatello – his comparison of them with the head and hands of Pope John XXIII and with Michelozzo's head and hands of Bartolommeo Aragazzi is conclusive in favour of the attribution. He calls them 'a last hurried contribution' by Donatello before the tomb was despatched to Naples. The rest of the effigy he assigns to an assistant – the working method presumed being that the head and hands, the most difficult and expressive parts, were cut by Donatello himself, while the drapery and decorative details were left to a less skilled hand.

Martinelli also attributed the Christ in the canopy to Donatello. Here entire agreement is less easy. He assumes that all of this little figure is finished or so nearly finished as to make no matter. This is not so: the face and the front part of the hair over the brow, the locks at the side and the beard are finished, but not the rest. Clearly it was decided, as with the Virtues below, to bring up the essential parts and leave the rest in its relatively unfinished state. Martinelli's first argument in favour of his attribution, that the figure is dramatically foreshortened for optical effect at so great a height and that its form is the result of deliberate mathematical calculation is unconvincing. The dimensions of the figure (approx. 2 ft. 7 in., 48 cm.) which is shown not quite down to the navel, if doubled, prove that it was conceived in terms of naturalistic size. When every allowance has been made, there still remains an uncomfortable disproportion between head and body. But if Martinelli's observations on the quality of the figure are restricted to the face and to those parts of it which are fully worked, it is impossible to deny their force. He cites the delicacy of the relief, its subtle pictorialism of working, its typological similarity to the heads in Donatello's *Trinity* of the *Tabernacolo di Parte Guelfa*. To these qualities he could have added that sense of the complexity of planes and a skill in rendering them which are without parallel in the sculpture of Michelozzo.

Martinelli has left open the problem which, if any, of the sculptures of the tomb are by Michelozzo. As H. W. Janson pointed out long ago, the only marble sculptures securely known to be from Michelozzo's hand are those of the Aragazzi tomb, executed after the Brancaccio tomb. Comparison with these is the first test for establishing whether or not a sculpture is by Michelozzo. But in the case of the Brancaccio tomb the test is complicated by another problem, that of execution, since some of its figures, as well as being incompletely finished, are conspicuously inferior in execution to conception – most markedly of all the Virtues. In order to judge whether or not any of the figures on the tomb are by Michelozzo the eye has to ignore their actual quality of carving. Once accident of this kind is separated from essence, all their characteristics suggest that they were designed by Donatello, not that they were designed by Michelozzo. In contrast with the sculptures of the Aragazzi tomb, whose naturalism is colder, more self-conscious, less coherent, they are instinct with vital life, with Donatello's *fierezza*, even the two clumsier Virtues, those on the left and right. Their awkwardnesses are awkwardnesses of execution, not of conception. Typologically, for instance, the Virtues, especially the middle Virtue, and the two angels speak Donatello's hand; they find close parallels in the two figures of the *Annunciation* in Santa Croce (a work undocumented, but which certainly dates from the early 1430s or before). And the two little trumpeting angels must also have been designed by him. Even if the putti on the Aragazzi tomb were not so different, their completeness of vitality would suggest a design by Donatello. And it should be noted that the putto on the left clearly recalls in type the right-hand angel on the Cossa sarcophagus.

This division of labour is consistent with all that we know of the two sculptors and their collaboration. Donatello must quickly have become conscious that Michelozzo would never equal him as a figure-sculptor – Vasari, who greatly lauds Michelozzo, remarks that for all the excellence he attained by his diligence in study, he found the art difficult to master.[25] Equally Donatello must also have grasped that he himself would never be interested enough in architecture to be as much at ease with complex architectural design as his partner. It is significant that the one work in which Michelozzo was left to design and execute both figures and architecture was the Aragazzi tomb, destined for a church in a small and remote town off any main highroad. The documents that we have, as far as they go, also support this interpretation of their roles in the Brancaccio tomb. It is Donatello whom we find in Pisa, working on the monument and supervising its execution, not Michelozzo. Probably Michelozzo provided working drawings, wooden models and dimensions for the architecture: from these skilled masons would certainly have been able to work under Donatello without much need for interference or supervision from Michelozzo. The carving of the figures was a very different matter: this was a much more difficult task, exacting the master's constant eye.

But if the design of the figures is entirely from one hand, their execution must be the work of several. The effigy and the two angels are by far the finest of the carvings in the round or in high relief on the tomb, and must be essentially autograph works by Donatello, though certain parts of them, for instance, the Cardinal's mitre and drapery, were probably carved wholly or partly by assistants. The Virtues, like the Virtues on the Cossa tomb, must be the work of assistants, so inferior is their execution to their conception, though a hasty, last-minute botching by workshop hands of these relatively unfinished sculptures may partly explain their defects. The half-length figures in the lunette pose rather more complex problems of attribution. Judging by the form of the right arm the St. John Baptist is likely to be, in part, the work of the assistant who carved the torso of the left-hand Virtue. The face is by a better hand. In style and execution the Madonna and Child seem nearest to Michelozzo of all the sculptures on the tomb, both in their merits and weaknesses. The St. Michael is possibly by the same hand. The two trumpeting angels are very unfinished, as we saw, and for this reason, justice has not been done to them. They are essays in the lifesize nude in the round, a theme not previously attempted by Donatello, though his awakening interest in it as he turned more and more to the antique is already evident in the tiny child angels on the knob of the staff held by San Lodovico, executed some three years previous to the Brancaccio tomb. For this reason alone they are unlikely to have been consigned to an assistant. In its present condition the angel on the right is less good than his companion, where the accomplished treatment of the nude is conspicuous. The close relationship of these angels to the Siena putti has been denied,[26] largely, it may be suspected, from a failure to understand that they differ from the bronze figures, so masterly in the virtuosity of their movement and the subtleties of their *contrapposto* because they have a different function in the general design of the work for which they were conceived. Had they been fully finished, the classical smoothness and rotundity of form of the Siena figures would have been anticipated, allowing for the finish of marble, which is softer and deeper than that of bronze.

As with the Cossa monument, Donatello's domination of his assistants was so great that their individual hands cannot be surely isolated. Their presence is revealed by inequalities of treatment, not by stylistic idiosyncrasies. The only names we know of possible assistants are the two already mentioned in connection with the Cossa tomb, Nanni di Miniato and Pagno di Lapo Portigiani. Nanni, as we already know, was in Naples in 1430, working as an assistant of the Florentine sculptor Andrea di Onofrio, a friend, like Nanni himself, of Donatello and Michelozzo, on the tomb of King Ladislaus, which was begun in 1428. But as we have seen, what Nanni says of Michelozzo's debt to him suggests that he worked for Michelozzo in Florence, and if so, he cannot have worked on the Brancaccio tomb. Pagno di Lapo on the other hand is more than likely to have worked on the Brancaccio tomb, for he is known to have worked for eighteen months with Donatello and Michelozzo. Significant in this context too is the statement made on 8 August 1428 by Pagno's father, Lapo, that the work for which he had been hired was now finished. His last words, 'No judgement can be made until the account is made out, for the said Pagno is away and the said masters are in Pisa' have been taken to mean that the two masters were in Pisa busy with the despatch of the Brancaccio tomb. This seems unlikely, now we know that a month before the Cardinal's two nephews had handed over their uncle's foundation to the Seggio di Nido. There are other reasons why Donatello and Michelozzo should have been in Pisa at that moment, winding up their workshop there for example, or waiting for marble from Carrara. In the late nineteenth century Tanfani-Centofanti[27] conjectured that the Pisan mason-architect Pippo di Gante, who built Giuliano di San Giusto's chapel in the Carmine for which Masaccio painted the altarpiece, and carved an altar and a tomb-stone for Giuliano which were placed in it, may also have assisted Donatello. But without further documentary evidence his conjecture must remain a conjecture: indeed only new documents can be expected to reveal the names of the assistants-hired by Donatello and Michelozzo.

This disjunction of the tomb into its separate components for the purposes of attribution must not be allowed to obscure how closely Michelozzo and Donatello collaborated in its overall design. For the dimensions of the figures and of the architecture are carefully proportioned to each other, so that the music of corresponding measures is repeated throughout the tomb. In spite of the loss of the original plinth relations between figures and architecture are easily discerned. The whole height of the middle Virtue and ratios of it are dimensions that recur again and again. The entire tomb, excluding the finial, is five times the whole height of the Virtue. The columns from base to the base of the capitals are twice her height: the arch and pilasters above are the same height. The width of the tomb from the mid-points of the columns is twice her height bating 10 in. (25·4 cm.), so that they frame the tomb in a square. The sarcophagus is a quarter of the height of the column including its capital. The capital is one-sixth the height of the column, and one-third of the column. Its width is her whole height and a half and the width of the *Assumption* is half her height. The navel was taken as the centre of the figure by its designer, and if the measurement from navel to the roots of the hair is taken as a radius, the whole figure is enclosed in a circle – as Ghiberti[28] declares in his *Commentari* that it ought to be. This has more than an ideal significance when we find that the radius of this imaginary circle – corresponding to half the height of the figure – is the diameter of the inner laurelled medallion framing Christ in the canopy.

It is perhaps an exaggeration to claim that the Brancaccio tomb, as some scholars have done, is the archetype of the *quattrocento* tomb. Apart from any other consideration archetype is far too strong a word in this context, suggesting as it does an abrupt break with the past. In conception the tomb is essentially a grandiose canopied tomb of the type devised by Gothic sculptors for personages of high estate, secular and ecclesiastical, and its iconography continues the tradition of the *Trecento*, indeed is its most eloquently articulated expression. Since both its general form and iconography were so evidently prescribed by Cardinal Brancaccio, it would be remarkable if it were otherwise. The changes from the past are stylistic, in the artistic form given to the various elements that compose the tomb. Throughout all the architecture below the canopy, forms and ornaments borrowed from antiquity are substituted for Gothic forms and ornaments. Instead of twisted colonnettes there are Roman composite columns, their fluting in all probability imitated from the celebrated fluted columns on the Arch of Constantine: the front of the sarcophagus is patterned by Corinthian pilasters and the back of the tomb by Roman composite pilasters: a classical round arch replaces a Gothic pointed arch and is framed by twin Corinthian pilasters and a heavy classical cornice. And, if anywhere, it is here, in this motif of a classical arch framing a sarcophagus that the tomb heralds later Florentine tombs.

Such translations are typical of the transition from one style to another, and as might be expected, certain features of the tomb are still Gothic in feeling or design. Gothic in feeling is the relative profusion of ornament – the scallops, the rosettes, the little panels of red marble, the band of coloured inlaid marble running across the entablature, all motifs which break up the surfaces of the members with their sumptuousness and colour into the smaller,

125

richly decorative units, so delightful to International Gothic taste. Gothic too in feeling are the two pairs of twin pilasters, which seem too light and thin to sustain the burden of the heavy cornice above. Gothic in design is the canopy; indeed so Brunelleschian are the forms and ornament of the rest of the architecture that some scholars have roundly called it an obtrusive archaism imposed on the sculptors by the peremptory will of Cardinal Brancaccio. In reality its confident presence, in all the fullness of its 'mixti-linear' outline and of the broad Late Gothic foliage of its crocketing and finial, is an un-mistakable token of the transitional character of the tomb and of the eclecticism of the early decades of the *quattrocento*, when the latest inventions of Gothic art were still powerfully attractive even in Florence, even to artists who were enthusiastic for antiquity. For this type of 'mixti-linear' canopy was in fact a novelty in Florence, where it had first been used so recently as 1408–10 by the Florentine sculptor Niccolò di Piero Lamberti on his great doorway for Or San Michele (no. 128). In 1414 it was copied by Ghiberti on his *Tabernacolo dell' Arte di Calimala*, also on Or San Michele, and it can be found in certain parts of the Duomo erected *c.* 1413. Michelozzo has modified the purely Gothic character of these examples of the motif, transforming its convex lower segments into sections of a perfect circle and so giving it what Morisani rightly calls a semi-Renaissance character, which in its less insistent verticality is more in keeping with the rest of the architecture below. Far from being an archaism in 1425–6, the 'mixti-linear' canopy continued popular among Florentine sculptors and architects for at least another decade afterwards. It was used again by Ghiberti on the Porta del Paradiso (1425–52), by Michel-ozzo himself on the façade of Sant' Agostino in Montepulciano (no. 141) and by Bernardo Rossellino on the tympanum of the portal of the Misericordia in Arezzo (1434–5).[29]

We find moreover that in the design of large-scale tombs the Gothic preference for a strong vertical termination, preferably in a pointed motif, kept its hold in Florence into the middle years of the century – not surpris-ingly since height was a prerequisite for tombs of greatest dignity. The climax of Bernardo Rossellino's Bruni tomb in Santa Croce (after 1444) is not the great classical arch in which the sarcophagus stands but a Gothic shield encircled by a laurel wreath and held by two putti whose bodies form the two sides of a sharp triangle. Even Desiderio da Settignano's Marsuppini tomb (after 1455) culminates in a tall vase from which flames shoot upwards: two laurel swags held by putti depend from its neck and with their convex curves form a gentle triangular apex to the tomb.

In its clarity and simplicity of articulation within a dignified architectural framework the Brancaccio tomb is greatly superior to the multiplicity of statuettes and reliefs, the picturesque polychrome colonnettes and profuse crocketing and pinnacling of such late Gothic tombs as the Minutolo tomb,

126

its immediate predecessor. The decorative treatment of some of its parts, notably the two pairs of twin pilasters, with their apparently capricious incorrectness and the use of inlays in coloured marble, has been criticised, unfairly and in the interests of an abstract architectural orthodoxy, for the same principles of exposition were not applied to tombs as to buildings. Only Brunelleschi was sufficient of a purist in the *quattrocento* to object to the interruption of his clear lines and surfaces by patches of colour. Even if every fresco were to perish from walls and doorways, the coloured reliefs of the Della Robbias would remain to prove how greatly colour was valued in the *quattrocento* as a means of relieving the severity of architecture. The façade designed by the humanist Alberti for Santa Maria Novella is as rich as any Gothic façade in its decorative use of coloured marbles. The gilding and inlays of the Brancaccio tomb when it stood against the rear wall of Sant' Angelo, behind the altar, not only relieved it against the wall behind but struck the entering worshipper or visitor with admiration of its magnificence. A soberer treatment would have done the Cardinal less honour.

Chapter VI · The Aragazzi Tomb: a literary quarrel

THE SOLE IMPORTANT WORK OF SCULPTURE which Michelozzo executed without the help of Donatello was the grandiose, but long dismantled and dismembered tomb of the Apostolic secretary Bartolommeo Aragazzi in the Pieve (now Duomo) of Montepulciano, in southern Tuscany. Aragazzi ordered the tomb during his lifetime, probably in the spring of 1427, for Michelozzo, listing it in his *catasto* return as one of the commissions he and Donatello had had in hand during the time of their partnership, adds that 'no price will be fixed for it until the work is finished: it is to be valued by common friends and may be of greater or less expense according as the intention may be changed and so no estimate can be made beforehand. We have received 100 florins to have marble brought.' Aragazzi died on 29 June 1429, but in his will he provided for the completion of his tomb. We next hear of it in the famous letter from Leonardo Bruni to Poggio Bracciolini describing Bruni's encounter on a country road outside Arezzo with carts carrying pieces of the tomb, 'marble columns, two statues not fully finished, and bases, arched segments and capitals.' The oxen yoked to the carts had stuck in a difficult patch of the road and workmen were trying to push them along and smoothing the way with pick-axes.

Bruni, surprised at the unusual sight of carts travelling along that particular road, especially carts laden with marble carvings, rode up to the workmen and asked them what their troublesome load was and where they were carrying it. One of them looked round and wiping the sweat from his face, exclaimed, probably with more elegance in Bruni's humanist Latin than in his own vernacular Tuscan, 'May the gods curse all poets, both those past and to come.' Bruni, taken aback by this reply, inquired, 'What quarrel have you with poets? In what way have they been troublesome to you?' 'In this way', answered the man. 'This poet here, a foolish, puffed-up man, who has lately died, ordered a marble tomb to be made for himself. That is the reason why these marbles are being carted to Montepulciano, but it is my belief they will never be got there on account of the badness of the roads.' More and more curious, Bruni asked, 'What is all this? Has a poet died lately at Montepulciano?' 'Not there', said the man, 'in Rome. But in his will he provided for a tomb to be set up to himself in his native place. This figure you see here is his statue, and this other one is a statue of his father, which he ordered to be placed beside his.' Putting together the name of Montepulciano and the death of the poet, Bruni recalled, or so he says, that a certain Bartolommeo da

Montepulciano had lately died in Rome, leaving some money. He asked the man whether this was the poet of whom he spoke and was told that it was. 'And is it on account of this ass,' exclaimed Bruni, 'that you curse poets? Do you think him a poet, who knew no science or learning, and surpassed all other men together in folly and vanity?' 'I did not know him,' answered the man, 'when he was alive, indeed I never heard his name spoken, but his townsfolk think him a poet, and if he had left a little more money, would think him a god. And had he not been a poet, I would wish no curse on poets.'

As Bruni rode off, so he tells Poggio, he began to ponder within himself those words of the workman in which he had called Aragazzi foolish and puffed-up for having ordered a marble tomb for himself as he lay dying in Rome. How true they were. No one, he reflected, who feels any confidence in the immortality of his own glory ever took thought for his tomb; he believes himself sufficiently commended to posterity by the fame of his great deeds and the splendour of his reputation. What can a tomb, which is a dumb thing, do for a wise man? What is viler than to have one's tomb remembered, one's life forgotten? Neither Cyrus nor Alexander nor Caesar, the three greatest generals of past ages, had troubled to raise tombs to themselves. Cyrus, indeed, the most ancient of the three, a great warrior, a wise legislator, the founder of a mighty line of kings, had ordered in his will that his body should be laid in the earth, with no marble monument above it, for the earth produces flowers and crops and pleasant and precious trees, and no man could desire a nobler substance for his tomb than these. 'But I insult the memory of these great heroes by producing them as witnesses to my censures of this vilest of mankind. Yet if three such excellent heroes have been lauded for avoiding this ambitious vanity, how greatly is this sort of pride to be mocked in one who was the dregs of mankind. Shall you' exclaims Bruni in an indignant apostrophe, 'shall you order in your will that marbles are to be brought for you from a great distance, that a tomb is to be made for you and statues raised to you? For what merits, I pray? For your science when you knew none? For your letters, when you scarce knew four of them? For your life and character, when you were the most fribbling of men, full of a singular folly, and did nothing from wise counsel, everything with rashness and presumption? Yet if his character was undeserving, perhaps his descent was honourable, and his birth from an itinerant merchant, with a midwife for a grandmother and a fanatic for a mother make him worthy of a statue and a marble tomb? Or was it on account of the money you had hidden underground that you deemed yourself worthy of a statue? Surely this was the thing that prompted the thought. But in very truth did not the Pope demand that same money as having been stolen from him by you when at last it came to light after your death? What will you inscribe on your tomb, pray? What deeds, what actions will you have celebrated? How your father drove his asses and his wares from fair to fair? How your grandmother nursed new-born babes and waited on women in childbirth? How your mother flitted about the churches, her hair all dishevelled? How you heaped up money by theft? How the Pope demanded that money back? Such is the sum of your deeds, such is the glory of you and yours, which are of that sort, that had you been a little wise and not, as throughout your life, so on your deathbed carried away by your own folly and presumption, you would have provided in your will that just as you once hid your money so your family were to hide you underground, lest this vanity and ambition of your tomb give matter for ridicule and complaint.'[1]

The burden of Bruni's diatribe is that Aragazzi, though unworthy by his birth of a great and lofty tomb, had ordered just such a tomb for himself as if he had been a Pope, a cardinal, a bishop or a great secular lord. Surprisingly, the answer which this famous letter received in its own day has long been forgotten. After Bruni published his collected letters in 1438, they came into the hands of a young humanist, the Benedictine monk, Hieronimo Aleotti (1412–80). Aleotti, like Bruni, was from Arezzo. He was a friend and protégé of Frate Ambrogio Traversari, the Camaldolese friar who was the great promoter of Christian humanism in his generation, and also of Aenea Silvio Piccolomini, later Pope Pius II, with whom he had studied at Siena. Aleotti, after spending two years at Foiano as a solitary, had been chosen in the autumn of 1439 to accompany Bartolommeo Zabarella, Archbishop of Spalato, on a mission to France for Pope Eugenius IV, who was then residing at Florence. It was in Florence, early in October 1439, that Aleotti read Bruni's assault on Aragazzi's memory. It must have seemed all the more outrageous to him because it was addressed to Poggio Bracciolini, one of the dead man's dearest friends. In his indignation he wrote a satirical epistle in reply. So much we learn from Aleotti himself and from a note inserted at the head of a copy of his epistle which was made at some date in the third quarter of the fifteenth century at the end of a Virgil written for Messer Corrado Bellarmino of Montepulciano,[2] where Bruni's diatribe against a famous fellow-townsman had evidently been much resented. 'Leonardo of Arezzo' this note reads, 'had written against that most excellent and prudent man Bartolommeo da Montepulciano, Apostolic Secretary, after his death, as appears from the book containing the letters of the same Leonardo. When Hieronimo of Arezzo read this letter, he was angered by the unworthiness and turpitude of the thing and wrote against Leonardo, but suppressing his name. He addressed his answer to Poggio, that most eloquent and learned man, while the Curia of Eugenius IV was residing at Florence. Poggio gave this letter of Hieronimo to read to Aurispa, Cencio, Biondo and Carlo of Arezzo,[3] men of great learning and Apostolic Secretaries, who all agreed with laughter and joking that Leonardo had been stung with well-deserved reproaches in return for the reproaches and invectives he had falsely and unjustly hurled against the dead Bartolommeo of Montepulciano.' Here follows Hieronimo's letter.[4]

Hieronimo of Arezzo to the most famous and eloquent Poggio. As you may easily discover from my society, which shall be very frequently yours if you so desire it, I am by nature rather retiring and shy. From this cause, if I love any man, if I contemplate any man's virtues and ornaments of learning, I cannot entirely disclose the virtue of that man or my love for him in his own presence, lest I thereby incur the suspicion of adulation. Although I have always taken the greatest care to avoid that detestable vice in my letters, yet I know not how it happens, if I have just cause to praise anyone, I can accomplish the task more faithfully and comfortably with the pen than with the tongue, as if a letter seemed in some way to blush less and to be less suspicious in itself. Your reputation, most famous Poggio, is so celebrated, so certain and fixed, and is spread so far and wide abroad that none who treat of it afresh need fear the suspicion of flattery from any quarter. For he who exalts you cannot so much be censured as a flatterer as he who refrains from your praises can be censured for great neglect or sloth or malice if he have power to sound them properly. Wherefore, my Poggio, I am troubled by no light care, inasmuch as I am not of such fluency or genius as to trace out one tittle of your virtues and ornaments. Accordingly I shall cast the task of praising you on to the shoulders of those who seem better able to perform it amply and comfortably. It shall be my part merely to admire your knowledge of letters, whether of the common or recondite sort, and the concinnity of your prose, the elegance of your diction and the weightiness which is mingled in so marvellous a manner with the festiveness of your prose. In these things you are easily superior to all men of this our age in the judgement of the men of greatest learning. Next I shall admire your great humanity of nature, wherein you rise in my opinion above the men not only of our age but of almost all centuries past and gone. For with what humanity did you receive me for the first time yesterday, that is, if we may call the twilight a part of the day. O happy for me that day (or night if you so prefer to call it) on which I first drew near to Poggio! How affable and easy you showed yourself to me: had you known me familiarly for many years, you would have had no duty to attempt more than you did at that first meeting, to me most truly pleasant and delightful. For if one of these two things by itself, that is extraordinary skill in letters or singular humanity, makes a man worthy of praise, how much the more excellent shall these two things appear when in company and conjoined to each other in one and the same man. And it has ever been my opinion that humanity without letters is more to be esteemed than letters without humanity.

On which matter I made a witty joke a few days ago. Whilst a certain friend and I were walking by the church of Santa Maria, it chanced that there came towards us one who by most men is held excellent among the learned, advancing with slow step and measured pace. My companion said to me that a very famous man was approaching, one admirably skilled in invective, most of all against dead men. But I pretended not to see him and passed him by without any sign of reverence or even of customary courtesy. My companion asked me wherefore I had not bowed my head to a man so lettered and so well known to me, 'Let him go in an evil hour', I replied, 'I envy neither him nor his letters. For truly he is an ass to whom all good offices and humanity are abhorrent.' Whence you may perceive, my Poggio, that I esteem moderation and humanity so highly that I hold learning, however great, without humanity of light account but am wont to admire and venerate humanity without learning. If you feel differently, I shall gladly yield to you and not be pertinacious in error. But these two things yoked and compounded together in one man make that man a great and admirable man, worthy of all praise. Great men of that sort I, from a boy, have ever revered and embraced with all my heart. Wherefore I congratulate myself wonderfully on having lately obtained such a one in you – for I trust to that free and noble and most humane nature of yours not to be rejected by you. If, therefore, you will account me as one among your sons, I have no fear that you will ever be disappointed of your good opinion. Farewell and be happy (*most reverend father and lord*). Florence 1439.

Unfortunately for the cause of human nature Aleotti very soon regretted that in a first movement of anger he had allowed so much indignation to his pen. News of his epistle soon reached Bruni's ears. Greatly alarmed at having offended the powerful Chancellor of the Florentine Republic, Aleotti wrote him a letter on 18 October which was as deferentially humble as its predecessor had been vehemently indignant.

> To the most eloquent Leonardo of Arezzo.
> Giovanni Bacci,[5] who has the greatest care of your good name, came to me today and said that you have taken a ill notion or suspicion about me, to wit, that I have written something against your reputation to that excellent and most learned man, Poggio. Overwhelmed by the suddenness of the thing and by my astonishment, I lamented that unhappy fate of mine, by which, though leading so very innocent a life and injuring none by word or deed, I am yet now so harassed by the envy of detractors that I have incurred the suspicion and hatred of a man whom I revere among the foremost, whose name I honour even in his absence, whom I have ever cultivated, and lauded to the skies. Would I censure Leonardo of Arezzo, that most grave and learned man, for disorderly manners and ignorance? Would I, who am devoted to all men of letters, even to those whom I have never beheld, inveigh against my fellow-townsman, a man of such eloquence? Am I of such evil disposition or so mad of mind that I should disparage the excellent and most honourable Leonardo of Arezzo to the excellent Poggio of Florence? No, not even if I were that sort of man, which I am not, who abuses the art of speaking ill, not among good and grave men, but among naughty and light-headed jesters. For no man, not even a stupid one, is ignorant that scandal-mongers are unwelcome and unpleasant to good men. Do you think me so entirely demented as to dare sneer and speak ill of you to those who are your greatest friends? For who is there that does not know how Leonardo and Poggio have ever been conjoined by a singular goodwill towards each other? Not only the

volumes of your letters which have circulated throughout all Italy but the very stones themselves shout this out. Wherefore may God send that man an evil fate who by feigning such dire lies to my injury has sought to arouse a man of your worth into hatred of me. If I learn who he is from you, I shall tell him to his face that he lies in his filthy throat and impure jaws. I believe my letter is with Poggio and I shall procure you a sight of it as quickly as possible. In the course of writing it I toyed wittily with a certain noisy brawler, who is full of bile and always carping at the manners and writings of others, though for the rest very learned. He has been hostile to me for a long time, and has often attacked me in words and in his writings, calling me a hypocrite and an apostate, but I have suppressed his name from moderation, nor could anyone extort from me to name him by his own name. And if any perverse interpreter has twisted a vice so obscurely struck at by me into an attack on your surpassing virtue, myself I should deem him neither friend nor favourer of yours, since he seems to feel otherwise than he ought concerning your character and excellence. Had I the letter in question by me, I would send it to you to read at once, but I shall arrange with Poggio for it to be carried to you as soon as may be. For if you are such a man as I and all others believe you to be, you cannot interpret and twist that morose and perverse nature which I appear to have censured and branded in my letter, into meaning yours. I was going to come to you today with the same Giovanni Bacci to visit you and purge myself in person, but by chance it happened that you were away, so I was told, and stay in the country. Since we shall move from Florence the day after tomorrow, as I believe, on our way to France, I may have no opportunity of seeing you before our departure, and so I have determined to write this short apology, short for this reason, that I may neither seem to acknowledge the crime by keeping silence completely, nor yet to wish to disguise my fault by excess of speech and artifice of words. I am yours, I have been the crier and trumpeter of your praises and learning and such I ever desire to be, not that I am capable of illustrating them by my tongue or by my pen, but according to the ability of my poor little genius it was my wont to sing them out like a crier, not to adorn them like an orator. It shall now be the part of your prudence and gravity to drive far from your society, nay far from your ears, all evil-speakers, murmurers, double-tongued detractors. Until now I have ever honoured your famous name, and once again, I am determined ever to love you, whether you wish for my love or no. Farewell. Florence, 18 October 1439.[6]

Bruni's satirical letter and Aleotti's ineffectual reply suggest that we shall do best to make a closer acquaintance with Bartolommeo di Francesco Aragazzi and his native town of Montepulciano, so as to understand the kind of man he was and the sort of place he came from.

Chapter VII · Montepulciano and the Aragazzi

THE MODERN VISITOR TO THE Tuscan hill-city of Montepulciano sees first the great brown walls which enclose its roofs and towers, and then, after passing through the stately sixteenth-century Porta a Prato, begins a steep ascent through streets lined with lofty Renaissance façades in grey-gold travertine. The impression of magnificence is indelible, but deceptive for our story. The great palaces of Montepulciano, like the wealth of its noble families, date from the sixteenth century, when the splendid and lucrative careers in the Church of certain townsmen enabled them to rebuild their family houses on a more sumptuous scale, with nobly designed façades of stone. The earlier palaces and houses of Montepulciano, like the still surviving Palazzo Neri Orselli Bombagli and the house of Politian, were Sienese Gothic in design, and built neither wholly nor in part of costly stone, but in a warm dusky-red brick.[1]

Although no building or work of art belonging to an earlier century than the *Dugento* survives in Montepulciano, the town is none the less of some antiquity. According to legend it was founded by Lars Porsenna, who was king of the great Etruscan city of Clusium (Chiusi) in the valley below. Pride in this illustrious origin prompted the Comune of Montepulciano to commission in 1520 from the sculptor Andrea Sansovino a large terracotta figure of Porsenna. Vasari describes this work as 'a singular thing', but only its head now survives.[2] However, Porsenna's very existence has been doubted in recent times, and the tradition of Montepulciano's Etruscan origin finds few supporters now, especially as no Etruscan remains have been discovered on the hill-top site of Montepulciano itself, but only at scattered places in the country-side below.[3] The tradition of a Roman temple of Mercury which once stood on the top of the hill where the medieval Fortezza now stands seems to have as little foundation, and the first certain date in the history of the town is 713 or 714, when the *Baptisterium a sancta Matre ecclesia in castello politiano* is named as one of the eighteen parishes whose jurisdiction was disputed between the bishops of Arezzo and Siena. The quarrel had already lasted more than sixty years, and was to last for five hundred more until in 1224 the Pope decided it in favour of the bishop of Arezzo.

During the early Middle Ages the town occupied only the Sasso, a great calcareous rock on the summit of the hill, and was fortified by its escarpment as well as by walls and gates, as can still be seen in the model of the town (no. 130) held by Sant' Antilia in the great altar-piece which Taddeo di

Bartolo painted in 1401 for the high altar of the Pieve of Santa Maria, the mother church of Montepulciano, the *Sancta Mater Ecclesia* of 713–14 and now the cathedral. The Pieve of Santa Maria and the Palazzo del Comune originally stood facing each other on the Piazza near the upper end of the Sasso. In accordance with Tuscan custom all the churches founded later in the *plebatus*, or parochial district of Santa Maria were dependent on the Pievano or priest of Santa Maria. The population of the town seems to have risen considerably in the twelfth century, for in 1195 the Bishop of Arezzo is found quarrelling with the Bishop of Chiusi over an oratory which the Bishop of Chiusi had built in Montepulciano 'because a great part of the people of that castello had gone from his bishopric to live there.'[4] Another token of this emigration, which was probably provoked by the increasing swampiness of the Val di Chiana and the chronic state of war prevailing there, is to be found in the dedication of a church below the Sasso to Santa Mustiola, the patron saint of Chiusi. During the late twelfth and thirteenth centuries the town spread down the slope below the Sasso, and by 1337 it was divided according to the Sienese system into three wards, known as *terzieri*, that of Santa Maria on the Sasso, and those of San Francesco and Sant' Agostino below. This division persisted until the middle years of the fifteenth century.[5]

Not all the space enclosed by the battlemented town walls was filled with houses. During the Middle Ages Montepulciano consisted of eight long and irregular *contrade* of houses, cottages and palaces, interrupted and surrounded by orchards, *poderi* and vineyards. R. Caggese has described it as a typical example of the *comune curtense* or *comune di castello*, half-way between a rural and an urban commune.[6] Politically the town emerged from obscurity in the twelfth century, during the struggles between Guelf Florence and Ghibelline Siena. Like all the smaller communes which lay between the territories of the two great rival cities, it vibrated for centuries between independence and dependency first on one and then the other. In strict law, as a result of the administrative divisions of the Emperors, the town formed part of the *contado* of Siena, so that its ultimate, if distant suzerain was the Emperor himself and its immediate overlord Ghibelline Siena. But in spite or because of Siena's undoubted rights, Montepulciano fought obstinately for independence, all the more because the townsmen were predominantly Guelf in sympathies. The town was important both to Siena and to Florence because of its strategic position above the Val di Chiana and between the Via Francigena and the highway into Umbria, and there was fierce contention between them for its possession. To escape from the Sienese Montepulciano made a voluntary submission to Florence in 1202, but during the century of intermittent warfare that followed it passed more than once from Florence to Siena and back again. The foundations of a form of communal government were laid after the triumph of Charles of Anjou and the Guelfs in 1266. On 24 June

135

1267 the *sindaco* of Montepulciano swore an oath of fealty to Charles as Imperial Vicar of Tuscia, receiving in return confirmation of the town's old privileges and a grant of new ones.

Like most Italian communes the town fell during the fourteenth century under the domination of a single family. The ascendancy of the Del Pecora was established by Guglielmo, who in 1301 bought a house on the meadow in front of the Pieve and transformed it into a palace. The power of the family was founded on its nobility – they were related to such illustrious houses as the Malaspina and the Conti Guidi – and on its wealth. They were Guelf, and the Guelf party was in ascendancy in Montepulciano during the first decades of the century, so much so that in 1337 it enacted new statutes 'for the exaltation and peaceful and tranquil state of the Guelf party and of the men of the said town.' But from the middle of the fourteenth century the town was racked by the rivalries for power which sprang up among the Del Pecora, as among all families of *signori* in fourteenth and fifteenth century Italy. Siena and Perugia both sought to exploit the struggle for sole authority between the cousins Jacopo and Nicola del Pecora[7] and their sons. In the end Giovanni del Pecora succeeded in expelling his cousin Gherardo in 1385, together with his followers and all Sienese officials in the town, and claimed full independence of Siena. However, in 1387 Florence arbitrated in an agreement by which Montepulciano consented to submit to Siena for fifty years. This compromise lasted only a year, and in 1388 Giovanni's faction once again expelled its rivals and the Sienese *Podestà* and offered the town to Florence.

The outraged Sienese, unable to obtain redress by negotiation, allied themselves with Gian Galeazzo Visconti, the dreaded lord of Milan, and the Florentines hastily withdrew a garrison they had sent to Montepulciano and restored the town to Sienese rule. But Siena refused to break off its alliance with Visconti, and Florence once again seized Montepulciano. In 1390 the town formally placed itself under Florentine lordship, agreeing to pay a tribute of salt to Florence, to surrender all fines levied for political causes into the Florentine treasury, and to receive its *Podestà*, its *Capitano del Popolo* and its *castellano* from Florence. Giovanni del Pecora surrendered his rights in return for a pension and certain privileges. The peace of 1404 between Florence and Siena confirmed Florence in the lordship of Montepulciano. A Florentine possession it remained until the nineteenth century, except for a brief period between 1495 and 1511, when the townsmen, angered by the expulsion of the Medici, placed themselves once more under the suzerainty of Siena. The end of Sienese power did not end the prestige of Sienese art in Montepulciano and Sienese painters continued to work for patrons there until the middle decades of the fifteenth century, when Florentine art gained the ascendant.

From the last decades of the thirteenth century the government of Montepulciano was vested in an elected council of five men known at first as the *Domini Quinque*, and later, from the 1370s or thereabouts, as the *Priori*. They held office for two months, but the shortness of this term is deceptive, since those eligible for election seem to have constituted a close-knit oligarchy of merchants – there was a rule disqualifying all magnates, judges or notaries. In addition to administering the business of the town the *Domini* or *Priori* had the right to call assemblies of the townsmen, to keep four hundred men in their service, and before the submission of the town to Florence in 1390 to appoint the *Podestà*. The statutes of 1337 which secured the power of the Guelfs in Montepulciano gave them the right to elect the members of the *Consiglio Generale*, whose numbers varied from 150 in 1337 to 88 in the second half of the fifteenth century, but only in conjunction with certain other officers whose authority was even weightier in the Comune. These were the *Capitani di Parte Guelfa* (*Capitanei Partis Guelfe Fideles Sancte Romane Ecclesie*) who first appear in the second half of the thirteenth century. The *Capitani* were entitled to take part in all the meetings of the *Priori*, and in most of the town elections, and assured the influence of their party by nominating those who were to elect their successors.

On 25 November 1372, after a struggle by the artisans against the narrow ruling oligarchy, a modified form of government was introduced which lasted throughout the decades with which our story is concerned. A *Gonfaloniere del Popolo* (*Vexillifer populi de artibus et de arteficibus*) was to be elected together with five *Priori*. He was to be supreme head of the town, and the *Priori* were to pay him all reverence and honour. The *Capitani di Parte Guelfa* still kept their share in the government. Each of the *terzieri* of the town also had a *Gonfaloniere*, who was assisted by a committee of four members and whose responsibilities were chiefly military. A second *Consiglio* was instituted known as the *Consiglio del Cinquanta*, whose fifty members were elected from the *Consiglio Generale*. They had the right to elect the *Priori*. It was also their duty to approve the expenditure of the Comune and to appoint those of its officers who by custom had to be *forestieri*, that is, born outside a ten-mile limit round the town. As all business had still to be initiated at the meetings of the *Gonfaloniere*, *Priori* and *Capitani* before it could be proposed in the two *Consigli*, real power remained in their hands. The executive and judicial authority of the town was vested in the *Podestà*, who held office for six months. After a long resistance by the town full civic rights were granted to the inhabitants of the *contado* in 1374.[8]

To understand fully the history of Aragazzi and his tomb it is also essential to know something of the ecclesiastical state of Montepulciano in the early fifteenth century.[9] The principal church of the town, as we have seen, was the Pieve of Santa Maria. Like most collegiate churches of its type in Northern Italy and Tuscany it was served by a college of canons, who formed a chapter, and lived together in common in a presbytery or *canonicato* on the endowment of the church. From at least as early as 1217 the chapter was headed by an Arciprete, whose dignity was superior to that of an ordinary *pievano*. In 1337 the statutes mention him as head of the local ecclesiastical court, and he was without question the principal church dignitary within the circuit of the town and its district. But the endowment of Santa Maria was not large: in the declarations for the *catasto* return of 1427 it was valued at only 280 florins, 14 *lire*, 8 *soldi*, less than the endowment of the chapel of the Annunziata within the church, which with property valued at 305 florins, 13 lire, 7 *soldi* was the richest of all the ecclesiastical foundations of Montepulciano. Santa Maria's endowment was in fact worth no more than the property of the average small Florentine notary of the day. It consisted of various *poderi* and pieces of vineyard, and of other land in the town and its *contado*, two houses, and a shop on the piazza, and was burdened with a tax to the bishopric of Arezzo.[10]

The town also contained three or four parish churches, notably Santa Lucia and San Bartolommeo which had been founded *c.* 1200 on the slopes of the hill below the Sasso. But the devotion of the townsfolk centred on the convents of friars, all founded during the great spiritual revivals of the thirteenth century. The Franciscans arrived in 1218, settling at first outside the town and then in 1256 moving inside its walls. The Servites came in 1262 and the Augustinians towards the end of the century. The date when the Dominicans founded their convent is not known, though it was certainly in existence by 1296.[11] Sant' Agnese Segni, the local saint of Montepulciano, placed the convent of Dominican nuns she founded in 1306 just below the town under their care.[12]

None of these convents was wealthy. In the *catasto* returns for 1427 the value of the endowment of the Dominicans was returned as 215 florins, 13 lire, 8 *soldi*, and that of the Augustinians as 238 florins, 3 lire, 11 *soldi*. The sanctity of its foundress had made Sant' Agnese rather richer than the others, for its endowment was valued at 494 florins, 10 lire, 2 *soldi*. Hence the need for the pious contributions which the town allotted every year for their support: hence too the meritoriousness of gifts and legacies from individual citizens. Both kinds of benefaction were made readily, for the townsfolk of Montepulciano shared the common late medieval belief that the friars were superior in holiness to the secular clergy and the old monastic orders. But the conventual buildings and churches were small and simple: all the churches were built of brick, even San Francesco, and only Santa Maria dei Servi had a façade of stone, with a portal in the *trecento* Gothic style.

We know something of the economic life of Montepulciano. During the thirteenth and fourteenth centuries there were companies of wealthy merchants in the town, some Sienese, some of townsmen, who traded in the saffron, so much valued in the Middle Ages for dyeing cloth and in cookery, that was obtained from the crocus and *guado* plants grown in the fields around Montepulciano.[13] Saffron from the *contado* of Siena was reputed to be the best, and there exists a record of a sale in 1347 of 45,000 pounds (Pisan weight) of *guado* made by merchants of Montepulciano to two merchants of Valencia for 800 florins. On 29 December 1379 the *camarlingo* (treasurer) of the Comune farmed out the town-duty on local-grown saffron for a year to one of the townsmen for 240 lire (probably *lire cortonesi*). The wine of Montepulciano, still famous in Tuscany, and panegyrised by Francesco Redi in a famous line of his *Bacco in Toscana* as *d'ogni vino il re* was already in high esteem and an article of commerce by the middle of the fourteenth century.[14] By the 1420s there was an Arte dei Lanauoli, or guild of cloth-merchants in the town. Dr. Ilio Calabresi, the local historian of Montepulciano, tells me his researches have given him the impression that the town was prosperous during the fourteenth century.

Francesco Fabiano Benci, the seventeenth century historian of Montepulciano, wrote in his manuscript history of the town's great families that the Aragazzi were both 'ancient and noble'.[15] As its *capostipite* he gives a certain Ragazzo, who can be identified as the '*Ciutius qui vocatur Ragazius quondam andree*', *italice*, Ciuccio di Andrea, who is mentioned in a notarial document drawn up in Montepulciano on 23 September 1303.[16] Ragazzo had three sons, Messer Nuccio, whose title indicates that he took a doctor's degree in law, Paolo, who figures in documents dated 15 December 1330[17] and 2 January 1331, and Puccio. Messer Nuccio's son Bartolommeo had two sons, Messer Jacopo, born *c.* 1348, who entered the Church and became Arciprete of Montepulciano at some date between 1389 and 1400, and Francesco, father of our Bartolommeo Aragazzi, whose tomb has preserved both his own memory and that of his relations. Since Francesco declared himself to be '64 years of age or thereabouts', in February 1429, he must have been born *c.* 1365.[18] The two had a sister, Monna Gabriella, born *c.* 1354, who in 1429 was living 'old and ill', with her brother Francesco.

Nothing is known about the line in life of their father, Bartolommeo, but in all probability he was a man of some standing and substance, if only because Messer Nuccio had engaged in the honourable and lucrative pursuit of the law. Bruni claims that Bartolommeo Aragazzi's grandmother had been that thing discreditable in Bruni's eyes – a midwife. Whether this accusation is strictly true is uncertain: uncertain too is whether it applies to the younger Bartolommeo's paternal or maternal grandmother. But it certainly reflects one truth about the Aragazzi family, which is that it belonged to the mercantile and professional oligarchy of Montepulciano, not to that aristocracy of magnates which the statues of 1337 had excluded from all share in the government. Francesco Aragazzi was a merchant. Bruni speaks of him, as we saw, scornfully, as a peddling merchant who drove his asses from fair to fair. And from a mention in his *catasto* return of 1429 of money owed him by a certain Guglielmo di Giunta for Florentine cloths it seems likely that he was not a manufacturing merchant but a trader, who sold the grain, wine, oil and saffron produced by his lands and carried goods from one market to another to sell them at a profit. But we should think of him less as a pedlar than as an itinerant *mercator*, whose mules must often have passed through the gates of Siena, laden with bales (*torselli*) of cloth wrapped in white felt just like the four, one white, one brown and two black who are being driven into the city by a muleteer dressed in a red tunic in Sano di Pietro's painting (no. 131) of the *Virgin obtaining the protection of Pope Calixtus III for Siena* (c. 1456).

In Montepulciano Francesco was a man of standing, active and influential in the public life of the town. On 29 June 1413 the Comune paid him 43 lire for his expenses as *oratore* to the Nove in Florence over a question regarding cattle. On 29 November 1415 he received 8 lire 18 *soldi* for his expenses as its 'oratore' to Magister Onofrio di Giovanni in Siena 'in order to procure the said Magister Onofrio to accept the office of master of grammar of this Comune.' During these years the affairs of Montepulciano were greatly involved with the Jews, the only moneylenders who could then practise usury without subterfuge. Francesco was a prime mover in an attempt to get the townsfolk out of their grip, and on 30 July 1418 was 'paid for several various and diverse expenses and for various motions taken by him for the defence of the Comune against the claim of the Jew Venturello'. The sum he received was quite large, 312 lire 10 *soldi*.[19] He went the rounds of the town's public offices and honours. He was *Gonfaloniere del Popolo* of Montepulciano on 30 August 1418, when he and 'his fellow-lords priors of the said Comune' were paid 6 lire 'towards the expenses of a dinner given to the Podestà', and specifically for 'two *stanne* of white wine'. In November 1422 he was one of the councillors of the *Consiglio Generale*. On 3 September that year he had been elected one of the twelve *Officiales super speculo* for 1423: it was the duty of this body to administer the scrutiny of those eligible for public office. At the end of the month following he was chosen one of the three *Regulatores gabellarum* for 1423: their duty was to supervise the collection of the dues imposed on goods and cattle passing through the town-gates, an important source of revenue for the Comune. On 6 December 1427, when his name had again been drawn for *Gonfaloniere del Popolo*, it was agreed that 'for the benefit, utility and honour of the Comune Francesco di Bartolommeo . . . may be permitted and allowed to enter and embark on the said office at the time that best pleases him, even though he is absent at the beginning of his tenure, and to exercise it up to the end from whatsoever time he shall come in spite of the rule to the contrary which thereby may be infringed'. In May 1429, the year of his death, he was again serving as one of the Councillors of the *Consiglio Generale*.[20]

Probably there were still lingering loyalties in Montepulciano to Siena, with which the town had so long been linked, and since Francesco must have witnessed, perhaps even taken part in the transfer of allegiance to Florence in 1390, it is significant that he belonged to the Guelf, that is, the Florentine party, which was also of course the party of merchants like himself. On 15 April 1428, his was one of twelve names submitted to scrutiny for election as one of the six salaried *Capitani di Parte Guelfa*, two from each *terziero* of Montepulciano, who sat with the *Priori* and *Gonfaloniere* of the town. He was one of the two *Capitani* who were elected for his *terziero* of Santa Maria, and is recorded as proposing motions in this capacity on 1 and 3 November.[21] During the same years certain of the churches and convents of Montepulciano were being repaired or rebuilt. The Comune took a lively part in these good works, supporting them with grants from the town revenues and even extending its care to a close supervision of the morals of the religious, particularly of the nuns, who were of course mostly the daughters or sisters of the townsfolk. For some churches and convents it appointed an *Opera* or board of works, whose members, known as the *Operai*, maintained and improved the state of repair of the church entrusted to them, or if necessary advanced the work of its reconstruction and adornment. Like the other offices of the town that of *operaio* rotated at certain intervals. By 1429, when Francesco is recorded as one of the three *Operai* of the Dominicans, he had probably already held the office several times and for more than one church and convent.[22]

Even from such a career of public office it is already conspicuous that Francesco di Bartolommeo Aragazzi was not quite the itinerant pedlar of Bruni's venomously eloquent letter. We know, in fact, that he was a close friend 'most conjoined in love and charity in Christ', according to his son, of the Camaldolese friar Ambrogio Traversari, who was, as we have already seen, one of the group of scholars now labelled Christian humanists for their deep piety and because they applied the new learning to the revival of patristic studies, especially of the Greek Fathers.[23] Such a friendship implies that Francesco was deeply devout, and if Bruni's contemptuous words about the frantic devotion of Bartolommeo's mother are true or near the truth, then the atmosphere of his household must have been austerely pious. Certainly Francesco's bequests in his will to two confraternities in his native town, that of Santo Stefano 'called the confraternity of the grown men' and that of the Virgin suggests that he was a member of both. The *Compagnia di Santo Stefano*, founded in 1303, got its name *dei Grandi* because it taught prayers and psalms to boys who were later admitted to it when they were 'grown men' (*grandi*), that is, twenty years of age or more. Its members met on feast-days to recite the Office of the Virgin and to hear mass, said the penitential psalms during Lent and took communion at certain fixed times of the year.

The confraternity of the Virgin, also known as the *Confraternità dei Neri*, which was instituted on Good Friday 1303 and still exists in Montepulciano as the *Arciconfraternità di Misercordia*, concerned itself with works of mercy. It gave assistance to the sick and poor, nursed dying members, washed their bodies after death and accompanied them to the grave, gave spiritual comfort to those condemned to death, celebrated anniversaries in suffrage of their souls and those of dead members, provided dowries for poor girls and maintained a hospice for poor travellers and pilgrims. Thus one of these two confraternities represented the practical, the other the contemplative side of medieval devotion.[24] For Francesco's tastes in reading there is naturally less evidence, but his bequest of a Dante to a certain Agnolo Spinelli suggests that he read the secular devotional literature popular with pious Tuscan merchants in that age.[25]

For Montepulciano Francesco was a man of property and wealth – in 1418 he was one of the twenty-five citizens who had to pay a *prestanza* of 4 florins imposed on 12 August that year.[26] It is from his *catasto* return of 1429 that we learn the value of what he possessed, and the kind of income it brought him. The long list begins with his large dwelling-house, valued at 330 lire, in the *contrada* of San Donato (now known as the *Strada della Fortezza*), one of the three *contrade* on the Sasso. In this house, which lay beyond the Palazzo del Comune and Pieve of Santa Maria, with a deep cellar beneath, he lived with his family and with his brother Jacopo, the Arciprete. It had a garden, a plot for vegetables rather than for flowers, which is listed separately in the *catasto* as *uno casalino a orto* in the same *contrada*, with the explanation that 'the said *casalino* is a garden for the use of the house, and no profit is drawn from it'. Francesco also had another house with a *bottega* (shop or workshop) in the *contrada di Talosa*, one of the other two streets on the Sasso, which still runs down from the piazza to the right of Palazzo Tarugi. This *contrada* was also known as the *Mercantia*, and as this second name implies, was the trading and business street of Montepulciano. Francesco's house and shop were valued at 180 lire, and were let to Nicolo di Papi for 12 lire a year. These two main properties head the list, and after them comes the usual string of small houses, parts of houses, *poderi* and pieces of land, acquired by investment or inheritance, in which much of the fortune of medieval Tuscans consisted. Francesco had, for example, among his properties, a house, a part of a house and a cottage in the *contrada di Voltaia*, and a house with a yard behind it in the *contrada di Collazzi*, all let out to yearly rent. From a vineyard and a small piece of cultivated ground known collectively as the Vigna degli Apostoli which lay beside his dwelling-house in the *contrada* of San Donato Francesco obtained twenty barrels of wine and twenty *metadelle* of oil yearly – no doubt by letting it out at *mezzadria* (share-cropping) or *a fitto*, that is for a certain term of years in return for a fixed rent in kind or money. Besides this he had other pieces of mixed cultivated land and vine-yard, both inside and outside the walls of Montepulciano. From one 'with a *palazuolo* on it' in San Cervagio, for instance, he received hay and more oil, from another sixteen barrels of wine and two pounds of saffron. Besides this *podere* at San Cervagio his properties outside Montepulciano included pieces of land near the village of La Strada, at Abbadia Argnano, in the village of Villanuova and in that of Castel Vecchio.[27] He also owned a mill on the stream called La Parcia which runs by Chianciano below Montepulciano: this he let to a miller in return for a yearly payment of 60 *staia* of wheat.

In 1416, moreover, he had bought for 76 gold Sienese florins a holding of about 10 *staia* of land a mile outside Siena, partly vineyard and partly cul-tivated ground. The enjoyment of it he had assigned to his cousin Monna Balda, daughter of the late Ser Francesco Naldi of Siena, in return for the gift of her dwelling-house in Siena, which lay 'in the *terziero* of San Martino, in the *contrada* and *compagnia* of Rialto and Cartagine, beside the house of Mino di Paolo da Monterone and Maestro Martino di Bartolommeo, painter of Siena. Which house [has] before and behind the Via del Comune. Which house and property the said Monna Balda is to enjoy all the time of her life, and then it is to fall to me or to my heirs. I have no profit from it, but I wish to advise you of each and all of my possessions.' This last remark was for the benefit of the *catasto* officials, whose natural suspiciousness of all such returns must have been augmented by the riots with which townsfolk of Montepulciano had greeted the law of 1428 extending the *catasto* to the *contado* of Florence.

In addition to these properties in land, Francesco owned valuable livestock, which in 1429 was being grazed on a share-basis by Agnoluccio di Maria and his sons on their land in the village of Acquaviva, near Montepulciano. He had entered into partnership with Agnoluccio on 4 December 1426; their agreement was to last for six years, at the end of which the herd was to be divided into two halves. The cattle now numbered 70 steers; the cows had produced 26 calves since the beginning of the partnership. Francesco and Agnoluccio estimated the value of the whole herd at the very considerable sum of 350 florins. Because Francesco had provided the cattle he reckoned that at the date of the *catasto* Agnoluccio and his sons were entitled to only a quarter of the herd. Agnoluccio was also grazing 4 mares which Francesco had bought for 15 florins 'and so I must have the first profit from them'. They were now estimated to be worth 35 florins, of which Francesco's share was 25. There can be no doubt then that Francesco was the capitalist who had bought the stock, and he notes that his partners, who were probably only *contadini*, owed him 24 florins 3 *soldi* for the *gabelle* or customs-dues which had been paid on the beasts as they passed through the gates of Montepulciano 'and for other things'. The *contadini* on his lands outside Montepulciano

143

were rearing other animals for him: one was grazing 5 oxen worth 45 florins and 2 young female asses worth 14 florins, another 3 oxen worth 33¾ florins and a young female ass worth 9. Nanni di Nuccio had in his charge a flock of 28 sheep, valued at 14 florins, and Gianpaolo at Abbadia Argnano had an ox with which to till Francesco's ground and a female ass. For 3 florins Francesco had bought from Biagio di Cenni at La Parcia a herd of 6 swine. Besides all this livestock he owned a store of grain. Some of it had not yet been paid to him by the cultivators of his ground, but 300 *staia* were already laid up in his house. However, wrote Francesco, although the current price was said to be 5 *soldi* per *staia* 'you would not get 3, and were it not for the ready money I have in hand, of which I have some provision, I could not live off selling grain and wine.'[28]

His *catasto* return also lists Francesco's investments and assets in ready money. He had not yet made up accounts with Filippo and Domenico di Bernabò degli Agli and partners, Florentine merchants with whom he had invested money, and could make no return at the moment of what they owed him, but would do so after the arrival of Aldobrandino di Giorgio the Florentine *Podestà*.[29] But the next entry begins: 'Afterwards, because I did not feel well, I could not come before Aldobrandino, and so I have advised to write down what I believe to be owing to me by Filippo and Domenico di Bernabò degli Agli and partners, for I think it will in truth be not much more or less, and I believe it to amount to 2,000 florins. And it is on these that I live for my expenses, and pay the dues of the Comune of Florence and of Montepulciano, and for clothes, shoes and the other things that give occasion for expenditure.' Besides this large deposit of capital, no doubt invested on a profit-sharing basis, Francesco was owed 149 florins and some *soldi* by Guglielmo di Giunta of Florence as a final payment for some Florentine cloths. After Francesco's death the moneys due from the Agli and Guglielmo di Giunta were found to amount in fact to 2136 florins.

In the *campione* or return which the Florentine *catasto* officials compiled from the declarations they had received Francesco's entire fortune was valued at 3728 florins 14 *soldi* and his *valente* or property liable to taxation at 3378 florins 14 *soldi*. He was therefore one of the two or three wealthiest men in Montepulciano. Even by Florentine standards he was rich. According to the scale of wealth in Florence during the first half of the fifteenth century as established by Martines,[30] he would have ranked there in the upper five per cent income group, among the smaller international merchants and landowners of medium fortune. His wealth, then, if it did not rival the greatest of Florentine fortunes, was enough to make him a great man in Montepulciano. Indeed he was probably one of the richer inhabitants of the Florentine *contado*. If family groups are excluded, the wealthiest citizens of Prato in 1428-9 were the wool merchant Andrea del Gatto and his son, who had a fortune worth

3235 florins, some 500 less than Francesco, but a very much larger sum than was possessed by any other citizen of Prato.[31] Bartolommeo Aragazzi could have answered Bruni, himself only the son of a small grain-merchant from Arezzo, in Bruni's own words to Niccoli. 'For what reason then do you scorn my birth? To touch on the matter lightly, I had parents and forefathers who were free-born and honourable: I might add, if it concerns this matter at all, that they were not without wealth and had filled every honourable office of a free city.'[32]

Messer Jacopo Aragazzi, Arciprete of Montepulciano and Francesco's brother, is another person of importance in the history of his nephew's tomb. It was he who obtained the first accession of honour to the dignity of Arciprete. On 9 April 1400 a bull of Boniface IX granted him the right to use a crozier and mitre, the two principal insignia of a bishop, and that of ordaining to minor orders. The Pope also withdrew the Pieve of Santa Maria from the diocese of Arezzo and made it *nullius diocesis*, that is, immediately subject to the Holy See. Naturally, these privileges, the first advance in that slow but persistent ascent which in 1561 elevated Montepulciano into a diocese and its Arciprete into a Bishop, were hotly contested by the bishops of Arezzo, and in 1480 another Arciprete, Messer Fabiano Benci (1423–81) a powerful and much trusted official of the Papal Curia, had to procure a second bull from Pope Sixtus IV renewing and confirming them.[33] Messer Jacopo's aspiring character is also reflected in the huge and costly altarpiece of the *Assumption, Annunciation* and *Coronation of the Virgin*, which was commissioned for the high altar of Santa Maria from the Sienese painter Taddeo di Bartolo, probably in celebration of Boniface's bull. Completed in 1401, it is the other great artistic magnificence of the modern Duomo besides the pieces of the Aragazzi tomb.[34]

In 1429 Messer Jacopo, aged eighty years and ailing, was living in Francesco's house. His tenure of the *arcipretura*, after a first blaze of glory, had become highly unsatisfactory to the chapter of Santa Maria on account of his persistent non-residence in the *canonicato* attached to the Pieve. Either he held or had come to hold the benefice in conjunction with some greater benefice or dignity, perhaps in the Papal Curia, though there seems to be no record of his presence there, or else he had lived all the time in his brother's house, neglecting the comfort of his canons. At a meeting held on 16 September 1431, shortly after his death, the chapter passed a resolution imposing the obligation of residence 'in the church of the Pieve' on the next Arciprete 'since the said late Messer Jacopo never dwelt nor lived in the said church of the Pieve of Santa Maria, whence the said church and Pieve and chapter suffered many and innumerable losses. . .'[35]

The exact birthdate of Bartolommeo Aragazzi, better known to his contemporaries as Bartolommeo da Montepulciano, is unknown, but from his father's birthdate of *c.* 1365 and from dated events in his later life it can be fixed as *c.* 1385. In all likelihood he learnt the rudiments of Latin grammar from the schoolmaster (*magister gramatice*) maintained by the Comune of Montepulciano. In 1429 the Comune allotted 230 lire as a year's salary for the schoolmaster, only 20 lire less than for the town doctor.[36] At about the age of fifteen Bartolommeo went to University, probably at Perugia, Siena or Florence, and took a doctor's degree in law, presumably after the usual ten years' course. He then entered the Curia of John XXIII as a Papal *scriptor*. It is as a *scriptor* that he figures in the first known document to contain his name, a letter from John XXIII dated 29 April 1411,[37] shortly after the Pope's entry into Rome. The *scriptores litterarum apostolicarum* were officials of the Papal Chancery. It was their task to write out bulls and documents on parchment in the style of the Papal chancery on the basis of minutes prepared by the abbreviators from petitions approved by the Pope. After they had completed their redaction, it was taken to the *corrector*, an official of great responsibility, who examined it, compared it with the original minute and verified any documents concerning it produced by the petitioner.[38] In 1373 there were a hundred *scriptores*, and the office was one that was eagerly sought after, for in the words of Poggio Bracciolini, it was both 'profitable and conjoined to honour and dignity'.[39] Consequently an influential recommendation was usually necessary to obtain one of the coveted vacancies.

It seems probable then that Bartolommeo was helped to procure an office in the Papal Curia by his influential fellow-townsman, Messer Francesco de' Piendibeni, one of the first of the many sons of Montepulciano who rose to dignity and wealth in the Church during the fifteenth and sixteenth centuries, each in true Italian fashion giving a helping-hand to fresh aspirants from his native town. Francesco di Ser Jacopo di Ser Piendibeno, after studying law and rhetoric at Bologna and Perugia, had begun his career as a notary.[40] He became an Imperial Judge, and in 1392 attracted the notice and patronage of Pope Boniface, who made him Chancellor of Perugia and shortly afterwards summoned him to the Curia, where he served first as an *abreviator*, then as a *scriptor* and finally from February 1396 as a *secretarius*. Francesco was a learned man, a humanist and poet,[41] and a friend of Coluccio Salutati, the first of the great humanist Chancellors of Florence. It was he who at Salutati's request succeeded in obtaining an office as Papal *scriptor* for the young notary Poggio Bracciolini, who was to become one of Aragazzi's closest friends. Salutati thanked him for this piece of patronage on 9 February 1404, and in a letter to Poggio written some days later bade him always to honour and reverence Francesco as his 'father and lord'. Francesco continued to serve Boniface's successors as a *secretarius*, and was sent by them on a number of important diplomatic missions. After the secession from Gregory he followed the Council of Pisa and rose to higher favour than ever under John XXIII.

During many of these years he was a colleague of Leonardo Bruni, who asked to be remembered to him in a letter of 13 September 1416 to Poggio Bracciolini in Constance.[42] John made him Bishop of Arezzo late in 1413, and Francesco remained faithful to him to the last, accompanying him through all the adventures and miseries of his flight, enforced return and deposition. He enjoyed equally high favour under Martin V, who made him a referendary, gave him the important financial office of *taxator domorum et rerum curialium* and sent him in 1419 to Naples as one of the three great dignitaries charged to crown Giovanna d'Anjou as Queen of the Kingdom of Sicily. He went back to Montepulciano to die, and after his death there in 1433 was buried in Santa Maria, in a marble tomb of which only the effigy, a lumpish provincial sculpture, now survives.

To be appointed a Papal *scriptor* Bartolommeo must already have been a proficient Latinist. The earliest of his few surviving letters, written to Ambrogio Traversari on 21 January 1417,[43] proves that as might be expected he commanded a polished epistolary style. He was either already a friend or soon became one of the Florentine scholar Niccolò Niccoli (1364–1437) the mentor of Tuscan humanists in the early fifteenth century and the owner of a splendid library of the ancient classics and of a collection of antique gems and sculptures. In his letter to Traversari, already cited, Bartolommeo called Niccolò 'easily the first man of our times in studies of this kind'. Now, at the Papal Curia, he met the celebrated Byzantine scholar Manuel Chrysoloras (*c*. 1350–1415) from whom he set himself to learn Greek. Chrysoloras had been invited to the Papal court by the Cretan Alexander V, who had the cause of reunion between the Eastern and Western churches much at heart, but only reached Bologna about the middle of 1410, after the death of Alexander V and the election of John XXIII. The cause of reunion was also taken up by John, who attached Chrysoloras to his service and soon afterwards sent him to Constantinople with letters to the Patriarch. He had returned to Bologna from this mission by 24 December 1410, and it was probably during the next months that he met Bartolommeo and began to teach him Greek. 'I loved that great man so dearly', Bartolommeo wrote to Traversari, 'that so far as I was able and it was allowable, I never departed from the conversation of such a Father, and tried to become more learned from his wisdom: nor was there a single day spent in sweetest familiarity with him on which I did not know myself made better by it'. Chrysoloras was no mere grammarian, and from him Bartolommeo learnt not only the Greek language, but Greek and Byzantine philosophy, obtaining an intellectual formation which was incomparably richer than anything he can have received from the arid study of the law.[45] For in one of his letters Bruni inveighs against the narrowness of contemporary jurists, and their prosaic absorption in the matter-of-fact legal business.[46] A true humanist, Bartolommeo preferred to their dry and worldly pedantry the pursuit and study of the thought and literature of antiquity, the practice of poetry and fine Latin.

Chrysoloras and he followed John on his triumphant journey to Rome in April 1411 and ignominious flight to Florence, where the Curia, unlike the Pope, was allowed by the Signoria to lodge inside the walls. And if Bartolommeo had not yet met Niccoli, it must have been now that he made his acquaintance. Presumably he left Florence with John in October 1413, and then journeyed in the Pope's train to Constance. It was in Constance, on 16 December 1414, that he finished copying out the *De fato et fortuna* of Coluccio Salutati.[47] This book, Salutati's second longest work, was written *c.* 1396–8, and though it has never found its way into print, enjoyed some popularity in its own day, for at least thirteen manuscripts of it are known to survive. It is divided into five tractates, *De ordine causarum, De fato, De fortuna, De casu, Unde clades pervenerint Perusinae.* Their principal theme is the problem of free-will. Salutati propounds the orthodox Christian doctrine, taking Augustine as his principal authority, and rejects all pagan opinions on fate and fortune.[48] Aragazzi's studies were interrupted three months later by John's flight to Schaffhausen. He was one of those who obeyed John's peremptory order of 24 March to his Curia to leave Constance and join him in Schaffhausen. He accompanied him on his second flight to Laufenburg, perhaps from loyalty to Francesco da Montepulciano as well as to the Pope, and it was he wrote out the bull of 8 April which John sent from Laufenburg to Constance announcing to the Council that he had been driven yet farther in his flight by fear.[49] After John's deposition and imprisonment he remained in Constance, in the service of the Council, and on 27 March 1416 he and another secretary wrote a letter sent by the Council to King Ferdinand of Aragon asking him to arrest and imprison Benedict XIII.[50]

To the great grief of all the humanists Chrysoloras died in Constance on 15 April 1415. Bartolommeo now turned to a fellow *scriptor*, the Roman humanist, Cencio de' Rustici, an older and more advanced pupil of Chrysoloras, for assistance in his Greek studies. On Cencio's advice he copied out many of the shorter dialogues of Plato, two treatises of Chrysoloras, one, the *Protagoras*, on friendship, the other on fortitude, and Chrysoloras's letter to the Emperor John Palaeologus comparing Old and New Rome, that is, Rome and Constantinople. He also engaged in a literary correspondence with Guarino of Verona, another pupil of Chrysoloras, whom he may have met in 1413, when Guarino went to Florence. It was probably Guarino who made Aragazzi known to the Venetian humanists Francesco Barbaro and Andrea Zulian, with whom he shared a common bond of discipleship to Chrysoloras. 'It would take too long', he wrote in 1417 to Traversari, 'to describe the kindness and humanity with which Guarino of Verona, Francesco Barbaro and Andrea Zulian treat me'.[51] In a letter of 9 November 1415 to Zulian,

148

Guarino asks him to give a heartfelt salute to Poggio and to Bartolommeo 'that most humane and most learned man'.

Another of Guarino's letters, dated 9 February 1416, was written in reply to one from Bartolommeo.[52] After lamenting the death of Chrysoloras he answers an enquiry from Bartolommeo for a copy of a little work he is rumoured to have composed about some late translations from the Greek and the errors made in them by certain learned men. He has written no such work, nor would he be so arrogant or uncharitable as to take pleasure in satirising illustrious men, who like him have studied in the school of Chrysoloras. Who for instance, could be more refined, excellent and pleasant in character, virtue, learning and genius than Leonardo Bruni, or offer a more perfect resemblance to Cicero? Would Bartolommeo in his high prudence be good enough to contradict any persons who falsely assert that Guarino has been guilty of so ignoble a proceeding. As regards any translations of his own for which Bartolommeo may wish, Guarino will willingly let him have his performances, though they are not to be compared with what the learned men of whom he has just written have done. To guide Bartolommeo in his choice, he has translated the *Calumny* of Lucian, seven of Plutarch's *Lives* and the same author's elegant work on the education of children. And he ends by recommending himself to Poggio and to Cardinal Zabarella, who was evidently a patron of Bartolommeo. The whole letter leaves the impression that either from jealousy or dislike, Bartolommeo was not unwilling to hear criticisms of Bruni's translations from the Greek. But its subject-matter also shows that after the storms of John's flight Bartolommeo had resumed the tranquil pursuit of his literary studies. Some of that winter he spent copying out for himself part of the Chronicle of Prosper of Aquitaine, a task he completed on 8 February 1416.[53] Sometime later he copied out after it Cencio de' Rustici's translation of Aristides' *Sermo Bacchi*, Poggio's famous letter to their mutual friend Niccolò Niccoli describing the baths at Baden, and a Greek and Latin vocabulary.

Meanwhile Poggio was embarking on his famous hunt for manuscripts of ancient authors in the libraries of Germany, France and Switzerland. In the early months of 1415 he acquired, possibly in Cluny, more probably in Constance, a codex of Cicero's speeches from the Cluny library containing the *Pro Cluentio* and also the *Pro Roscio Amerino* and the *Pro Murena*, both then unknown. From these Bartolommeo seems to have made extracts. In June and July 1416 Cencio de' Rustici, Poggio and he rode out together from Constance to the nearby monastery of St. Gall in order to make new explorations. Their success probably exceeded their liveliest hopes, for they found part of the *Argonautica* of Valerius Flaccus, Asconius's commentary on five speeches by Cicero, another, anonymous, commentary on four of the *Verrines*, and most important of all, a complete Quintilian. They transcribed these manuscripts hastily and copies of Bartolommeo's transcript of Valerius Flaccus and Asconius still survive. The Valerius Flaccus had a colophon dated 16 July, the Asconius one dated 25 July 1416. Both were made at St. Gall. Aragazzi also copied out in Constance Antonio Loschi's commentary on four of Cicero's speeches.

Bruni was overjoyed at the recovery of a complete Quintilian, but contemptuous of the other finds and of these labours of transcription. 'Although I am pleased about the discovery of both Asconius and Flaccus', he wrote slightingly to Poggio in September, 'I do not consider that any great labour need be spent on them, since Latinity would be little the less if neither of them had ever existed. But Quintilian, the father of rhetoric, the master of oratory, is a man of such sort that when you have delivered him from his long and harsh imprisonment among the barbarians and sent him hither, all the peoples of Tuscany ought to rush together to congratulate him, and I am surprised that you and those who were with you did not lay eager hands on him at once, but instead preferred to transcribe slighter works rather than this one, which I dare affirm is more wanted by the Latins than any other after Cicero's books on the Republic. . . .'[54]

In January 1417 Bartolommeo went again to St. Gall, bent on new discoveries. According to Francesco Barbaro, some of the cardinals had commissioned Poggio and him to make new expeditions at the expense of the Council: one of these generous patrons of the new learning seems to have been Cardinal Branda da Castiglione. Bartolommeo gave an account of his experiences in the letter to Traversari already cited. This was written from St. Gall on 21 January. It followed a first letter now lost, and other letters to Bruni, with whom therefore he must still have been on friendly terms, at least outwardly, and to Antonio da Pistoia. He had found the great library of St. Gall in a deplorably neglected state. 'I entered the prison-house of ancient manuscripts, where I stumbled on the book of Flavius Renatus Vegetius, an illustrious man, concerning the ancient military discipline. I determined to copy him, since he is rich in eloquence and excellent precepts, and lays open the foundations of ancient Roman generalship, and he may be profitable to our studies, whether we fight in the camp, or more gloriously in Christ. I have also obtained an ancient manuscript concerning the meanings of words which is excerpted from the books of Pompeius Festus, a book far from useless to students and of wonderful genius. Now, most illustrious sir, having completed these manuscripts and brought them to light, I am girding myself for a journey on which, God willing, I set out on 24 January, to another monastery, of Augustinian Hermits, in the bowels of the Alps. There, so I hear, is a large store of such ancient manuscripts. When I return thence, I shall still have to visit three monasteries. Though they are of very difficult access, rough and rocky (for there is no access to visitors save through the precipices of the Alps and of rivers and forests) yet I know that the path of virtue is exceeding full of labours and difficulties. Afterwards I shall write as you ask a very full account of the situation and condition of each. I enclose a short list of many of the books, but not of all, for a day would scarcely suffice to write one out, and I get entrance into them only with difficulty. I would prefer that you should send me a little note of those works which appear to be lost or thrust out of sight by some fate into dark places. Then would I attempt to persuade this little body of mine not to shrink either from the difficulties and any other hardship of the road or from the waxing cold of the Alps in the labour of reviving them.'[55]

But perhaps the journey proved too much, for on 6 July, five months later, Francesco Barbaro was writing to Poggio that he must prosecute the search all the more vigorously 'because the sickness of our Bartolommeo has made this task more peculiarly yours. Just as I was hoping that his zeal and vigilance would bring no small contribution to letters, by some ill chance of his and evil fate of ours we are fallen from a great hope. Alone therefore must you do so much, that by your care and toil we may bear the less heavily concerning this task Bartolommeo's sickness, though certainly it is most painful to all lettered men.'

The news of Bartolommeo's discoveries was received with excitement by the humanists of Italy, and on 4 October Guarino asked his brother to report the names of the books Bartolommeo had found and whether they included any new texts, 'for in things of this kind I take the greatest delight.'[56] Barbaro had already written to Poggio in that same letter of 6 July 1417 that 'these seeds of letters, which by your work and labour are to be carried down from Germany into Italy, in future days shall be called Poggiana and Montepolitiana'.[57] And he declared, all unconscious of the future, 'None would think it wrong if I were to decree to you and your colleague a statue in the temple of the Muses, not armoured, not equestrian, not gilded, but habited in the toga and of bronze.' He lists the books the pair had found, Tertullian, Lucretius, Manilius, Silius Italicus, Ammianus Marcellinus and the three grammarians Caper, Eutyches and Probus. It was Bartolommeo, or so it would seem, who brought into Italy on his return from Constance the first copy of Silius Italicus known to the humanists, one made for him by a German scribe.[58] Barbaro's prophecy was partly correct, for it is to these journeys of discovery among the libraries of Switzerland that Aragazzi owes his small share of posthumous fame. His enthusiasm in the collecting of books is also attested by a Martianus Capella,[59] which he acquired and corrected, and by a fourteenth-century Plutarch which once belonged to him and is now in the Vatican library.[60] A large folio, it now lacks about 224 leaves, but still contains twenty-eight of the lives, the *De vita et poesi Homeri*, the *Consolatio ad Apollinem* and the *Consolatio ad uxorem* (incomplete). On the verso of the last complete leaf are three notes in different hands. The first records that it was bought in Constantinople by a certain Piero d'Agnolo for the firm of Jacopo d'Anichino, merchants of Ancona. The second records that it was bought with money furnished by '*Messere Bartolommeo di Francesscho di Bartolomeo da montepulciano*', and the third is Bartolommeo's own inscription of ownership. This Plutarch seems to have been bought for him in 1415 or 1416, while he was in Constance, for in the same letter to Traversari, so often quoted, he thanks him for sending a list of its contents: 'it was very delightful to me to learn what works of that author had been brought for me from Greece to Italy'.

The letter concerns more than the rediscovery of ancient texts. Bartolommeo's prime motive was to ask Traversari for his friendship. Though Chrysoloras and Cencio had both sounded his praises, though his father Francesco was so 'closely conjoined to Ambrogio in love and charity in Christ', yet Bartolommeo had neglected to open a correspondence with him, a neglect now repaired by Traversari's courtesy in writing the first letters. To this new friend, therefore, he shows himself, 'as nature made me; cheerful, gentle and mild, and what will be even more grateful, you shall have me as you would wish'. Their common studies will promote their mutual love, and Bartolommeo humbly asks the monk to help him become a more virtuous man. 'For I am not such a man as is delighted by vain things, by honour or glory, or such as swells at the pomp and ornaments of his body. All boastfulness is abhorrent to my conversation, all adulation, all pride of mind, than which no pest can be blacker, heavier, more damnable. Woe unto me, man born of clay, that in the day of my calling must return to ashes: let it not then be that one who must give account before the tribunal of Christ of our husbandry in that brief life we live should be puffed up even in dreams with pride of mind or vain glory.' If as Cicero says, nothing is sweeter than exchange of goodwill and community of study, it is also true that nothing attracts men more to each other than likeness to each other, 'for it will assuredly be conceded that good men love good men – that is, if I, a sinner, can be esteemed a good man – and draw to themselves those excellent in virtue and manners as if into near relationship'. These sentiments of humility and piety testify to Aragazzi's reverence for the saintly Traversari, as well as to a sense of his own unworthiness as a Christian which blended with his joy and pride in his studies. Such a self-portrait is very different from Bruni's acrid sketch of vanity and folly, though admittedly Bruni was writing years later, after Bartolommeo had long basked in the sunshine of Papal favour under Martin V.

In July 1417 Poggio departed together with a copyist on a new excursion through the libraries of France and Germany. Bartolommeo did not go with him, but remained in Constance, where the Council, by deposing Benedict

XIII on 26 July, now removed the last formal obstacle to unity. On 9 September the cardinals presented a petition to it praying for the institution of a conclave; on 8 November a conclave was opened, and three days later Cardinal Oddo Colonna was elected and took the name of Martin V. Bartolommeo was already in his service as a *scriptor* by 11 December 1417, when Guarino wrote to him from Venice to solicit his aid in obtaining a place in the Curia for his pupil Francesco Bracco.[61] On 1 January 1418 he drew up a safe-conduct for the three Ethiopian delegates to the Council, who were now returning to their homeland.[62] Martin V left Constance for Italy on 16 May. Bartolommeo followed in his train to Florence and was one of the witnesses who signed the act recording Baldassare Cossa's formal renunciation of the Papacy in June 1419.[63] During the eighteen-month sojourn of the Papal court in Florence Bartolommeo must have renewed and extended his friendships among the humanists of the city. He would certainly have been thrown into company with Bruni, who was now Chancellor of Florence.

On 9 September 1420, Martin and the Curia left Florence for Rome, which they entered on 28 September. In Rome Bartolommeo was to spend the remaining nine years of his life, singularly favoured by the Pope, who 'loved him above all others', wrote Pope Pius II in his *De viris aetate sua claris*.[64] In 1421 or 1422 he became a Papal secretary, and was soon one of Martin's confidential advisers. There is a curious glimpse of him at work that year with his friend and colleague, the humanist Antonio Loschi, who had already had a long career in the Curia. On 31 December 1422, a vendor of parchment was paid 18 gold florins for three hundred parchments 'of medium size' for Papal briefs which Loschi and Bartolommeo were to write 'to certain kings, princes, prelates, knights and other notable persons in the parts of Germany, Hungary and Bohemia' warning them against the Hussites and their followers and accomplices.[65] Another of Bartolommeo's colleagues was Cencio de' Rustici, who had been made a secretary by Martin on 28 November 1417, only ten days after his election. Their experience of the business of the Curia as well as their fine Latin made these humanists desirable acquisitions for the new Pope. Bartolommeo's eventual primacy in favour is perhaps reflected in the addition he made to the rules of the Papal chancery in 1425 of two new regulations concerning the duties of the Vice-chancellor which had been approved by the Pope.[66]

The Papal secretaries wrote the Pope's secret letters, that is, his letters concerning diplomatic and administrative matters. They were chosen from the *scriptores litterarum apostolicarum* or from the *scriptores papae*, who were attached to the Apostolic Treasury. The choice was probably a personal one made by the Pope, and the secretaries sometimes retained their original office. Bartolommeo, for example, is described in 1425, after he had been a secretary for at least three years, as a *litterarum apostolicarum scriptor*. Alter-

L

natively they might be given high office in the Chancery, for example, as *correctores* or notaries or protonotaries. In any case the Pope would give them benefices for their subsistence and reward – the Curia was a place where pluralism had ample room. The office and importance of the secretaries were of comparatively recent date. In the earlier decades of the fourteenth century the Popes had entrusted their more important and confidential letters to their notaries, but from as early as 1341 we find mention of three *secretarii*. In the later days of the Avignon Papacy their numbers increased and by the accession of Urban V (1362) the distinction between them and the notaries had become blurred. And from Urban's reign onward each Pope by a natural development seems to have had one particular secretary who was his confidential counsellor. Niccolò de' Romani, secretary to Urban V and later to Gregory XI, was a man of great influence, deep in the Pope's affairs. The little we know of their role does not reflect the real importance in the Curia of such personages.[67]

However, since part of Bruni's diatribe against Aragazzi turns on his rank in society, it is worth pausing to consider what was his standing simply as a Papal secretary. The importance of the secretaries in their own eyes can be gauged from an indignant letter written by Bruni himself to Pope Martin when the Consistorial Advocates claimed the right to precede them on ceremonial occasions. Bruni reminded the Pope that the office was one held by men of great eloquence and learning, such as even the Roman See might boast of employing. A simple test of the rank of an office is the dignity of those who have held it. 'The office of secretary is consonant with the dignity of bishop, and brings no shame on it. Assuredly there were very many examples of this before our time, but in our own days Francesco (da Montepulciano), Bishop of Arezzo and Bartolommeo (Capra), Bishop of Cremona, are two who remained in the office of secretary after they had been made bishops.' Bruni adds a lively sketch of the duties of the secretaries and of the history of their office. All the Pope's letters and rescripts are written by them in the first instance. 'Is there one who must receive the secrets of the Pontiff? Let a secretary stand close by the Pontiff's side, and watch his face and wait not only on his words, but on his nod . . . we see Papal Notaries preferred before bishops by ancient custom for this one respect alone: it was not received that they should precede bishops on account of their dignity, but for convenience's sake, since they took down the sacred words of the Pontiff and put his orders into writing, whence arose their name of notaries. If therefore their office has become obsolete, as we see, and nothing is left them of it but the empty name, and the secretaries have taken their place and do about the Pontiff's person those things which they formerly did, let the Advocates bear the secretaries' precedence in honour with the same patience that the bishops formerly bore the preference of the notaries. . . .'[68]

There are two glimpses of Aragazzi's role as the Pope's confidential secretary in the despatches of a Florentine ambassador in Rome, Rinaldo degli Albizzi. In a despatch of 14 October 1424 Rinaldo describes how the Pope during an audience 'immediately in my presence summoned Messer Barto-lommeo da Montepulciano his secretary, to whom he committed the writing of a letter in the very same words I was able to dictate'. On 14 August 1425 Albizzi reported that the Pope had ordered Bartolommeo to write a letter to Giovanni Varano, Lord of Camerino, 'and then the Pope committed the said letter to Messer Bartolommeo da Montepulciano, and according to what the Treasurer sent to tell us, it was much fuller than he had made offer to us. We have since been at pains to obtain the said brief, but have not yet had the minute of it, for Messer Bartolommeo tells us that it is needful to discuss it with the Pope.'[69] His access to Martin and his office gave Bartolommeo influence, and perhaps it was because that influence was once powerfully exerted in favour of Florence that the epitaph on his tomb described him as *'conservator reipublicae'*, saviour of the Republic.[70] Is it necessary to point out that if he was so light-headed and foolish as Bruni makes out, he would hardly have become the Pope's intimate counsellor as well as secretary? But whether his favour with the Pope made him presumptuous is perhaps another matter.

In the tenth year of his reign (November 1426–7) Martin made Aragazzi a referendary.[71] Referendaries received all petitions addressed to the Holy See, examined them, read them to the Pope and advised him on the answer to be returned. The office was not at this date an official one in the Chancery; rather it was a private office bestowed by the Pope on personages of high standing whose abilities and experience he respected. According to Pius II, Bartolommeo had become so dear to Martin that he employed his as sole referendary and entrusted all affairs to him.[72] Pius cannot have meant this statement literally, since Martin is known to have had at least seventy-eight referendaries; he must have meant rather to suggest that intimate influence, favour and trust which Bartolommeo possessed with the Pope and which made him 'a participant in all his counsels', to use the words of the epitaph on his tomb. Luigi Milanesi da Prato had enjoyed a similar position in the Curia of Pope John XXIII: in fact such confidential secretaries were the ancestors of the later Secretary of State. No doubt Bartolommeo expected to rise eventually to the more splendid and public honours of the cardinalate, but of this dignity Martin was notoriously sparing, for he was not anxious to raise up contumacious rivals to his supremacy. And in 1428 Aragazzi was still only some forty years of age.

Bartolommeo's career in the Curia can only be explained then by his role in the conduct of Papal policy and affairs. During its last years he was kept busy with onerous business that was laid on his shoulders. 'Many wished to persuade me after our Bartolommeo's death' wrote Poggio to Niccoli on 23 July 1429 'that I should shoulder the burden of the many things that he sustained, and that I should insinuate myself into the inner councils of the Pope and undertake the government of affairs of my own initiative. But I am extremely averse from such counsels, nor have I any wish to push myself any further forward, but rather to draw back'.[73] Bartolommeo must now have had less and less leisure for his studies and for poetry. Yet he still continued to interest himself in philosophy and even in the collecting of manuscripts of the classics. On 17 May 1427 Poggio wrote to Niccoli that Bartolommeo was trying to obtain a manuscript of Lucretius which Poggio had discovered at Hersfeld in Germany in 1417, and caused to be transcribed. Unwisely he had lent this transcript to Niccoli, who had failed to return it, and Bartolommeo was finding negotiation with Heinrich von Grebenstein and the other monkish owners of the original difficult 'for they are barbarous and suspicious'.[74]

The only intimate glimpses of Bartolommeo's life with his fellow secretaries and humanists in Rome are to be found in the letters and other writings of Poggio, who had rejoined the Curia in the spring of 1423, after his return from England. In a letter of 1 January 1424 to Bruni in Florence,[75] he describes a banquet given by Antonio Loschi at Poggio's instigation to Poggio himself, Bartolommeo, Cencio and Bartolommeo de' Bardi. For significantly Bardi, whom we know to have had no small hand in the Brancaccio tomb, now reappears as an intimate of Aragazzi's circle. The feast was paid for by conscience-money which had been handed over by a priest on behalf of a man who had defrauded the Papal secretaries of some lawful dues under John XXIII. Poggio was greatly diverted by such scrupulosity, and he and his fellow-guests ate and drank in high spirits. 'The banquet was splendid and festive, full of laughter and jokes, and what mattered more, excellent wine, which gradually made us merrier and more talkative. At first the conversation was about serious matters, smacking of wisdom, but little by little as those at table grew warmer wisdom turned first to jocularity and then to shouts, but not so loud as to exceed due bounds; and at last, worn out with eating, drinking and argument, we departed.'

Bartolommeo and Poggio, as we have seen, were especially close friends. On 11 September 1428 Poggio sent Niccoli a description of a day's excursion the two of them had made from Genazzano, Martin's country castle, to which the Pope and Curia had retreated from the heat of Rome.[76] 'Bartolommeo and I went to Ferentino together, he for the sake of relaxing his mind, I to seek out antiquity, together with a friend of ours, who had offered to give us a meal.' Although the heat was burning, Poggio clambered about the walls and citadel, marvelling at their great size, and copied out an inscription he found inside a cave-tomb. Bartolommeo on the other hand rested in the shade – a clear proof that he did not share Poggio's eager interest in the stones of antiquity. For this reason alone is would be unwise to attribute to him any responsibility for the style in which his tomb was executed.

Poggio also laid the scene of his first important literary work, the *Historia Convivalis Disceptatiua de Auaricia & Luxuria* in Bartolommeo's *vigna* near the Lateran, which was then surrounded by plots of land, vineyards and gardens. He imagines that Antonio Loschi, Cencio de' Rustici and other Papal secretaries had been invited to dine there one summer's day 'as is the Roman custom'. After a dinner enlivened by the wine of Montepulciano, sent to Bartolommeo from his home-town, the conversation turns to the merits of San Bernardino, the Observantine friar then preaching in Rome. Poggio had his full share of that traditional contempt for the friars which was the reverse of the devotion they were also accorded, and makes some of his interlocutors criticise Antonio Loschi's enthusiastic admiration of Bernardino's sermons. Bartolommeo remarks that the two great vices of mankind are avarice and lust, which the preachers do nothing to uproot. Lust is bad enough, but avarice is even worse and Bernardino has not even touched on it. He proposes a disputation on these two vices, but Loschi declares that he would prefer an attack on avarice, 'for I fear it may be necessary for us to become avaricious on account of the slenderness of our fees, with which we can scarcely support the dignity of our office'. After some polite waiving of the honour Bartolommeo agrees to open the disputation. Cencio makes a courteous reference to his *prudentia* as an encouragement, and after he has concluded a declamation against avarice as a hatefully selfish and antisocial vice, Loschi declares: 'Many things have been said by Bartolommeo, in my opinion much to be commended, wherein I praise his gifts of mind, for although he is kept very busy in the wearisome business of the Curia, yet he devotes so much time to these studies that he can speak not without elegance of such things.'

The dialogue continues with a claim made by Loschi that lust is a fouler vice than avarice, as the search for profit works to the prosperity of society, prompts many creditable deeds and does not impair the general usefulness of citizens. He is opposed by Andreas of Constantinople, who had supervened at the opening of the disputation. Andreas distinguishes between avarice and the legitimate pursuit of profit, and condemns avarice as a selfish and pernicious vice. Cencio and Bartolommeo agree enthusiastically with him and he clinches his argument by citing the authority of St. John Chrysostom and St. Augustine, to which Bartolommeo adds those of Lucian and his own Silius Italicus, regretting that he is not more familiar with Chrysostom. Antonio says that he himself is glad to have taken the part of misers, since he has had the opportunity of hearing such excellent words, and with a modest speech of thanks from Andreas the dialogue concludes.[77]

In a letter to Niccoli of 10 June 1429[78] answering Niccoli's observations and criticisms Poggio explains the relation between the opinions he assigns to his speakers in the dialogue and their real characters. 'For I wish this should be your sentiment about their characters. In my opinion Antonio and

Bartolommeo are perfectly generous. I had assigned the primary role of blaming avarice to Cencio, who is held to be avaricious, and of defending it to Antonio, who is almost a prodigal, and I had done so deliberately in order that a miser should attack avarice and a prodigal defend it. But Antonio would by no means allow this. "Say what you like, about me', said he 'but it is ridiculous and insupportable for Cencio to speak against avarice". So as there were no other personages who could be put into my dialogue, I assigned all that to Bartolommeo, for want of speakers.'

Bartolommeo had a certain reputation as a Latin poet, but only some epigrams to Martin V and one or two other poems are known to survive. One poem in elegiacs was copied out during the second half of the fifteenth century into a miscellany of verse now in the Riccardiana Library, under the heading 'Sequentia Carmina Edidit Bartolomeus felicis vero recordationis Martini Pope Vti Secretarius ac Referendarius Vir doctissimus'. It voices a cyclical theory of history. Man collects Riches with much care and labour: Riches generate Pride, which causes the destruction of cities and peoples, for it brings War. War generates poverty, cold and hunger, and Poverty begets a humble race of men, content with little, and so brings a peace that lasts for centuries. Peace is graced with all human blessings, bringing with her happy lives and riches. But with Riches the turn of the cycle begins once more, and after this manner Fate alternates a happy state with a sad.[79]

When Bartolommeo de' Bardi died at the beginning of November 1428 it was Aragazzi who wrote the letter of condolence which Pope Martin sent to Giovanni de' Medici. 'To our beloved son salutation and our Apostolic benediction. Inasmuch as many examples of the fragility of our human life daily appear before our eyes, one has newly occurred here which must grieve both us and thee, and which we cannot relate without tears. After Bartolommeo de' Bardi, thy faithful and beloved son and ours had sickened for ten days, oppressed by heavy fevers, he migrated to the Lord with a speedy death. We grieved and still grieve at his decease. Not that anything evil has befallen one who has been translated in the flower of his age to the life of the blessed and recalled to our better home, but because of our affection towards thee we cannot but feel thy grief. For he was a man of great prudence, experience and virtue, by whose death we shall feel no small loss and thou, beloved son, hast lost very greatly. For he governed all the affairs committed to him by us and by thee with singular goodwill, honesty and diligence and studied to increase thy greatness and honour with singular zeal. Yet we must bear this mischance patiently and endure with a calm mind whatever it hath pleased God to ordain. We exhort thy prudence therefore to bear the will of God with a calm mind, and since thou ever lovedst him as a son in life, return him this one thing in death, to be moved by no grief, but to pray for his soul, which requireth from thee neither tears nor lamentations, but pious alms and orisons to God. For as he departed this life in the best disposition and contrition, so we may rightly hope for the salvation of his soul. For the rest, beloved son, hold without doubt that we shall have thy honour and estate and that of thy company with all our old affection ever in cordial commendation at the Roman Curia and in what other places we can in all that may occur (as thou hast ere now been able to perceive) though but one of thy least clerks had remained in the custody of thy affairs. For thou knowest our singular affection and goodwill towards thee and all thine, whose honours and advantage we willingly prosecute at all times. Given in Rome at SS. Apostoli under the Fisherman's ring on the sixteenth day of November in the eleventh year of our Pontificate. B. de Montepulciano.'[80]

We shall find that Aragazzi had a large sum in the bank of Cosimo de' Medici, then depositary to the Papal Treasury, and although this is an official letter of condolence we have seen that he was on terms of private friendship with Bartolommeo de' Bardi. Were Cosimo and Bartolommeo then among the '*amici comuni*' mentioned by Michelozzo in his *catasto* return of 1427 as those who were to assess Aragazzi's tomb when it was finished? It is more than likely that they were, and in all probability Niccolò Niccoli was another, for he, we now know, was an intimate friend of Michelozzo.

On 26 June 1429 Aragazzi died, cut off unripe (*immature absumpto*), laments his epitaph, at the age of forty-four or thereabouts. He fell a victim to the plague which broke out in Rome that month and drove the Pope and the Curia into flight. On 9 July Poggio wrote to Niccoli from Anagni excusing himself for his silence: 'I had been shocked and terrified by the death of Bartolommeo de Montepulciano, a most illustrious man and one of my dearest friends: in addition came the sudden and unforeseen departure of the Pope.'[81] Because Bartolommeo made his father his heir, an abstract of his will was added to Francesco's *catasto* return later that year. From it we learn what was previously unknown, that he was a cleric, for it calls him '*chericho e segretario del Santo Padre*'. It would seem then that according to a common practice in the Curia he had taken minor orders in order to enjoy benefices – Poggio, Bruni and Alberti all did the same. From minor orders it was always possible to resign and marry, and yet while one held them the road was open for promotion to high ecclesiastical dignities. Since Bartolommeo is shown without a priest's tonsure on his tomb, we can be sure that he advanced no further than minor orders, but nevertheless he had had to obtain the usual licence from Martin to make a will. For by the right of spoils (*jus spolii*) the Pope was entitled to all the property of a cleric who had been collated to reserved benefices, as was Aragazzi's case. But even when the Pope took a cleric's estate it was customary to allow the dead man's debts and other liabilities and the expenses of his exequies to be met from it and to allow his heirs to retain his patrimonial inheritance and anything he might be supposed to have earned for himself.[82] Martin left all Aragazzi's bequests of furnishings, goods and ready money undisturbed. Contrary to Bruni's assertions, he even permitted his father to keep the huge sums which were found hidden in his house and *vigna* after his death. But he exercised his rights by taking Aragazzi's house, which stood by or close to the palace of SS. Apostoli where he himself resided, and his *vigna* by the Lateran.[83]

Francesco survived his son only three months. He died on 29 September, and an abstract of his will was also entered into his *catasto* return. From these two abstracts and the rest of the *catasto* return we can fill out the picture of the Aragazzi family as it was in 1429. Francesco, we already know, was living with his brother the Arciprete and his sister Monna Gabriella in his house in the *contrada* of San Donato. Bartolommeo's mother was dead, long dead, judging from the ages of Francesco's other surviving children – all daughters – by his later wives. But one daughter at least whom he had had by her was still living, Monna Antonia, now the widow of Mariotto di Conte of Arezzo. Antonia had been given a dowry of 500 florins by her father, but in 1429 he still had to pay her 350 florins of it 'for which she has a writing in my hand'. The fourteenth-century dowries of the daughters of Florentine notables ranged from 400 to 1000 florins, and so Antonia had received a good marriage-portion, suitable to her father's wealth and position. On the death of their husbands dowries became the property of daughters, and it was for this reason that Antonia held a *scritta* for 350 florins from her father. Her brother-in-law Michele had repaid her 150 florins, and Bartolommeo had made his sister a gift of 300 ducats – the equivalent of as many florins. These, for some reason, Francesco had taken from her 'and they remained in his hands'. Perhaps he thought them safer in his care, or perhaps according to the harsh manners of the time towards widowed daughters, he believed he had a better right to so great a sum.[84]

After the death of his first wife Francesco had married again. By his second wife he had one surviving daughter, Monna Ghita, the wife of Papi di Nanni. His second wife had also died, probably *c.* 1419, and by 1429 Francesco had taken a third wife, Monna Tita, aged 25, by whom he had had three little daughters, two of whom were still out at wet-nurse. The eldest of the three was named Caterina. In the Middle Ages the hazards of child-birth, super-added to the other endemic ills of life – from 1348 most notably the plague – shortened a woman's expectation of life even more miserably than a man's. Francesco's three wives make up a typical matrimonial history of the time.

From the abstract of Bartolommeo's will it is obvious that he had accu-mulated a great fortune during his years in Papal service. Even after the *vigna* by St. John Lateran and the house by Santi Apostoli had been taken by the Pope there was plenty left to soften the loss. In the bank of Cosimo de' Medici – in other words, the Roman counter of the Medici bank which had formerly been managed by his friend Bartolommeo de' Bardi – there was a deposit of 1200 ducats and in that of Francesco degli Alberti one of 1300 ducats. Hidden in his house, his *vigna*, and his *chassa* (strong-box) were florins 'of various sorts' to the value of 4696 ducats. Their discovery made a great sensation, not surprisingly, for this was an enormous sum, and the sensation still echoes in Bruni's letter. But even if Martin at first demanded all this money, as Bruni asserts, he did not press his claim, for its seizure would have been mentioned in the *catasto* return, where on the contrary it is listed as money received from Bartolommeo's estate.

Aragazzi clearly lived in the manner of a high Roman prelate, for his household furniture – such things as his bed, his books, his hangings and other '*ornamenti di chamera*', his stuffs of linen and wool – were valued at 1000 ducats. And besides these he had plate which was sold to Francesco degli Alberti for 497 ducats and other plate, of 38 lb. weight in all, valued at 300 ducats. 21 rings, partly of gold, partly of silver, valued at 100 ducats, were found in a bag. In his stables were 3 mules, valued at 50 ducats, and 4 horses, valued at 60. Between ready money and valuables then, Bartolommeo left a fortune of 9503 ducats, the equivalent of as many florins. A notion of the degree of wealth this represented can be formed from some contemporary fortunes of Florence. With a net capital of 11,000 florins Leonardi Bruni was in 1427 the seventy-second wealthiest man in that wealthy city, where only about 150 heads of some 9866 who made returns in the *catasto* of that year reported net assets of 6500 florins, and only 137 households net assets over 7000 florins.[85] Bartolommeo's fortune set him in the second line of the front rank of wealth, below the vast riches of the city's greatest capitalists, but still affluent even in comparison with its solider citizens.

It would be idle to hope that such great sums of coined money, such comfortable property, such valuable possessions, merely represented Bartolommeo's accumulated savings from the revenues of his benefices and his income as a Papal secretary. It was of course always possible for a Pope to enrich a favourite servant. Vespasiano da Bisticci tells how John XXIII made up 200 florins a servant had stolen from Bruni by giving him a bull taxed at 600 florins to expedite.[86] And in fact Martin had lavished rich benefices on Bartolommeo. On 28 September 1425 he conferred on him a canonry and prebend in the cathedral church of Liège worth 50 marcs of silver yearly. The value of the benefice having been wrongly given in the original bull as only 30 marcs, Bartolommeo received letters of revalidation on 7 February 1426. In the margin of these it was noted that he had received them without payment of fees since he was the Pope's secretary. Already on 27 January he had obtained a dispensation from the obligation of residence. That same year, on 19 June, Martin gave him the archdeaconry of Famenne in the diocese of Liège, vacant because the protonotary Hermann Dwerg had obtained the late

Cardinal Rainaldo Brancaccio's archdeaconry of Condroz in the same diocese. Famenne was worth 60 marcs of silver and yet once again the bull was expedited without fees. A year later the ever vigilant Dwerg obtained the even richer archdeaconry of Hesbaye, whereupon the equally vigilant Bartolommeo secured for himself that of Condroz, probably by arrangement with Dwerg. Condroz, valued at 80 marcs of silver, was conferred on him at Genazzano on 28 July 1428, and a few days later, his close friend and fellow townsman, the abbreviator Angelo da Montepulciano, bound himself in Bartolommeo's name to pay the taxes that were due before the bull granting the benefice could be issued. From the general distribution of his benefices made by the Pope after Bartolommeo's death we learn that he also held the church of St. Géry at Haeltert in the diocese of Cambrai. 60 marcs of silver were equivalent to 300 Papal florins, so that from his benefices in the Southern Netherlands alone Bartolommeo was receiving in 1429 an annual income – at least in theory – of about 950 Papal florins. And he held other benefices in Germany and probably elsewhere.[87]

Yet to some degree Bartolommeo's riches must represent bribes and pickings of various kinds, offerings made to secure Bartolommeo's influence with Martin, offerings made to secure and expedite the preparation of important bulls and letters. Bartolommeo's store of plate and rings and the diversity of coins found in his hidden treasure were just the sort of gifts in kind and money made by eager or grateful suitors at the Papal Court: and the concealment of so much of his hoard is suspicious, for it seems to suggest that he was afraid to run the risk of disclosing the amount of his secret profits, even by depositing them in the comparative secrecy of a bank. But it would be rash to conclude that by the standards of his day he was exceptionally corrupt or even avaricious – as we have seen, his reputation was rather for liberality. All the humanists made large fortunes in their careers as Papal or chancery officials – Bruni after all had heaped up more wealth than Aragazzi during a slightly longer career for much of which he too had been a powerful and much favoured Papal secretary. Although Poggio returned gross assets of 566 florins in the *catasto* of 1427, the figure probably includes only his assets in Florence and its *contado*, not those in Rome. By 1458 in any case his fortune had risen to gross assets of 8500 florins, placing him among the richest of Florentines.[88] The system of present-giving was recognised and endemic in the Curia, and none of his contemporaries blamed Bartolommeo for making the most of his opportunities. Even Bruni preferred to slur him with theft rather than with taking bribes. Honour and wealth were after all what men sought at the Curia.

Bartolommeo made various kinds of bequests in his will. Some were charitable legacies for works of mercy intended to assist the salvation of of his soul. He left 400 ducats to provide dowries for girls who were to be chosen by his father Francesco. Antonio Casini, Cardinal of San Marcello,

was to distribute 500 ducats 'for God' as he thought best. Casini (d. 1439) a
learned Sienese and a friend and correspondent of Bruni, was made Bishop
of Siena in 1409, and on the departure of John XXIII for Constance, had
been left as his governor of Bologna. Martin made him a cardinal on 24 May
1426. He, like Aragazzi, was one of the small group of Martin's intimate and
trusted counsellors, and was also a figure of the first importance in the Curia
because of his office as Apostolic Treasurer. He had a reputation for charitable-
ness, which explains why Aragazzi chose him to distribute his pious legacy.[89]

To the monastery of Sant' Alessio Bartolommeo left 100 ducats. In 1426
the decadent religious life of Sant' Alessio had been revived by the introduc-
tion of eight monks from the newly reformed congregation of Monk-Hermits
of St. Jerome. They were headed by the congregation's austere and learned
founder, Lope (Lupo) of Olmedo (1370–1433). Frate Lope, whose tomb-
slab can still be seen in the church of Sant' Alessio, restored the prestige of the
basilica as a spiritual centre and promoted the cult of the two Roman saints,
St. Alexis and St. Boniface, to whom it is dedicated. In 1424 he had obtained
a bull from Martin authorising him to found his new congregation and
appointing him its General for life. The congregation had been established
under the rule of St. Augustine, but Lope soon added to its austerities,
borrowing some of his constitutions from the Carthusians, notably one which
forbade his monks to study, either in their convent or at the university, 'since
knowledge swells heads, while charity edifies'. He repeated this absolute
prohibition in 1429 in a rule drawn from the writings of St. Jerome for which
he obtained Martin's approval. His own days were passed in the severest
penitence: he fasted for six or seven months of the year, usually on bread and
water, wore a hair shirt, flagellated till his stripes were bloody, and slept on a
plank.[90] Aragazzi's deep veneration for this penitential ascetic, whose ideal
of holy ignorance was so different from his own, appears in a bequest to him
of 60 ducats to clothe the poor and to hold a service of obsequy 'as shall best
please him'.

His affection and reverence for a milder austerity of Christian virtue, for
the golden Christian humanism of his friend Ambrogio Traversari, he expressed in a legacy of 100 ducats to Ambrogio's convent of Santa Maria degli
Angioli in Florence. Both Cosimo de' Medici and Niccolò Niccoli were
admiring friends and patrons of Traversari and of Santa Maria, and the connection between Ambrogio and Bartolommeo may have linked him to Cosimo
and bound him by yet another tie to Niccoli. It may also explain the bitter
enmity of Bruni. Bruni had not only had a fierce quarrel with Niccoli from
1421 to 1426, but jealous at finding himself obliged to share with Traversari
the honour of restoring classical Latinity and envious of the monk's favour
with Cosimo and Lorenzo de' Medici was moved to attack him covertly in an
oration *Contra hypocritas*. Monk and chancellor were already on bad terms

by 1432.[91] Probably it is no coincidence that Hieronimo Aleotti, who answered Bruni's diatribe against Aragazzi, was an especial favourite and protégé of Traversari. However, it seems that there was no open quarrel between Bruni and Aragazzi before 1421, for in a letter written on 15 February of that year Guarino speaks of letters he has sent to Aragazzi and others praising Bruni's wisdom, erudition, loftiness of mind and friendship towards him.[92]

For distribution among the members of his household Bartolommeo left 200 ducats, a sum which suggests that it was a household of some size. We know that it must also have been one of some state, for among his familiars were ecclesiastics of degree. There could be no clearer indication that in the Curia he was regarded as a man likely to rise high in the Church, certainly as high as a bishopric, perhaps as high as the cardinalate, when he would be able to open lucrative and honourable careers to the members of his household. We know the name of one of them, Heinrich Maiszheim, canon and scholasticus of St. Victor outside Mainz. When Maiszheim was given the church of Bilsen in the diocese of Liège in May 1426, he received the bull without paying any fees because he was a 'familiar of Messer Bartolommeo da Montepulciano'.[93] To his young fellow-townsman, Messer Angelo (Grasso?) da Montepulciano, also a friend, admirer and correspondent of Traversari, and yet another in the long succession of Montepulcianesi who made profitable careers in the Curia, Bartolommeo left 100 ducats.[93]

Two nieces, daughters of one or other of his sisters, received 200 florins towards their dowries. For the immediate succour of his soul Bartolommeo left 15 ducats to be spent on five hundred masses. But he provided much more liberally for its future welfare and for that of the souls of the other members of his family. As an endowment for his chapel and for its chaplains in the Pieve of Santa Maria in Montepulciano he left 600 ducats, so providing a maintenance in perpetuity for masses to be said for his soul at its altar. Nor did he forget his tomb. 'He leaves that a sepulture be made for him in Montepulciano, which he had given out to be made while yet living, which will cost 1000 ducats when it has been brought here.' No more bequests are listed in the *catasto* return, but it specifies two other expenses which were to be set by the tax-officials against the assets of Bartolommeo's estate. The first was a sum of 200 ducats, laid out in exequies held at Rome for Bartolommeo and in bringing his body to Montepulciano. The second was a sum of 21 ducats, expended on a tomb-slab cut to commemorate his memory in Rome.[94] Deduction made of all these liabilities, Francesco inherited 5907 ducats from his son.

When Francesco died in his turn on 29 September, he left his brother, Messer Jacopo, Arciprete of Montepulciano, as his heir-general. To his wife Monna Tita, who evidently came of a wealthy family, he left 800 florins, the amount of her dowry. To the three little daughters he had had by her he left 700 florins each to provide them with dowries. To his daughter Monna Ghita he bequeathed 350 florins over and above the dowry he had already given her, while Monna Antonia, her step-sister, received 200 florins. By a further bequest he added 12 florins to be divided between the two. The two daughters of Agnolo di Riccio were left a legacy of 40 florins, while to Agnolo Spinelli, who as we already know received his Dante, he also left a mule – the two bequests being valued jointly at 30 florins. These were his bequests to the world, amounting to 3532 florins in all.

To the Church he left very nearly as much. The largest bequest of all was one of 1600 florins to the Augustinians 'to wall their church in Montepulciano'. To this legacy we shall return, for it is of great significance for the date of a noble work of architecture. The Dominicans, whom he had served as an *Operaio*, received 600 florins, 'to wall a church of San Luca in Montepulciano'. Other churches and convents also received bequests, but much smaller ones: the church of Santa Maria Maddalena on the Monte Chiancianese 200 florins, the friars of San Giovanni at Poggiuolo 50 florins, the church of San Lorenzo in Montepulciano 10 florins, the church of Santa Lucia another 10 florins, the church of San Biagio below the walls of the town (the predecessor of Sangallo's beautiful High Renaissance church) 20 florins. To the *compagnia* of Santa Stefano he left ten capes valued at 5 florins and to that of the Virgin 10 capes and a bed with its coverings valued at 15 florins – no doubt for the hospice the confraternity maintained. The remaining bequest was much larger, 550 florins to make three pairs of 'paramenti da chiesa' probably embroidered altar frontals. These legacies amounted in all to 6242 florins, to which the *catasto* return adds 250 florins expended during Francesco's sickness and on his funeral. It seems that Bartolommeo's ducats were more or less the equivalent of florins, so that Francesco's estate amounted at his death to 9825 florins, of which his brother Messer Jacopo would have inherited 2795 florins.

One of the executors of Francesco's will was his relative Ser Giovanni di Bartolommeo di Naldino or Naldini (b. 1382 or 1383–after 1445) a notary of Montepulciano. Ser Giovanni played an important part in the history of the Aragazzi tomb and it is necessary to know something about him. In 1429 he was living in the *contrada di Cagnano*. Although his taxable property was estimated in that year as worth only 181 florins 5 *soldi*, he was a person of weight in the affairs of Montepulciano.[95] On 31 March 1419 he was paid for writing out the *sindacatus* or report on the retiring Florentine *Podestà* and that of the retiring *notarius camparie del Comune* Ser Silvestro di Lodovico of Volterra. In the next years he rose to higher things. On 6 December 1427 he is mentioned as one of the councillors of the Comune: on 25 January 1428 he was chosen as one of the three *deputatores* who apportioned its annual revenues: on 6 February he was appointed one of two members for the *terziero* of San Francesco who were to sit on a commission of enquiry into the perennial problem of the Jews. On 20 March he was made *officialis catasti*. His name was drawn on 21 December 1433 as *Cancelliere* of the Comune, and from that time onwards he appears again and again as *oratore* from the Comune to Florence.[96] On 20 November 1435 he was made a 'lord and governor' (*dominus et gubernator*) for life of the Spedale di Santa Maria (also known as San Cristoforo) and on 10 September 1438 he was chosen for the *terziero* of Santa Maria as one of the *operai* of Sant' Agostino.[97] His name still recurs frequently in the town records during the 1440s: it was he who as *camarlingo* (treasurer) of the Ufficiali della Fabbrica paid on 27 February and 31 December 1445, sums amounting to 750 *scudi* in full satisfaction of the façade of the Palazzo del Comune of Montepulciano, for which Michelozzo had given the design in 1440.[98]

The Agnolo Spinelli who received a legacy of 40 florins was also an executor of Francesco's will, but since he does not appear in the subsequent history of the Aragazzi tomb, we can turn to another personage who figures in it very greatly. This was Don Battista di Giovanni di Paolo, Prior of the Vallombrosan priory of San Pietro, known as San Pietro della Parcia because it stood in the village of Petroio near the stream of La Parcia, the stream on which Francesco, it will be remembered, had a mill. The priory can only have been small – quite often in medieval Tuscany a Prior was merely a single monk who had been sent to officiate and administer a church belonging to his order – and its solitary distinction was that in 1327 its Prior Ranieri had been made Bishop of Chiusi. And by the third quarter of the fifteenth century it had sunk to such a state that in 1480 Messer Fabiano Benci was able to obtain a grant of the *priorato* and bestow it as an endowment on the chapter of Santa Maria.[99]

On 15 January 1430, before the scriveners of the *Officiali del catasto*, Don Battista added a declaration in his own hand to Francesco's *catasto* return attesting that all it contained was true and declaring himself to be the nephew of Francesco and the cousin of Bartolommeo. He was using the terms with true fifteenth-century looseness, for he was a grandson of Paolo Aragazzi, not of Bartolommeo, Francesco Aragazzi's father.[100] But he was none the less a blood relation, the son of Giovanni di Paolo Aragazzi, a notary who is recorded as buying property in a deed of 1390.[101] If the family tree constructed by Benci in the seventeenth century is to be trusted, his grandfather Paolo was the brother of Messer Nuccio, Bartolommeo Aragazzi's great grandfather. But the synchronism is not perfect, and in any case the irregularity of medieval Tuscan usage, in which a man was sometimes described by his grandfather's name or that of the *capostipite* makes for uncertainty in matters of kinship. But as a relative and as executor of Bartolommeo's will and of Francesco's, Don Battista's role in the making of the tomb was to be of primary importance.

Chapter VIII · The History of the Aragazzi Tomb from Documents

T O COMPLETE THE HISTORY OF THE TOMB and of those concerned in its making we must follow their vicissitudes as registered in documents until it was set up in Santa Maria in 1438. Those vicissitudes can now be told for the first time with reasonable fullness. In order to form some impression of how much time Michelozzo gave to the tomb during the years before its completion we shall take into account his other activities in so far as they are recorded. Bruni's letter must have been written after Bartolommeo's death on 26 June 1429 and before the death of Pope Martin on 20 February 1431, and so either in the autumn of 1429 or in the dry months of 1430 when alone it would have been possible for heavy carts carrying pieces of marble to be drawn over the roads of Southern Tuscany.[1] By the end of 1430, then, the framework of the tomb – its columns and their bases, some arched pieces – and the two effigies were sufficiently shaped out to be despatched from the workshop in Florence to Montepulciano. There is a ready explanation as to why Bruni found the two effigies only partly finished. It was common for marble sculptures which had to be sent any distance to be left rough in order to prevent irremediable damage to delicate or fragile parts – noses, the edges of drapery, for example, or areas in high relief. Unlike painting, sculptures, once injured, cannot be restored without resorting to the unattractive device of adding new pieces of marble. Normally, perhaps, as we saw with the Brancaccio tomb, carvings were worked up to a point that would allow the last strokes and the final polishing to be carried out accurately and swiftly after they had reached their place of destination.

But to some extent the degree to which they were finished must have depended on whether their final home was to be far or near. In the case of the Brancaccio tomb Donatello and Michelozzo preferred to set up a workshop in Pisa rather than expose their carvings to the risk of overturning or to the other dangers which made land-journeys hazardous in the fifteenth century. Its pieces were then sent by ship in a finished or near-finished state to Naples. They also saved themselves the time and expense required to transport the blocks of marble all the way from the quays of Pisa, at which they were landed from the quarries of Carrara, to Florence. In the case of Montepulciano no such economy was possible, and Michelozzo probably judged it prudent to rough out the sculptures in Florence and then send them on to

Montepulciano to be finished there, since the town was only one or two days' ride away. In Montepulciano he would easily have found a *bottega* in which to work – perhaps even a sculptor's or mason's *bottega*, for at least one is known to have existed there in the 1430s, that of Giovanni di Sino da Montepulciano *intagliatore*.[2]

During the early months of 1430 Michelozzo cannot have been very busy with the monument, since he, like Donatello, was fully occupied with Brunelleschi's over-ingenious scheme for bringing Lucca into submission to Florence by flooding it with the waters of the river Serchio, which were to be diverted for this purpose into the low ground surrounding the city. Brunelleschi surveyed the walls of Lucca between 2 and 8 March 1430, and on the strength of his report the Florentines decided to attempt his scheme. Michelozzo, who had already taken advantage of the war against Lucca to ask Averardo de' Medici for a place of *sotto scrivano* on a galley for his scapegrace brother Giovanni, vacant because its holder had been sent to the Florentine camp, was engaged to put the plan into action together with Ghiberti, Donatello, and the engineer Domenico di Maltese. He was at Lucca from 20 March onwards and on 29 April he fixed his salary there retrospectively at a florin a day. But in a letter to Averardo de' Medici of 1 May he is already complaining that the success of the ditch he is digging round Lucca is threatened because the captains of the Florentine army refuse to give him men for it, using them instead on building bastions. Two days later, on 3 May, he repeated the same complaint in another letter to Averardo. As is well known, the result of the scheme was not what had been so confidently expected. The river, instead of flooding Lucca, flooded the Florentine camp, and the army had to withdraw. Michelozzo was awarded a final payment of 50 florins on 14 June and Brunelleschi had to endure the humiliation of hearing taunting songs about his failure sung by little boys in the streets of Florence.[3]

By the time of our next information about Michelozzo's movements, which comes from a letter he wrote on 28 December 1430, he was in Padua. The letter is written to Averardo de' Medici, the cousin and ardent supporter of Cosimo, through whose bank in Pisa Donatello had been paid some of the advances on the Brancaccio tomb. It speaks of a work of art, perhaps a piece of goldsmith's work, which Michelozzo was making for Averardo's son Giuliano (d. 1467). 'Because I shall stay here for some days yet, I pray that you will arrange with Andrea de' Pazzi, who is Signore of the Mint, that my place (of die-engraver) may still be kept for me, though I am sure you have done so up till now. The reason for my delay here is a little work I have nearly finished which Giuliano wishes to give to a friend of his.' Andrea di Guglielmo de' Pazzi had entered on his term as one of the two *Signori* of the Mint on 27 November.[4] Presumably Michelozzo had fled with Giuliano and his company from Florence, where the plague was then raging, to North

Italy. Giuliano is known to have gone first to Padua and then to Venice. In Venice, where he stayed from 21 September until 1 October, he was welcomed by Jacopo Donato, a great friend of Cosimo and Lorenzo de' Medici, who gave him lodging in a house he owned at Padua which was 'very well furnished'. Cosimo de' Medici took refuge in Verona, where he was joined by his brother Lorenzo. At the beginning of November, Lorenzo, on an alarm of plague in Verona, took Cosimo's children and fled to Venice, which like Padua was free from the plague. Giuliano occupied himself with the affairs of the bank, but on 6 December he was hoping that the plague would soon be over in Florence. And on 27 December we find him thinking of paying a visit to Verona for a few days – hence Michelozzo's explanation to Averardo as to why he was staying behind. Michelozzo's brothers recorded in the *catasto* return they made at the beginning of 1431 (not 1430, as is always said) that they expected him back on 18 February. They could make no return of his property and affairs, so they declared, because of his absence, but they thought he had a number of accounts to be settled, including one 'with some person in Montepulciano or else with the Comune of the said town.'[5]

Michelozzo's occupations in Tuscany came to a halt in the late spring or early summer of 1432 when he went with Donatello to Rome for a famous sojourn which seems to have lasted until March of 1433. On 27 November 1432 the *Signori* and officials of the Florentine Mint for the term 28 May to 27 November 1432 met together and complained that Michelozzo had altogether failed to do his work as die-engraver that term, having been 'continuously absent on his own business.' They therefore appointed Maso di Niccolò Scarlattini in his place, and as a caution to Michelozzo retrospectively awarded to Maso Michelozzo's salary and perquisites for the entire six months past. The *Signori* and officials who entered on their tenure of office on 28 November re-appointed Michelozzo as die-engraver 'but because he is otherwise prevented' charged Maso di Niccolò to carry out the duties of the post 'as would the said Michelozzo if he were here'.[6] On 25 December 1432, the *Operai* of the Madonna della Cintola of Prato, with whom Donatello and Michelozzo had contracted in 1428 to make a new pulpit for the display of the relic of the Virgin's girdle, became impatient at the delay and commissioned Pagno di Lapo Partigiani to go to Rome to fetch back '*Donatello e el chompagno*'.

Michelozzo was certainly back in Florence in April when his name reappears in the accounts of the Prato *Operai*.[7] He heads his *catasto* return of that year with the date 30 May and in it he notes: 'I have several works in hand in my art of carving which are begun, and for these I have taken part of the money for which there is no price fixed. And therefore I shall say later if I gain or lose by them.' But now, from a recent discovery made by Dr. A. de la Mare, we know that Michelozzo also spent some of the winter of 1432 in Montepulciano, for on 28 December 1432 the humanist Niccolò Niccoli sent him a letter there from Florence. Its familiar affectionateness as well as its contents show that humanist scholar and humanist artist were bound to each other by close friendship and common interests. The letter also reveals that Francesco da Montepulciano was known to Niccoli and Messer Giovanni da Montepulciano, his brother, even better known. It runs:

To Michelozzo, sculptor and dearest brother, in Montepulciano. My sweetest Michelozzo. Had I known you were in those parts, I would have written to you some time before. Last night I fell in by chance with Leonardo di Giorgio and heard it from him, which was very pleasing to me because I can give you a little bit of trouble in my service, which I know will be pleasing to you because of your kindness. On the 23rd I was in Bibbiena at the house of Esau Martellini and at the same time the Lord Bishop of Arezzo stayed for some days in Esau's house while making a visitation of the benefices of his diocese. And conversing with him often about many things as usually happens, among other things mention was made by me of Vitruvius on architecture, and the bishop told me that by chance as he came from Gaeta towards Rome he found by the roadside – the name of the road I cannot recall at the moment, whether it was Via Appia or some other – the tomb of the said Vitruvius, large and of marble, and carved on it were letters which declared it to be his tomb. And he also added that he had a copy of the said letters on a piece of paper, and said he had taken them down with his own hand. I besought him to make me a copy of them, and he said he would do so on his return thither, but that he had the said letters among the things he kept locked up which he could commission no one else to search among, but when he returned thither he promised to serve me. I now hear that he is there and also his Messer Giovanni. I beg you to visit the Lord Bishop on my behalf and to commend me to him and beg him to suffer you to borrow his copy of the said letters so that you may take a transcript of them in your own hand. And then send it to me in a letter, keeping a transcript of it so that if the letter should be lost you can send me a transcript of it so that I may have one. Michelozzo mine, here is need of a little solicitude, and pray lay it on Messer Giovanni as from me to make the business his care and when you have taken the letters down let it not be a trouble to you to send them me in a letter.

And I enjoin on you yet another labour. At the same time I was with the Bishop at Bibbiena I heard from him that he had Cato the Censor on agriculture in a most ancient book in Lombard letters, which book I should dearly like to have for fifteen days, long enough to compare it with a copy I have which is very corrupt so that I may emend it and then I would send it back to him immediately. And I beg you, be you my guarantor, and promise him I will restore the book quickly to him and I beg you also to lay it on Messer Giovanni as from me to persuade the Bishop to serve me with it, and should he wish for any book from me I will serve him with it before he asks. I am so liberal of my books to others that it seems to me I may ask similar favours of others with a bold front. Take you that way which it best seems to you may issue in this effect and I shall immediately send it back safe. Commend me to Messer Giovanni and tell him that Messer Leonardo of Arezzo (*i.e.* Leonardo Bruni) has shown me the commentary that he (*lacuna of two words*) of Montepulciano and that they were greatly prized by him and that similarly they were delightful to me and that if I can do anything for him here let him advise me of it, for I shall hold it a favour to serve him.

If I take such confidence in you be not surprised, for if you ask of me you shall find me ever ready at your pleasure. It is your kindness that has moved me to give you so much labour, be patient therefore. May Christ keep you safe for me. 28 December 1432. Your Niccolò Niccoli. Infinite salutations from Florence.

Michelozzo may also have been in Montepulciano at this time because of a commission he had received in 1432 from the Republic of Florence to carry out regular work, probably of inspection and repair, in the fortress (*cassero*) of the town. No annual salary was assigned to him and a debt of 10 florins was still outstanding to him for the job in 1457. His connection with the tomb no doubt procured him the commission.[8]

It will already have become more than obvious that Michelozzo, like Donatello, was much favoured by Cosimo de' Medici – later he was to be Cosimo's architect in all his major buildings. By the coup d'état of 7 September 1433 Rinaldo degli Albizzi and the Albizzi faction drove out Cosimo and the leaders of the Medici faction. According to Vasari, Michelozzo went voluntarily with Cosimo into exile. If this is true, he either left Florence with Cosimo on 3 October or else followed him shortly afterwards to Padua and then to Venice, returning from exile on 1 October 1434.[9] And certainly Vasari's story has been accepted by art historians and in virtue of it an important influence in the development of Venetian architecture has been assigned to Michelozzo. But it is in fact a question whether the contemporary documents bear it out. Although no die-engraver was appointed to the Mint for the term 28 May – 27 November 1433, the assembled *Signori* and officials of the Mint declared on 27 November that 'as Michelozzo di Bartolommeo and Maso di Niccolò both intromitted themselves in making the said dies during the said term, and as each of them made some of the said dies' they would retrospectively appoint and pay them both as die-engravers for the term elapsed, the usual salary to be divided between them. No names of die-engravers are recorded for the term 28 November 1433–27 May 1434, but coins were certainly struck during this period, and on 28 May 1434, when the next term began, Michelozzo and Maso di Niccolò were appointed joint die-engravers.[10] Nor do the documents concerning the Prato pulpit at all square with Vasari. There are entries in the accounts of the *Operai* for December 1433 and September 1434 which imply that Michelozzo was in Florence at both those times. If Michelozzo really did join Cosimo in exile, then the early months of 1434 are the only time when he can have done so. But all in all it seems far more likely that Vasari was recording a confused tradition of Michelozzo's sojourn in Venice and Padua with Giuliano di Averardo de' Medici in the winter of 1430.

We must now turn back to catch up with events in Montepulciano. In a document of 11 September 1430 we find Messer Jacopo the Arciprete busy discharging the liabilities of the estate he had inherited from his brother and his nephew. Bartolommeo had received a deposit of 75 florins – for what purpose is not disclosed – from a certain Jacopo di Mino di Angelo of Montepulciano. In his will Francesco had ordered this sum to be repaid to Jacopo di Mino, and the Arciprete had now faithfully discharged this trust, as Ser Niccolò di Angelo Nicolai recorded in a *refutatio* drawn up in the presence of three witnesses, one of whom was Ser Giovanni di Bartolommeo Naldini and another Don Battista. By 14 June 1431 the aged Messer Jacopo had become unable to discharge his duties as Arciprete and had appointed Don Battista his Vicar. Between that date and 16 September he died, leaving Don Battista and Ser Giovanni with the task of executing the wills of Francesco and Bartolommeo, a task which, as we shall see, they discharged well and faithfully to the utmost of their power.[11]

During 1435 and 1436 Michelozzo seems to have been more or less continuously in Florence. We know that he was busy with the tomb and had brought it nearly to completion in 1436, for in his *catasto* return of 1469 he says that he worked on it '*insino nel 1436*'. Although he made this entry some thirty years later, contemporary documents show that he was making a precise, not a vague record. The first of these is a petition presented to the Priori of Montepulciano on 21 May 1438. In it Michelozzo recites that 'several years have now passed since I was commissioned by the happy memory of Messer Bartolommeo di Francesco, your townsman, to make a certain tomb of marble, as is known to each and every one of you, of which a good part was made in those times (*più anni sono che . . . mi fusse dato affare una certa sepultura di marmo come a ciascuno divoi e noto laquali insino inquellj tempi ne fu buona parte lavorata*). Then the work halting and perfection not being given to the tomb, I was moved to give it perfection in letters written by your *Comune* to the *Signori* of Florence, our lords. Wherefore coming into their presence, it was alleged by me that the halt was in respect that from whatsoever cause the inheritance had come to such a pass that it could not be seen by me whence at the end of the said work the payment for it was to come.'[12]

The sum of 1000 ducats left by Bartolommeo to pay for the tomb was of course an enormous one, representing a considerable proportion of the entire Aragazzi inheritance after payment of the legacies made by son, father and uncle. Yet there would have been money enough and to spare, had it not been for the difficulties in which a law-suit brought by Vanni di Cola, a merchant of Fermo in the Marches, involved the estate of Francesco di Bartolommeo. The first mention of this suit in the archives of Montepulciano occurs on 21 September 1435, when Don Battista appealed to the Comune to send an *oratore* to Florence at his expense 'because the heirs and the goods of the inheritance of Francesco di Bartolommeo have been and are being molested by the *Podestà* of the city of Florence.' It was agreed that an *oratore* should be sent to Florence to defend the rights of the inheritance, and also the rights of the Comune, which claimed that by the terms of its treaty of submission to Florence all cases concerning the property of its own citizens came under its own jurisdiction.[13]

Nothing seems to have been done until 8 May 1436, when the Comune appointed *oratori* to the *Signoria* of Florence and as their first commission ordered them to procure that 'the sentences given against the inheritance and the goods of the inheritance of Francesco di Bartolommeo of Montepulciano by the *Podestà* of Florence at the suit of a certain merchant from the Marches, and similarly all process which has been formed or condemnation that has been given in the said cause may be revoked and made null and void, since neither the said *Podestà* nor any other has jurisdiction in this town or its *contado*, saving only their citizen, the *Podestà* of this town, according to the terms and agreements entered upon and made between their Magnificent Comune and this their most faithful Comune.'

At first their suit was successful, for on 21 May the sentence in favour of Vanni di Cola against the heirs and goods of Francesco was annulled. But Vanni di Cola or his representatives at once entered a petition praying for that sentence to be given effect. The Florentine *Signoria* wrote to the Comune of Montepulciano asking it to send a representative to Florence to show cause why the sentence should not be carried out. On 9 June the Comune replied that it would at once send someone to justify what had been done 'in these last days . . . in conservation of the rights of this your most faithful people.' Two days later the *Priori* decided to send an *oratore* for this and other business in Florence. But from Michelozzo's petition and from subsequent events it is evident that their protests were unsuccessful and that the Florentine sentence was put into execution, so reducing considerably Francesco's inheritance and bringing the completion of the tomb into peril.[14]

This was not the only travail Francesco's family had to undergo. It would seem that his daughter Caterina, who was evidently the eldest of his three daughters by his third wife Tita, had been married without permission from the Florentine *Ufficiali dei Pupilli*, who had care of wards. Early in May 1437 the Florentine *Signori* wrote to the *Podestà* in Montepulciano ordering him to take her away from her husband's house, and place her in custody. The *Podestà* carried out these orders with all gentleness and propriety. His *cavaliere* went with three *donzelli* to arrest her, but first called her mother-in-law and other women from the neighbourhood to accompany her to the house deputed by the *Priori*, that of Monna Caterina di Duccio di Paruta and her daughter Monna Antonia, 'most worthy widows' and her relations. Nevertheless, all Montepulciano was scandalised and indignant and Caterina's relations moved to effect her release. The Priori met together on 17 May and commissioned Ser Giovanni di Bartolommeo di Naldino to go as their *oratore* to Florence to make a strong protest and a prayer that Caterina might be restored to her husband and not taken away from Montepulciano, since the intention of her father had been that she should marry and remain there and her uncle the Arciprete, had signified the same by his will. This time the plea was successful, and the Comune wrote a profuse letter of thanks to the *Signori* on 7 June, at the same time acquitting their *Podestà* of any undue harshness in the affair, Ser Giovanni having apparently rather blackened his conduct in Florence in order to enlist sympathy.[15]

Michelozzo dropped work then on the Aragazzi tomb in 1436; indeed in 1437 he returned to Ghiberti to work with him on the second bronze doors of the Baptistery. And when pressed and solicited by Don Battista he refused to take up his chisels again on the ground, as we shall see, that he had not received all the monies due to him for the work he had done. At last, after the summer of 1437 had passed without him coming out to Montepulciano Don Battista had recourse for assistance to the town. On 12 September a pressing letter of recommendation from the Comune to the *Signoria* of Florence was composed for him.

> *Magnifici et potentissimi domini nostri singularissimi.* The venerable Don Battista, prior of the abbey of San Pietro of the order of Vallombrosa and our most beloved fellow-townsman has recourse with devotion and very great faith to your Excelsa Signoria in order to obtain help and favour by which Michelozzo .... (*sic*) sculptor, your citizen, may come to finish a certain chapel and tomb of marble (*una certa cappella et sepultura di marmo*) of our most famous townsman Messer Bartolommeo di Francesco, which was commissioned from the said Michelozzo and by him begun. As by this same Don Battista your Magnifica Signoria may be fully informed, whom we most instantly pray to lend your usual favour to the said Don Battista, by which the wish of this Messer Bartolommeo, as he left in his will, may be fulfilled. Such a work will be merciful and acceptable to God. And for it we shall be bound to your Excelsa Signoria, to which we ever humbly recommend ourselves. Ever ready to obey the commands of your most magnificent and victorious Signoria. Given in the town of Montepulciano on 12 September 1437.[16]

In spite of the financial disaster of the law-suit, then, the Aragazzi executors were resolved not to endure the shame of leaving the tomb unfinished. The *Signoria* of Florence listened favourably to Don Battista's suit, and gave a decision which met the claims of both parties. What was done in Don Battista's favour appears from an agreement drawn up by Ser Jacopo di Silvestro, notary of Florence, on 30 September between Michelozzo and Don Battista and Ser Giovanni di Bartolommeo 'executors of the testaments and last wills of the said Messer Bartolommeo and of the said Francesco his father.' Its preamble sets out that whereas Michelozzo had promised and bound himself to make a tomb for the body of Bartolommeo Aragazzi in the Pieve of Santa Maria in Montepulciano, and whereas he had long ago begun the said tomb and finished the greater part of it and has received part of the price of it and whereas he now claims that he ought to have the greater part of the said price and so delays completing it and whereas a promise must be made anew to the said Michelozzo or to his representative of paying what shall remain due on account of the said tomb after he has completed it, a deposit of money is to be made to pay for the remainder of the tomb and a document recording the deposit is to be drawn up, according to the command in writing of the *Priori* and *Gonfaloniere* of Florence. And Michelozzo is desirous to show himself willing in deed to complete the tomb and perform all things incumbent upon him.

Accordingly Michelozzo, so the instrument recites, and Leonardo di Giorgio di Messer Jacopo del Biada and Jacopo di Benedetto di Zenobio acting as his bondsmen, and Ser Jacopo di Silvestro acting as a public person promise to Prior Battista di Giovanni, acting on his own behalf and on that of the absent Ser Giovanni di Bartolommeo, that within twenty-five days of a promise to pay the rest of the money to Michelozzo or to his representative he will present himself in Montepulciano to finish the tomb and will finish it within six months. Michelozzo and his bondsmen also make an equally solemn promise that should Michelozzo have received more money than is a fair price for the tomb – its price was to be determined, as usual, by an estimate on completion – then he would restore all the excess moneys to the two executors. The act concludes with solemn attestations that Michelozzo, Leonardo and Jacopo di Benedetto have indeed promised and sworn to perform all that was contained in it and have bound themselves to do so under dire pains and penalties.[17]

Michelozzo's petition of 21 May 1438 continues his side of the story. The Florentine *Signoria* had also taken measures to secure his interests. As a result of a letter they had sent to the *Consiglio* of Montepulciano, the *Consiglio* obtained for Michelozzo payment for the tomb to the amount of Michelozzo's own estimate. To take up the petition at the point where we left it: 'Don Battista, prior of the Parcia, who was present and the demanding party, promised me in the hands of our *Signori* that provided I came to Montepulciano with my workmen to carry on with the said work, he would give me such satisfactory security that I should be quite clear and satisfied to the amount of what might still remain outstanding to me for the said work. And to give execution to these things, our *Signori* wrote to your *Podestà* here that in this matter he should take such measures that the said effects should follow from them. Wherefore the *Podestà* by the authority of his court and in pursuance of your orders in the ordinary manner on his bench adjudged and by his sentence assigned to me as the most proper creditor all the goods of the said inheritance in such quantity as might come up to what I was clear was still rightfully due to me.'

The phrase 'by the ordinary method on his bench' refers to the custom by which the *Podestà* of Montepulciano sat every judgement-day with the judge and gave sentence on cases that came up before the court. Now the reason for Michelozzo's petition to the town was that he could find no purchaser for the Aragazzi properties, since there was no guarantee that the sale would be held valid after the completion of the tomb – it will be remembered that by the contract of the previous September Michelozzo was bound to restore any excess sums he might have received for the tomb after its price had been fixed by estimation. He therefore prayed the Comune to find him some means of guarantee 'so that I may sell the said properties in such a manner that the purchaser may be secured. So doing you shall be cause that the will of the testator shall be fulfilled and that your town shall be honoured by the work. And I shall be able to praise myself entirely that I have been moved by your *Signoria* to finish this work and the said work will not remain imperfect, which could not happen without blame of the parties considering the reasons.'

Not all the *Priori* were favourably inclined to this petition. Next day Battista di Ser Modesto moved that Michelozzo should be ordered to finish 'the work of the said tomb and sepulture which he is bound to finish so that when it is effectually and wholly set up and finished the accounts and calculation between the said Michelozzo and the heirs of the inheritance of the said Francesco may be inspected. When those accounts and calculation have been returned and inspected, and if the said Michelozzo shall be found to be owed anything by the said heirs then let the Comune give him help and lend him all favour so that he may be effectually and wholly satisfied.' Nevertheless the *Consiglio Generale* resolved that the Comune should act as guarantor to the sale. On 24 July the *Priori* formally sanctioned its resolution. But when the motion went forward that same day to the *Consiglio Generale* for validation, the *Consiglio* decided, probably as a result of pressure from the friends and relations of the Aragazzi, that Michelozzo ought not to be allowed more than the security of the property. By 57 votes to 5 it resolved 'that the motion given and obtained and deliberated upon elsewhere by the *Consiglio Generale* of its own will may be put into full execution. With the condition that the said Michelozzo must complete the whole work and job entirely and perfectly and then his account shall be inspected and if he still has to receive any money then he may sell part of the property of the said inheritance of Francesco di Bartolommeo and the Comune of Montepulciano shall be bound in law to maintain the sale of whatever is sold to the purchaser of the said property.'[18] Clearly the councillors felt that it was safer and fairer to make Michelozzo finish the tomb before enforcing his claims.

From the tenor of these documents it is evident that the greater part of the tomb had been carved and all its pieces had been brought to Montepulciano by the middle of 1436. For what they insist on is that Michelozzo must come to Montepulciano, finish the tomb and set it up in the Pieve. No doubt all that remained to be done was to finish one or two sculptures that were only roughed out, to give some final strokes to others, to add the final polishing and the final gilding and to set up or more probably finish setting up the tomb in its destined position. And we know for a fact that Michelozzo did finish the tomb in that same year of 1438, for an inscription, since destroyed, which Ser Giovanni di Bartolommeo di Naldino caused to be carved on the tomb to celebrate its completion after so many trials, proclaimed: 'FIDELIS AFFINIS ET COMPATRIOTA MIHI EXECUTOR FUIT/SER JOANNES BART.ᵉ ANNO DNI 1438' (Ser Giovanni di Bartolommeo, faithful relative and fellow-townsman was my executor. In the year of our Lord 1438).[19] Since Montepulciano is bitterly cold in the winter, it is more than probable that Michelozzo had completed the tomb by the end of the autumn. He must in any case have finished by 25 December 1438, when the year of Montepulciano ended, unless for some reason Ser Giovanni used the style of Florence, whose year ended on 24 March 1438/9.

Unfortunately the conditions about payment laid down by the *Consiglio* left room for further dispute. The straits to which the Aragazzi inheritance was now reduced can be surmised from a letter of 31 March 1438 written by the Comune of Montepulciano to the *Signoria* of Florence. In it the Comune commends to the sympathetic consideration of the *Signoria* the case of Monna Cristofana di Cecco di Berto. Her daughter had been set down by Francesco for a dowry of 20 florins from the 400 left by Bartolommeo to dower un-married girls. The inheritance, as we know, had now descended to the hands of Don Battista, 'who is of the order of Vallombrosa, and the said legacies are not paid because he alleges that he cannot be burdened with them saving with licence from the abbot of Vallombrosa, his superior.' The Comune therefore 'moved by justice, mercy and piety, recommends the said Monna Cristofana and the other poor and miserable girls to whom the said legacy belongs to your *Magnifica Signoria*, praying it with most instant affection to deign to procure that licence may be granted by the abbot so that the said Don Battista may be burdened here by (the officers of) our *Podestà*, to whom may it please your *Magnifica Signoria* to write ordering them to do summary justice as is rightful in matters of pious mercy to poor folk.'[20]

It is without surprise then that we find on 31 October 1439 a motion laid before the *Priori* arising from a disagreement over the price of the tomb between Michelozzo and Don Battista. The disagreement followed almost immediately on the estimate of its just price made, according to fifteenth-century custom, by two experts. Now the tomb was finished, the Comune was more concerned for the dowries of the poor girls of the town than for anything else. 'Since the tomb or sepulture of Messer Bartolommeo di Francesco di Bartolommeo has been finished and securely set up, and a difference has sprung up concerning it between Maestro Michelozzo of Florence, on the one side, and Don Battista prior of the Parcia on the other. Therefore for the interest of the Commune it seems good that all the residual estate of the said Francesco or of the said Messer Bartolommeo should pass into the hands of the fraternity and *opera* of the Pieve of this town and that provision be made from the said goods and their appurtenances for the marriages of girls.'[21] The motion then came before the Consiglio Generale, which met later that same day. Here Michelangelo di Niccolò proposed that if Maestro Andrea and Maestro Maso, the two sculptors who had been employed to value the tomb, were in agreement about the valuation, they should come before the *Consiglio*. And if they then declared themselves in agreement, their valuation should hold and be observed, and there should be no further proceeding in the matter. But if otherwise, then the *Consiglio* should act as it saw proper. Michelangelo's proposal was passed by 43 votes to 20, and with it the dispute vanishes for ever from the minutes of the deliberations of the *Consiglio*.[22]

Neither Don Battista nor Michelozzo was satisfied. Whether or not the two sculptors had settled their valuation, and whether or not the Comune had accepted it, Don Battista still considered it exorbitant. And he had strong sympathisers in the Comune, for next January, when he decided to take his case before the *Signori* of Florence, he received a warm letter of recommendation. 'Magnificent and potent fathers and our most singular lords. The venerable Don Battista, Prior of the Parcia, our most beloved townsman, has recourse to you concerning a certain difference he has with Michelozzo, master sculptor and your citizen, on account of the amount of payments made for a marble tomb made here with sculptured figures, of which your Magnificent Lordships may have full information from him. For which cause finding him to be a simple and pure man with most ardent affection in those things which with reason and honesty [word omitted] Your Lordships will understand that favour may be shown to him [and] we recommend him to your Magnificence. And each and every pleasure and favour that shall be shown and done to him by Your Magnificence we shall esteem as shown and done of grace to our own selves. Ever ready to obey the commands of Your *Magnifica Signoria*. Given in the town of Montepulciano, on the fourteenth day of January A.D. 1440.'[23]

This plea was effective enough to stay or prevent Michelozzo from any legal proceedings against Don Battista. Nevertheless he did not abandon his claims, and in his *catasto* return of 1457 he listed a debt of 60 florins, a sizeable sum, as still owing to him 'by the heirs of Messer Bartolommeo di Francesco of Montepulciano in full payment of a tomb I made for him about twenty years ago.' The same debt appears again in his *catasto* return of 1469, only three years before his death, this time as due 'in full payment of a chapel and a tomb.'

This mention of a chapel leads us to the question of where in Santa Maria the tomb was erected. It is not easily answered, for the old Pieve was razed to the ground in the late sixteenth and early seventeenth century to make room for the present Duomo, a larger, more ambitious structure. And not a great deal is known about the earlier building. Unlike the present Duomo, it did not face Palazzo Tarugi, but the side of the square on which the Palazzo Comunale stands. Some notion of it can be formed from depositions taken at Rome in January 1599 as to the state of the diocese of Montepulciano.[24] The witnesses describe it as old, with a vaulted roof and 'three little naves', that is a nave and two aisles in English terms, with two rows of columns – but both vaulted roof and naves are said by Spinello Benci to have been erected by the Arciprete Fabiano Benci[25] and so were later than the Aragazzi tomb – as small, too small for the population, one witness deposed, not too small, deposed another. It had a choir, which in 1597 had seats of walnut for the bishop and other dignitaries, and a campanile, which still remains and may have been built in the third quarter of the fifteenth century by the Checco di Meo who constructed the façade of the Palazzo Comunale to Michelozzo's design.[26] At the time of the enquiry the bishop's residence seems to have been more or less the old *canonicato*. It adjoined the church (as it still does) and is described as 'narrow and small, with few rooms.'[27] The impression is of a typical small Romanesque Pieve of a kind which still survives in some numbers in Tuscany, most notably at San Quirico d'Orcia, and which is sturdy and compact and to Northern eyes unambitious in scale and decoration.

Such churches were not designed to contain private chapels, which were added to meet the demands of later ages, obsessed by an anxiety to provide for masses to bring the souls of the founder and his family more quickly through Purgatory into Paradise. It is therefore virtually certain that the tomb was not erected in a previously existing chapel. Probably foundations of this kind were a recent ambition in Montepulciano: it was only in 1421 that Messer Jacopo Aragazzi had conceded a chapel to the wealthy Benedetto di Michele di Fighi, who by his will of 8 July 1423 ordered for it an altar-piece representing the Virgin Annunciate, with his patron saint St. Benedict on one side and St. Dominic, to whom the chapel was dedicated, on the other. According to the Abate Parigi, writing in 1836, the Aragazzi tomb stood 'in a chapel on the right hand of the high altar of the old Pieve of Santa Maria.'[28]

So far as can be collected from the episcopal visitations held before the final destruction of the church, this tradition is largely correct, for the altar of Sant' Angelo with which it was associated is listed immediately after the high altar in all of them. The probability then is that the tomb stood at the end of one of the three *navicelle* (little naves) mentioned in 1597, that on the right of the church. But whether it stood in a chapel specially built by Michelozzo or even in a chapel at all, is another matter.

The essential feature of a chapel was a separate altar, not a separate structure. Thus we find that the Piccolomini altar, in the cathedral of Siena, commissioned in 1481, and consisting of a flat arched framework enclosing an altar and set against the wall of the nave, is described in all the contemporary documents as a *capella*.[29] The combination in the Aragazzi monument of altar and tomb in fact constituted a chapel, just as much as the more usual combination of altar and altarpiece. As we shall see, the height of the tomb, so far as this can be established, and the evidence of the one description that survives of it, suggest that Michelozzo did not create a special architectural setting, and that it was simply set against the wall like the Piccolomini altar-chapel. Accordingly, we should perhaps visualise it as rising originally against the right wall of the nave at the altar end of the church.

Chapter IX · The Fragments of the Tomb

AFTER IT HAD BEEN SET UP in the Pieve of Montepulciano, a remote town lying off the great highroads to Rome, the Aragazzi tomb was forgotten in the great world. It was copied, as we shall see, by Agostino di Duccio while working in Perugia, but even Vasari, though born in nearby Arezzo, seems to have visited Montepulciano only once, to judge from what he says of Andrea Sansovino's terracotta statue of Lars Porsenna. He attributes the tomb to Donatello, mentioning it briefly as a work made by him after his return from Rome in 1434, and describes it vaguely as decorated with 'a most beautiful history'. It survived the sixteenth century undamaged, but not the seventeenth. In 1561 Montepulciano had been made a bishopric, and a bishopric must have a suitable cathedral. The first Bishop, Spinello Benci, began the work of demolishing the old Pieve by pulling down the sacristy and part of the library in 1583–4. The town took up his scheme with enthusiasm and Bartolommeo Ammanati, the great Florentine architect, was invited to design a new Duomo. Ammanati submitted his plan and model in 1588, but the work of construction did not begin until 1593, a year after his death. And it was suspended almost immediately by the election that October of a new *Soprintendente della Fabbrica*, Guido de' Nobili, who was dissatisfied with Ammanati's design. Accordingly he called in another architect, Ippolito Scalza of Orvieto, who produced a design which was accepted after the Grand Duke's architects, Buontalenti and Maestro Raffaello, had pronounced it superior in all respects to Ammanati's project.[1]

Construction began after 23 May 1594, and by 1612 work on the nave was well under way, for on 13 October of that year Cristina of Lorraine, Dowager Grand Duchess of Tuscany, who had been granted sovereign possession of Montepulciano during her lifetime by her son, the Grand-Duke Cosimo II, issued a decree permitting the chapels of the new Duomo to be assigned 'to those who shall ask for them in order to adorn them, provided they make that acknowledgement which is proper for the benefit of the Fabric. Then let the old Duomo be razed to the ground so as to widen the Piazza, according to the design, and let work on the middle nave then be continued with its materials.' This decree was put into effect in 1616, when the old church began to be demolished. With it was pulled down the Aragazzi tomb, 'many pieces of it being broken', wrote the Abate Parigi in 1836, 'either through carelessness or else, as tradition relates, from animosity'.[2] Was this animosity against the surviving representatives of the Aragazzi family or was it resentment that the most splendid tomb in Montepulciano should belong to a family whose standing was now much humbler than that of the Benci, Cervini, Nobili, Bellarmini, Tarugi and other great noble families of the town which had risen to wealth and eminence in the sixteenth century and were now living in stately palaces. In any case the tomb was soon without the protection of Bartolommeo's collateral descendants, for the last of the Aragazzi, Dionigi di Ser Jacopo, died during the seventeenth century. Moreover by then the family were almost certainly without the means and the will to reassemble the monument fittingly after so much of it had been broken.

Its splendour survived as a living tradition in Montepulciano. Thomas Dempster, writing his *De Etruria Regali* between 1616 and 1619, was told of it by a certain Gregorio Fanti, and mentions in his catalogue of the illustrious sons of the city that 'Bartolommeo, named Politianus, of uncertain family, was buried in his native place in a magnificent tomb, in the year 1438. On it is a double eulogy, which I do not transcribe.' In 1641 Monsignor Spinello Benci (d. after 1648), the first historian of Montepulciano, who must have seen the tomb intact, since he was born *c.* 1565, wrote that 'Pope Martin had as one of his familiars a certain Bartolommeo da Montepulciano, whose father and family are unknown, though his marble tomb in the destroyed Duomo, adorned with marbles, with statues and with bas-reliefs by the famous sculptor Donatello sufficiently testified that he was a person of rank. As may still at present be seen, the dead man was sculptured in that dress of familiars of the Pope which is used in the Pontifical Chapel. The inscription was on a plate of bronze, with three stag-heads, the arms of Bartolommeo, which three stag-heads may be seen carved on the façade of Sant' Agostino in our city. In the said inscription it was affirmed that he had been a counsellor and favourite of Martin; there was no mention in it either of the charges or offices that he held, nor of how long he lived, nor of when he died.'[3]

One or two local historians mention the tomb in the eighteenth century. Padre Giuliano Bartoli defends Aragazzi against Bruni's malice in his life of S. Agnese da Montepulciano and speaks of his 'superb mausoleum, rich with statues, emblems and most delightful ornaments, which later, to the sorrow of connoisseurs, was dismembered so that the plan of the new Duomo might be carried forward'.[4] In 1815, during what seems to have been a general re-ordering of the Duomo, the effigy of Bartolommeo was placed to the left of the main door in a low niche, tastefully framed by a canopy in *quattrocento* style. Above it was set a slab with the inscription:

AMATORI PATRIAE   CONSERVATORI REI PUBLICAE
BARTHOLOMAEO ARAGATIO VIRO DOCTISSIMO
APUD MARTINUM V.P.M. CONSILIORUM PARTICIPI

IMMATURA MORTE PRAEREPTO. A(*nn*). AB. INC.
MCDXXIX
INCLYTUM MIRIFICAE ARTIS MONUMENTUM
POSTERI. POSUERUNT. QUO POSTEA
NON SINE. SUMMO LIBERALIUM ARTIUM
AMATORUM. DOLORE. DIRUTO
SIMULACHRUM. EIUS. DIU NEGLECTUM
NE TANTI. VIRI. MEMORIA. PENITUS DELERETUR
POLITIANA. PIETAS. HIC. COLLOCANDUM CURAVIT
ANNO. MDCCCXV

The first part of this inscription is adapted, as we shall see in a moment, from the original epitaph on the tomb. The effigy is described in the second part simply as having been 'long neglected'. Certainly Benci's words in 1641 imply that it was still to be seen in the Duomo at that date. Yet according to Fumi,[5] writing in 1894, it was discovered in 1815 together with the other surviving pieces of the monument buried in the choir of the Duomo. However this may be, in the same year of 1815, the much damaged effigy of Francesco da Montepulciano was also mounted in a similar niche in the corresponding position on the other side of the doorway.[6]

It was also in 1815 in all probability that six other pieces of the monument preserved in Montepulciano were set in their present positions. They consist of a frieze carved with putti and garlands, two bas-reliefs, two statues in the round, and a figure of *Christ Blessing* carved in high relief. The two reliefs are now mounted on the first two piers of the nave, one on either side, fronting the entrance. The frieze is set on top of the high altar, and the two statues in the round stand on pedestals to either side of the same altar. The figure of *Christ Blessing* is set against the rear wall of the right transept, more or less immediately to the right of the high altar. All six sculptures were already set in these positions by 1839, when they were seen and described by Emmanuele Repetti, the great topographical historian of Tuscany.[7] To them should be added the much less well known bronze plaque bearing Aragazzi's arms and epitaph, which now has a piece broken off from the bottom (no. 93). It is inscribed:

AMATORI PATRIE
CONSERVATORI
REIPVBLICE BAR
THOLOMEO DOC
TISSIMO APVD MA
RTINVM QVINTVM
PONTIFICEM MAXI

183

MVM CONSILIORV
M OMNIVM PARTICI
PI IMMATVRE ABS
(*sumpto*) POSTERI
(*dedicaverunt et*)
(*benemerenti*)

The missing portions indicated in italics are known from a document whose acquaintance we shall make in the next chapter.

At some date after the destruction of the tomb, probably after the re-mounting of the other pieces in 1815, two angels belonging to it vanished from Montepulciano. They reappeared in England during the middle of the nineteenth century and were shown in the Special Loan Exhibition of works of sculpture and decorative art held in 1862 at the South Kensington Museum (now the Victoria and Albert Museum), the first and possibly the greatest exhibition of its kind ever held, and with its nine thousand or so items an overwhelming testimony to the omnivorous tastes and bottomless pockets of English collectors. The angels were lent to the Exhibition by a Mr. H. H. Nugent Bankes, who had bought them as sculptures from 'a destroyed tomb or altar-piece, formerly in the Duomo of Perugia'. After the Exhibition they were left on loan at the Museum, which finally acquired them in 1904.[8] Some years before, the great German art-historian Wilhelm von Bode had recognised that they were by Michelozzo and had once formed part of the Aragazzi monument.[9] His attribution has been unquestioned ever since.

Before attacking the knotty problem of the reconstruction of the monument,[10] it is indispensable to familiarise ourselves with these sculptures that survive from it, all executed in gleaming white Carrara marble. The great base (nos. 47–8) now mounted on the high altar is 12 ft. $\frac{7}{8}$ in. (3·68 metres) long, and 2 ft. $4\frac{3}{4}$ in. (73 cm.) high, and $6\frac{7}{8}$ in. (18 cm.) deep. The first thing to notice about it is its remarkable condition: it has not received the knocks and rubbing we should expect if it had been set at or near ground level. Such breaks and damage as it shows it obviously suffered in the course of dismantling and remounting. It is made in four horizontal sections. The first is a plain and narrow plinth. On this rests the second section, composed of a moulding ornamented by a stem of fruit, berries and leaves wound with a ribbon, a concave moulding and a moulding decorated by four cables also bound by a winding ribbon. The left and right corners of these two sections are made of separate pieces of marble neatly fitted in. Above rises the third and principal section, a frieze decorated with the usual motif adapted from an antique garland sarcophagus, winged child angels (*spiritelli*) holding with playful liveliness of pose and gesture swags of fruit, leaves and flowers. One antique sarcophagus with this motif, that re-used in the thirteenth century for the tomb of Luca Savelli (d. 1266) in Santa Maria in Aracoeli, Rome (no. 118) was almost certainly known to Michelozzo. Ruched ribbons curl outwards to form decorative swirls above and below the swags. A ledge of acanthus running along the base of the frieze establishes a rational depth in which the angels can move freely in space, and they stand on it with their feet turned inwards or sideways or poised with much verve of invention (no. 48). In order to increase the illusion of depth the ribbons are made to fall or lie along it. Although these motifs make a formal pattern such devices introduce an artful naturalism which is enhanced by the various ways in which the swags are suspended and the avoidance of strict symmetry in the arrangement of the child angels – the middle one is not posed in the centre of the frieze, but a little to its left. Above the frieze runs the fourth and last section, a cornice richly moulded and decorated with classical ornament, acanthus, dentils and bobbins.

The effigy (no. 46) is 6 ft. 6¾ in. (2 metres) long and its approximate diameter is 1 ft. 6⅞ in. (48 cm.). It is set in its niche at a tilt, a feature as we shall see, almost certainly not without significance. Aragazzi's head does not lie flat in profile on the pillow beneath it but is inclined towards the spectator. The eyes are closed in death. He wears a long robe whose stiff collar is fastened tightly round his neck: his hands (no. 61) emerge from the turned-back edges of its ample sleeves and are crossed composedly on his body as they were crossed on his death-bed. Over the robe he wears a short mantle (*cappa*). Attached to this is an ample chaperon hood which is pulled up over his head. Spinello Benci, it will be remembered, describes this costume as that worn by members of the Papal *familia* (household) at pontifical ceremonies. There is early fifteenth-century evidence that this was indeed the formal costume of some officers of the Papal household, for among the list of concessions and reforms drawn up for Pope John XXIII to lay before the first Session of the Council of Constance was one that no prelates should come to the Palace or the Curia without a mantle (*cappa*).[11] Like the effigies of Cossa and Brancaccio then, the effigy of Aragazzi is robed in the deceased's ceremonial dress. The same costume appears in some late fifteenth-century representations of the Papal suite, for example in Carpaccio's *Meeting between St. Ursula and Pope Ciriacus* in the Accademia at Venice. The significance of the pulled-up hood can only be conjectured. As Aragazzi had died before promotion to any great ecclesiastical honour, and so could not be shown wearing a mitre, it may be that Michelozzo hit on it as a means of giving the face an effective frame. But more probably it represents a usual custom in laying out the dead: thus the figure on the tomb-slab of Fra Angelico, dated 1455, in Santa Maria sopra Minerva, Rome, is shown with the cowl pulled up round the head, which rests on a pillow, and with hands composed as in the Aragazzi effigy.

Robe, cape and hood are arranged in simple, heavy, flowing folds. Along the front side of the body, below the right sleeve, is a mass of close, ridged folds, expressing where the stuff has fallen of its own weight. The form of the legs beneath is suggested by the transverse folds across the knees, which for a little bend the lines of the folds. Similarly, the gathering of the folds on the upper edge of the sleeves marks the swell of the muscles of the upper arms and the bend of the elbows, while the thick folds and deep hollows of the lower part of the sleeve render the movement of the stuff as it falls over the lower arms and rests on the robe beneath. Michelozzo has solved with admirable skill his main difficulty – how to impose an overall pattern on the drapery without confusion or unnaturalness. His guiding principle was to represent the forms of the stuff as it would fall or be arranged on a body lying flat on its back. Hence there is little or nothing that is entirely decorative in the treatment: pattern is evoked by the unforced repetition of the lines of the folds.

In style the face (no. iii), which is a portrait, and was surely copied from a death-mask, is modelled on Roman portrait-sculpture. From Roman portrait-sculpture derives the emphasis on structure, the prominent cheek-bones, the heavy brow, the firm chin. The features are articulated in a few simple, severely defined planes, the borders of the cheeks are marked by two bow-shaped ridges on either side of the nose, the mouth is firmly outlined, the channel between nose and mouth as firmly sunk. Between the eyebrows is indented a deep cleft and there are three deep furrows on the brow. This austerely generalising realism is very Roman, and it is not surprising to find that the thick eyebrows are rendered after a formula which reappears constantly in Roman portrait sculpture from the Late Republic onwards. Even those parts of the hair that are visible are disposed with an eye on Roman models.

The head rests on the usual stiff pillow, enclosed in an embroidered cover fastened by buttons at the side. The ornament of the cover, though richly designed, is also rendered with severity, each motif standing up with polished surface from the roughened ground. The border consists of panels of those imitation Cufic letters, whose originals, inscribed on glass or woven into textiles, had first captivated Western fancy in the thirteenth century. The panels are separated by pointed ovals enclosing Florentine lilies. Within the border the cover is decorated with circles linked by a small rosette at the junction: each of these circles encloses a diaper containing the stag's head of the Aragazzi arms. On the inscribed slab set up in 1815 the full arms of the family are shown as *or, three stags heads, with a label of three Florentine lilies*. But in all probability this blazoning conflates the decorative lilies of the border with the authentic charge, for the Aragazzi arms as carved on the façade of Sant' Agostino (no. 141) which is contemporary with the effigy, display only three stags' heads. The pillow was originally enriched with bronze tassels set in holes pierced in the front corners (because of the stucco in which the cushion is set at the back it is impossible to be certain whether all four corners once had such tassels); there are still remains of one in the left hole.

Aragazzi appears once more in the two reliefs. These are now made up with a broad strip of stucco on either side and are set in stucco frames coloured to imitate black marble. If these early nineteenth-century additions are ignored, the dimensions of the marble are the same in both reliefs, that is 2 ft. 6¾ in. (78 cm.) long by 2 ft. 5½ in. (75 cm.) wide. The two may have been carved in one with their frames, like the *Assumption* on the Brancaccio sarcophagus, in which case these would have been too large and too broken for retention in 1815. But it is far more likely that they were always separate panels and that the present dimensions of the carved area are the original ones. In both spatial depth is created by the traditional device of a protruding base, and the top curves inwards for the same purpose. The upper border, curiously enough, has a bevelled, not a vertical edge. The composition of both reliefs is distributed in the same manner. In each it is divided vertically into three sections, with a large group in the centre and flanking figures on either side. The repetition of the pattern establishes a correspondence between the two reliefs and is all the more satisfying because the same personages, with one exception, appear in both.

One of the reliefs (no. 49) has always been recognised as a representation of Aragazzi and his family. So classical is it in feeling and treatment that some have seen in it an imitation of those antique sarcophagus reliefs in which husband and wife hold each other by the hand. Michelozzo may have known this type of funerary relief, but his direct inspiration was a type of sarcophagus in which the motif is used to represent a wedding. A famous Antonine example carved with scenes from the life of a Roman general, is in the Palazzo Ducale, Mantua (no. 121) and was much copied during the Renaissance. But it is not certain that it was already known in the early fifteenth century and Michelozzo is much more likely to have been acquainted with the motif from the antique sarcophagus which was incorporated in the thirteenth century in the tomb of Cardinal Guglielmo Fieschi (d. 1256) in San Lorenzo fuori le mura, Rome (no. 120).[12]

For the moment we shall not search either for the identity of the unknown personages who figure in the relief or for the meaning of their actions, but content ourselves with taking a survey of it as a composition. On the left is Aragazzi, in a costume which is different from that of his effigy, for he is clad in his *tabarro*, a type of long gown traditionally worn by jurists, doctors and by the Papal *scriptores*, with a short mantle over it whose hood or chaperon is fastened across the back of his neck and over his right shoulder in what is possibly the traditional 'transverse' manner Burckhardt described in 1484.[13] Beneath it he wears a tight-fitting shirt: on his head is a *berretta* of standard fifteenth-century type. His costume here is in contrast with the ceremonial garb of the effigy. Aragazzi gives his right hand to a tall, severe, stately matron, who clasps it and looks into his eyes (no. 51). She is dressed in a heavy robe (*guarnacca*) and a tunic (*gonnella*) with tight-fitting sleeves. Her heavy cloak (*mantello*) is crossed on her breast in the fashion of a Roman matron. It falls behind her left arm in a long transverse fold which rests on her flexed left knee and then is folded backwards to finish in graceful horizontal curves over her foot. Over her head she has pulled up the hood or chaperon (*cappuccio*) attached to her cloak: under it she wears a wimple (*soggolo*), a sign that she is a reverend matron.[14] The sombre colours of such a costume in real life can be divined from the dress of the two old women who come to visit the young mother on the *desco da parto* attributed to Masaccio now in Berlin: they wear black cloaks, black robes and a white wimple. On her left stand two youths. The one next to her has his legs astride, turning his head, with its classical deep cut hair, to gaze at the cleric standing at the other end of the relief (no. 52). The other youth clasps the head of the old woman and raises his right arm in salute to Aragazzi. Both are clad only in light cloaks, not *quattrocento* mantles but classical cloaks, which are gracefully draped and wound round their naked bodies in classical fashion. Behind them, in much lower relief, another youth, similarly cloaked, strains forward, raising his hand in eager salute to Aragazzi.

Clutching at the four figures in front are three chubby little boys, quite naked. They are fitted into the interstices which are made by the four as they stand sideways gazing at each other. One stands on tiptoe so that his right hand can reach the clasped hands of Aragazzi and the matron. With his left he holds the wrist of the next child, who stretches eagerly up to clasp the hem of the matron's cloak. The third *putto*, in the same eager pose, puts his arm round the thigh of the second youth, where it is held by the left hand of the first. Closing the composition on the right stands a tall cleric wearing a robe and a long cloak, and a *cappuccio* whose turned-over collar is also the edge of the hood or chaperon hanging behind. He lifts his eyes upwards, and holds his *cappuccio* with his left hand. Like Aragazzi and the old matron, he wears pointed shoes: the feet of all the others are naked. His costume, though clearly ecclesiastical, is not easily identifiable. It is not a typical monk's or friar's dress since it lacks the characteristic cowl, nor does it seem to be that of a secular priest. Most likely it is that of a canon regular. If so, in all likelihood the old cleric was a former *arciprete* or canon of the Pieve of Montepulciano. Behind him stands a girl, with a dimpled chin and long waving hair parted in a smooth line down the centre, her eyes turned towards the principal group on the right. Her neck, throat and the left side of the upper part of her chest, are bared, which indicates that she too wears classical, not *quattrocento* costume.

All these figures are disposed on two planes after the manner of a classical relief. The composition links all the figures, but Aragazzi, the matron, the youths and the children are bound into a tighter group, whose ties are the outstretched arms of the matron, continued on the left by the arm of the child. The two pairs of clasped hands, both on the central horizontal axis of the relief, and one more or less on its centre-point, are emphasised by the lines and actions of the figures so as to emphasise the indissoluble love uniting them. The rise and fall of their arms and shoulders in alternatively inverted V-forms establishes rhythm and pattern within the relief, too great symmetry being avoided by the usual skilful variations. The turned head of the inner youth brings the old cleric into emotional unity with the main group, and the youth and girl behind are linked with it by their gaze and by the youth's saluting hand. Aragazzi himself is singled out with beautiful cunning of design. Whereas the two innermost little boys are given the same clinging pose in right profile and stretch up their right arms parallel to each other, the little boy who stands in front of Aragazzi is set a frontal pose and lifts himself and his two arms in lively action.

The interweaving of limbs and bodies in high relief on a single plane is sedulously imitated from classical sarcophagi reliefs. The tall figures occupying almost the entire height of the relief space are also inspired by classical relief style – perhaps the reliefs on Trajan's column. Their faces are treated with the same solid Roman realism as the face of the effigy. We have already seen that the motif of the relief was derived by Michelozzo from an antique sarcophagus and the type of the little boys and youths also suggests the imitation of antique originals. The first youth, with his loose ruffled hair, may be a direct quotation from some ancient sarcophagus relief, probably one representing a mythological subject – his striking pose and costume suggest a hunting scene. His curious, almost agonised expressiveness, in such strange contrast with the restraint of the others, is to be explained as a search for an antique effect, rather than in terms of his personal history. In all the figures the iris is marked by an incision and the pupil by a drill hole, *all'antica*.

It was also from antique models that Michelozzo learnt the dynamic freedom of movement he has given to the three boys. Daringly he shows them with head upturned, both frontally and in profile. In spite of some awkwardnesses their plastic vitality is complete: Michelozzo has rendered with studious attentiveness the forms created by the play of their muscles and the curves of their flesh. The youths too have active, almost heroic poses, but their bodies are animated by marking the folds of the flesh, the structure of the bones, the tension of the muscles. Their lips are parted, as in speech. Aragazzi, the old woman and the old cleric are more statuesque, as befits their age and dignity, but their eyes and hands express their feelings. Their draped figures are skilfully contrasted with the nude or partly nude figures set between and the strong tubular folds of their dress create sharp alternancies of shadow and light which throw up the smooth round bodies of the youths and children.

Naturally Michelozzo did not master entirely the secrets of antique relief style. He succeeded in grouping his figures with dignity and charging them with emotional meaning, but at the cost of some forcedness in design and execution. The legs of the two youths develop from their bodies unconvincingly; the left leg of the first youth is arbitrarily flattened to make room for the left leg of the second youth, swelling out again rather disconcertingly below it, and it is better not to search for the whereabouts of the second youth's right leg. Drapery conceals a similar arbitrariness in the management of planes in the body of the matron, whose stance is strained to make room for the child. The convex posture of the old cleric, though rhythmically satisfying in its echo of the lines of the matron's dress, also seems strained and too obviously designed to produce a satisfying space for the head of the girl behind. The slanting gaze of the girl's eyes is rendered awkwardly – here, as in some other parts of his sculptures, Michelozzo's execution is not quite equal to the ambitiousness of his design. But for all its awkwardnesses the relief is one of the noblest and most fascinating works of art of the early Renaissance.

The same severe classicism is conjoined to the same severe naturalism in the other relief (no. 50). Here the Virgin blesses Aragazzi in the presence of eight of the figures who appear in the other relief – the girl behind the old cleric is omitted, probably because there was no room for her, and girls in Michelozzo's day were less important than members of the other sex. Michelozzo has attempted to give all the personages who appear in both reliefs the same features. He did not meet with perfect success, perhaps because they are mostly shown from different aspects, perhaps too because of his style, which is a generalising one, concentrating on broad structure and form, not on that careful study of particulars which is a major secret of successful portraiture. But as we shall see, he has an excuse in that most of his portraits were certainly imaginary. For iconographical reasons he designed the relief to give more suggestion of spatial depth than its companion, but so strongly did he feel the influence of classical relief style that even here he has ensured that the first two planes are dominant by carving the figures on them in prominent relief, thrusting what remains into an accessory role. Even the two cherubs who hold up a garland of leaves and fruit behind the Virgin's head and before her throne push themselves forward into the middle plane, so creating a very classical superimposition of motifs. Michelozzo could have them do this without sacrificing verisimilitude, for he has made them true cherubim, with four wings, and so their little bodies must not be thought of as stretching backwards in space, but as terminating more or less below the chest in two wings, of which Michelozzo has shown only one in each case (see no. 53). It is only the swooping curve of their bodies as they hold up the garland and at the same time turn their heads inwards in eager contemplation of the Virgin that seems at first sight to suggest the contrary. And yet their garland is designed so as to suggest a graduated recession. On the left it passes over the knob which surmounts the arm of the throne, on the right it is held up in the air and passes above and a little behind the front of the corresponding knob. Michelozzo's constant anxiety to avoid monotonous, unnatural symmetry probably inspired this concession.

The Virgin (nos. 50, 54) as of right, dominates the composition. She sits on a great throne which is really a Renaissance version of a Gothic throne – its polygonal base can be seen between the feet of the three children below. Her dress is the usual dress of young married women in the *quattrocento*, a broad cloak over a low-necked robe. Michelozzo has not attempted the difficult task of rendering the sides of the throne in correct perspective: they are simply turned inwards at an angle to meet the back, with the outspread effect characteristic of *trecento* thrones. Against it the Virgin's head forms the apex of a narrow triangle whose base is the curved horizontal made by the heads of the children as they cling to her legs. Her gilded halo, which originally protruded above the upper edge of the relief, but is now broken off, emphasises her divine supereminence above the human beings who kneel or stand in adoration to either side of her throne.

The halo is set exactly in the centre of the upper part of the relief, so as to stress that the Virgin has inclined her head, and turned herself on her throne in order to lay her right hand on the head of the kneeling Aragazzi. On her knee sits the Child, a short cloak loosely draped in classical fashion over His naked body. In His right hand He holds a pomegranate, the apple of Paradise: He presses His left hand against the upper part of His chest, and looks down smilingly on Aragazzi. His head forms the apex of a second, smaller triangle whose base is again the heads of the three boys below. Two of these stand in right profile, their heads upturned towards the Child, their arms outstretched in a single curve to embrace the Virgin's body. The third is posed frontally, pressing his little body against the Virgin's left thigh. The order of these poses exactly reverse that of their poses on the other relief. Together with the Child they form a central group of naked or near naked putti whose chubby rounded forms and lively action contrasts with the draped or partly draped figures disposed in solemn adoration on either side of the throne.

The most prominent of these is Aragazzi. Now he has no *berretta* on his head, out of reverence to the Virgin, and his hair is visible for the first and only time. He kneels, his hands joined in a prayer which is answered by the Virgin's blessing, wearing the same robe as in the other relief, though now by kneeling he has pulled the stuff tightly and smoothly over his knee, in contrast with the strong ruckling folds into which it elsewhere falls of its own weight and by the pull of his movement. Behind him stands the cleric, his right hand resting on Aragazzi's shoulder in a gesture of affection – just such a gesture as appears in the double portrait in the Louvre of *c.* 1518, attributed to Raphael, where the rear figure, who has been identified as Raphael himself, rests his left hand on his friend's shoulder. The cleric rests his left hand against the arm of the throne and gazes reverently at the Virgin and Child. On the other side is a close-knit group. The three youths of the other relief (see no. 50), wear the same cloaks over their naked bodies, differently, though still classically draped. So classical is the full roundedness of their nude forms and their hair, copied from the hair of antique sarcophagus figures and busts that one acute late nineteenth-century scholar even muddled the identification of their sex, though it is unmistakably male in the context of the early *quattrocento*.[15] The first kneels with his hands crossed in adoration over his breast, his head upturned in devout contemplation of the Virgin. On his brow he wears a fillet, possibly as a symbol of virginity. Behind kneels the second youth, resting his hands on the shoulder of the first. The third youth stands behind him, gazing at the Virgin and Child, his left hand clasping the second youth affectionately round the shoulder. Between him and the Virgin's throne, her hands on the shoulders of the first youth, stands the matron, her eyes also devoutly turned to the Divine Persons. We have already looked at the cherubs hovering above, but it may also be noted in passing that each has a fillet of different design, the one on the left wearing a ribbon, the other a garland composed of a stem of laurel with a rosette in the centre of the brow.

The faults of this relief are conspicuously the same as those of its companion. The Virgin's body is flattened to excess to make room for the body of the Child, and it is difficult to discover how the legs and feet of the first kneeling youth could conceivably find room in the space behind him. The left arm of the cherub on the right is flatly treated so as to keep it well behind the head of the youth beneath. Yet Michelozzo has saved himself in spite of such awkwardnesses. The relief has all his austerely strong humanity of feeling, which animates its solemn ordonnance with grave and simple emotion. It speaks a classical language of its own, less graceful than Ghiberti's, less vivid, immediate and ardent than Donatello's, but like early Latin, at once noble and colloquial. During many decades these two reliefs were to remain the only attempts made by Italian sculptors to reproduce on tombs the form of classical relief sculpture. They are stripped of all accessories of setting or costume except for those which are strictly indispensable, like the Virgin's throne. The costume in which the figures are dressed is plain, and plainly treated, and nude forms are boldly and convincingly introduced. Although space is established for the action by the traditional device of a projecting base, Michelozzo has rejected Brunelleschian perspective and, in spite of a little wavering, the other pictorial devices of his contemporaries, for a stern neo-classicism. As the humanists revived in their writings the vocabulary, syntax and idiom of their classical models, so he has revived for the sarco-phagus of the Aragazzi tomb the vocabulary, syntax and idiom of classical relief sculpture.

Yet he could not revive it completely. Aragazzi, the matron, the cleric are clothed in the full costume of their time and place, not in classical drapery. Clearly the familiar dilemma which for centuries faced all artists and human-ists wanting to describe modern realities in antique style had posed itself to Michelozzo in all its sharpness – for the first time, perhaps, to any sculptor. In answer he took that middle course of acknowledging the modern, but adapting and harmonising it to a predominantly antique vocabulary which was recognised as an acceptable solution to the same difficulty even in Neo-classical times.

For reasons that will appear in the next chapter it is convenient to move next to the two statues. In spite of their heroic masculinity of pose and thew and muscle, they have been constantly and absurdly identified since the late nineteenth century, as Virtues – that is, as female figures.[16] The absence of breasts, always carefully marked by sculptors of Virtues, as for example on the Brancaccio tomb, ought to have disposed of this notion as soon as it was first mooted. But once again the question of what they represent must be left unanswered for the moment; we shall consider them here simply as figures. One or two things should first be noted about them as a pair. To begin with, although both are executed in the round and offer rewarding side-views, they are primarily intended to be seen from the front, and are designed with strongest emphasis from this view. This gives them a flatness as of a relief sculpture. The difference in finish between the front, highly wrought and polished and the back, which is left slightly rougher, proves that the effect was calculated. It also gives a precious indication of how they were originally set. Both figures are the same height 5 ft. 8⅛ in. (1·73 metres) and are carved in one with narrow bases, which are now much broken and damaged, but were once the same shape and size.

The head of the figure which now stands to the right of the high altar (nos. 64, 65) of the Duomo is a little inclined to its right – an inclination the sculptor has been careful to emphasise by incising creases in the right side of the neck. The slight curve so begun runs right through the figure and ends in the out-thrust right foot. It expresses only the body's response to the strain of supporting the heavy gilt cannelated object (no. 64) which the figure holds in its hands, for the eyes (which are left blank, and are not incised and drilled like those of the effigy and the figures in the reliefs) look serenely, even loftily outwards. In arranging the drapery, copied from late antique togaed Roman statues (see no. 65), Michelozzo was torn between the need to make it identify the figure and the desire to make it express the body's action. He was not entirely successful in reconciling these two purposes, though at first sight he has created a fairly satisfactory disposition from the front. Only when the eye begins to disentangle the components of the drapery does a certain incoherence appear. The figure wears a tunic with a V-shaped neck. One of the tunic's sleeves can be seen turned up on the right shoulder: the other is concealed by the heavy cloak. It would seem that it is fastened down his right side, for in the act of grasping the attribute the upper part over the chest has been ruffled up into deep, horizontally slanting folds and the lower part has swung over to his left side. The edge now runs from the sleeve on the right upper arm, passes under the heavy cloak, and emerges at the top of the right thigh to fall with a curving movement to the ground by the right heel. The voluminous folds of the cloak are disposed with great complexity. Its interpretation is impeded by the unpolished state of the back, which has left some of the forms behind without the sharp definition essential for legibility. After mantling the back completely except for the neck, it passes over the right shoulder and right elbow in two wisps or bands, the first vertical and held to the body apparently by the pressure of the attribute, the second, which emerges from a bunched-up area of the cloak behind, winding over the elbow and then falling down the outside of his right leg. On his left side, where all its weight is cast, it is pulled up over the left arm and then runs across the tunic, where it was held by a belt or strap, now missing – if ever present – on to the right thigh, where the right hand holds up its end. As it crosses the chest its slanting horizontal folds become muddled with those of the tunic, and even the smooth polish of the gleaming white marble fails to soften away the clumsiness of the junction. Again this complicated disposition is intended to suggest that an energetic movement has preceded the now tranquil stance.

In spite of all this forcedness of effect, in spite too of the slightly grotesque device by which the right hand holds up the cloak-end to reveal a heroically bared leg, the figure has *fierezza* and nobility. The lower part of the legs and the front part of the feet are garbed in buskins, or rather classical military socks ruckled up on the upper side. The feet themselves are shod in classical sandals, composed of thick-shaped soles and two straps which join to make a third between the big toe and its neighbour. Socks and sandals seem to be copied from the military footgear worn by Roman soldiers in some of the reliefs of the column of Marcus Aurelius – notably that at the base of the column which shows the Roman troops crossing the bridge of boats across the Danube. Michelozzo may have a little misinterpreted his original, but we shall see his choice of a classical military source is not without its importance for solving the mystery of the figure's identity. Over the brow is bound a fillet, a plain band which runs under the hair to fall in two ribbons on the nape of the neck behind. The narrow base is much rubbed and broken into a jagged edge. When complete it was about $23\frac{1}{2}$ in. (60 cm.) square. In all likelihood the right side is original: if so, the present position of the figure should be slightly adjusted. Michelozzo took much of his inspiration for this figure from Donatello, notably from his David (1408–9, 1416; see no. 136) and his St. George (1421).[17] As in these sculptures of Donatello, the canon of tall slender grace, inherited from Gothic art, is translated, but with far less ease, from an abstract linearism into naturalism. But Michelozzo's figure is more classical in effect than Donatello's carvings, partly of course because it is more frozen, partly because Michelozzo lacked Donatello's expressive power.

The effect of the other figure (nos. 62–63) which is the more successful of the two, is now rather marred by its present placing, which is the result of an error made when it was first set up on the left side of the altar in the early nineteenth century. The position in which it was intended to be seen would be restored by turning the long straight front section of the base, which now runs away at an angle, to align it with the front of the modern pedestal. The correct frontal view of the figure would then reappear (see no. 63) and especially the graceful poised action of the feet, and the strong incurving movement of the upper part of the body would become an expressive, not an oddly strained *contrapposto* when set in right relation with the lower part. The head would be thrown sharply into profile, the attribute into greater relief, and the pose into its full suggestiveness of movement arrested in contemplation.

The weight of the figure, like that of its companion, rests on the left leg. The right is flexed in an easy pose, the foot turning lightly and gracefully outwards. It wears a long loose sleeveless tunic, imitated from a classical *chiton*. Caught round the waist by a belt which is hidden by the fall of the stuff, it then falls in two broad folds and in a number of narrow, lightly rounded folds which smooth out over the knees. The fall of the heavy stuff has halted on the bridge of the left foot, creating a pattern of horizontal and slanting creases across the leg above. Once more the eyes are blank. The hair is not bound by a fillet and its curls seem ruffled by the wind. The feet are bare, not shod in sandals. The right leg and right arm of the companion figure are treated with careful tracing of sinew and muscle and precise description of structure and joints, but in the arms of this figure there is even more intensity of effort to reproduce bone and muscle and sinew and the forms they make under the movement and stresses of a given action. In spite of a little exaggeration in the protrusion of the elbow-bones of the right arm, the heavy sinewy muscularity of these arms is powerfully plastic in effect, much more so than the turning neck, which is stiff and rigid.

Behind this figure we can discern more clearly than usual the terracotta model which Michelozzo undoubtedly made for all his sculptures before proceeding to cut them or have them cut in marble. Vasari records that he learnt the scientific naturalism, founded on a study of human anatomy, which was one of the great innovations of the Florentine Renaissance. 'In his youth Michelozzo practised sculpture with Donatello and also drawing, and although it came to him with difficulty, yet he none the less went on improving himself with clay, wax, and marble, after such fashion that in the works he later made, he always displayed genius and great virtue.'[18] The success of these two standing figures is not to be judged by the success with which they incorporate Michelozzo's studies from the life. Only in certain parts do they record the lessons of anatomy; as wholes they are modelled, loosely rather than imitatively, on classical sculpture, just as their garments, though naturalistically arranged, are styled on classical garments. But if the aspiration to ideal beauty redeems them from the charge of mere awkwardness, there is none the less in Michelozzo's sculpture in the round a struggling imperfection. He had the power to create movement and majestic forms, but not the plastic genius to inform his whole creation with a vital unity. But even at their most cumbrous these statues are arresting, so sincere is their conception, so resolute their execution.

The great figure of Christ in Benediction (no. 59) is relatively free from these faults. It is not carved in the round but in very high relief, with a flat back, and as now, so originally it must have been set against a flat surface. It measures 6 ft. $\frac{1}{2}$ in. (1·84 metres) in height and is on an average 2 ft. $5\frac{1}{8}$ in. (74 cm.) wide. The right hand is raised in blessing, and the head bends downwards (no. 66) so that the eyes look on the recipients of the blessing. The left hand once held a metal cross which is now missing, with the result that the groove into which it was fixed between thumb and index finger is visible with awkward effect. The weight rests on the right foot, which is drawn back, while the left leg is advanced, so that it almost seems as if Christ were moving forwards on his supporting clouds. Only the upper bank of those clouds is original: the rest are modelled in stucco and were added in the early nineteenth century when the figure was set up in its present position in a frame of stucco simulating marble. The head (no. 68) is rather reminiscent of Ghiberti's St. Matthew (no. 135). The face and beard are shaped as a pointed oval, the soft beard ending in two symmetrical curling points. Over the beard fall the long curling moustaches, and the hair too is arranged in curling pointed tresses on the forehead. Once more the features are strongly articulated and firmly rendered, with two incised clefts between the brows, prominent cheek-bones, high ridges marking the inner edges of the cheeks. The expression is serene and benign, as becomes the personage and the action.

The noble head, the majestic torso and the graceful flexion of the body recall classical statues of gods and emperors. Michelozzo could not make a figure representing the Son of God in His glory more than partially nude, but in baring the great chest and the upper part of the belly (see no. 66) he was being a daring innovator in the cause of reviving the classical nude. For except in the cycle of the Crucifixion, where Christ's nakedness was intended to move to pity, He had always been shown fully clad. Even here much of the form is that of the heavy, simple drapery, which with its mass and slanting spread conceals the curving outline of the body beneath. As in the two figures just discussed it also disguises the relative slenderness and elongation of the body – all three have long legs. The conception and arrangement of the drapery is nearer to the masterly simplicity of the effigy. Christ wears a great cloak, which is partly held by the pressure of the thumb and index-finger of his left hand against his thigh. Down his right side, below the fold which makes a sleeve, it is shaped into a succession of great pendant V-folds, as a pattern conventional, but here treated naturalistically, with much emphasis on the sag and swell of the heavy stuff. The edges of the cloak, by contrast, are rendered in a decorative sequence of sinuous folds, obviously Gothic in ancestry. The flat surface of the drapery over the left leg stresses the slight flexion underneath. But if the cloak is turned back, creased and folded for the sake of making it interest the eye, its great folds are so smooth that they seem modelled in terracotta.

This figure has sometimes been described as St. Bartholomew,[19] on the supposition that it represents Aragazzi's patron saint. The emblem of St. Bartholomew is a knife, and the long narrow cylindrical groove in the left hand can never have been intended to hold the flat curved handle of even a small fifteenth-century knife (see no. 129), let alone of one of the kind usually shown in representations of St. Bartholomew, which was the large sort used by butchers and tanners in allusion to the Apostle's martyrdom by flaying. As other attributes of St. Bartholomew in Tuscan painting Kaftal gives a flayed skin or a banner, and in Central or South Italian painting a scroll or a book.[20] None of these fit here, and in any case the clouds beneath the feet make the identification an iconographical impossibility.

Other scholars have seen that the figure must represent Christ, and have suggested that it represents the Christ of the Resurrection. There is some early sixteenth-century evidence for the use of the motif the Christ of the Resurrection at the apex of a tomb. The chapel-tomb of Cardinal Francesco Piccolomini, later Pope Pius III, in the cathedral of Siena, which was begun in 1485 and later continued by Michelangelo, who never completed it, was to have been crowned, according to a letter of 1511, by a 'Cristo in resurrezione', more than *due braccia* (4 ft. high, 1·22 metres) with two smaller child angels with trumpets in their hands flanking it on either side. The connection between the motif of Christ in Resurrection and the believer's hope in the salvation of his soul is obvious, and was already made by the middle of the fifteenth century, when Giovanni Dalmata carved a figure of the enthroned

Christ blessing, with the wound required by the iconography of the Resurrection pierced in his right side, for the tomb of Pope Nicholas V (d. 1455) in St. Peter's.

It is less easy to say if the Aragazzi Christ is a *'Cristo in resurrezione'*. There are no wounds in his side or on his hands, as can be seen very clearly from the left hand, where the wound from the nail would show conspicuously had it ever been marked by the sculptor.[22] Comparison with Luca della Robbia's lunette of the Resurrection, made *c.* 1450 for the door of Sagrestia Vecchia of the Duomo in Florence makes clear these essential differences. As a subject from the cycle of Christ's death and Resurrection the Risen Christ is sometimes shown – in Luca della Robbia's relief, for example – with naked shoulder and breast, which is perhaps what suggested the identification of the Aragazzi Christ as the Risen Christ, the groove in the left hand being supposed to have held the pole of a pennon, Christ's normal attribute in the Resurrection, symbolising his victory over Death. But again comparison with Luca della Robbia's relief shows that in it Christ grasps a true fifteenth-century pennon with a long pole which if stuck in the ground would reach up to his shoulder. From the position of the left hand of the Aragazzi Christ it is obvious that he cannot have held so long a pole, since there is no room for the lower part of it. What he held was clearly the lower end of the short cylindrical stem of a cross, not the middle part of a tall pole. But the presence of the cross is an exceptional feature, and in this sense the conception of the figure was probably influenced by the devotion of the patrons, who wished to affirm their own faith and that of Bartolommeo and Francesco in man's redemption by the cross of Christ. Given the traditional role of Christ on such tombs, the figure can be identified merely from the clouds beneath its feet as a Christ in Glory.

As beautiful as the Christ, perhaps even more beautiful, are the two adoring angels now in the Victoria and Albert Museum (nos. 56–58). Of these the one which faces right is 3 ft. $2\frac{1}{4}$ in. (97·2 cm.) high and 3 ft. $3\frac{1}{2}$ in. (100·3 cm.) wide. His companion is 3 ft. $1\frac{1}{8}$ in. (94 cm.) high and 3 ft. $1\frac{1}{2}$ in. (95 cm.) wide. Unfortunately, they have suffered damage; both have been drastically cleaned, and the lower part of the face and the throat of the other have been destroyed and restored in marble. More complex is the problem of the front wings. In both angels the section of wing adjoining the shoulder is extended by two pieces. These differ in the colour of the surface from the rest of the figures, and it has been suggested that they are a restoration. But in the case of both wings, it is only the colour that differs, and the four pieces are carved in exactly the same manner, including the detailing of the feathers, as the sections of wing adjoining the shoulders of the angels. As it is inherently improbable that a restorer making up or adding a wing would execute a restoration in two pieces, irregularly joined, it becomes important to notice that the shoulder of the rear wing of the left-hand angel was executed by Michelozzo in two separate pieces of marble. If we look at the front wings again with this in mind, we see at once that they are original, but that each was carved in a separate piece of marble, which was originally joined to the first section along the same vertical edge as now. The other two breaks across the tips of the wings are fractures that have been rejoined with the same skill found in the other restorations of these angels. We shall see in a later chapter that there is a perfectly good explanation why Michelozzo allowed himself to carve the wings in marble of a different colour.

Both angels look upwards with their hands crossed across their breasts in adoration, no fluttering of drapery distracting the eye from the steadfastness of their serene absorption in Christ. The convex curves on which their design is based render with marvellous urgency the intensity of their contemplation. As always, they are carefully individualised in dress. The angel in left profile wears a tunic, caught around the chest by a girdle and round the waist by a broad belt, a loop of which dangles below the swell of the gathered stuff. Round his shoulders is a scarf. His companion has a fillet over his brow, and a sleeved shirt buttoned at the ends under his tunic. Above he wears a heavy mantle slung from his left shoulder, with an aperture in the right side forming a great oval whorl of drapery. In Masaccio's fresco of the *Tribute Money* in the Carmine St. Peter wears his cloak in the same fashion, with the same whorl-shaped effect on the right side.

Finally there is a fragment of stone curtain, last seen by Emilio Marcucci in the 1880s in the magazines of the *Opera* of the Duomo of Montepulciano and reproduced by him on the right upper corner of his reconstruction of the tomb (no. 112) where he has used it as the right-hand horizontal loop of his draped curtains. This fragment is said still to exist in Montepulciano, but its whereabouts are unknown.

With sculptures of this period it is natural to ask if a system of proportion was used in designing the two figures in the round, the Christ and the angels. Professor Charles Seymour has suggested that Michelozzo employed the *exempedum* proposed during the 1430s by Alberti in his *De Statua*. According to this canon the module of the foot, repeated six times, gives the measure of the figure. Seymour claims that it is exemplified in the figure to the left of the high altar of the Duomo. This canon would also apply to the companion figure, but it seems not to fit the Christ or the two angels. Possibly therefore some other module, now lost to us with the architecture of the tomb, is the key to the proportioning of the sculptures.[23]

Chapter X · The Tomb Reconstructed · Sant' Agostino and its Sculptures

WITH THE ROMANTIC MOVEMENT and the revival of interest in Christian Art the Aragazzi tomb became once more admired and studied, though at first, because of Vasari's attribution, as a work of Donatello. In 1839 Gaye, publishing part of Michelozzo's *catasto* return of 1427, declared that the tomb was 'one of the loveliest things that ever came from Donatello's chisel' and that 'the two reliefs . . . are superior to any other effort in this kind of work known from his hand.'[1] Charles C. Perkins (1823–86) of Boston, the first historian of Italian sculpture in English, collected the earlier printed references to the tomb with his usual thoroughness, and published the first long admiring account of it in his *Tuscan Sculptors* of 1863. Like his predecessors he too believed the tomb to be by Donatello. 'Nothing . . . in the whole range of Donatello's sculptures surpasses in beauty one of the two bas-reliefs which represents the Madonna seated. . . . All Donatello's best characteristics are to be found in this work, which is admirable in composition, masterly in handling of form and treatment of surface, lovely in the winning grace of the children, and in the perfect sweetness and tenderness of the infant Saviour. The second relief . . . is scarcely less fine. . . .'[2] In October 1879 and May 1880 John Addington Symonds visited Montepulciano and described his impressions in an essay which is a most perfect evocation of the 'lordliest of Tuscan hill-towns', of its skies and landscapes. Symonds was deeply impressed by the fragments of the tomb. 'On the left hand of the central door, as you enter, Aragazzi lies, in senatorial robes, asleep; his head turned slightly to the right upon his pillow, his hands folded over his breast. Very noble are the draperies, and dignified the deep tranquillity of slumber. Here, we say, is a good man fallen upon sleep, awaiting resurrection. The one commanding theme of Christian sculpture, in an age of pagan feeling, has been adequately rendered. . . . This marmoreal repose of the once active man symbolises for our imagination the state into which he passed four centuries ago, but in which, according to the creed, he still abides, reserved for judgement and re-incarnation. The flesh, clad with which he walked our earth, may moulder in the vaults beneath. But it will one day rise again; and art has here presented it imperishable to our gaze. This is how the Christian sculptors, inspired by the majestic calm of classic art, dedicated a Christian to the genius of repose. . . . The boys of Montepulciano have scratched Messer Aragazzi's sleeping figure with *graffiti* at their own free will. Yet they have had no power to erase the poetry of Donatello's mighty style. That, in spite of Bruni's envy, in spite of injurious time, in spite of the still worse insult of the modernised cathedral and the desecrated monument, embalms him in our memory and secures for him the diuturnity for which he paid his twenty-thousand crowns.'

Like all nineteenth-century critics Symonds was captivated by the two reliefs and especially by the 'loveliest interlacement' of the 'masterly panel' of Aragazzi and his family. 'Nothing in the range of Donatello's work surpasses these two bas-reliefs for harmonies of line and grouping, for choice of form, for beauty of expression, and for smoothness of surface-working. The marble is of great delicacy and is wrought to a wax-life surface.' The two statues Symonds identifies as Fortitude and Faith – was he the first to make this mistake? – and perceptively notes: 'The former reminds us of Donatello's St. George; the latter is twisted into a strained attitude, full of character, but lacking grace. What the effect of these emblematic figures would have been when harmonised by the architectural proportions of the sepulchre, the repose of Aragazzi on his sarcophagus, the suavity of the two square panels and the rhythmic beauty of the frieze, it is not easy to conjecture. But rudely severed from their surroundings, and exposed in isolation, one at each side of the altar, they leave an impression of awkward discomfort on the memory. A certain hardness, peculiar to the Florentine manner, is felt in them. But this quality may have been intended by the sculptors for the sake of contrast with what is eminently graceful, peaceful, and melodious in the other fragments of the ruined masterpiece.'

The impressions of another famous visitor must be our last. On 1 November 1890 Paul Bourget spent a night in Montepulciano and drew a sketch of the town in his *Sensations d'Italie*. Unlike Symonds, Bourget was greatly drawn to the two statues of the 'Virtues'.

L'une, prétend-on, représente la Foi. C'est une femme résignée et douce qui tient un flambeau dans sa main. Elle semble sourire à la Mort, puisqu'elle sourit sur un tombeau. . . . L'autre statue est celle d'une femme aussi, aux traits durs, à la chevelure courte et bouclée. Elle serre dans ses bras un encrier. Sans doute sa main a laissé tomber la plume avec laquelle, froidement, elle se préparait à noter une observation. Pas une ride ne défigure son visage, convulsé pourtant d'angoisse; mais sur ce front, autour de ces lèvres encore jeunes, il n'apparaît pas non plus une seule fraîcheur de traits qui permette de croire à la possibilité d'une sensation heureuse, à l'habitude d'un laisser-aller. Toute l'irrémédiable tristesse d'une grande force impuissante se lit sur cette face dont la beauté avait pourtant vaincu la vie, et ce serait la Science, prise d'épouvante devant l'invincible enigme. Jusqu'à cette heure, on le sent, elle a si altièrement suivi sa route, qu'arrêtée en présence d'un problème à jamais insoluble elle ne se rend pas encore. Mais tout son être se crispe, ses yeux ne pleurent pas, sa bouche ne gémit pas, seulement elle ne peut plus bouger, fascinée par un spectacle

> *qui confond sa raison sans qu'elle le nie, stupéfiée de ce qu'elle comprend et ne comprend pas. Le mélange de réalisme et d'Idéal tourmenté qui se lit sur ce visage, l'âpre sécheresse de facture avec laquelle toute la statue est traitée et son intensité d'expression transforment cette oeuvre, conçue en pleine Renaissance, en une illustration anticipée d'un poème de Poe ou de Baudelaire. Cette créature est si touchante à la fois et si sèche, si désespérément malade et brisée, et pourtant l'orgueil en elle corrompt la douleur. Cet orgueil empêche, il empechera toujours que la tristesse ne devienne l'élément de salut et de révélation. Cette âme angoissée souffrira indéfiniment sans rien faire qu'ajouter la souffrance à la souffrance, comme les ténèbres s'ajoutent aux ténèbres et dans une nuit qui n'aura pas d'aurore. . . .*

And believing that it is '*un grand principe en voyage, de rester sur une sensation d'extrême beauté quand on l'a rencontrée,*' Bourget looked at no other work of art in Montepulciano, satisfied with his vision of '*une cathédrale où frémit à jamais ce marbre dans lequel j'aime à reconnâitre l'image de la Science impuissante.*'[3]

But now together with critics and travellers, content to receive and to express only the impressions of the moment, came architects and scholars, anxious to reconstruct the monument in its original form. The first published attempt was the work of Ingegnere Emilio Marcucci of Bibbiena, in 1885. Marcucci, who had been commissioned to make a design for a projected restoration of the tomb, sent his drawings (no. 112) to exhibitions in Florence and Bologna and also had them reproduced in the architectural journal, *Ricordi di Architettura.*[4] Marcucci assumed that the tomb rose directly from the ground and that the frieze now set on the high altar was its base. He therefore made the frieze the facing of a low plinth, on which he set pilasters about two feet from the front to frame the tomb and create a deep recess. From each of the console-capitals of these pilasters he hung a shield bearing the Aragazzi arms. The recess he topped by a heavy entablature, whose frieze echoed the design of the frieze at the base, and he surmounted the whole by a canopy copied from the canopy of the Brancaccio tomb. On the plinth he placed the sarcophagus, supporting it on six feet shaped as stag-heads in allusion to the charges of the Aragazzi arms. On the front of the sarcophagus he set the two reliefs, placing that of Aragazzi and his family to the left, and framing them with pilasters of which the middle one was made broader and decorated with a *targhetta* for the inscription. The effigy he laid, not immediately on the sarcophagus, but on a bier. The sarcophagus stood partly within and partly without the recess, flanked by the two statues in the round, which were placed in front of the pilasters in the same relation to each other as now on either side of the high altar. From the top of the recess he hung a canopy modelled on that of the Cossa tomb. Beneath this, on the rear wall of the niche, he set the figure of Christ Blessing in a flaming mandorla. The background of the recess was richly patterned, and in the centre of the canopy was a medallion encircling a bust of Aragazzi turned in three-quarter profile to the left on a shell-shaped ground. Marcucci's death fortunately prevented the execution of this astonishing project.[5]

Although Marcucci's reconstruction was entirely fantastic, mingling motifs from the early and late *quattrocento* in the unhappiest and most unhistorical way, and with no use of evidence from documents to support its too imaginative recreation of the original appearance of the monument, much of it was taken over by Fritz Burger in 1904[6] for what purported to be a more scholarly reconstruction (no. 113). By 1904 Bode had attributed the two angels in the Victoria and Albert Museum to Michelozzo and to the Aragazzi tomb, and Burger arranged his design so as to accommodate them. He kept to Marcucci's general lines: the frieze in the base, a recess framed by pilasters and surmounted by a canopy, the effigy resting on a bier, set on the sarcophagus, the two statues flanking the sarcophagus in front of the pilasters. His only changes are made in a purist spirit. The frieze now rests on a plinth, like the frieze of the base of the Cossa tomb. The sarcophagus rests on four claw feet, the shields have been taken down from the pilasters, the console-shaped capitals have been removed to make room for more orthodox early *quattrocento* capitals supporting volutes on which the cornice is made to rest. The canopy itself is a correct classical pediment enclosing a rather Baroque motif of a circular laurel wreath with two pendant swags. Burger's great change was in the recess. Marcucci's curtain and mandorla are swept away and Christ is set against the background without any frame. Around Him are four adoring angels, two on either side of His shoulders, two – those now in the Victoria and Albert Museum – on either side of His legs, their lower part being concealed by the effigy. And having recognised the blessing figure as a Christ, Burger gave Him the long cross He undoubtedly held and to all four angels complete wings.

Both these reconstructions are so arbitrary as to be useless, and we must attack the problem of the original design of the tomb as if they had never been made. A first and great difficulty is Bruni's mention in his letter of two effigies, one representing Bartolommeo Aragazzi, the other his father Francesco. There are no known precedents in Tuscan tomb-sculpture for two effigies and on this rather narrow ground some scholars have doubted Bruni's testimony. Fortunately the documents assembled by Fabriczy and another document which has lain for centuries unpublished in the Archivio Vescovile of Montepulciano make it possible at last to solve this and the other mysteries of the tomb in so far as the disappearance of so many of its parts permits.

This document is so crucial, clearing away as it does some fundamental misconceptions, that we must begin by studying it so as to establish the framework within which the tomb has to be reassembled. In 1584 Pope Pius V, as part of his campaign to enforce on the Church at large the stricter regulations of the Council of Trent, ordered a general visitation of all dioceses in order that scandals and abuses might be discovered and removed. The visitation of Montepulciano was carried out by the Reverend and Illustrious Angelo Peruzzi, Bishop of Sarsina. Monsignor Peruzzi began his visitation on 30 January in the Duomo, still it will be recalled, the old Pieve of Santa Maria, going from chapel to chapel, examining, criticising, and recommending while his remarks were carefully noted by an attendant ecclesiastic, to be entered up in a formal record which was then preserved for the use of the next Visitor. In due course he reached the Aragazzi chapel, on the right-hand side of the high altar.

> The altar of Sant' Angelo is of brick, with its own portable altar and furnished with a decent enough frontal, but it does not have suitable candlesticks and so (the Visitor) ordered that care be taken to provide candlesticks and a decent cross. To this altar are attached two beneficed titles, of which the first is called Sant' Angelo the first, which is held by the Reverend Canon and Abbot Fiorenzo Bellarmino. It has as real property sixty *staia* of good ploughland and a house in the city with the obligation of saying mass on alternate Sundays and on two days of every week and with a tax for the University. The other title is called Sant' Angelo the Second, and is held by Don Giulio Cini, canon of this same Church. As its real property it has one piece of good ploughland of four *staia* or there-abouts, a vineyard and a house and as was alleged also an olive grove, both bordering (the house) with the obligation of saying mass on alternate Sundays and on two days in the week and both chaplaincies are called whole chaplaincies. . .
> And when the same Reverend Visitor saw that on the altar itself there was no picture but in place of a picture there was a marble sarcophagus (*loco Icone haberi sepulchrum unum marmoreum*) with two marble statues and other very many figures carved in the marble itself, made as it appeared in the year 1438 with bronze plaques and an inscription of this tenor, viz. *Amatori patriae Conseruatori Rei-publicae, Bartholomeo/doctissimo apud Martinum Quintum Pontificem Max.ᵐ/ Consiliorum omnium participi, immature absumpto/posteri dedicauerunt et bene-merenti.* And on the base of the said sarcophagus there is this other inscription, viz. *Fidelis affinis, et Compatriota mihi executor fuit/Ser Joannes bart.ᵉⁱ anno dñi 1438.*
> Which the same Most Reverend Lord Visitor judged extremely indecent, and ordered the tomb itself to be removed from thence forthwith and in its place to be put a handsome painting or picture with the image of that same saint to whom the said benefices are entitled. If this cannot be done without scandal, he ordered the tomb itself to be removed, and the titles to be taken away and transferred to another of the altars in the said church with all their honours and obligations and rights and appurtenances.[7]

It was the second of Monsignor Peruzzi's alternatives that was adopted. During the second visitation of the diocese of Montepulciano, held in 1610, 'the Most Reverend Lord Visitor found that the command concerning the demolishing of the altar of Sant' Angelo had been fulfilled according to the form of the command made in the Apostolic Visitation, which he approved, and was informed that the two titles of the benefices, the one of Sant' Angelo the first and the other of Sant' Angelo the second have been transferred to the altar of Santa Caterina. The first is held by Don Lodovico Aragazzi. . . .' The altar of Santa Caterina was the next altar but one in the church: Peruzzi had recommended in 1585 that at least one of the two chaplaincies should be transferred to it. Seven years later, in October 1617, by which date all the altars of the old church to which chaplaincies were attached had been demolished, Cardinal Roberto Ubaldini, another Visitor, transferred them once again, this time to the new altar of the Holy Sacrament. Both still exist in the cathedral.[8]

To a scandalised Counter-Reformation bishop, then, we owe the only known description of the Aragazzi tomb before its demolition. It is only a partial description, for the Visitor was not concerned with describing a work of art, but merely with the immediate removal of that part of it which was offensive, namely the sarcophagus, standing as it did in the position that ought to have been occupied by a holy image to attract the devotion of the faithful. Nevertheless the Visitation establishes that the altar was a combination of altar and tomb, in fact the *cappella seu sepultura* of the contemporary documents. It also establishes three other significant facts. The first is that the tomb did not rise immediately from the ground, like the Cossa and Brancaccio tombs, but began several feet above it, probably rather above some 3 ft. 11 in. (1·14 metres), the height of the altar of 1432 in the Old Sacristy of San Lorenzo. The space beneath was occupied by a brick altar, which as we shall see, was probably set against a plinth supporting the main structure of the tomb. The tomb began then above the rear of the altar, occupying the place of an altarpiece. And we now know that there was indeed a second effigy resting on the sarcophagus, and that Francesco's image lay beside that of his son, as that son had ordered in his will.

The first piece to consider in fitting together the surviving fragments of the tomb is the great frieze now set in the high altar of the Duomo, measuring as we saw 12 ft. $\frac{7}{8}$ in. (3·68 metres) by 2 ft. $4\frac{3}{4}$ in. (73 cm.). From the description in the Visitation it is clear that the position it now occupies corresponds to its original position and that it was set above the altar like a predella. The mystery of why it has suffered no damage from feet and brooms is therefore explained: it was always set at a height above the ground. The altar in front of it may have been so designed as to leave room for two caryatid figures of Virtues on either side, as on the tomb of Cardinal Enrico Minutolo in the Duomo of Naples (no. 103). But in the Minutolo tomb the design is so managed that the Virtues support the sarcophagus, which on this account is made longer than the altar and predella beneath. For this there is good iconographical reason. The function of Virtues on tombs is to support the sarcophagus: placed elsewhere they lose their symbolic role in the general iconography. Since the Aragazzi sarcophagus was shorter than the carved base on which it rested, as we shall see, immediately above the altar, there was no room for supporting Virtues even at its corners. Hence it is virtually certain that no Virtues formed part of the tomb unless they were carved in relief on extensions of a plinth to either side of the altar, a very doubtful possibility.

The two sides of the base measure $6\frac{7}{8}$ in. (17·5 cm.). At the end of each of them is a ring from which the garland held by the child angels is suspended. The ribbon that hangs beneath the top of the ring and the cut-off bow that fastens the garland to it are purely decorative devices for filling space, and the sides as we have them are evidently complete. But since they are so short they cannot be taken as indicating the entire depth of the monument. It follows that the base served as a decorative frontal to a deeper whole created by the columns or pilasters that Bruni saw lying in the carts on the road to Montepulciano. There are two possibilities about the placing of these columns or pilasters. The first is that they stood at the corners of the base as we have it now. But there is no trace either of the mortar or of the damage that we should expect if columns had been set on those corners and then taken down: hence this is a most implausible hypothesis. The alternative is that they stood on extensions of the base attached to the ends of the sides. And since the rear edges of the sides do not terminate in a moulded border, the presumption must be that an additional member was indeed joined to them. On these then the columns or pilasters stood.

At this date the Latin term *columna* was used indiscriminately both of columns and pilasters, and it is not possible to assert positively whether it was pieces of column or pilaster or indeed of both that Bruni saw lying in the carts. If the front of the tomb was framed by columns, then it was presumably open at the sides, like the Brancaccio tomb. Given the design of the base, the height to which the sarcophagus was raised, and the presence of two effigies, the arguments in favour of this solution are strong.

From the description in the Visitation it is obvious that the sarcophagus rested on the carved base, immediately above the altar. For what scandalised Monsignor Peruzzi was the usurpation by a tomb containing uncanonised bones of the place of an altarpiece. By the stricter notions of the Counter-Reformation he was quite justified, for this is an honour that ought to be reserved for the bones of saints and even to them is rarely accorded. If a row of frontal statues of saints or of the Divine persons had decorated the base his scandal might have been less. But the child angels who decorate it did not placate him, for they are not posed in the proper relationship of image to worshipper. We can also deduce that although the tomb presented several representations of Divine personages, of which that in the relief of Aragazzi and his family in adoration of the Virgin and Child was nearest to the ground, none of them were set in a position that made them suitable for worship in the eyes of Peruzzi's orthodox post-Tridentine piety. Indeed the first thing which the sarcophagus offered to the eye was the inscription commemorating Ser Giovanni di Bartolommeo's merits as an executor, for this was inscribed on its 'pedestal', by which Peruzzi evidently meant the moulded base which it must have possessed like all sarcophagi of its date and kind.

Extraordinary as such a disposition now seems, in the laxer days a century and a half before the Council of Trent it had not been so uncommon as Monsignor Peruzzi's indignation might suggest. It was, for instance, not unusual in Naples, where the tomb of Cardinal Minutolo (no. 103) is still a striking example of it.[9] And other similar tombs must have been dismantled in Naples and elsewhere because of post-Tridentine disapproval. One still survives in Venice, the now fragmentary tomb of Doge Marco Cornaro (d. 1368) in SS. Giovanni e Paolo.[10] The arrangement was in fact a natural, if extreme development of the practice of placing monumental tombs in funerary chapels immediately behind the altar, where they would make a constant appeal to the prayers of the celebrant and worshippers. But unlike the Aragazzi tomb the Minutolo and Cornaro tombs both mitigated the irregularity in some way. The Cornaro tomb has a carved altarpiece with statues of the Virgin and Child, saints and angels in niches above the effigy, while the Minutolo tomb has a row of saints in niches in a predella above the altar and a *Nativity* carved on the central panel of the sarcophagus.

Since Aragazzi's effigy is 6 ft. 6¾ in. (200 cm.) long, the sarcophagus, according to custom, can have measured only a few inches more, protruding a little beyond the head and feet. Its front face will have been recessed in relation to the lid and base, which were surely moulded, like the lid and base on the Cossa and Brancaccio sarcophagi. On its front face, as has always been recognised, and as Peruzzi's description now proves, were set the two sarcophagus reliefs. A detail of their execution implies that they were set above eye-level; the hair of the children in the relief of Aragazzi and his family is only lightly modelled at the back, with rather slight indications of the forms, which by contrast are strongly and fully marked at the front. As we have seen, neither relief has borders at the sides, and originally they must have been framed by pilasters like those on the Brancaccio tomb. Possibly they were slightly recessed within their framework like Donatello's *Assumption*, but if so for decorative rather than for spatial effect.

Trecento and early *quattrocento* sarcophagi carved with two reliefs are unusual: most have either a single relief extending their entire length or more frequently three reliefs, either a single central subject-relief framed by panels containing heraldry or other symbols, as on the Brancaccio tomb, or a central subject-relief flanked by panels containing saints. But as we shall see the presence of two subject-reliefs is explained by the iconography of the tomb. The Peruzzi Visitation also implies that the bronze plaque inscribed with Aragazzi's epitaph (now 27 cm. in height) was set on the sarcophagus, where indeed one might expect to find it. The reliefs are both 2 ft. $5\frac{1}{2}$ in. (75 cm.) wide, and the plaque is $8\frac{1}{4}$ in. (19·5 cm.) wide, so that the reliefs must have been placed to either side of a narrower central section in or on which the plaque was set. In or on, for the plaque may either have been set on a blind panel or else sunk in a specially shaped recess. It is now broken, and the shield bearing three stags' heads described by Benci and the last two lines of the inscription as given by Peruzzi are entirely missing. When complete, its probable height was about 35 cm. to 40 cm. Indeed the likeliest figure is about 39 cm., which is half the height of the reliefs to either side. This figure allows approximately 2·4 cm. for each of the missing two lines of the inscription, and about 7 cm. for the stags' heads and a blank space to set them off. Assuming that the plaque was set on a blind panel and that each pilaster was approximately 2 in. (5 cm.) wide, we find that a width of approximately 2 in. would be left on either side. But this can only be a speculation, and the front may have been rather differently scanned. Clearly Michelozzo intended the inscription, which could not be conspicuously lettered on the monument, should stand out by reason of the size and the rich dark brown colour of the plaque and by means of its letters in relief. Its tall vertical shape would also draw the eye.

It will already have been noted that the Visitation speaks of bronze plaques in the plural – either from a slip of the pen, or else because Ser Giovanni's inscription on the 'pedestal' was also lettered on a bronze plaque. The way in which the description in the Visitation is set out suggests that the second alternative is the more likely.

If the sarcophagus extended to about 7 ft. (2·13 metres), then there would have been a graceful interval of at least $2\frac{1}{2}$ ft. (76 cm.) between it and the framework on either side. In reality the interval was probably larger, depending on how far away the columns or pilasters of the framework stood on the wings of the plinth. From the measurements of the effigies it is possible to calculate more exactly the approximate depth of the sarcophagus. The effigy of Aragazzi measures 1 ft. $6\frac{7}{8}$ in. (48 cm.) across and the effigy of Francesco must have measured very much the same. They would have been laid side by side with a small interval between them, and with a little space at the wall side, so that at the very least the sarcophagus must have been about 3 ft. 10 in. (1·17 metres) to 4 ft. (1·22 metres) deep and possibly a little more. Aragazzi's effigy was evidently the outer one, if only because the bronze tassels of his pillow clearly overhung the edge of the sarcophagus just as those of Cossa's pillow overhang the edge of his bier. The side of his effigy lay therefore more or less flush with the edge of the sarcophagus, like the effigy of

Brancaccio. We can also surmise the approximate height of the sarcophagus: since the reliefs are 2 ft. 6¾ in. (78 cm.) high, the whole sarcophagus chest, including base and lid, will not have been less than about 3 ft. 10 in. to 4 ft. (1·17 metres to 1·22 metres) high.

There were in fact precedents in other parts of Italy for placing two effigies on one sarcophagus on family tombs. One parallel may be cited here because it is so close in date to the Aragazzi tomb, the tomb of Francesco and Niccolò dell' Anguillara (d. 1406 and 1408) in the church of San Francesco at Capranica, near Sutri in Latium (no. 124). And the tradition continued late into the century, for on Agostino di Duccio's tomb of Matteo and Elisabetta Geraldini, erected in 1477 in San Francesco, Amelia, but carved in Perugia, not far from Montepulciano, husband and wife lie side by side on the same sarcophagus. Indeed Agostino's tomb (no. 122) certainly betrays a knowledge of the Aragazzi tomb and perhaps gives us some idea of how Bartolommeo and Francesco lay side by side.[11]

A more problematical question is whether the effigies were horizontal, or, as on the Anguillara and Geraldini tombs, tilted. It will already have become obvious that they were set at a level at least 9 ft. (2·74 metres) above the ground, the height arrived at by adding the probable heights of the altar and sarcophagus to that of the base without making any allowance for the possibility that the whole tomb was raised on a low step. Set so far aloft, would both effigies have been visible if the surface on which they lay was horizontal? Almost certainly not. Now as we saw, the Cossa and Brancaccio tombs show a consciousness of the problem of keeping the effigy visible while raising it to the lofty height consonant with the deceased's high estate. Cossa's head, it will be recalled, is turned outwards in part answer to the difficulty, and Aragazzi's head is also turned outwards for the same reason. But this device can in no way have helped to disclose the parallel effigy of his father. Yet from the account of Peruzzi we know that both effigies were visible.

It is therefore worthy of notice that whoever re-set Aragazzi's effigy in 1815 set it at a tilt, deliberately so, for the effigy of Francesco de' Piendibeni, which was re-set at the same time in a matching niche on the other side of the main doorway is laid flat. Another point which may not be without significance in this connection is that the upper borders of the two reliefs are bevelled, whereas the lower borders are plane. The tilted effigy, if unusual in Tuscany, was common elsewhere in Italy, both in the *trecento* and during many decades of the *quattrocento*. All these arguments amount to a strong presumption that the lid of the Aragazzi tomb was also tilted. If it was so, then in all probability its further side was attached to the rear wall of the tomb recess for further support. It is also likely that the sarcophagus rested directly on the floor of the recess, not on feet, and that the effigies rested directly on the sarcophagus, as had always been usual in tomb design before the Cossa tomb.

We must now turn to the two figures in the round standing on either side of the high altar. While these were identified as Virtues, it was impossible for iconographical reasons to place them anywhere except below the sarcophagus. Indeed it has even been claimed that they were caryatids which supported the sarcophagus like those of the Brancaccio tomb. But this is one function that they can never have performed. No sarcophagus was ever sustained by their hands, or even uplifted on their heads, for the hair of both is delicately chiselled and finished, with grooves marking out the separate locks and their forms and with no sign of the abrasion they must have suffered if they had supported a sarcophagus. Where then did they stand on the tomb? The answer lies in their identity. The clue to this is supplied by the broken-off attribute held by the figure standing to the left of the altar. This is the foot of a candlestick, and the figure is therefore that of an angel. Pairs of angels holding candlesticks had been common on altars and tombs from the early *trecento* and possibly from at least the late *dugento*. Two, for example, stand on either side of Giovanni Pisano's marble Madonna and Child on the Scrovegni chapel altar in Padua (executed *c.* 1305–6): allowing for differences of date and style, they are strikingly similar in pose and dress to Michelozzo's figure (no. 114). There are also candlestick-bearing angels on other *trecento* altars. Alberto Arnoldi made two for example to attend his Virgin and Child (1359–64) on the altar of the Bigallo, and two are set on the altar-piece above the effigy of Doge Marco Cornaro. Angels holding candlesticks also appear on the sarcophagi of tombs in North Italy and the Veneto, notably on the tomb of Jacopo da Carrara, now in the Eremitani, Padua (commissioned 1351).

The other figure is rather differently dressed and holds what at first sight appears to be a very different attribute (no. 64). Yet in reality it is only a more magnificent form of candle, for it is a *tortitia*, that is, a great cannelated wax torch of the kind used at splendid ceremonies both religious and secular. Both tapers and *tortitiae* were employed in funerals, of which they made one of the great expenses. It was customary to give *tortitiae* to the principal mourners and great dignitaries, as we saw in Del Corazza's account of the ceremonies after Cossa's death, while lesser personages held tapers. The cannelated shape of the *tortitia* is already found imitated in stone in the great Paschal candlesticks made during the thirteenth century in Latium and Rome, and the form has survived in Italy for large candles to this day. The bearer of this great gilded candle can therefore be identified as a second angel. Angels bearing *tortitiae* of this form are shown in the relief of the *Death of the Virgin* from the tomb of Cardinal Philippe d'Alençon (d. 1403) in Santa Maria in Trastevere, which incidentally before its dismemberment was another tomb set immediately above an altar. They bear them too in the Botticelli work-shop tondo of the *Virgin and Child attended by seven angels*, in East Berlin.

Wax was costly in itself during the Middle Ages, and in addition candles for great ceremonies were often elaborately painted or gilded. At the saint's mass in St. Peter's which concluded the canonisation of St. Brigit of Sweden on 8 October 1391, the Cardinal of France, one of the commission of three cardinals who had concluded the process, brought as his oblation 'two great lighted *tortitiae* covered with gold' – just like the attribute of our figure. And the advocate and each of the five proctors of the cause offered a large candle of white wax 'worked with roses and flowers, green, white and red.'[12]

His great gilded torch indicates that this angel is of higher rank than his companion. His youthful aspect and the martial nature and set of his dress, the latter so obviously modelled, we remember, on that of Donatello's *David* are other pointers to his identity, which is established beyond doubt by the dedication of the altar and chapel to Sant' Angelo, that is Michael, Prince of the Archangels. We have already seen in discussing the Brancaccio tomb that Michael, greatest of the archangels, and therefore of those two lowest degrees of angels who descend to earth on the errands of Heaven, was the protector of the souls of the dead and their conductor to judgement and the Beatific Vision. We saw too that for this reason he often received the dedication of funerary chapels such as Aragazzi's. Yet although it may have been this dedication that led to the representation of so mighty an archangel as a mourner at the tomb, we know from the scandal expressed by Peruzzi that he did not stand above the altar in the orthodox central position for veneration.

There is nothing remarkable in the presence of these two angels, for we have seen that angels often appear on tombs, sometimes simply coming to fetch the soul of the dead man, sometimes performing the last rites or mourning at his exequies. What part do they play on the Aragazzi tomb? The answer is they are mourners taking part in his exequies before carrying his soul into Heaven. The lesser angel holds the humbler candlestick of the mourner of lesser degree, Michael the *tortitia* of the great dignitary. The iconography then exalts the virtues of the deceased: so great were they that the angels share in the grief and reverence of man.

To this, the entire sentiment of the tomb, we shall return when we come to discuss its iconography as a whole. At the moment it is more pressing to consider where and how the two angels were placed on the tomb. Angels might be placed behind the sarcophagus, like the angels of the Brancaccio tomb, but the elaborate working of the front view of both figures suggests that this was not the convention Michelozzo observed on the Aragazzi tomb. Moreover, the sarcophagus was very deep and there is a high degree of probability, as we have seen, that it was attached to the wall at the rear. More important still, the poses of the two figures, with the lesser angel looking downwards in profile on the effigies beneath while Michael turns his eyes on them with imperial serenity imply that they stood apart, at some distance from each other. Clearly then they were set in the most frequent position of all, to either side of the sarcophagus, even though they are not drawing back the curtains of the death-bed like most angels set in this position. Again the conclusion is forced on us that the early nineteenth-century placing of the figures on either side of the high altar designedly reproduced their original position on the tomb so far as was possible, and that they stood Michael to the right and the other angel to the left, possibly a little to the rear of the front of the sarcophagus. Once their true identity and placing are established and with them their role in the meaning of the tomb, their artistic conception can be understood. Far from being the stiff and frozen figures they have been called, they participate in the action of the tomb with the serene and dignified emotion of angels: seen contemplating the effigies, they had a dramatic meaning which they have now lost, so that their action seems strained and empty of significance.

Since there was an interval of at least $2\frac{1}{2}$ ft. (76 cm.) on either side between the end of the sarcophagus and the framework, the two angels would have fitted into the space allowed even by this narrowest calculation. But the need to isolate them a little in space without too much cramping is an additional argument for believing that the framework rested on wings extending from either side of the present base. It is also an argument for thinking that the front supports of the tomb were columns, not pilasters. Above the sarcophagus, filling almost all the entire height of the upper section, was the figure of Christ, His hand raised in blessing looking down on the two effigies below, the two angels in adoration on either side. We can be sure that this group formed the entire upper section if only because of the height of the Christ, which is 6 ft. $\frac{1}{2}$ in. (1·85 metres), it will be remembered. And since the tomb must already have been at least $12\frac{1}{2}$ ft. (3·81 metres) high below the cornice, it is obvious that there cannot have been further figures above the Christ. Moreover a figure of Christ blessing forms the iconographical culmination of all such tombs. It will become evident when we discuss the iconography of the two reliefs why there can have been no intermediate figures of saints or of the Virgin and Child interceding for the souls of the deceased. Here it is enough to stress the benign and gracious aspect of Christ as He looks down on Bartolommeo and Francesco.

There still remain two problems. How were the adoring angels related to the Christ, and what was the design of the framework that enclosed the upper part of the tomb? The angels have not been truncated at the base and there can have been no additional figures in the composition, if only because of their great size. Yet as set on the tomb itself they cannot simply have been severed just below the knee-line as they are now: the effect would have been much too abrupt, even when seen from several feet below. There must have been a feature that softened and at the same time rationalised such a termination. Like the Christ, in fact, and like so many other adoring angels in *quattrocento* art, they must have been borne on clouds. And this is no arbitrary solution. It explains the oval hollow in the right corner of the lower edge of the angel on the left, and the similar hollow in the left corner of the lower edge of the angel on the right. Into these there evidently fitted small clouds shaped as pointed ovals like the original marble clouds that still remain beneath the feet of Christ. On the tomb cloud motifs of this kind must have had a certain structural value, serving as pedestals to help in supporting the weight of the figures. If we follow the angle of the eyes of the angels as they look upwards at Christ, we see that they must have been placed with their heads slightly below His shoulder level. As they are virtually half the size, this must have created a satisfying division of the Christ into four equal parts, of which they filled the middle two. It is possible that a cornice ran below the feet of Christ, if only because his feet extend forwards to a degree that would have made a swelling group of clouds beneath them protrude rather forcibly if set independently of such a cornice. Such a feature would also have helped to carry the weight of the figure.

The width of the angels and Christ, if added together, gives a total of 9 ft. $\frac{1}{8}$ in. (2·75 metres). An interval must be allowed between the heads of the angels and the figure of Christ, and also some space behind the tips of the wings of the angels, so that we should reckon about 12 ft. (3·66 metres) for the total span of the rear wall of the upper section. This corresponds very well with the dimensions of the frieze at the base of the tomb, which measures, as we recall, 12 ft. $\frac{7}{8}$ in. (3·68 metres). There still remain two problems. In the first place, how did Michelozzo conceal the different colour of the marble pieces in which he carved the front wings of the angels and the joins in the marble? These features of the two angels suggest that the tips of their wings as well as their rear sides were concealed by the curtains of which, as we have seen, a fragment still survives. These were presumably draped to simulate bed-curtains like those on the Brancaccio tomb, and were no doubt looped up in the same way (see no. 57) to disclose the heavenly vision of Christ justifying Francesco and Bartolommeo.

The presence of the curtain explains the shape of the lower right edge of the right-hand angel. The corresponding or lower left-hand edge of his companion angel is a pleasing silhouette, but the lower right-hand edge of the right-hand angel is less satisfactory in outline. Certainly the loss in its upper section of part of the rounded fold on the return edge of the scarf has distorted the form here, for the curved folds of the scarf below are continued on the edge, so that in this area it is evidently complete. By contrast the edge of the four final folds belonging to the tunic beneath is left rough, but bears chisel marks, suggesting that it has been shaped. Evidently it was concealed by a drape of the curtain.

If the relationships of these three figures in the upper part of the tomb have been recomposed correctly, then it offered a rather more contemporary treatment of space than the two reliefs in the sarcophagus. For the poses of the angels, with their fore-shortened rear wings and their free movement imply a three-dimensional treatment of space, though Michelozzo with his severer sense of design and robustly austere and generalising sculptural style probably did not attempt the pictorial richness of Ghiberti or the atmospheric unity of Donatello. The different spatial conception of the upper part signalises the oscillation imposed by the revival of the antique on an early *quattrocento* sculptor. At this date humanistic art had to catch most of its knowledge of the antique from sarcophagi – these must have prompted Michelozzo to emulate a classical relief style on a sarcophagus of his own carving. Yet even on the sarcophagus the nature of his subject-matter demanded a Christian imagery which drew Michelozzo to the spatial naturalism of his own time, and led him to produce in the relief of Aragazzi receiving the Virgin's blessing a work suspended, so to speak, between classical and modern relief style. In the upper part he had for reasons of iconography to represent the infinite of Heaven, and here naturalism of spatial treatment had to be unhampered. And as we shall see, after his neo-classical enthusiasms had worn off it seems that Michelozzo returned to the gentle naturalism, with some classical borrowings, in which early *quattrocento* Florence had nurtured him. The austerity of the three figures implies that Michelozzo did enough in the upper part of the tomb to create an illusion of depth, but avoided any elaboration of detail that might interfere with the sculptural purity of his composition.

Can we determine the design of the framework which enclosed the upper part of the tomb? On iconographical grounds alone the probability is that there were no figures above the Christ and angels. The rear wall of the upper section was in all likelihood framed by pilasters, on the analogy of the Brancaccio tomb, and these were surely united to the two columns at the front of the tomb by transverse architraves. It is the form of the topmost section of all that poses the most intriguing problem. As the tomb was executed during a decade which was still one of transition it may well have incorporated both Gothic and Renaissance forms, and been topped by a lunette in mixed style as on the Brancaccio tomb. But we must take very seriously the possibility that for the first time on any Renaissance tomb an arch of pure antique form rose above the head of Christ, enclosing the whole depth of the recess. For there is one factor that might well have inclined Michelozzo to use an antique arch for his framework. A lunette would have added considerably to the height of the tomb, which must already have risen some 17 ft. (5·18 metres) above the ground at the level of the top of Christ's head. An arch on the other hand would have provided a suitably monumental termination without adding so greatly to the tomb. If an arch was used, the Aragazzi tomb was the prototype of the great

214

tombs of Renaissance Florence – those of Leonardo Bruni and Carlo Marsuppini, for example, to name only the most famous – in which an arch
imposes a unifying framework on the whole.

Now that we have more or less reconstructed the tomb, it becomes possible
to interpret its iconography. To begin with the two reliefs. That in which
Aragazzi clasps the hand of the grave matron has always been recognised as a
representation of Bartolommeo and other members of his family, but it has
usually been interpreted as a scene in which he bids farewell to them on his
departure for the shores of death. From what we now know of the Aragazzi
family it is obvious that this must be a mistaken interpretation, since Bartolommeo survived his mother and all his brothers and sisters except Antonia.
Bode approached the right answer when he suggested that the group is a
representation of the deceased and his family of a kind found on ancient
tomb-reliefs.[14] The dominating figure is Bartolommeo's dead mother. The
three youths and the three putti, who are either wholly naked or lightly
draped in classical costume must be his dead brothers. The girl in the right
background must also be a near relation, surely a sister, for all she seems
to watch rather than to take part in the action. She too must be dead, since
she wears an ideal classical costume. In all probability a sad history of death
from the plague lies behind this scene of a dead mother and her six or seven
dead children. During the late fourteenth century a number of plagues
swept Tuscany; that of 1399–1400 was particularly terrible, almost as terrible
as the Black Death of 1348 itself. It was not unusual for the plague to destroy
whole families or the greater part of them: the devout Sienese notary Ser
Cristofano Guidini, for example, records that he lost his wife and six of his
seven children in little more than a month during the plague of 1390.[15] The
dates of Francesco Aragazzi's later marriages, so far as they can be conjectured, seem to point to just these years for the death of his first wife. The
cleric who stands on the right contemplating the scene with eyes raised
upwards must also be a dead relation: he cannot be Bartolommeo's uncle
Jacopo if only because he is not a representation of a very old man – Jacopo,
it will be remembered, was eighty years of age in 1429. Probably he is a maternal or paternal uncle who died before the tomb was carved.

By linking all the figures through gesture or expression Michelozzo has
emphasised the intensity of a family's love. But unlike the classical reliefs
which inspired it the relief is not a static group portrait: the main group is
moved by more than the expression of deep affection. Two of the youths
raise their hands in an eager salutation of welcome to Aragazzi on the extreme right, and the putti are jumping for joy. There can only be one explanation of these gestures. What we are shown is Aragazzi's reunion in Heaven
with his mother and his dead brothers and two other near relatives, one
probably a sister. The scene of the second relief is also set in Heaven. The

215

cleric now makes one with the others, resting one hand on Bartolommeo's shoulder and the other on the side of the Virgin's throne with an innocent familiarity which speaks the homeliness of the society to which he and his sculptor belonged. The Child smiles on Bartolommeo, pressing His left hand on His chest, but it is His mother, not He, who lays a blessing hand on Bartolommeo's head. And in that blessing hand laid on Bartolommeo's head the relief differs from other representations of a dead man praying for the intercession of the Virgin. The Virgin's gesture means that the praying Bartolommeo has received the grace of her prayer to her Son for mercy on his soul and His gracious and benign acceptance of her prayer.

There exists at least one close earlier parallel to this scene, a relief (no. 116) of the 1330s attributed to Tino di Camaino which is now in the National Gallery, Washington. It shows the Virgin seated on a throne, blessing a kneeling woman presented to her by St. Clare on the left, while the Child, standing on her left knee, raises His hand in blessing. St. Francis stands on the right: behind him and the kneeling woman stand two adoring angels, while above two more angels hold a rich cloth of state – the Gothic equivalent of Michelozzo's Renaissance garland – behind the Virgin.[16] The cleric and Bartolommeo's mother stand in token of their dignity as the elder members of the family. It is possible that they rest their hands on the shoulders of its younger members to testify that they have guided them in the way of Christ – certainly some such feeling, rather than the mere desire to squeeze so many persons into two compact groups, must account for their stance in an attitude resembling that of patron saints, which would otherwise be so irreverent in mere mortals permitted to approach the Virgin's throne. Indeed their gestures seem chosen to suggest that even though they are not patron saints – who present mankind to the Virgin with a different gesture of the hands – yet they are the human counterparts of saints. And since no saints figure on the tomb, there is even stronger reason for thinking that those who commissioned the reliefs felt a pious reverence for the memory of the cleric, and for that of Bartolommeo's mother, whom we know from Bruni's scathing reference to have been so deeply devout.

The majestic full-length figure of Christ blessing, though mightier and grander in aspect than the little half-length figures of Christ blessing on earlier tombs, symbolises just as they do the hoped-for admission of the deceased to Paradise and the Beatific Vision. Here the manner of His appearance, standing on clouds, adored by angels, looking down benignantly on the effigies beneath, His hand raised over them in blessing, declares that He has justified the soul of Bartolommeo, according to His promise to His Mother in the relief below. Hence the angels and the blessed welcome Aragazzi and Christ receives him into glory as the great words in the first part of the commendation service in the Roman Breviary beseech that he will be welcomed and received. 'I commend thee, very dear brother, to God Almighty, and I commit thee to Him whose creature thou art, so that when thou has paid the debt of humanity by the intervention of death, thou mayest return to thy maker who formed thee of earthly clay. As thy soul leaves its body may the shining company of angels meet it. May the company of judgment of the Apostles come out to greet thee. May the army of white-robed and triumphant martyrs meet thee. May the lily-bearing troop of radiant confessors surround thee. May the choir of rejoicing virgins take thee and the embrace of blessed rest in the bosom of the patriarchs enfold thee. May the face of Christ Jesus appear mild and cheerful to thee, and may He deign to number thee with those who sweetly wait on Him. Mayest thou never know what shuddereth in the darkness, what howleth in the flames, what paineth in torments. May foulest Satan with all his servants yield at thy coming, may he tremble as the angels accompany thee, and flee into the vast chaos of eternal night. May God arise and may His enemies be scattered and may those who hate Him flee from before his face. As smoke vanishes, so may they vanish, as wax melts before the face of flame, so may sinners perish before the face of God. And may the just eat and rejoice in the sight of God. Therefore let all the legions of Hell be confounded and may the ministers of Satan not dare to hinder thy path. May Christ deliver thee from torment, Who was crucified for thee. May Christ deliver thee from death, Who deigned to die for thee. May Christ the Son of the living God set thee among the evergreen pleasaunces of his Paradise, and that true shepherd acknowledge thee among His sheep. May He absolve thee of all thy sins and set thee on His right hand among the number of His elect. Mayest thou see thy Redeemer face to face, and present and ever in attendance behold the truth most manifest with happy eyes. Numbered therefore in the ranks of the blessed, mayest thou possess for ever and ever the sweetness of divine contemplation.'[17] The two adoring angels symbolise for the worshipper the world of Paradise into which the Christian hopes for admittance after death, for they are angels of those highest orders that wait constantly before the face of God, eternally absorbed in contemplating and glorifying Him: Michael and his companion angel belonging instead to that lowest choir which passes between Heaven and earth as messengers between God and man.

As on the Brancaccio tomb, then, the iconography of the Aragazzi tomb assembles the personages of Heaven of whom the souls of the dead stand in most need, Christ, the just but merciful judge, the Blessed Virgin, who will incline her Son to mercy by her tender prayers, the angels who conduct the souls of the dead before the face of Christ and into Paradise. While it was still intact the tomb's rising array of reliefs and figures must have imaged with solemn grandeur the world of heaven towards which the prayers of the dying and those who prayed for them after death were so beseechingly offered. They would fix the intention of those who said mass from age to age at the altar under the tomb on the need to continue the succession of masses to bring the soul of the founder and his relations, who might be languishing in Purgatory, into the bliss of Paradise. The thoughts of those who chose the theme are probably mirrored in that other prayer of the commendation service which invoked a blessing on the tomb of the deceased after his bier had been carried to it. 'O God, who hast founded the earth and made the Heavens, who hast given fixed places to the stars, who hast restored man, a prisoner in the bonds of death, by the absolution of baptism, who has noted in the book of life Abraham, Isaac and Jacob, that were buried in the double cave, to be blessed as princes of all glory, so mayest thou bless this tomb of thy servant N, that thou makest him here to rest and deignest to lay him in the bosom of Abraham, Isaac and Jacob. Thou who hast willed that those who believe in Our Lord Jesus Christ should trample on the bonds of hell, and rise again, and that they and the members of their body should be resurrected, look down, O Lord, upon the fabric of this tomb. May thy Holy Spirit, Lord, descend upon it, so that by thy will there may be quiet sleep for thy servant in this place and on the day of judgement a true resurrection with all thy saints by the grace of Our Lord Jesus Christ, who with thee and thy Holy Spirit liveth and reigneth for ever and ever.'[18]

Yet this iconography, while it invokes the prayers of the living, proclaims a pious belief about the souls of the dead it commemorates. For it declares that Aragazzi and the other dead members of his family have entered into salvation. The difference between it and the Brancaccio tomb is that between a pious hope and a pious belief. The Brancaccio tomb expresses a pious hope for salvation after death; on the Aragazzi tomb the hand of the Virgin, laid in blessing on Bartolommeo's head, the hand of Christ, raised in blessing as He looks down on the effigies of Bartolommeo and Francesco, unambiguously assert a pious belief in that they have been justified and entered into Heaven. Astonishing as the sentiment may seem, when applied to ordinary uncanonised human beings, there are many parallels for it in epitaphs on late fourteenth- and early fifteenth-century monuments. Many contemporaries attached the stigma of worldliness to Pope Boniface IX, but his relatives inscribed on his tomb, not only that he was a patient listener to the woes of the poor, but that if his bones now lie within his tomb 'his lofty soul rose on wings of bliss to Heaven and shines before God, a new source of light'. Of Cardinal Adam Easton (d. 1398) his epitaph in Santa Maria in Trastevere says that 'death gave the last and supreme gifts of Heaven'. Cardinal Cristoforo Maroni (d. 1404), buried in St. Peter's, 'lies here in the body, but his soul sits among the stars'. The soul of the saintly Cardinal Luca Manzoli (d. 1411), who was entombed in Ognissanti at the expense of the Signoria of Florence 'flew up into Heaven'. According to the epitaph of Cardinal Pietro Stefaneschi

(d. 1417) 'the earth covers his bones, but his soul stands in glory in Heaven'. And 'the pious soul' of Cardinal Angelo de Anna de Sommaripa (d. 1428) 'flew back into the angelic courts', according to his tomb in Santa Maria de Porta Nova, Naples. The epitaph of Cardinal Branda da Castiglione (d. 1443) declares that 'the Almighty Father brought me out of the prison of this earthly world and set me in the lofty region of Heaven'.[19] These pious declarations enunciate the same devout paradox as Pope Martin's letter of 1428 to Giovanni de' Medici informing him of the death of Bartolommeo de' Bardi. On the one hand Martin speaks of his pious belief that since Bardi had died a good death he had gone to heaven, yet on the other, he does not fail to make a pious recommendation of his soul to Giovanni's prayers.

The Aragazzi tomb was not the first in which the pious belief that the deceased has entered into Paradise was announced in visual form. The relief (no. 117) on the sarcophagus of Tino di Camaino's tomb of Bishop Antonio degli Orsi, in the Duomo of Florence, executed in 1321, shows the Bishop in Heaven, kneeling before Christ, to whom he is presented by the Virgin herself. The Virgin's train is held by a praying female saint, behind whom are two other saints and three angels. Immediately behind Christ's throne, his hands also clasped in prayer for the Bishop's soul, stands St. John Baptist, the patron saint of the Bishop's see of Florence, and behind him are St. Peter and St. Paul, the princes of the Apostles, and three more angels. The front angel of each of the two groups has his hands crossed in adoration like the youths on the Aragazzi relief, while the last angel on the right rests his crossed hands familiarly on his companions' shoulder. With book resting on His left knee, Christ raises His right hand to bless the Bishop and admit him into Heaven.[20]

On the tomb of the Neapolitan Grand Admiral Luigi Aldomorisco, (d. 1421) carved by Antonio Babboccio in 1421, the long relief (no. 125) set in the front of the sarcophagus shows two scenes in continuous narrative. Above are two scrolls with French inscriptions which explain their meaning. On the right an angel leads the admiral's soul into Paradise, leaving his family and household plunged in grief: on the left Aldomorisco kneels by King Ladislaus, who died about the same time. The King rests his hand protectingly on his Admiral's shoulder as the two of them are brought by St. Anthony and St. Amatus into the presence of the Virgin and Child, who are enthroned in Paradise, attended by angels and by St. Cecilia and St. Catherine. The inscriptions leave no ambiguity as to the meaning of these scenes. The first reads: 'This shows . . . the bold and noble knight Messer Louis Moriske left his household all disconsolate and went with the angel of God to be shown the glory of . . . holy Paradise'. The second, 'See how St. Amatus and St. Anthony carry the noble Prince and puissant King Ladislaus of Durazzo who bears with him the noble and potent knight Messer Louis de Moriske and present them to the Virgin Mary and her son Jesus Christ in the glory of Paradise where St. Cecilia and St. Catherine dwell.' And on the other side of the sarcophagus (no. 126), among the angels and saints of the court of heaven, St. Anthony and St. Amatus rest their hands protectingly on the shoulders of Ladislaus and Aldomorisco as the Virgin presents them to Christ, who raises His hand in blessing.[21]

The imagery of the Aragazzi tomb starts important questions about its chronology, for it is impossible that Bartolommeo himself can have chosen it. To answer those questions we must turn again to the early documents about the tomb. In his *catasto* return of early July 1427 Michelozzo expressly declares that the tomb is to be set up in Montepulciano, that no price has been fixed for it, that one will be agreed by the estimate of common friends after the tomb has been completed, that the tomb is to be of greater or lesser expense according as Aragazzi's intention fixes itself (*secondo si mutasse di pensiero*), that Donatello and he have received an advance of 100 florins to have marbles brought. By the middle of 1427, then, Aragazzi had not made up his mind about the design of his tomb. After all, he was only in his early forties and not expecting to die soon, and though his uncle was eighty and his father sixty-four, there was no pressingly immediate need for it. Nor had the two sculptors as yet procured the marbles for which they had received an advance: there was no reason for them to hasten work on the tomb if Bartolommeo was in no hurry for it, especially as they were behindhand with both the Cossa and the Brancaccio tombs.

The ordering, quarrying and transporting to Florence of the Carrara marble needed for the tomb must have taken a certain amount of time, even if it came on the two boats Michelozzo and Donatello had bought for their own use. The probability is that by the date of Aragazzi's sudden death on 26 June 1429 little more had been done than the procuring of it. The entry in Francesco Aragazzi's *catasto* return which records that in his will Bartolommeo had ordered 'that a tomb be made for him in Montepulciano, which he had given out to contract while yet living, which will cost 1000 ducats when it is brought here' must have been made between 1 July 1429, the earliest date when news of Bartolommeo's death and of the contents of his will can have reached his native town, and January 1430, when Don Battista certified the correctness of the *catasto* return. 1000 florins were allowed against Bartolommeo's estate for the tomb, and the enormousness of this sum, 150 florins more than the price of the Cossa and Brancaccio tombs, suggests that Bartolommeo had made no further payments for the tomb after his first advance of 100 florins for marbles. Hence it is more than probable that the first detailed, as opposed to general instructions that he gave for it were made on his death-bed and set down in his will. Indeed Bruni says that it was in his will that he ordered an effigy of his father to be laid beside his own.

Such a command is in itself an indication that little or nothing had as yet been done towards the execution of the tomb, for so large and important a sculpture, requiring a much deeper sarcophagus and therefore a much deeper setting for the whole tomb would hardly have been added to it as an after-thought, even by a death-bed testator.

These conclusions fit perfectly with Bruni's description of the two effigies as 'half-finished' when he saw them. His letter is undated, but must have been written between Bartolommeo's death and the death of Pope Martin V on 29 February 1431. It also seems to imply that Francesco was already dead by the time he met the carts stuck in the road with their burden of carvings. Hence the crux of interpretation turns on his remark that Bartolommeo was 'lately' (*nuper*) dead. Given the looseness of the terminology of time in the fifteenth century and Bruni's probable intention of implying scornful indifference for the news of Bartolommeo's death, 'lately' cannot necessarily be interpreted in modern terms as meaning a few weeks or months. Francesco died on 29 September 1429, and it is most improbable that the framework and effigies would have been exposed to the hazards of a winter journey from Florence to Montepulciano, especially if that part of the road which lay between Arezzo and Montepulciano was so bad and so little frequented by wheeled traffic as Bruni declares. Dr. Hans Baron proposes to date the letter between April and October 1430,[22] but since Michelozzo was at the camp before Lucca from March until June of that year and in Venice or Padua from September onwards, July or August are the months of 1430 in which Bruni is most likely to have seen the carts and their burden.

It follows that the framework and the two effigies must have been roughed out by July or August 1430, at the prompting first of Francesco, and after his death of Messer Jacopo, Prior Battista and Ser Giovanni. Clearly it was they who decided on the imagery of the tomb; only on this supposition can its proclamation of Bartolommeo's entrance into Paradise be explained, or the formula employed in the epitaph: BARTOLOMEO . . . POSTERI DEDICAVERUNT ET BENEMERENTI (Posterity dedicated (this tomb) . . . to the well-deserving Bartolommeo). The death of Francesco in September 1429 must have halted work until his estate was settled up and firmly in the hands of Messer Jacopo. And Messer Jacopo's own death in August or early September 1431 must have produced another delay while Don Battista wound up his old relation's affairs and took possession of the inheritance. Michelozzo was in Monte-pulciano in December 1432, either for the work on the fortress with which he had been charged by the *Signoria* of Florence, or for negotiations about the tomb, or for both purposes. But progress on the tomb must have been partly interrupted by Michelozzo's journey to Rome with Donatello from June 1432 until April 1433. It is a question whether the two sarcophagus reliefs were executed before, during or after this excursion. If we assume that his sojourn in Rome converted Michelozzo as it converted Donatello from an eclectic classicism into something very like Neo-classicism for two or three years, then the reliefs most probably date from late in 1432 or 1433, after Michelozzo came back from Rome to Florence. Such a dating, obligatory on the evidence of subject-matter, also fits better than any other with the style of the reliefs, since it makes them contemporary or nearly so with Donatello's Cantoria and his reliefs for the Prato pulpit, both begun in 1433 and 1434, and both works in which Donatello too has attempted a classical relief-style.

The two statues of angels are also very classicising, far more so than the other large-scale figures on the tomb, and it is reasonable to suppose that they are contemporary with the reliefs. We have seen that Professor Charles Seymour has suggested that in the figure of the lesser angel (which he believes to be female and to represent Faith) Michelozzo employed the earliest Renaissance canon for the human figure to be formally enunciated in a literary treatise, the *exempedum* recommended by Alberti in his *De Statua*. This canon, in which as we know the module of the foot, six times repeated, gives the height of the figure, certainly seems to be exemplified in this statue. But since there is a possibility that Ghiberti, Michelozzo's first master, may have used a six-part canon so early as 1415, it cannot be assumed as a proven fact that Michelozzo used the *exempedum* in consequence of an encounter with Alberti, either in Rome, where Alberti was living from 1432 onwards, or in Florence, where Alberti came in the train of Pope Eugenius in June 1434, remaining there until April 1436. In any case there must always be a doubt whether such theories of proportion were the inventions of those who first wrote them down, or whether they circulated orally among artists before being ennobled with all the dignity of a learned system by the learned author whose interest they caught.[23]

The figures of Christ and the adoring angels are so assured in design and execution, particularly the angels, that they were probably the last sculptures of the tomb to be carved. Significantly these are the figures which are most reminiscent of Ghiberti in feeling and style: they mark the beginning of that return to a more Gothicising manner which followed Michelozzo's neo-classical experiments. The probability is then that the reliefs and the two standing angels date from the later months of 1433 and early 1434 and that the Christ and the adoring angels belong to 1434–6. Most likely all the figures and reliefs of the tomb, and not only the two effigies, arrived in Montepulciano partly finished and were stored there until Michelozzo and his assistants could ride out to complete and polish them. Probably their inception and completion were irregular by our notions – Michelozzo being the sort of artist who was careful to be paid his due for every part of the work as he proceeded, so that progress probably corresponded to payments rather than to the pressure of inspiration. In his *catasto* return of 1469 he himself says he worked on the tomb *'insino nel 1436'*.[24] According to the new contract of September 1437 and his petition of May 1438 he had carved the greater part of the tomb 'long ago', in 1429 and the years immediately following. Certainly when he downed tools in 1436, after the disastrous lawsuit which so reduced the Aragazzi inheritance, not very much remained to be done. The presumption is then that the greater part of the tomb was brought near to completion during the four or five years after Aragazzi's death.

The Aragazzi tomb is not a humanist monument in the sense that it reflects the taste of a humanist patron. The humanist elements it contains are stylistic, and were contributed by Michelozzo, not by the small-town merchant, the small-town notary and the two small-town clergy who were his patrons. The imagery of the tomb was traditional: only its style belonged to the new age. Even its basic design, as we have seen, had prototypes and parallels in Naples, Rome and Venice. Yet its most prompting inspiration was surely one singularly important and very recent predecessor in Florence itself, no less than Masaccio's fresco of the Trinity in Santa Maria Novella (no. 115). Since Professor Procacci rediscovered the lower part of this great painting, representing an altar-table with a tomb-chest and a cadaver effigy lying upon it, much has been written about its significance.[26] Nevertheless its real meaning has gone unrecognised. It is a combination of tomb, altar and altar-piece like the Aragazzi tomb, simulated by *trompe-l'oeil* devices, above all of course by a novel and brilliant use of geometrical perspective. In other words, it is a simulation in paint of a funerary chapel. The skeleton lying on a tomb-chest protruding from a recess under the altar-table is a cadaver tomb of a type very rare in Italy, and possibly unprecedented in Tuscany itself, but familiar, even commonplace in Northern Gothic art, in France, Germany, England and the Netherlands. One wonders what tomb seen and admired beyond the Alps inspired the *Gonfaloniere* Lorenzo Lenzi, and his wife, who kneel before the chapel to left and right, to commission this painted reminder of mortality on the wall beside his tomb-slab. The inscription that runs above the effigy is one that frequently appears on cadaver tombs IO.FV.G(I)A.QVEL. CHE.VOI.SETE: E QVEL CHI (O) . SON . VOI . ANCHO . SARETE (*Once I was what you are now, and what I am now that shall you be*).

Within the chapel are the Virgin and St. John and the grandiose figures of the Trinity. Here Masaccio has not carried through completely his painted simulachrum of an architectural chapel, perhaps because he did not wish to press his imitation of reality to the point of painting simulated sculptures, unlike his Flemish contemporaries, since this would have been highly inconvenient to his overriding desire for an effect of illusionistic recession. Into his *trompe-l'oeil* painting of a chapel he has introduced divine figures of dramatic grandeur, allowing himself to transform the chapel's altar-piece into a visionary scene.

There still remains one last little mystery. In his diatribe *In Pogivm Floren-tinvm Antidoti Libri Qvatvor* the humanist Lorenzo Valla accused Poggio Bracciolini of having intrigued against him to prevent him from obtaining the apostolic secretaryship which had become vacant by the death of his uncle Melchiorre Scribani. Poggio, it seems, had poisoned Antonio Loschi's mind against Valla by telling him that Valla had criticised Loschi's poems 'on this account forsooth, because when speaking at the house of Cipriano da Pistoia of the tomb of Bartolommeo da Montepulciano I had said that the poem composed by Antonio in elegiacs and inscribed on Bartolommeo's monument was not so excellent as others he had written in hexameters and that Bartolommeo had been the better poet in that kind of verse and very nearly the best of all. Which I said, both because it was my opinion and because it had been his wont to encourage me to study.' This episode occurred after Melchiorre Scribani's death of the plague in the late summer of 1429,[27] and so can be dated to the autumn of that year.

Now there is no record of a verse epitaph on the Aragazzi tomb in Monte-pulciano, which in any case had only been begun by the autumn of 1429, if then. Hence another explanation has to be found for Valla's story. One might be that there was no room on the tomb for Loschi's epitaph: even six lines of elegiacs take up a certain amount of space when carved as an inscription and in fact Bartolommeo's brief epitaph had to be squeezed on to a small bronze plaque. Alternatively, like a number of epitaphs written later for Leonardo Bruni, it may simply have been a tribute to the dead man's memory couched in the form of a laudatory epitaph. But since Valla had seen the epi-taph and had seen it moreover carved on Bartolommeo's 'monument', by far the likeliest explanation is that it was carved on that slab (*lapide*) commem-orating Bartolommeo's memory, which we know to have been made in Rome during the summer of 1429 at a cost of 20 florins.[29] Yet the epitaph on the bronze plaque was evidently composed by one of Bartolommeo's humanist friends, Poggio perhaps or Loschi, so much does it aspire to antique majesty and brevity in its formula and choice of words. Accordingly it is the sole token on the tomb of that literary humanism which has been claimed as its inspiration.

The full explanation of why Aragazzi had so ambitious a tomb erected to himself will probably never be recovered. But some things we can conjec-ture. Was his motive merely vanity and vainglory, as Bruni scornfully sug-gested? Vanity and vainglory certainly entered into the making of the tomb. But before determining of what sort, we must consider once more the cir-cumstances of Bartolommeo and his family at the moment of his death. In the first place we know that his death came suddenly and early, shocking his friends and relations, and before Bartolommeo had taught himself to expect it. On this point the evidence of his life and of his epitaph is unequivocal. It is far more likely then that it was his father's age of sixty-four, so much nearer to death in the ordinary course of things, that moved him to commission the tomb. But this does not account for its size and magnificence. Here we must remember that Bartolommeo was more than an eloquent secretary in the Pope's service and that the nature of his office does not suggest his real importance at the Curia. He was the Pope's confidential and trusted adviser, with a part in the management of policy and affairs, just such a person in fact, as might well feel confident if Papal favour continued – and Martin, we are told, loved him 'singularly' – of advancement to the cardinalate. Probably the Aragazzi tomb is a monument to ambition frustrated by death.

It was August Schmarsow[30] who first saw in 1893 that the façade of the convent church of Sant' Agostino (no. 141) in the lower part of Montepulciano must be the work of Michelozzo. He made the attribution simply on stylistic grounds, and failed to notice an important clue, that the arms carved on the enwreathed shields of the second storey are those of the Aragazzi.[31] In 1902 Bode confirmed Schmarsow's ascription by pointing out that the design of the façade had been adapted from the design of the Brancaccio tomb.[32] Although the attribution to Michelozzo has been generally accepted, the date given to the façade, and indeed to the church, has varied from Morisani's date of c. 1430 to Saalman's date of c. 1450–60.[33] The true date can now be established from what we know of the history of the Aragazzi family and from unpublished documents.

The Augustinian friars arrived in Montepulciano during the second half of the thirteenth century, and are said to have begun their first church in 1285 and to have completed it in 1309.[34] Almost certainly it was a small and humble edifice, in spite of the quarter of the century it took to build, and during the late fourteenth century a new and more ambitious church was begun. It was already in progress by 1384 when there is a mention of the *opus nove ecclesie Sancti Agustini*.[35] The Comune regularly elected *Operai* to supervise the fabric and allotted a certain sum to the work from its revenues at the beginning of each year. On 28 January 1429, probably to speed up lagging progress, it gave 200 lire, quite a considerable sum for Montepulciano, to the '*Ecclesie nove beati Agustini terre montispolitiani pro elimosina et fabrica ipsius ecclesie et eius expensis.*'[36] Francesco di Bartolommeo's legacy in September of the same year arrested these grants of money, and also the election of *Operai*, since for some years it must have seemed that his huge bequest would be amply sufficient to complete the work. We may surmise that Messer Jacopo Aragazzi and Prior Battista obtained a design for the façade from Michelozzo in 1430 and that the local *travertino* of which the façade is built was soon being hewn out of the quarries in the slopes below the town, near Chianciano. But the difficulties in which the Aragazzi inheritance was involved from 1435 onwards brought work on the façade to a halt as well as work on the tomb, and in the case of the façade it was not resumed until the beginning of the next century. Hope for its completion in the 1430s was finally abandoned on 10 September 1438, when the *Consiglio* of Montepulciano proceeded to an election of *Operai* 'for the new church of Sant' Agostino', one of them being Ser Giovanni di Battista Naldini.[37]

The aspect of Sant' Agostino still reflects its history. Set back a little from the line of the ascending brown street, its noble façade of grey travertine, veined here and there with gold, comes with sudden and breathtaking surprise on the visitor. But a closer inspection shows that except for its façade the church is of brick: the façade is a front of costly magnificence to a large plain building behind. The brick is just the material we should expect to be used in the ordinary way of things for a convent church in medieval Montepulciano and except for what was altered during the restoration of 1784–91, when the transepts were pulled down and the apse was shortened, the rest of the fabric behind the façade dates from the late fourteenth and early fifteenth century, wholly or largely before the windfall of Francesco di Bartolommeo's legacy in September 1429. It is the façade then that concerns us here.

The pilasters and capitals at each of its ends are repeated in travertine at the sides, forming pier-shaped corners, behind which the brick walls of the nave run backwards. The façade itself rises from a podium, which has a moulded base and a frieze decorated with sunk Gothic quatrefoils, each containing a central boss. It is demarcated into three horizontal divisions by three heavy cornices, the last surmounted by a gabled pediment. At either end the composition is closed by a projecting member, left plain on the second division, but on the lowest division decorated with twin projecting Corinthian pilasters and on the uppermost with blind panels surmounted by twin Corinthian pilasters. On either side of the portal two sunk blind panels are divided by a Corinthian pilaster, only slightly relieved against the wall so as not to disturb the closing effect of the terminal pilasters. The portal (no. 141) on the other hand, is framed by Corinthian pilasters in bolder relief. In the portal the style of the design changes from Renaissance with some Gothic detail to Gothic with some Renaissance detail. Its sides slope inwards at an angle, and although its lunette, which contains three half-length terracotta figures of the Virgin and Child, St. John Baptist and St. Augustine, to which we shall return presently, is of Renaissance form, it is framed by two Gothic pinnacles and a Gothic canopy like that of the Brancaccio tomb, richly crocketed with heavy Late Gothic foliage alternating with a trefoil plant ornament. Each of the two spandrels on either side of the plain medallion in the centre of the canopy – plain now, but was it originally intended for a fresco? – contains a rosette resting on broad Gothic foliage. And the finial surmounting the canopy is a typically Late Gothic finial. Canopy and pinnacles rise the full height of the second division of the façade. To either side of them is a pair of blind Gothic niches similar to those on the façade of the Palazzo Comunale of Montepul-

226

ciano, erected from 1440 onwards to a design by Michelozzo.[38] They prove that it still pleased Michelozzo to advance and recess, to hollow and smooth a façade after the Gothic manner, even if his version of that manner was the austere Tuscan one. Above each of these pairs of niches are the laurel medallions which contain pointed shields carved with the three stag heads of the Aragazzi arms.

The cornice of the second division is narrow, but projects strongly: it terminates that part of the façade which was erected between 1430 and at the latest 1438. According to the inscription DIVO.AVGVSTINO.SACRVM. OPERA. ET. FRATERNITAS.CLERICORVM AVGUST. PERFECERVNT.MDVIII which runs along the top of the third division, the upper part was finished in 1508[39] at the joint expense of the *Opera*, and the Augustinian brethren of Sant' Agostino.[40] Comparison with the church of San Barnaba in Florence, which Michelozzo also built, suggests the façade was finished according to his original design, with some modifications in the decorative details.

The building history of the Palazzo Comunale of Montepulciano, which has recently become known to us in detail from an admirable article by Professor Saalman has to be considered for the building history of that part of the façade of Sant' Agostino which was completed during the 1430s. On 16 October 1440 Michelozzo was formally invited by the *Consiglio* of Montepulciano to furnish a design for a new façade to the Palazzo del Comune and for the remodelling of some of its interior rooms, since both façade and rooms were threatening to collapse. Michelozzo made the required design, but the execution of it was entrusted by the Comune to two Florentine master masons, Cecho and Mechero da Settignano, who had begun their work by 7 April 1443. Mechero soon disappears from view, but Cecho remained in charge of the work through all the vicissitudes and delays caused by the usual money difficulties until its completion in 1465. Hence it is not impossible that Michelozzo merely made a design for the façade of Sant' Agostino and that its execution was handed over to a master mason. On the other hand, for some years after 1430 Michelozzo must have come to Montepulciano regularly – after 1440 he had no particular reason for going there – and we know that in 1432 he was employed by the *Signoria* on work in the fortress of the town, a commission which suggests that he may have taken masons there. Moreover, Francesco's legacy 'for the walling of Sant' Agostino' amounted for some time to a large enough sum to interest him personally in the work. One glance at the façade is enough to tell us that Francesco and his executors intended it to be a costly and splendid memorial to his piety, and both in design and execution it is much finer than the Palazzo Comunale. Although its stones were cut and worked locally, the probability is that Michelozzo himself supervised it when in Montepulciano, and during his absences left it in the hands of a skilled master mason.

227

The terracotta sculptures of the lunette (no. 70) also suggest that he kept the work under his own eye until money ran out. Schmarsow discovered that these were ascribed locally to the fifteenth-century sculptor Pasquino da Montepulciano, who, so it was said, had taken as his model for the Virgin a beautiful woman of Montepulciano named *La Zingarella*.[41] The *Memorie* of the church in which all this was circumstantially related have disappeared, but the tradition sounds a late one. Pasquino, even though little or no figure sculpture known to be from his hands survives, was never a forgotten figure, for he is mentioned by Vasari as a pupil of Filarete and (wrongly), as the sculptor of the tomb of Pope Pius II.[42] Accordingly, he lived on in the memory of his fellow-citizens as a legitimate object of local pride. Schmarsow seems to have divined the case correctly, for he quite rightly discounted the attribution of the lunette sculptures to Pasquino as a mere piece of speculative anti-quarianism. Instead he attributed them to Michelozzo, comparing the Virgin and Child to the Virgin and Child of the Aragazzi relief and the St. John to the terracotta figure of the same saint modelled by Michelozzo after 1444 for the chapel of Antonio da Rabatta in the Annunziata at Florence (nos. 73, 74). To justify his ascription of the St. Augustine to Michelozzo he could find only two details of costume – the thick cords of the mantle and the rosette on the glove, rather oddly describing the latter, which is merely a customary ornament of medieval episcopal gloves, as 'Michelozzo's signature'.

In reality the attribution of these sculptures to Michelozzo poses a problem which escaped Schmarsow, though his ascription is certainly correct. They are from the hand of a mature and accomplished sculptor, even if the St. Augustine (no. 71) which is less good than the other two, may be largely by an assistant. Their style belongs to the middle 1430s, and there are unmistakable analogies between them and the Aragazzi reliefs. The Child especially is extremely close to the Child of the relief of the Virgin blessing Aragazzi (no. 54) even to the disposition of the curls on the left cheek and the cast of the drapery across the body. The St. John is gentler and less ascetic than the St. John of the Annunziata, but there are obvious similarities between his head and that of the Christ of the Aragazzi tomb, and he has the muscular, sinewy arms proper to a figure by Michelozzo. The long slender fingers of these three figures, if they are not so like the strongly structured hands of the Aragazzi effigy as Schmarsow claimed, are certainly paralleled in the hands of the figures in the relief of the Virgin blessing (no. 50). And the draping of the cloaks which both the Baptist and the Virgin wear has the amplitude and bold simple folds characteristic of Michelozzo. There are no such marked analogies between the figures of the Aragazzi tomb and the St. Augustine, but the figure was evidently designed by the same hand as the other two.

Yet the general style and handling of the figures, particularly of the Virgin and Child and of the Baptist, is far less rigid and constrained, far less unequal

than that of most of the Aragazzi sculptures, as Schmarsow recognised. There
is a greater sense of plastic unity, of greater ease in the management of poses
and of planes. However, as we saw, this increased freedom also appears
in the two angels and to some extent in the Christ of the Aragazzi tomb.
Hence it would seem likely on stylistic grounds alone that the Sant' Agostino
figures were modelled *c.* 1435, and this date is confirmed by the history of the
façade and of the Aragazzi inheritance. Michelozzo has now moved then
towards a lighter, more elegant, more Gothicising manner, in which classical
elements are still used, as in the Child, but only in a subordinate role. This
style will be that of Michelozzo's few later sculptures; less awkward and un-
even, it is at the same time less interesting and remarkable than his classicising
manner.

Although the Sant' Agostino terracottas fit smoothly into Michelozzo's
stylistic evolution – indeed without them we should lack a key moment in the
transition to his later style – their comparative softness has no parallel either
in his earlier or later work. Something of this sweetness of character may be
due to the subject: the Virgin is shown in a tender act of maternal love, about
to give suck to the Child. And the grave gentleness of St. John's expression
may be intended to match this motif: though his scroll is inscribed EAD.
(*Ecce Agnus Dei*, that is, Behold the Lamb of God), he is pointing, not to the
Christ of the Baptism, but to Christ the Holy Child. By contrast, Michelozzo's
two other representations of the Baptist (nos. 74, 77) are much more rigid
and austere. Yet it is also tempting to suppose, with Schmarsow and Janson,
that Michelozzo was now beginning to come under the influence of another
great Florentine sculptor, Luca della Robbia. The resemblances between
Luca's lunette relief of the *Resurrection* above the door of the sacristy of the
Florentine Duomo, completed in 1443, and the lunette of the Aragazzi tomb
are strikingly close. And later Michelozzo is known to have worked with
Luca in the Cappella del Crocefisso in San Miniato al Monte and at Im-
pruneta, designing tabernacles for which Luca made the sculptures, and again
in the Duomo, casting Luca's bronze doors for the sacristy.

Chapter XI · The Prato Pulpit· Michelozzo's Last Sculptures

DESCANTING IN 1721 on the merits of his native city of Prato, Dr. Giuseppe Maria Bianchini numbered among its terrestrial blessings the healthiness of its air, the abundance and purity of its water, the fertility of its countryside, the dignity of its buildings, the sufficiency of its traffic, the wisdom of its magistrates, the number of its monasteries and convents, schools and charitable foundations. 'But to all these things', he continued, 'which are common to so many other cities in even greater abundance, it was the will of Heaven to add a most precious Gift, a Sacrosanct Gift, so singular that no other city can boast of such a one. And this is the Girdle of the Virgin Mary, which has been preserved in Prato for many centuries, and is there venerated with tender Christian devotion no less by the peoples of Tuscany than by strangers of every condition and degree.' To the history of this relic, 'as great in respect of all other relics as the Queen of the Angels is greater than all the Saints' he then addressed himself.[1]

Let us read it in a *trecento* Tuscan legend of the Girdle which he printed.[2] This relates that when Our Lady departed this life, the Apostles all met together at her bedside, saving only St. Thomas, who was away preaching in India. They dressed her body, girdling it with a beautiful girdle, and laid it in a new tomb in the Valley of Jehosaphat. Meanwhile St. Thomas was caught up in the air and set down on Mount Olivet, where he lifted up his eyes and saw Our Lady being carried up body and soul by the angels into Heaven. Calling to her in a loud voice, he begged for her blessing and for a token to prove that she had indeed been taken up into Heaven. Our Lady blessed him, and unloosening her girdle, gave it to him. He went down with it to the Valley of Jehosaphat, where he met the other Apostles, who rebuked him for his absence from the death-bed of Our Lady and told him that because of his incredulity he had not been thought worthy to assist at her death. In reply St. Thomas asked where the body of Our Lady lay, and when the Apostles showed him her tomb, declared that she was not within. The Apostles, unbelieving, opened the tomb, and marvelled to find that Our Lady was in truth not there. Then St. Thomas revealed what he had seen and showed the girdle which the Virgin had given him as a token. And thereupon the other Apostles begged his forgiveness.

This story, which so evidently buttresses the doctrine of the bodily Assumption of the Virgin, dear in the Middle Ages to popular devotion and to the Franciscans, but vehemently opposed by the Dominicans, was openly doubted by the Dominican Sant' Antonino in the early fifteenth century.[3] But the saint discreetly separated the authenticity of the story from that of the Virgin's girdle, observing 'that it may with piety be believed that her Girdle is on earth; it is said to be at Prato and is there exhibited to the people.' In Prato itself belief in both legend and relic was fervent and unquestioning. For there the girdle's later history was circumstantially known. Desiring to return to India. St. Thomas had left it with a certain good man of Jerusalem, whose family handed it down from generation to generation until in the twelfth century it came into the hands of the last of their line, a married priest, who had one daughter, named Maria. At that time there was living in Prato a poor man named Michele, who could do no good for himself at home and so decided to try his fortune overseas. He took himself to Jerusalem, where he met the wife of the priest and his daughter Maria. Maria fell in love with him and he with her, and the priest's wife had them married secretly, giving Michele as her daughter's dowry a basket or reeds containing the girdle and bidding him go back with Maria to his native land for fear her husband should discover the marriage.

Michele returned safely to Prato in 1141, and set up as a tanner in a little house opposite the Pieve of Santo Stefano in Borgo (now the Cathedral of Prato). To safeguard his treasure he slept over it every night, even though every night he was cast out of his bed for this want of respect. At last, in or about the year 1174, as he lay dying he summoned the Proposto of Santo Stefano, gave him the girdle and told him its history. At first the Proposto was incredulous. He put it into his dormitory, which was also his treasury, but after strange and terrifying sounds had been heard at night from the casket containing it he took it with him to a house he owned outside the walls of the town. But that very night as he lay down to sleep a fire broke out, and he and his companions were forced to escape from the house. Next morning, astounded to find the house had suffered no hurt, he perceived at last that the relic he had been given was in very truth the Virgin's Girdle. He had a box of silver-gilt made to contain it, but at first concealed the whole matter from his flock, for fear he should be accused of imposture and greed if he announced that his church had become the owner of so astonishing a relic. Only after the girdle had miraculously cured a woman possessed by three devils did the townsfolk learn that Prato now possessed such a holy treasure.

Traditionally the veneration of the girdle in Prato dates back to c. 1178. It became the custom to exhibit it publicly on certain feast days to a great throng gathered in the square outside the church, and c. 1211–14 a special pulpit of wood and stone was constructed for this purpose on the south front.[4] On 31 July 1312, two days after an unsuccessful attempt to steal the girdle and sell it to the Florentines – not yet masters of Prato – by a certain Giovanni di

Ser Landetto nicknamed Musciattino, the town decided to build a special chapel in which it might be securely housed. Ground was purchased for this in 1317 and there are payments relating to its construction from that year until 1322.[5] On 13 April 1330 the *Consiglio* of Prato decided to replace the old wooden pulpit used for the exhibition of the Girdle with a new and splendid pulpit of white marble, carved with an *ystoria* of the Girdle on one side and an *ystoria* of St. Stephen, the patron saint of Prato, on the other. At each of its two corners was to be an angel made in such fashion as to hold a wax torch (*tortitium*) in order to light the exhibition of the Girdle.[6]

From the wording of the *Consiglio*'s resolution it is clear that the Comune had already considered and accepted a design for the new pulpit, but although it appointed three *Operai del Pergamo* (*operarii perbii*) that same October, nothing happened until the end of 1337, when payments begin for marble and to a certain Maestro Lupo who was to carve the pulpit. It seems that in the end the project came to nothing, probably because of the quarrels between the town and the *Proposto* over the offerings made to the Girdle. The towns-folk became convinced that the *Proposto*, who was now usually an absentee ruling the church through a Vicar, and the chapter of the Pieve were mal-administering these, and in 1346 some of the magnates and populace of the town went in force to Santo Stefano, removed the Girdle from its Chapel, and transferred it to another altar on the south side of the nave. Here a priest who was by birth a Pratese, but not a member of the chapter of Santo Stefano, had it in his custody. The moneys offered to the Girdle now passed into the custody of the town of Prato, which in 1348 appointed an *Opera* composed of four *Operai* and a *Camarlingo* to receive and administer them. The dispute was settled amicably in 1350 when it was agreed that the town should have a share in the custodianship of the relic and that the offerings should be divided between the Proposto and the chapel. But from henceforward the responsibility for surrounding the relic with all due state and splendour was primarily that of the town, and c. 1422 it was delegated entirely into the hands of the *Opera*.[7]

In 1357 the scheme for a new pulpit was revived, and the Sienese sculptors Niccolò di Cecco del Mercia and his pupil Sano together with the Florentine Giovanni di Francesco called Fetto began carving a pulpit which was decor-ated with subjects from the life of the Virgin. Payments for it continued until 1360.[8] This new pulpit gave satisfaction until the translation of the relic in 1395 to the newly built chapel on the left side of the church at the beginning of the nave, immediately behind the façade, in which it is still housed. The old pulpit was set on the outside of the opposite wall of the nave, under the first blind arch, and the Pratesi, ever anxious for the safety of their precious Girdle, now felt that the distance between chapel and pulpit exposed it to risk, since it would be relatively unprotected when carried from the one to the other during its solemn exhibitions. Accordingly they determined to mask the old front of the church with a new and sumptuous façade, leaving enough room between the two to allow for a covered passage which would run from the chapel to a new pulpit to be constructed on the corner of the new façade.[9] In 1413 Niccolò Lamberti of Florence and his partners Giovanni di Donato and Lorenzo di Matteo of Fiesole, who had undertaken the building of the façade after a model by Giovanni d'Ambrogio, were ordered by the *Operai del Cingolo* to leave 'strong and sufficient' brackets at the corner for 'the new pulpit'.[10] But it was not until early in 1428 or just before that Michelozzo and Donatello were invited to submit a model for that new pulpit.

On 14 July 1428 a contract for its execution between the *Operai del Sacro Cingolo* and the Comune of Prato on the one hand the two masters on the other was formally drawn up by the *Cancelliere* of the Comune in the sacristy of the chapel of the Sacro Cingolo.[11] From its wording we can see that the two masters had divided their labour. Michelozzo had designed the architectural part, while the sculptural ornament was to be the work of Donatello. The foundation of the contract was a *modello*, either a drawing or an architect's model of wood, which Michelozzo and Donatello had made and now agreed to leave in the sacristy of the Chapel of the Sacro Cingolo. The contract describes this *modello* very precisely. The pulpit was to rest on the pier which had been raised for the purpose on the new façade; this Michelozzo and Donatello were to decorate with fluting so as to make it a fittingly rich support. The pulpit itself was to be wholly of white Carrara marble, and 'the work of the said pulpit must begin five and a quarter *braccia* (about 10½ ft., 3·2 metres) above ground, with a cornice on which there shall be two child angels (*spiritelli*) to serve as consoles, each two *braccia* (4 ft., 1·21 metres high), ornamented with foliage as the said model shows. And above the said child angels (*spiritelli*) a thick cornice carved with dentils, and above the said cornice a set of brackets carved with foliage and a cornice. And on the said brackets shall be the base of the said pulpit, and between each bracket and the next foliage or something else, according as it shall please those commissioning the work. And above the said base of the said pulpit shall be a round parapet (*paramento*), as the said model shows, divided into six spaces, in which are to be carved child angels (*spiritelli*) holding between them the arms of the Comune of Prato, as the said model shows, or something else, if it shall so please the said persons commissioning the work. Which parapet shall be composed of a floor of five and two-thirds *braccia* (about 11½ ft., 3·5 metres). The circuit of the outer part shall be ornamented with pillars and with cornices to serve as a frontal, as the said model shows. And as for that which may need to be done to the façade from the floor of the said pulpit to above, the said masters shall be held and obliged to give the form and the method of carrying it out and putting it in and to employ on it those masters that shall seem proper to them at the expense of the said *Opera*. . . .'

Michelozzo alone was present at the signing of this agreement, acting both in his own name and that of Donatello. For this reason, and because the contract addresses itself to him '*massimamente*' and is specific in its provisions for the architectural part of the pulpit and open as regards its sculptural decoration, which was to be either the essentially decorative motif of putti holding a shield charged with the arms of Prato or to be altered according to the later determination of the *Operai*, it is clear that for the moment Michelozzo was the master principally involved. Donatello was concerned at this stage only as the partner who would eventually undertake the decorative carvings once their subject had been decided. And significantly it was Michelozzo's own property that was pledged as security for the due fulfilment of the obligations he and Donatello had undertaken. The pulpit was to be finished and set up by 1 September 1429, four days before the Feast of the Nativity of the Virgin, a day on which it was customary to make one of the solemn exhibitions of the Girdle. On their side the *Operai* agreed to make a first payment of 350 florins, payable in instalments, 50 florins in August, October and January, 100 florins in April and 50 florins in July and September. After the work was completed it was to be valued and its price fixed by Lorenzo d'Angelo Sassi of Prato, a celebrated doctor of medicine. The moneys for payment were to be found from the income of the chapel, and the *Operai* in their turn pledged all the property of the chapel as security for their obligations.

We do not know how seriously the *Operai* expected the two masters to observe their undertaking to finish the pulpit in little more than a year. It was customary to insert clauses penalising masters for failure to fulfil their obligations in order to prevent too much procrastination, but patrons often knew that procrastination there would be.[12] Yet the *Operai* cannot have thought that no work at all would be done. Between 30 July and 21 November 1428 Michelozzo and Donatello are known to have received from them $100\frac{1}{2}$ florins, exactly the sum they had been promised. But as this time had passed without any visible results, the *Operai* became anxious. They deputed their *Provveditore* and a notary to go to Florence[13] to exact a formal undertaking from Michelozzo and Donatello that they would honour their contract under pain and penalty of repaying all and any advances of money they had received.[14] By this undertaking, made on 27 November, the two masters pledged all their own property as security for completion of the work, and their friend Andrea di Onofrio Nofri, sculptor of the tomb of King Ladislaus, also pledged his as their guarantor. After the signing of the agreement the two masters set hurriedly to work, as payments for their expenses made by the *Operai* during December show. But it was not until 8 December of the following year that they sent three cartloads of carved marbles to Prato. The *Operai* for their part kept up a steady flow of payments to them from December 1428 onwards.[15] It was not even interrupted by the absence of Michelozzo and Donatello in

Rome during the second half of 1432 and the first months of 1433, though from April 1431 the *Operai* made their payments to the two masters solely through the intermediary of Pagno di Lapo Portigiani or of others.[16]

Having honoured their financial undertakings they naturally became impatient when in September 1432 they found themselves still without a pulpit and with Donatello and Michelozzo away in Rome, showing no signs of returning to finish it. Through one of their number, the innkeeper Cambio di Ferro, they appealed for help to Cosimo de' Medici, the patron and banker of the two masters. Giovanni d'Antonio de' Medici, an agent of Cosimo's counter, was despatched to Rome with a letter from Cambio to Donatello, carrying in addition a verbal undertaking to the errant sculptor from Cosimo that if he came back he would suffer no financial penalty, but would be paid properly and in full. Donatello promised that he would be back for certain in Florence by the end of October, and would then bend himself with a will to the completion of the pulpit. 'He has,' wrote Giovanni d'Antonio to Cambio di Ferro on 11 October, 'many and legitimate excuses, so make no complaint of him, and do nothing against him, not even if any ask of you to do so, and especially that (word missing) for that would be an ill thing.' It was Cosimo's promise that had principally moved him to return, and so the *Operai* must keep their word as Cosimo had said they would. 'For know that he has no other possessions than his own two hands, so that if he has interposed this interval in serving you in such fashion as he well knows how, make him no worse provision for it.'[17] But October and November passed, and no Donatello or Michelozzo appeared. In December the *Operai* lost all patience and sent Cambio di Ferro to Florence to obtain letters from Cosimo de' Medici and others putting pressure on the absentees to return. On Christmas Day they commissioned Pagno di Lapo to carry these to Rome, making him a loan of 8 lire to pay his expenses and promising to see him well rewarded for his time and trouble if he was successful.[18] Pagno was back together with the two masters by 1 April 1433 when he received 16 lire for his expenses (later, in 1438, to be charged up against Donatello and Michelozzo) and Cambio di Ferro was paid 4 lire for the expenses of his mission to Florence.[19] On 9 April the series of payments to the two masters began once more.[20]

During their absence work had not entirely halted, for Pagno di Lapo, who had worked on the pulpit from at least as early as August 1430 continued to work on it until their return. From the beginning we find him being given payment for carved work, certainly architectural and ornamental, not figure-work, and receiving marble for carving from the store belonging to the Opera, superintending the transport from Pisa to Prato of marble from the quarries of Carrara bought by the *Opera* and bringing carved marbles – again certainly not figurated – from Florence. It was he who on 6 August 1432 handed in on behalf of Michelozzo and Donatello two sets of accounts showing

235

the moneys they had received from the *Opera*.[21] H. W. Janson must therefore be correct in contending that work on the pulpit went on during the absence of the two masters.[22] A few architectural members are all that Pagno himself is now known to have carved – two consoles and some panels of marble to be set between them are specified in a document of 1430 or early 1431[23] – but even so the architectural framework must have been some way advanced for their execution to be undertaken. And the three cartloads of carved marbles sent by Donatello and Michelozzo in December 1429 must have amounted to something, for in 1436 eight cartloads brought all the carved marbles for the new internal pulpit of the Duomo.[24] In all probability, therefore, Janson is right in thinking that much of the framework of the pulpit had been finished before the return of Michelozzo and Donatello from Rome. The likelihood is that it was nearing completion by September 1432, when the *Operai* began agitating for the return of Donatello. For as Janson points out, it was for the return of Donatello, who was to execute the sculptural part of the pulpit, that they were impatient. From now onwards Michelozzo played a secondary role.

The design of the pulpit as executed (nos. 78, 142) consists of a circular moulded base, with consoles above supporting the pulpit proper. The pulpit itself is composed of a moulded plinth projecting outwards a degree further from bottom to top with each successive moulding, a central frieze of seven sculptured panels separated from each other by pairs of pilasters, and a richly moulded and decorated cornice. The ribbon-bound laurel wreath, the dentils and the billets which enrich three of the mouldings of the base are motifs which recur on the base of the Aragazzi tomb, while the pairs of pilasters are evidently from the same family as those which appear on the Brancaccio tomb, whose architecture, as we have seen, was certainly designed by Michelozzo. The ordered profusion with which these ornaments are disposed is also characteristic of his style. Nevertheless, Dr. Lisner has contended in her remarkable essay on Donatello's early work as an architectural designer that the pulpit was entirely designed by Donatello, though under the influence of Michelozzo, and that Michelozzo merely advised him on the technical problems involved in fixing so heavy a load high on an exterior wall and also supervised the work while it was in progress.[25] Her case is too extreme, even if it is most improbable that Michelozzo evolved his design without consulting Donatello or accepting any of his suggestions for it. The stylistic reasons for attributing the architecture of the pulpit essentially to Michelozzo are not only strong in themselves, but are supported, as we have seen, by the trend of the document-ary evidence.

In 1433 some work still remained to be done on the framework of the pulpit, or at any rate on its supports, even though the old pulpit was taken down during July, in a spirit that time was to prove too sanguine.[26] For Donatello, far from concentrating on the Prato pulpit, at once accepted new commissions in Florence. By 10 July he was negotiating to carve for the Duomo the famous Cantoria whose reliefs are so close in spirit and invention to those of the Prato pulpit.[27] He also took up work again on the statue of the prophet Habakkuk, intended for the exterior of the Duomo (no. 134). All this although soon after his return the *Operai* had made, either by themselves, or much more probably, in consultation with him, changes in the subjects they wanted sculptured on their pulpit. This we can surmise from another change in the design which had been decided on before August 1433, the substitution of a bronze capital at the head of the external pier supporting the pulpit for the two angels standing on a 'cornice', originally proposed. The alteration is of considerable interest, for instead of the essentially Gothic motif of two weight-bearing figures it set at the top of the fluted pier an orthodox antique capital. The increased purism which this implies must have been inspired by the Roman sojourn of the two masters. But the fluting of the pier was never executed, and only one side of this bronze capital was cast (no. 142). On 1 and 8 August 1433 Donatello received a total amount of 9 lb. 11 oz. of wax for the model, and on 14 August another 4½ lb. Michelozzo received 4 lb. more on 28 August for the use of Donatello and himself, and on 25 September Simone their *gharzone* took another 6 lb. to Florence. During September, October, November and December the *Operai* also paid for bronze, brass and copper for the casting and iron, bricks, charcoal and rubble for the oven. By 9 December Michelozzo had finished the casting of the capital with the help of Matteo di Nanni and Lucha d'Antonio.[28]

Unfortunately, all that the documents make plain is that Michelozzo did the casting itself, for which he alone of the two partners was equipped by his experience as a goldsmith and metal-worker. Hence there has been much dispute as to whether it was he or Donatello who made the model for the capital. H. W. Janson has argued most strongly in favour of Michelozzo's authorship. He rightly emphasises that the unorthodox, frieze-like design of the capital, on which some scholars have founded an attribution to Donatello, is due to its position at the head of a thick, short pier, on which a regular classical capital could not have been fitted. And it should also be said that the unorthodoxy of the design is partly to be explained by the imagery of the whole design: the angels on this, the part of the pulpit nearest the ground, prelude the motif of rejoicing angels who dance and make music on the panels above.

But these considerations, if they account for the 'hybrid' nature of the capital, do not tell us which of the two masters made the design. Janson's argument from the ornamental motifs, which are close in design and treatment to those on the capitals of Sant' Agostino, is weakened, as he himself points out, by the fact that these belong to the current ornamental vocabulary of the day. As for the use of ribbons to fill empty spaces on the Prato capital, this is certainly paralleled on the base of the Aragazzi tomb, as Janson says, but it too is a motif that had been in general circulation for some years – it appears on Lamberti's tomb of Nofri Strozzi (1417) and on the base of the Cossa tomb. Nor do the putti on the capital seem to be so very closely paralleled by the Christ Child of the terracotta group in the lunette of Sant' Agostino or by those on the base of the Aragazzi tomb. They are easier and defter in treatment even than the Sant' Agostino Christ Child, which as we have seen was probably modelled *c.* 1435, when Michelozzo's style was becoming less stiff and classical, and they do not really resemble the putti of the Aragazzi base, even less those of the two reliefs, with which they must be more or less contemporary. That one of the putti on the capital repeats the pose of the left-hand putto holding the epitaph on the Cossa tomb is an argument rather in favour of Donatello's authorship than against it, since Donatello, contrary to what has been claimed, was not at all averse to economising in artistic invention. Not only does he repeat architectural motifs – as in the niche framing the effigy of Giovanni Pecci, which has the same design as the niches of the Cossa tomb – but there are several instances from these years of his repeating in miniature inventions he had already designed for use on a larger scale. The Virtues and music-making angels of the Siena font, which are reduced variations of the Virtues of the Cossa tomb and the trumpeting angels of the Brancaccio tomb are examples already encountered. The impish liveliness of the figures of the capital is very characteristic of Donatello and quite uncharacteristic of Michelozzo, who would certainly have produced a much stiffer and austerer composition.

Yet here too as always it is surely absurd to suppose that each of the two masters designed particular parts of their joint works in a spirit of stern and jealous determination not to allow his creative imagination to be corrupted by the other. Such a conception of artistic integrity belongs to the Romantic era, not to the *quattrocento*. And if we allow force to Janson's arguments for Michelozzo's authorship of the ornamental parts of the capital, we reach the solution of a 'hybrid' design which not only reconciles scholarly divergencies, but may well correspond to the reality of its origin. Is it necessary to point out in favour of this line of argument that Donatello was willing enough to compromise his 'artistic integrity' by entering into partnership with Michelozzo and by tolerating inferior execution in parts of works he had designed.

At one time there was also much discussion as to the original form of the capital and even as to whether the rest of it had been cast. For this second dispute Vasari was responsible, for he asserted in his life of Donatello that the missing half of it had been broken away and carried off by the Spanish troops who sacked Prato so terribly in 1512. But contemporary documents[29] prove conclusively that only the still existing half was ever cast and that this was a

238

cause of grievance in Prato. The half-finished state of the capital, it may be added, is yet another indication that the model was largely the work of Donatello rather than of the more business-like Michelozzo. Meanwhile on 3 August the *Operai* paid a certain Meo di Jacopo for lime he had brought 'for beginning to set up the pulpit on the wall.' During the same month three stone *ruote* were sent by Donatello and Michelozzo and on 25 August a note was made that the *Opera* had obtained a thousand bricks for the pulpit in several lots from the *Opera* of San Giovanni in Florence. On 8 and 18 August three masons were paid for work on the pulpit, notably for 'walling under it'.[30]

But after the casting of the capital all progress was halted by the dilatoriness of Donatello. Accordingly the *Operai*, annoyed to find themselves no better off for all their trouble, sought to bind him by a new 'composition and pact' which they made with him in the sacristy of the Cappella del Sacro Cingolo on 27 May 1434. Donatello alone figures in it by name, Michelozzo appearing simply as one of the 'others' who were his partners.[31] It was now stipulated that Donatello was to receive 25 gold florins for each of the reliefs 'which shall be placed by his own hand on or in the said pulpit,' and both sides agreed to abide by the 'composition' under a penalty of 200 gold florins. As in November 1428, Donatello was stung into temporary activity by this fresh obligation, and only twenty-three days later had finished the first relief. 'I promise you,' wrote from Florence the Pratese Matteo degli Organi, a famous builder of organs and one of the witnesses to the new agreement between Donatello and the *Operai*, 'that those of this place who understand such things all say with one voice that never was seen the like history. And he seems to me to be of a mind to serve you well, so that, now he is in a good disposition, it is needful for us to acknowledge it, for masters such as this are not to be found at all times. He prays me to write to you that in God's name you fail not to send him some money to spend these feast days, and I lay it upon you to do so, seeing that he is a man for whom any little meal is enough, and he is content with anything. So that, even if the *Opera* has to beg for it at interest, it is needful that he have some money, so that he may be kept in that good purpose in which he has begun, and the fault be not laid on us. In Florence, on the 19th day of June 1434.'[32]

The *Opera* obliged, sending 32 lire in two lots on 20 and 29 June, but to reap their reward they had to make new solicitations in Florence, and it was only on 2 September that Lancia the miller was paid 1 lira 15 *soldi* for carting three more reliefs to Prato.[33] These were unfinished and evidently were to be mounted up in order for it to be seen how they looked from the ground. And after this burst of energy things returned to their usual course, so that for two years nothing more was heard of the reliefs, though in the summer of 1435 Maso di Bartolommeo (of whom more in a moment) was sent to Florence

239

to see about their progress. Then in April 1436 Donatello took back the three reliefs Lancia had carted to Prato in order to finish them off, for only the first relief, that so highly admired in Florence, had been sent to Prato fully completed. It is true they were returned by 3 June, though only after a first unsuccessful demand for them from Prato, but when the *Operai* sent for Donatello to come to Prato that November, he 'laughed us to scorn'.[34]

Meanwhile, the *Operai* had pressed on with such other parts of the job as they could get finished by lesser but more reliable masters, principally the Florentine mason, smith and metal-worker, Maso di Bartolommeo.[35] Early in July 1434 they had a scaffold erected and put Maso and another mason to work setting up the brackets on which the pulpit was to rest, installing the panels of marble which were to go between them, and fixing the first *ruota* which was to rest on the brackets. The two seem to have finished all this by October[36] whereupon the *Operai* started Maso working from 2 November on the column which was to support a baldacchino above the pulpit.[37] In addition, being determined to wait no longer for the other half of the capital, or perhaps hoping to shame Donatello and Michelozzo into finishing it, they obtained a judgment from the *Podestà* of Prato compelling the apothecary Vannozzo di Piero of Prato, in whose custody the two masters had left the finished half, to surrender it to them, and then had Maso set it up immediately.[38]

After the column was finished in April 1435 they sought for a master to make the *baldacchino*, and on 26 July, having had the old one knocked down a few days before they contracted for a new one of wood with Domenico di Domenico da Prato. At the same time they had a *ruota* set on the column which was to support it.[39] They then put in motion work on the new internal pulpit from which the relic was to be exhibited to congregations inside the church. By the end of September 1436 or thereabouts the marbles for this inner pulpit had all been brought to Prato, and Maso di Bartolommeo had finished putting a lead roof on the *baldacchino*, so that there now remained only Donatello's reliefs to complete the work.[40] Accordingly, Maso was despatched on 17 November to Florence to reason with Donatello, and the aid of Cosimo de' Medici was again invoked. Once more Cosimo smoothed matters over by obtaining an advance of money for Donatello: the *Operai* made a formal promise of 100 *lire piccole* to Cosimo through their treasurer (*camerario*) on 22 April 1437, and on 14 May Donatello's *gharzone* Agostino, who has been identified as the youthful Agostino di Duccio, appeared in Prato and took away 20 *lire piccole*.[41]

After this Donatello gave no sign of life, perhaps because he felt that the *Operai* had not kept their promises about money as they should. For in order to induce him to finish the three reliefs Simone di Giovanni, an *Operaio*, had promised him in 1436 on his own surety and that of his colleagues 240 lire after he had completed them. Early in 1438 Simone appealed successfully to the Signoria of Florence to compel the *Operai* then in office to pay Donatello this sum so that he might be quit of his obligation. The *Opera* protested indignantly that the reliefs ought to have been finished years ago, and that they had already paid out such sums for them that even the work of the Florentine Duomo would not cost so much. In any case the promise had been made on condition that the reliefs were completed. In fact the reliefs had not been completed, namely in that the fourth was still unfinished. If the accounts between him and the *Operai* were examined, it would be found that he owed the *Opera* far more than the 240 lire he now claimed. The trouble was that 'Donatello has always led us after him wheresoever it pleased him, and there has never been found a board of *Operai* to put a bar effectively to his inconstancy, but we have always followed his inclination and treated him with pleasantness, and he quite the contrary, but now things shall not be so.' The *Opera* chose two *ambasciadori* on 4 March to make these representations to the *Signoria* and also sent copies of the original contracts for the pulpit and of the *stime* or reports on the work which it had obtained at intervals from various masters.[42]

The *Signoria* seems to have compromised the matter: on the one hand the *Opera* paid Donatello the 240 lire through Cosimo de' Medici's brother and partner Lorenzo on 21 July, and in return Donatello was forced to complete the reliefs[43] – by July indeed he must have done so. For work on setting up the reliefs on the pulpit began early in July and on 8 September the Girdle was exhibited from it for the first time.[44] On 17 September the *Opera* entered into its accounts that 'Donato di Nicholo and Michelozzo di Bartolommeo master sculptors ... are creditors on the said day for 700 lire for the making and carving of the seven panels of marble, carved and historied, made by the said Donatello and Michelozzo, which are the parapet and border of the pulpit of white marble over the piazza: for these they are to have for their mastery and for the white marble of the said seven panels in all 100 lire for each.' And now, in emulation or imitation of the *Cantoria* of the Florentine Duomo, the *Opera* decided that the background of each relief should be filled with gold mosaic, and on the same day they agreed to pay Donatello a sum unspecified for this work through Lorenzo di Giovanni de' Medici, Donatello undertaking to supply the gold.[45]

Marchini has very acutely used the chronology of the reliefs as it emerges from all these vicissitudes to fix the date of one of them. When the pulpit was dismantled during the war for safe storage it was found that the last relief on the side wall (no. 79) was carved with a second pilaster on the right-hand side where it had been set in the wall. Marchini deduces,[46] surely correctly, that it must have been the very first relief of all, the one that was sent to Prato in 1434 after exciting so much admiration in Florence. For

R   241 as he points out, if it was carved for its present position, the second pilaster would not have been necessary. And the high quality of the relief also supports his argument. Of the remaining six reliefs we know that three were sketched out in 1434, two of them being finished in 1436, while the third was hurriedly completed by July 1438. The other three reliefs had been hurriedly begun and completed between March and July 1438. Too much should not be made of the haste with which some of the reliefs may have been carved, since they were all quite evidently executed with considerable speed – even the first and most highly admired was produced, as we saw, in the space of a month, more or less, and two months later the next three had been brought on far enough to be sent to Prato for trial on the pulpit.

The chronology of the remaining six reliefs has to be founded on an assessment of their quality. It is universally agreed that all the reliefs were designed by Donatello, but at one time it was also maintained that they were entirely the work of his assistants, and they were distributed among various hands, Michelozzo coming in for his share. There can be no doubt that Donatello made liberal use of assistants, all the more because the reliefs were to be set high above the ground so that minute delicacy of modelling would be so much wasted work. In a famous passage Vasari records his opinion that Luca della Robbia made the mistake of overworking the carving of his *Cantoria* (executed from 1431 to 1438) whereas the rough and bold figures of Donatello's *Cantoria* stood out with much more effect from below. But the view that Donatello left the Prato reliefs entirely to assistants is exaggerated. There is evidence from contemporary drawings and squeezes as well as from Matteo degli Organi's letter that the reliefs were much admired, and this alone ought to make us sceptical of such an opinion. It was first propounded some four and a half centuries after the reliefs had been set high on the corner of Santo Stefano, by which time weathering had coarsened many surfaces. Donatello's calculated roughnesses and audacities of effect have been distorted accordingly, all the more because of the spatial composition of the reliefs, to which we shall return in a moment. Hence it is even more dangerous than usual to assess rigidly and arbitrarily differences of quality in the reliefs and to distribute them among different hands, especially using only binoculars and photographs.

In recent years the impurities of the atmosphere of modern industrial Prato have accelerated the progress of their ruin, so that when the reliefs were again dismantled in 1971 for conservation treatment in Florence they were found to have scaled and flaked grievously. But the close inspection of them at ground level which I was kindly allowed to make inclines me to think that rather more of them is probably by Donatello's hand than it is customary to allow. Professor Marchini, who knows the reliefs better than any other scholar, is also of the opinion that at least one of them is fully autograph, the central relief (no. 80).[47] He is more hesitant about the second relief, the first to be executed, though recognising its great merits. But in my view it too must be called autograph if we use the term in the sense in which it should be used of any fifteenth-century work of art, that is, as meaning a work preponderantly executed by the master himself. Two of the remaining reliefs (nos. 81, 82) are certainly entirely by Donatello's assistants, so flatly and coarsely do the forms incarnate his design. In the first of these reliefs (no. 81) Michelozzo may possibly have lent a hand, since there are resemblances between the putto on the extreme left and those in the Aragazzi reliefs. The putto on the extreme right seems to be by the same poor hand which carved most or all of the other relief. The incompetence of these two panels suggests that they may well have been the last of the reliefs to have been carved, and that they were begun and finished by assistants in a rush to complete the work within the time fixed by the Florentine *Signoria*.

For it is important to remember the erratic nature of workshop assistance in the fifteenth century and later. At times parts or whole pieces of work were left entirely to assistants. These are usually the easiest to recognise. But assistants also finished off work begun by the master or else the master finished off work they had begun. In such cases, and especially when the assistant was talented or merely competent – and we have seen by now that Donatello and Michelozzo employed hands and helpers who varied from the incompetent to the accomplished – recognition becomes more difficult. At our date the controlling factors in the making of any given work of art were the degree of interest the master himself took in it, or the importance he might attach to certain parts of it, and the pressures, more or less effective according to circumstances, brought to bear on the master by patrons anxious to get their commission completed. As these factors fluctuated, so did the contribution of assistants. The remaining three reliefs seem to reflect this state of affairs in differing degrees. One (no. 83) has such ease in its variety of movement and such fullness and richness of form that it must be largely the work of Donatello, perhaps nearly as much as the two others which seem to be autograph in our sense of the word. For here too the accomplishment with which the audacious classicism and dynamic movement of the design is realised were surely beyond the ordinary workshop sculptor of this date – one has only to compare Michelozzo's Aragazzi reliefs with it to see the difference between the same aspirations fully and incompletely achieved.

Another of the reliefs (no. 84) is nearly as good. Only in the last relief (no. 85) is the participation of assistants, probably including Michelozzo himself in the heads of the two putti in the foreground, sensibly dominant. Since what we now have is a sequence of skinned forms designed by a sculptor with a masterly sense of what was required for telling optical effect it must be emphasised once again how important it is not to be too assertive in attribution. But if the two reliefs which are wholly the work of assistants are excluded, we are left with five panels for whose masterly movement and rhythms the hand of Donatello, carving or controlling to a greater or lesser degree, must be responsible. Too many complex formal problems have been posed and answered in them for them to be wholly the work of assistants except within certain bounds.

As we have seen, the hand of Michelozzo seems to be distinguishable, but it will probably never be possible to be certain which if any of the various assistants mentioned in the long sequence of documents concerning the pulpit executed other parts. We hear in December 1428 of Matteo di Bartolommeo, Donatello's and Michelozzo's *gharzone in bottega*, in September 1432 of another *gharzone* named Donato, in September 1433 of Bartolo di Giovanello and Betto d'Antonio 'who are in their employ', and in the same month of another *gharzone* named Simone. All these hands, besides Pagno di Lapo, his partner Papi di Piero, and his *gharzone* Chimenti di Luca, we have to reckon with, besides Maso di Bartolommeo and Agostino who may have been Agostino di Duccio.[48] And the impression given by the documents taken as a whole is not of a stable workshop, whose journeymen were the same from first to last, but of youths learning their art or men passing through the shop, of masons and other specialist craftsmen taken on for a time or hired for piecework. In fact, Donatello and Michelozzo had exactly the sort of assistance we should expect from all we know of the old irregular organisation of artists' workshops.

Each relief shows a *balla* or dance of child angels, dancing in a round in threes to the accompaniment of classical instruments, a cymbal, or a trumpet. To the severe nineteenth century, which saw in the Renaissance a revival of paganism, it seemed shocking that a pulpit intended for the exhibition of the Virgin's Girdle should have been adorned with infant bacchanalia. Yet all that had happened in reality was that the winged geniuses of antiquity have been changed into child angels, by a process of transmutation discussed in an earlier chapter. Kauffmann[49] suggested in 1935 that the decision to commission seven panels rather than six was prompted by symbolic considerations: he cited the Brancaccio *Assumption*, where the Virgin is carried heavenwards by seven angels. Certainly the *Operai* took their decision to increase the number of panels from six to seven deliberately and advisedly, since by the agreement of May 1434 they agreed to give Donatello 25 florins for each relief, so binding themselves to pay him more than they had originally intended, perhaps considerably more, since the new panels were to contain so many more figures than the old. As Kauffmann thought, the dancing and music making of the angels express their rejoicing at the Assumption of the Virgin into Heaven. *Assumpta est Maria in caelum et gaudent angeli. R. Laudantes benedicunt dominum* and again *Exaltata est Sancta dei genitrix Super choros angel-*

orum ad celestia are responses that ring throughout the office for the Assumption in the Roman Breviary. Each time the Virgin's Girdle is shown above the rejoicing choirs of child angels carved on the pulpit there is symbolised that exaltation into heaven above all the choirs of angels proclaimed in those responses. When the ground between the angel putti was filled with gold mosaic, and shone with the golden light of heaven, the symbolism must have been even more obvious. And so appropriate did the motif seem to the relic in whose honour it was devised that Maso di Bartolommeo used it again on the bronze casket he made to contain the girdle in 1447.

This programme, so much more significant than the simple and formal heraldic design originally proposed, was evidently chosen after April 1433, when Donatello resumed work on the pulpit, and before the new agreement of 27 May 1434. So close are the motifs of the pulpit to those of the *Cantoria* carved by Donatello for the Florentine Duomo that the question of priority of conception naturally arises. The *Operai* of the Duomo sanctioned the proposal for a new *Cantoria* on 10 July 1433, when they deputed Neri Capponi to commission it from Donatello and to arrange with him about its subject, price and date of completion. These had all been satisfactorily agreed on by 14 November, when it was formally settled that Donatello was to be paid 40 florins for each panel of his *Cantoria* if its workmanship was as good as that of the panels of Luca della Robbia's *Cantoria*: if it was better, then he might be paid up to 50 florins. Whether the design Donatello submitted in 1433 was that he eventually executed, or whether, as Janson has persuasively argued, his original design was for a series of panels like those of the Prato pulpit, the conclusion seems inescapable that the *Cantoria* was designed before the reliefs of the Prato pulpit.

Indeed, Janson has followed up his hypothesis with the suggestion that after Donatello had altered his first design for the *Cantoria* he put his original sketches or models for it to use in the Prato pulpit.[50] As he was to receive only half as much for each of the Prato panels as for the Florentine panels, this is very possible. But it is also possible that the *Operai* of Prato, seeing what magnificence the Florentines proposed for their new *Cantoria*, decided that they would like just such a design or something very like it for their own pulpit. Such imitative rivalry was frequent among fifteenth-century patrons, particularly, it is fair to suppose, among the less artistically sophisticated, such as the *Operai* of Prato – small notaries, innkeepers, apothecaries, wool merchants as they were – since it enabled them to feel some confidence about what they were going to get for their money. The fact that the reliefs were set with a ground of gold mosaic like that of the Florentine *Cantoria* is a strong presumption in favour of this interpretation, as is the complaint of the *Operai* in March 1438 that their pulpithad already cost more than the work (*opera*) of Santa Maria del Fiore.

In a brilliant essay on the relationship between Donatello and the antique Janson[51] has studied the classical sources of the Prato reliefs, where the antique is for a moment seen not as a repertoire of motifs to be quoted for learned enrichment but as a model whose forms and spirit are to be reproduced wholeheartedly. He points out that although the motif of the compositions is a round dance, the actions of the figures are derived from representations on antique sarcophagi of children boxing or engaged in athletic sports, and from small antique bronzes and terracottas depicting violent athletic action. In the reserves of the Museo Vaticano he has even found the identical Roman sarcophagus from whose boxing putti Donatello took the dancing putti for one of the Prato pulpit reliefs. It should be said that the early *quattrocento* recognised only one sharp division in the history of art, that between antique art and art in the antique tradition on the one hand, and modern art on the other. The distinctions between Hellenistic, Etruscan, Imperial Roman, early Christian and Byzantine art of which we are so sharply conscious were not made then or for centuries later, and even Romanesque art was sometimes confused, as in the case of the Florentine Baptistery, with the authentic art of antiquity and believed to be Roman, not Romanesque.

For *quattrocento* artists therefore all surviving works of art in a classical style were of equal value and interest, all the more so because relatively few were known to them. Donatello, though perfectly aware that there were distinctions of quality among them,[52] was not concerned with differences of date or style. Like his contemporaries he took from antiquity in a spirit that may now seem eclectic and empirical, but which in fact was realistic. For only by combining hints, suggestions and borrowings from his diverse and fragmentary sources could a Florentine sculptor of the Renaissance attempt to create new works using antique forms and in the antique spirit. Hence the importance to him of sarcophagi, small sculptures and gems. Moreover, the commissions he received were not for works in the genres of antiquity – only with the spread of humanism among patrons did portrait busts begin to be carved in Florence in the middle decades of the century. Even the medal did not establish itself as a current genre until the 1430s. During these years Florentine sculptors still worked exclusively in the genres which medieval art had evolved to express the beliefs of a feudal and Catholic society.

Moreover, they nursed other artistic ambitions in addition to the revival of antique forms. The foremost of these was naturalism, above all the systematised naturalism that sought to create the illusion of depth in space through geometrical perspective – a very Gothic ideal in its intellectualism, however much it seemed an ideal of antiquity revived to artists and humanists. From the contradiction between the search for pictorial illusionism, with its three-plane construction, and the realities of antique reliefs, with their two-plane construction, even Michelozzo at his most neo-classical was not able to escape completely, as we have seen. And after a few years of revivalism Donatello and he quietly resolved the incompatibility by jettisoning their neo-classical manner in favour of pictorial illusionism. In this they followed the preference of their age: later the logicalities of geometrical perspective, as soon as they had been pushed to the limits of the unreal, were abandoned for more plausible simulations of nature. Donatello's resolution of the dilemma posed to his fuller creative ambitions by the purist enthusiasm he had caught in Rome can be seen in the Prato reliefs and in the *Cantoria*. With great adroitness he has produced in both works a superficial aspect of antique relief – construction. Yet in reality his union of the forms and energetic actions of sarcophagus reliefs and antique statuettes with the gold mosaic of Early Christian, Byzantine and medieval Roman art is grafted into compositions which obey the concepts of three-dimensional space proper to his age. His dancing angels are not applied to a gold background, but dance their rounds in the golden light of Heaven.

The only note of colour now remaining on the pulpit is the green marble in which the capital of the column that supports the *baldacchino* is carved. Originally the egg and dart ornament, the laurel wreaths, the acorns of its various mouldings were all gilt, but the gilding has gone as has the red of the ribbon binding the laurel wreaths.[53] Gone too is the gilding of the bronze capital. The gold mosaic which once glowed between the white marble figures of the rejoicing angels has also disappeared, all save a few fragments, to be replaced by a ceramic mosaic of a dull, neutral tone. The underside of the *baldacchino* now glows no longer with the rich blue, relieved by gold and red in the coats of arms, that once enriched it. Even after it had received all these adornments the pulpit was still incomplete: the seven blind panels on its inside corresponding to the carved reliefs on the outside, were to have had decorated panels set between them, corresponding to the pairs of pilasters of the exterior. Only three of these carved uprights were executed, though since they are invisible from below they are not odd in effect like the unfinished capital.[54]

But it would seem that by September 1438 the *Operai* had either had enough of Donatello and Michelozzo or else had made up their minds to rest satisfied after the ground of the reliefs had been filled with gold mosaic. Or perhaps it was only that they were now too short of money to commission new work, for it was not until 1441 that they made their final payments to Domenico di Domenico and Maso di Bartolommeo for the *baldacchino* which the two masters had finished in 1436.[55] Certainly they made no final settlement with Donatello and Michelozzo, and they did not even meet them for the comparison and agreement of accounts which was customary. In 1443 Donatello left Florence for a ten years' residence in Padua, returning only late in 1454 or early in 1455. His departure effectively dissolved his partnership with

Michelozzo, but the two masters remained on the best of terms. In April 1455, after Donatello had returned to Florence, they determined to bring the *Operai* of Prato to a sense of their obligations. The courteous but firm letter which they wrote inviting the *Operai* then in office to meet them for an adjustment and settlement of accounts still survives, but what reply they received and whether they succeeded in extracting any money has not been discovered.[56]

After the completion of the Prato pulpit and of the Aragazzi tomb in 1438 Michelozzo undertook no more ambitious sculpture in marble. Henceforward he worked mostly as an architect in the service of Cosimo de' Medici and his son Piero. He certainly continued to design decorative carvings for his architectural work, though whether he sculptured them with his own now wealthy hands is another question. Vasari speaks admiringly[57] of the falcon holding the Medici device of a diamond ring through which passes a ribbon with the motto SEMPER (no. 92) which is carved in the lunette of the rear side of the Cappella del Crocefisso in the church of San Miniato al Monte. The Cappella, which was designed by Michelozzo for Piero de' Medici, was in fact a tabernacle built to enshrine an ancient painted crucifix which had come to be generally venerated during the fourteenth century as that whose Christ had bent its head to the eleventh-century saint Giovanni Gualberto, while still a monk at San Miniato, as a sign that his forgiveness of his brother's murderer was acceptable to God. By the middle of the fifteenth century devotion to the crucifix had increased so greatly that it was resolved to move it into the middle of the church and house it in a special tabernacle which was to be a chapel in miniature form.[58] On 27 June 1447 the *Arte di Calimala*, who had the fabric of San Miniato under their care, resolved that the altar of Christ Crucified might be adorned by any great citizen who should offer to make for it a tabernacle of great splendour and expense, but only on condition that no arms other than those of the *Arte* might be carved on it – a not unusual restriction in fifteenth-century Florence, where there was great jealousy for the honour and reputation of piety.[59] But on 10 June of the following year the *Arte* relented, and granted Piero de' Medici, the great citizen whose name had been discreetly omitted in its earlier resolution, permission to carve his arms on the 'marble adornment which he is making to the Cappella del Crocefisso,' provided always that the arms of the Arte were carved in the most conspicuous place of all.[60] Michelozzo's falcon must have been designed and executed shortly after this date. A very handsome carving, it is none the less the kind of work that by now, at fifty years of age, Michelozzo would certainly have left to one of the skilled decorative sculptors who abounded in *quattrocento* Florence.

This is borne out by the history of the marble tabernacle or chapel which Piero commissioned him to design *c.* 1447 to house the miraculous painting of the Virgin venerated in the Annunziata at Florence. Although Michelozzo designed this chapel, it was executed by his old partner and assistant in such architectural work, Pagno di Lapo Portigiani, who finished it in 1448 and proudly added his signature on the inside of the architrave.[61] A marble basin (no. 90), presumably once part of a lavabo, which is now in the Museo Bardini, is said to have come from the sacristy of this chapel, and hence is often attributed to Michelozzo. It is decorated with fluting imitated from an antique sarcophagus and ornamented with a medallion carved with the triple head which is a symbol of the Trinity: from this we can see that it has not even the most tenuous connection with Michelozzo's style. In the first version of his life of Michelozzo, published in 1550, Vasari says that Michelozzo carved for the Annunziata a marble *pila* or holy water stoup which stood at the entrance to the church and had a small figure of the Baptist *nel sommo*, that is, either in the centre or more probably at the back, and also a marble relief of the Virgin and Child which was set 'above the bench for candles'.[62] Michelozzo certainly undertook commissions for such ornamental works as holy water basins, for in December 1433 he obtained fifteen pieces of *Prato verde* marble from the *Operai* of the *Sacro Cingolo* 'to make stoups, so he said, for holy water'.[63] Evidently it was for some such purposes that Donatello and he wanted the other old or unwanted pieces of marble belonging to the *Opera* which they took as part of their pay. We do not know, unfortunately, for which church or churches Michelozzo intended to make holy water stoups, as there is no further mention in the Prato documents of this particular undertaking. The holy water stoup and its figure of St. John which he made for the Annunziata have long since disappeared, and a relief of the Virgin and Child (no. 91) now set above the bench in the portico of the Annunziata where candles are sold cannot be his – its style is much closer to Luca della Robbia (if indeed the relief dates from the fifteenth century at all). It has only occupied its present position since it was attributed to Michelozzo in 1922, when Lensi thought he recognised in it the relief described by Vasari.[64]

But the Annunziata does still contain one important sculpture by Michelozzo, the life-size terracotta statue of St. John the Baptist (nos. 73, 74, 77) which was commissioned by Messer Antonio di Michele di Forese da Rabatta, a descendant of a family which had moved into Florence from the Mugello in the fourteenth century, and had established itself among the ruling oligarchy. Messer Antonio was a banker in partnership with Bernardo Cambi, their bank having counters in London and Bruges. Politically he was an adherent of Cosimo de' Medici; on 1 August 1458, during the discussions before the passing of the law of the *parlamento* on 11 August, he urged that eight or ten persons be appointed to consult with Cosimo 'that very wise man,'[65] and that whatever they decided should be done. He commissioned the figure for his newly founded chapel in the Annunziata, which was dedicated to St. John Baptist. The chapel was begun in 1444, and the statue must have been modelled not too long after that date. Michelozzo may well have built the chapel – he had become *Capomaestro della fabrica* of the whole church by October of that same year – which would explain why he received the commission for the St. John. The figure was an altar-piece, rather an exceptional rôle for a single sculpture in *quattrocento* Florence, and stood above the altar in a niche of *pietra serena*.

That it was designed to occupy a niche is evident, for it is hollowed out at the back and its inner edges are left rough. At some date between 1546 and 1677 it was concealed behind an altar-piece of the Assumption, attributed to Perugino, which had originally been painted for the high altar of the church. This was set on the altar of the chapel, which was then rededicated to the Virgin of the Assumption. For a long time, certainly from 1677, the statue was attributed to Donatello, though not everyone believed it to be by his hand. Thus in 1684 Del Migliore, noting that the statue had now been removed from the chapel, tartly observed that while some thought it a work of Donatello, it could hardly be called one of his best things.[66] From 1828 it languished in the Secondo Chiostro of the convent, where Schmarsow saw it in 1886[67] and recognised it as a work by Michelozzo. By the early twentieth century it had been covered with a coat of whitewash (see no. 77): only in 1931 was it restored and set up in the left transept of the church.[68]

The figure is made in one with an oblong base. The saint stands with his weight resting on his right leg, so that his body is thrown into a gentle curve. Looking down at his adorers, he raises his right hand and points with its index finger in a traditional gesture symbolising his words 'Behold the Lamb of God' – the Baptist's index finger, it will be remembered, had been Cossa's legacy to the Baptistery. In his left hand he carries a cross (a modern replacement). He wears a short-sleeved tunic of goat-skin, held round his waist by an elegantly tied sash, and a broad cloak, which is extended by the action of his arms into a great arc of drapery patterned by broad, symmetrical folds. Visible is the same care as in the Aragazzi figures to mark the structure of bone, vein, sinew and muscle, but in keeping with the stylistic trend of the Sant' Agostino figures, the figure is treated with the more attenuated elegance of International Gothic. The face is long and pointed; the limbs and hands are slender and graceful, the hair is disposed in long waving curls and tresses. In all probability the figure was originally coloured and gilded, but no trace now remains of any such enrichment.

A similar Gothic elegance appears in Michelozzo's last dated sculpture, the St. John Baptist he was commissioned by the *Arte di Calimala* in 1452 to make for the great silver dossal of the Baptistery. The clothing of altars wholly in precious metal or the adorning of them with dossals and antependia of gold and silver had been a much favoured form of pious magnificence throughout Western Europe in Carolingian, Ottonian and Romanesque times, after the example of the Popes and Emperors who had enriched the churches of Rome with sumptuous works of the goldsmith's art from the time of the Emperor Constantine. In Northern Europe such splendours seem to have died out during the thirteenth century, probably for economic reasons, but like so many customs of earlier ages the tradition remained alive in Italy. The Pala d'Oro executed for the high altar of St. Mark's in Venice was completed in 1345. The silver altar of San Jacopo in the cathedral of Pistoia, consisting of a dossal and a three-sided antependium, was begun in 1287 and was continued with various changes of design until 1456, when it was finally completed. Already in the thirteenth century the *Arte di Calimala* had adorned the altar of the Baptist in the Baptistery with a silver dossal, decorated with subjects from his life.[69] But in 1360, stung by reports that silver altars of much greater splendour were to be seen in other Italian cities, notably in Rome, the *Arte* broke up their old dossal and commissioned a new one which it was intended should outshine all others in the whole wide world. How significant it is of the change from the earlier to the later Middle Ages that works of art so costly and ambitious were now undertaken by wealthy corporations of merchants, not by emperors, mighty bishops and abbots as in former times.

Begun in 1366 or 1367,[70] the execution of the dossal (no. 75) as of all such works, was protracted for a century and more, largely because of its expense, but also, or so it is said, because each relief was put out to competition. Every aspirant to the commission had to submit a wax model and these were then publicly exhibited so that the *Operai* appointed by the *Arte* could discover which was generally judged the best.[71] By 1425, possibly even by 1401–10, much of the rich Gothic framework of the altar, eight reliefs of scenes from the life of the Baptist and thirty of the statuettes filling the niches of the framework had been completed. All that now remained to be done, so the *Consoli* of the *Arte* recorded with gratification in 1425, was to fill the central arched 'tabernacle' with a large figure of the Baptist set in a frame of suitable richness.

But it was not until October 1445 that the *Arte* turned its attention to commissioning these final pieces, perhaps because all its funds had been needed for the expense of Ghiberti's second bronze doors. Even then all they ordered was the framework. This, as we know from recently discovered documents, was executed for them by two goldsmiths from Ghiberti's workshop, Tommaso di Lorenzo Ghiberti and Matteo di Giovanni. On 15 December 1445 these two masters were paid 46 florins 16 *soldi* in final settlement of the 169 florins due to them 'for the work they have done on the dossal and silver tabernacle of the Oratorio of San Giovanni.' To them, therefore, and not to Michelozzo as was once thought, is due St. John's gabled frame of ornate Late Gothic design, crowned with four statues of prophets, not now identifiable, but certainly four who were considered forerunners of the Baptist, and enriched on the piers with panels of saints in translucent enamel. The upper part of the niche which it encloses is adorned with a ground of blue enamel studded with silver stars.

Seven years later, in 1452, Michelozzo was given the commission to make the statue of St. John Baptist, perhaps after a competition, or perhaps because his statue of the saint in Messer Antonio da Rabatta's chapel had been greatly admired. The figure was to be one *braccia* and a twentieth high (slightly more than two feet) and was to weigh if possible a little less than eleven *oncie*. For the fashion Michelozzo was to receive 50 florins. In fact when completed the figure weighed 14 *oncie* 14 *soldi* and cost 206 florins, 41 *soldi*. Again the original books of the *Arte* recording the commission and its completion are lost, and we have to rely on Carlo Strozzi's *spogli*. But from what he noted it appears that the commission was first mentioned on f.12 of the book of *Deliberazioni* of the *Arte* for the years 1451 to 1454. Since Strozzi always kept to the style of the books from which he took his notes, and since he records three times that the commission was given in 1452, such an early position in the *Deliberazioni* probably means that the commission was awarded in April 1452 or thereabouts, since the year 1451 ended according to Florentine style on our 24 March 1452. Michelozzo seems to have worked with a certain expedition, for 50 leaves later came a note that 'the hairs of the said saint are gilded.'[72]

The silver figure (no. 76) repeats Michelozzo's terracotta figure made for Messer Antonio on a smaller scale, with only a few significant variations in the design. Its style too is the same, slender limbs, with muscles, bones and sinews strongly marked and terminating in long and elegant hands and feet. Some modern scholars, forgetting the close relationship between the two figures, so often noted in the nineteenth century, have surmised that Michelozzo used a rather old-fashioned Gothicising style to harmonise the silver St. John with the rest of the dossal. The truth is that, as we have seen, after passing through a neo-classical phase *c.* 1433–4, Michelozzo's style became one in which Late Gothic naturalism, as interpreted in Florence, is predominant. The figure wears the same costume as the Annunziata Baptist, a short-sleeved goat-skin tunic, gilded, and held by an elegantly tied sash of plain silver which is a feat of embossing, with a gilt border of lozenge-shaped flowers on a hatched ground at its end. The cloak, made in two sections soldered together, is also of plain silver except for a gilt border of imitation Cufic lettering. The hair, moustaches, beard and hair are gilt, as is the halo. In his distribution of the gilding Michelozzo has achieved that perfect balance between gilt and ungilt so characteristic of the best Gothic goldsmith's work and so masterly in its refined splendour of effect. The cross which the saint holds is a typical fifteenth-century Italian processional cross: it is hatched and gilt to the beginning of the shaft.

The principal differences between this figure and the Annunziata figure, apart from that of scale, are in the pose. Here the weight rests on the left leg and the head is turned leftwards, looking out towards the congregation whom the saint summons to behold the Lamb of God. In a sense this treatment is more dramatic than that of the Annunziata Baptist, which as the altar-statue of a private chapel is posed so as to enter into a closed relationship with the praying devotee beneath. Yet the design of the silver saint does not offend the limits of decorum imposed on altar figures by *quattrocento* notions, but images within them the rôle of the Baptist as the Precursor of Christ. In 1452, when it was made, the dossal was not in fact used as an altar-piece: on the contrary it was only displayed on the two great festivals of the Baptist, his Nativity (24 June) and the Baptism of Christ (13 January) which John XXIII had declared a feast-day in 1410 in order to gratify the devotion of the Florentines to their patron-saint. And it seems that for at least twenty years after the completion of Michelozzo's figure it was the custom to display it, not on the altar of the Baptistery, but on the font, which was almost always dry. Here it shone on the white marble, the gold and silver reliquaries of the church glittering in front of it.

We must always remember too that it was intended to be seen at some height from the ground, not at ground level, as now in the Museo dell' Opera del Duomo, where it is usually housed. Seen at ground level Michelozzo's figure appears awkward in its dimensions, too large for a statuette, too small for monumental effect. In fact Michelozzo seems to have taken the height at which it was intended to be seen into careful consideration, for he has made the feet disproportionately long and wide. And a little reflection soon shows that he solved the problems posed by the commission rather skilfully. He had to make a figure of the saint that would dominate a setting of the utmost intricacy and richness of surface. Not only was the framework made by Tommaso Ghiberti and Matteo di Giovanni elaborate and assertive in design and ornament, but it was framed by polygonal piers, niched, buttressed, crocketed, set with enamels. Across the top of the altar ran a heavy entablature of niches, each with its statuette. To either side of the piers the eight highly pictorial reliefs executed by late *trecento* goldsmiths extended themselves in all their opulence of figures and setting. Michelozzo evaded the snare of attempting to make his figure dominate all this by an exaggeratedly strained pose or by overwhelming richness of ornament. Instead his figure has a quiet pose and simple drapery, and stands out by reason of this relative simplicity, and because of the expressive gestures of its hands and the gilding of the goatskin, hair, moustache and beard. The result is at once an accord and a climax. The same dexterity appears in the matching of design to technique. The figure is so posed and worked that none of those sharp edges so disconcerting in sculptures executed in precious metal are presented to the eye. Michelozzo and his workmen could not avoid one or two cracks or holes as they raised the thin sheets of silver, but such defects were usual and were clearly accepted as inevitable in work of this kind by goldsmiths and their clients in the Middle Ages. They are in any case more conspicuous to the closely inspecting eyes of the museum visitor than they ever were to the worshipping eyes of a *quattrocento* Florentine congregation when twice a year they saw the figure of their patron-saint refulgent in gilt and silver against the softly glowing background of a simulated heaven of blue enamel and gilded stars.

Before we close this study,[73] let us pause for a moment to consider two last conclusions which emerge from it. First is that if the patrons we have encountered exercised their will in the choice of size, form and subject, they had little or no influence on the development of Renaissance style in sculpture beyond their readiness to accept works executed wholly or partly in it. To Donatello, to Michelozzo, not to Cossa's executors and heirs, not to Brancaccio, not to the Arciprete Jacopo, not to Priore Battista and Ser Bartolommeo, not to the *Operai* of Prato, belonged all that was new in the formulation and execution of the works of art we have studied. From the two artists sprang the first dynamic impulse to give traditional elements new stylistic forms. And so strong was that impulse in them that even in little Prato and remote Montepulciano they have left sculptures shaped with learned enthusiasm for the antique.

Probably it was the comparative passivity of their employers in matters of taste that enabled them to work their stylistic revolution. For their patrons evidently felt that the arts were the mystery of those who practised them, and though a high reputation might attract them to certain masters, they left the appraisal of their work to others of the craft, who gave their opinion in return for a fee. Yet there is an exception to this generalisation. Of all the figures who have passed through our story Cosimo de' Medici is the only one in whom we may suppose something of a consciously discriminating taste. Matteo degli Organi's letter of 19 June 1434 to the *Operai* of Prato in which he says that Donatello's first relief for the pulpit had been admired by the *intendenti* of Florence, shows that there were men in the city who had an eye sharpened to judge of the execution of works of art. And the Strozzi were already collecting antique sculpture in 1428, to judge from Nanni di Miniato's letters of 1428 and 1430. We know now that Cosimo played, or can be surmised to have played, a rôle in the history of all three tombs and of the Prato pulpit and that Vasari's account of his constant affection for Donatello and Michelozzo is fully borne out by contemporary documents. It seems natural to conclude then that his was the weighty influence or recommendation that procured the confidence of intending patrons, or even, in the case of the Cossa and Brancaccio tombs, the awarding of the commission. Accordingly he assumes something of the position of a mediator between the two artists and

254

the style they practised and the patrons from whom they obtained commissions.

We have traced the differing degrees of specification, suggestion or interference from patrons in each of the four great works we have studied. In the Cossa tomb Donatello probably received only very general directions about design and iconography, through the instrument of Giovanni and Cosimo de' Medici. To these he gave his own interpretation, partly under the influence of the restrictions imposed by the *Arte di Calimala*. Cardinal Brancaccio, on the other hand, evidently sent detailed specifications of size, form and subject-matter, largely, we must suppose, because his tomb was being made far from Rome, where he himself was living, and from Naples, where it was to be erected. As we have seen, he almost certainly gave them after a careful consideration of the tombs of two Neapolitan cardinals who had recently predeceased him. These we can fairly surmise him to have admired, since we know that he admired other carvings and paintings in the rich Late Gothic manner of Naples. Donatello and Michelozzo imposed then their style on his specifications. The cleavage between the ambience of Florence, where the Brancaccio tomb was created, and that of Naples, where it was erected, is proved by its failure to influence the sculptural style of Naples, which remained Gothic, exclusively or predominantly, for two decades more. As for Aragazzi's heirs and executors, they were content to order a tomb of the size and magnificence which their relative had destined for himself and to prescribe its subject-matter: in design and style Michelozzo had a free hand. And the *Operai* of Prato, though so anxious to be certain of getting full value for their money, accepted Donatello as an artist of the first rank to whose whims they owed deference.

In the works we have examined then the division between the contribution of patrons and artists is essentially that between the nature of the work commissioned, its general form and its subject-matter on the one hand, and style on the other. This is not to contest the influence of humanism in the formation of Renaissance sculptural style. Rather it is to define its action during the two transitional decades which have been our concern as an action exercised on artists rather than on patrons. From the whole tenor of what has gone before it will have become overwhelmingly obvious that the prime motive of patrons in commissioning great works of sculpture was religious. Even the tombs erected to honour the dead honour them with imagery embodying pious hopes and pious prayers for the welfare of their souls. In tombs and pulpit then the accidents of form are new: the substance of faith is still unchanged.